SUBJECTIVE PSYCHOLOGY

A Concept of mind for the behavioral sciences and philosophy by

William G. Quill

New York / SPARTAN BOOKS / Washington

Library of Congress Catalog Card Number 70-161473.
International Standard Book Number 0-87671-707-5.
Printed in the United States of America.

Sole distributor in Great Britain, the British Commonwealth, and the Continent of Europe:

The Macmillan Press Ltd.
4 Little Essex Street
London WC2R 3LF

Preface

The central problem confronting contemporary psychology, and in a less obvious though equally pernicious way the other behavorial sciences, is that it lacks a definitionally precise and comprehensive concept of human behavior. Since the psychological sciences do not have an exacting understanding of their primary units for analysis, knowledge claims issuing from these areas of inquiry may be brought into question generally as a direct function of the degree to which these sciences have oversimplified, and hence factually distorted, their objects of study. Progressively increased sophistication in experimental methodology, fortified even by methods uncritically imported from the formal, natural, and biological sciences, cannot in itself rectify the basic problem confronting psychology; fifty years of behaviorism renders this fact eminently clear. Alternatively, the ostensibly more robust theoretical formulations of human behavior articulated by developmental, Gestalt, and perceptual psychologies have, in fact, done little to extricate psychology from its definitional morass. This problem of definition has become so acute that Sigmund Koch, editor of the volumes entitled *Psychology: A Study of a Science*, has made, in a penetrating recent article, the following comments about the scientific status of modern psychology.

Whether as a "science" or any kind of coherent discipline devoted to empirical study of man, psychology has been misconceived . . .

Indeed, the pooled pseudo-knowledge that is much of psychology can be seen as a congeries of alternate—and exceedingly simple—images, around each of which one finds a dense, scholastic cluster of supportive research, theorizing and methodological rhetoric.

If one is drawn by unassailable scientific argument to the conclusion that man is a cockroach, rat or dog, that makes a difference. It also makes a difference when one achieves ultimate certitude that man is a telephone exchange, a servo-mechanism, a binary digital computer, a reward-seeking vector, a hyphen written within an S-R process, a stimulator-maximizer, a food, sex, or libido energy-converter, a utilities-maximizing game player, a status-seeker, a mutual ego-titillator, a mutual emotional (or actual) masturbator. And on and on . . .

My findings over the years suggest that while symptoms may vary, one syndrome is widely evident in modern scholarships. I call it AMEANINGFUL THINKING. The prefix has the same force as the A in words like AMORAL.

Ameaningful thought or inquiry regards knowledge as the result of "processing" rather than discovery. It presumes that knowledge is an almost automatic result of a gimmickry, an assembly line, a methodology. It assumes that inquiring action is so rigidly and fully regulated by RULE that in its conception of inquiry it often allows the rules totally to displace their human users. Presuming as it does that knowledge is generated by processing, its conception of knowledge is fictionalistic, conventionalistic. So strangely does it see knowledge under such aspects that at times it seems to suppose the object of inquiry to be an ungainly and annoying irrelevance. Detail, structure, quiddity are obliterated. Objects of knowledge become caricatures, if not faceless, and thus they lose reality. The world, or any given part of it, is not felt fully or passionately and is perceived as devoid of objective value. In extreme forms, ameaningful thought becomes obsessive and magical. (*Psychology Today*, September 1969.)

Most American and British psychologists throughout this century, obsessed by the desire to achieve the status of a rigorous science while simultaneously denouncing with equally pious fervor their "metaphysical" historical antecedents, have bungled into one form of unwarranted scientific reductionism after another. This erroneous course has been markedly facilitated by the heavily biased positivistic interpretation of the history of philosophy and science predominating these decades.

This essentially behavioristic movement in psychology managed in its most extreme forms to totally omit subjectively experienced mental variables from its theoretical definitions of human behavior (hence regarding 'behavior' strictly as that directly available to external observers), the accomplishment being widely regarded as a hallmark of scientific objectivity. It is precisely this concept of human behavior—one which thoroughly permeates the allegedly most rigorous approaches to psychology, the other behavioral sciences, and even current schools of philosophy—that I propose to refute. The refutation will not merely be "another criticism of behaviorism." It will entail a detailed and exacting study of the basic units for analysis, the presuppositions, and methodological assumptions that ANY systematic approach to studying human behavior—scientific, philosophical, or religious—must take into account if it is to tenaciously adhere to the basic concrete facts of human experience. Stated in this fashion, the possibility of attaining such an ambitious objective must impress the reader as surely remote. However, in fact, I will merely be reconsidering a small portion of the historically pertinent philosophical and psychological wisdom that must necessarily be consulted in any valid attempt to formulate a tenable definition of human behavior. Specifically, I will be reconsidering the classical mind-body problem, for it is herein, I contend, that the central problem confronting contemporary psychology and the related behavioral sciences is to be resolved. A clear implication of this mode of reasoning is that psychology cannot resolve its present impasse solely through more experimentation, for this was the principal error of this century. Rather, it is time to carefully re-examine its theoretical and methodological predispositions in light of the concrete empirical facts of experience and the relevant wisdom of the past, conditions for validation to which the former must ultimately be held accountable.

In precisely defining the basic units for analysis necessarily implicit in the concept of 'human behavior,' I discovered that my definition also included the fundamental insights of the historically great systems of psychology; namely, developmental, perceptual-Gestalt, and behavioristic approaches. Thus contrary to being exclusively critical of these major systems, I found that when they were contemplated in light of an empirically and logically sound comprehensive definition of human behavior, the entire constellation of factors could be neatly arranged into a general theory of psychology; one not antagonistic to the other biological, natural, or formal sciences!

Many of the technical terms used in subsequent chapters for formulating my concept of human behavior have deep historical roots, most notably in the works of Aristotle and Kant, and more recently in the views of Dewey, Cassirer, and Whitehead. I have taken the liberty of quoting extensively from those writings of Cassirer and Whitehead having profound significance for the subject of this volume.

I would like to express my deepest gratitude to Dr. Ralph Pippert and Dr. Leonard Erlich for their humane and insightful guidance into the realms of personal and intellectual knowledge. Finally, I am thoroughly appreciative of the unwavering assistance and continued sound advice I received from Dianne Littwin of Spartan Books in preparing this volume for publication.

WILLIAM G. QUILL
Graduate School
Northeastern University

Boston, Massachusetts
March 1971

Contents

To my mother and father

"Holding as we do that, while knowledge of any kind is a thing to be honoured and prized, one kind of it may, either by reason of its greater exactness or of a higher dignity and greater wonderfulness in its objects, be more honourable and precious than another, on both accounts we should naturally be led to place in the front rank the study of the soul."

ARISTOTLE

Acknowledgements

I would like to express my gratitude to the following persons, publishers, and firms who have been kind enough to grant me permission to reprint passages from works in which they hold the copyright:

Appleton Century Crofts, Educational Division, New York, from B. F. Skinner's *Cumulative Record,* copyright 1959, 1961.

Basic Books, Inc., New York, from J. A. V. Butler's *The Life of the Cell,* copyright 1964.

Cambridge University Press, New York, from Alfred North Whitehead's *An Enquiry Concerning the Principles of Natural Knowledge,* copyright 1919; *Concept of Nature,* copyright 1920; *The Principles of Relativity,* copyright 1922.

The Macmillan Company, New York, from B. F. Skinner's *Science and Human Behavior,* copyright 1965; from Alfred North Whitehead's *Adventures of Ideas,* copyright 1933; *Science and the Modern World,* copyright 1925; and from John Dewey's *Democracy and Education,* copyright 1916.

Minnesota University Press, Minneapolis, from Herbert Feigl's "The 'Mental' and the 'Physical'," and from Wilfred Sellers' "Intentionality and the Mental," both articles appearing in *Minnesota Studies in the Philosophy of Science,* H. Feigl, M. Scriven, G. Maxwell, eds., vol. II: *Concepts, Theories, and the Mind-Body Problem,* copyright 1963.

Psychology Today, from Sigmund Koch's "Psychology Cannot be a Coherent Science," copyright September, 1969.

John Wiley & Sons, Inc., Methuen and Co., Ltd., and W. Ross Ashby, New York and London, from W. Ross Ashby's *An Introduction to Cybernetics,* copyright 1963.

Yale University Press, New Haven, from Jacques Maritian's *Education at the Crossroads,* copyright 1943, and from Ernst Cassirer's *An Essay on Man,* copyright 1965.

Introduction

Currently, many of the most widely used theories for systematically investigating human behavior have presuppositional bases derived from what may be termed materialistic-mechanistic and materialistic-epiphenomenalistic philosophies. These philosophical systems are characterized, at least, by the following presuppositions.

1. Materialistic-mechanism is essentially the view (whether expressed as traditional Newtonian mechanics or more recent particle theories) that the universe is constituted of ultimate particles of matter, clustering together in determinate configurations that appear in dynamic interrelation with one another throughout space and time. Therefore, by conceiving these indeterminately numerous configurations of material particles dynamically occurring within a spatio-temporal framework in conjunction with such ancillary concepts as mass, velocity, inertia, gravity, etc., extraordinary fruitful mathematical and statistical formulations can be and obviously have been established as universally valid or, at least, highly precise statements of the *relations* manifested among given groups of material particles (or macrocosmically speaking, material bodies) at instantaneous moments of time.

2. Although there are somewhat different versions of this view, and even with regard to the one presented here many additional expository comments could be made, the primitive concepts "material particles," "motion," "space," and "time" are common to them all. Consequently, enough has been said to contemplate the theoretical conceptualization of mental phenomena that will logically follow from this philosophical position.

3. It becomes immediately evident that mental phenomena must necessarily be explained in terms of material entities occurring in instantaneous relations with one another, as these relations can be formally expressed in contemporary physical and biological theories.

4. In effect, then, regardless of how mental phenomena may be conceived, they must, in the view of materialistic-mechanism, be expressible in formally quantifiable scientific statements of dependent relations. Stated differently, it must be concluded that statements about mind can be completely reduced, in principle, to scientific statements about physical processes.

5. Another closely related, derivative theory from materialistic-mechanism is materialistic-epiphenomenalism. The latter places ultimate emphasis upon the same primitive concepts as the former, however,

with the qualification that mental processes, in some unknown way, occur as causally inefficacious by-products of their underlying physio-chemical (and ultimately physical) processes. This is to say, as it is most manifestly evident in a Skinnerian behavioristic psychology, for example, that any statements referring to the inner mental states of a human organism can be methodologically purged from scientific functional analysis for they unwarrantedly introduce variables not only inter-subjectively directly inaccessible to observers, but moreover, such statements do not refer to causal determinants of human behavior. Here the term "functional analysis" designates a systematic specification of given contemporary environmental stimulus conditions that interact with organisms' antecedently learned behavioral predispositions to determinately control organisms' response-behavior. These contingencies, alleged to in principle exhaust all possible efficacious factors involved in producing organismic behavior, are to be specified within a basic stimulus-response model, utilizing other relevant theoretical constructs such as "reinforcement," "operant," "reflex arc," etc., to facilitate behavioral explanation. Moreover, all behavioral contingencies are said to be directly inter-subjectively verifiable, thereby remaining consistent with the basic tenets of materialistic-epiphenomenalism.

6. The principal objective here is to refute the two materialistic theories briefly outlined above, to the extent that they are regarded as capable, in principle, of providing an adequate account of human mental processes. A scientific reduction of mental processes to their underlying physio-chemical correlates is logically untenable; and a behaviorism, investigating human behavior solely as it is ascertained directly through the external bodily senses, can in principle provide only a partial scientific account of behavior. Behaviorism maintains a concept of inner or "mental" states that is essentially erroneous. We will endeavor to propose a theory of mind both logically and empirically reconcilable with physical and biological scientific inquiry. Usage of the term "behaviorism" hereafter refers specifically to Skinnerian behaviorism.

To gain a better understanding of the very subtle manner whereby materialistic-mechanistic theories profoundly influence the thinking of both public and scientific mentalities, thus predisposing cultures imbued with a history of scientific achievement to adopt an overly reductionistic concept of man's uniquely human character, let us briefly reflect critically upon certain theoretical, methodological, and evidential tenets often erroneously regarded by philosophers, scientists, and laymen as fundamental to scientific explanation.

First, we will consider a materialistic assumption which is in one form or another basic to much natural scientific inquiry and hence seems to have an important influence on other areas of science, although in a far more subtle way.

1. Stated in its most general form, we will find ultimately that our universe is comprised of basic homogeneous material particles or configurations of particles occurring in dynamic, relative spatio-temporal interrelation with one another.

2. In fact, all physical theories must necessarily include hypothetical constructs positing ultimate entities, even though in practice theorists are not much concerned with discovering the real nature of these entities. Rather, the principal endeavor is to formulate constructs propitious for generating operationally fruitful mathematical and statistical formulae to ascertain precisely determinate relations among entities. Of course this complex abstract process is always concretely guided by a concern for rendering phenomenal occurrences explainable, and by the necessity for theoretical verification through "key" experiments. It is from these modes of emphasis that the scientific aims of prediction, control, and thereby explanation are fulfilled. But in all this, the assumption that entities, generally regarded as ultimately material—though this inference is *not logically necessary*, as we shall discover—exist in dynamic relationships to one another in space and time is logically primitive. After all, if mathematics and statistics are formal scientific disciplines that establish valid relations, the concept of relation is vacuous unless there are entities to be related.

Even the most abstruse scientific investigations must, however, begin with direct sense perception (e.g., in initially becoming aware of problematic phenomena) and hence, verificationally terminate in direct sense perception. It might be noted at this early stage of argumentation that a more general definition will eventually be ascribed to the term "perception" than that which is delivered through the external bodily senses. Thus from intersubjectively accessible initial phenomenal occurrence, contemplated in reference to previously acquired wisdom (e.g., information derived from prior relevant experimentation, theorizing, common sense, etc.), hypotheses are formulated and appropriate experimental procedures are contrived and eventually submitted to empirical test, thereby yielding results which often enhance theoretical understanding or suggest areas for revision.

1. In this essentially instrumental usage of knowledge the natural sciences particularly have made extraordinary advances in developing a theoretical understanding of many directly perceivable phenomena (an understanding obviously yielding innumerable concrete benefits in

our daily lives), to the extent that lawful, deductive explanations are available for various concrete phenomenal observations.

2. But it must be understood that the preponderance of this knowledge is theoretically factual, not empirically factual; that is, theoretical constructs, abstract axioms, postulates, their derivative formulae, etc., all of which are *not* directly observable in concrete external bodily sense perception, are products of thought adhering, primarily, to the principle of noncontradiction. Although the issue of fact and theory is a highly complex, and at present, indeterminate matter in the philosophy of science, we can legitimately maintain the distinction that theories and their constitutive constructs, axioms, postulates, formulae, etc., are, in principle, not directly ascertainable in direct external bodily sense perception. This is simply to say that we do not directly see, taste, smell, touch or hear such things as atoms, molecules, light waves, the *meaning* of formula, etc. Rather, we ideationally conceive them as instruments for facilitating our scientific inquiries.

3. More specifically, it must be said that theoretical elements exist psychologically as highly elaborate ideational predispositions for understanding phenomenal reality as it is directly perceived. In essence, then, theories have ontological existence in the minds of men, although they may be rightfully understood to essentially represent, linguistically, natural world correlates existing independently from individual human percipients. However, it *cannot* even be maintained that our theoretical ideas of atoms, for example, are in fact accurately representative of the independently existing entities to which they explanatorily refer. Rather, it is only justifiable to assume that our theories explain the behavior of merely those aspects of independently existing atomic entities that are ultimately directly perceived as sensory perception.

4. To make this distinction somewhat clearer, let us say, first, that we have made a distinction between the natural realm as it is directly perceived by individual human percipients, and an ideational symbolic domain used by percipients to render their perceptual content intelligible· In effect, these two realms are mutually exclusive, at least in the sense that they are spatially separated. But in contrast to the more problematic issue of man's relation to what are hypothetically conceived as, for example, the microcosmic entities "atoms," "light waves," etc., let us consider the simple entity, "tree." A tree has directly observable properties that are intersubjectively ascertainable, thereby rendering it a legitimate object of empirical knowledge. However, entities theoretically and hence symbolically characterized as atoms, for example, existing independently from human percipients, are far from being directly perceivable in the same way that we perceive a tree. We do not have intersubjectively

direct access to the intrinsic properties of atoms. Therefore, it is required that theoretical concepts of the structure of atoms be devised in accordance with the phenomenal representations of the independently existing entities to which we do have direct perceptual access. From this methodological approach, highly fruitful explanations for relevant phenomenal occurrence can be established by developing equations rigorously demonstrating the modes of relation among the theoretically conceived constitutive components of atomic entities, and clusters of these entities.

5. It may be concluded, then, that we have a clear concrete notion of the intrinsic character of the entity termed "tree," for it is an object of direct perceptual experience. But conversely, our concept of the intrinsic nature of the entity symbolically characterized as "atom" is unclear for we have no direct perceptual apprehension of its structure. However, the notions we do have, as they are ultimately grounded in the phenomenal representations of atomic behavior ascertained in experimental conditions, are highly determinate for they are of, essentially, the mathematically and statistically ascertained relations among theoretically postulated components collectively comprising the atomic model.

The point of our line of argument thus far is that in the modern historical development of the formal and natural sciences, man has fabricated an extraordinarily precise understanding of the mathematically, statistically, and geometrically ascertainable relations existing among the hypothetical or theoretical entities and their components, alleged to constitute, microcosmically, the grossly perceivable entities of direct concrete experience. However, this is to admit a view quite different from maintaining that we know, with the degree of certainty accomplished in establishing the relations amongst entities of the formal and natural sciences, the intrinsic character of independently existing entities ultimately constituting the "substantial" nature of the universe.

In fact, a major continuing problem for metaphysics, for example, is in attempting to formulate a reasonably clear notion of substance or a model fruitfully portraying the essential character of ultimate entities; one that is tolerably consistent with scientifically established knowledge of the microcosm and macrocosm as it is subject to ultimate verification through direct intersubjectively accessible perceptual experience.

Stated simply, it becomes evident that our great certainty about particular aspects of nature is grounded in formally ascertained relations, demonstrated to characterize the structure of natural scientific theoretical, hence hypothetically postulated, entities. This means, essentially, that our concepts of the many relations existing among entities are extremely precise, while our understanding of the intrinsic nature of the entities themselves is very vague indeed, particularly with regard to microcosmic entities. Consequently, our notions of the ultimate nature of reality must remain commensurately vague.

Nevertheless, the omnipresent danger of making an unwarranted materialistic inference (e.g., that the universe is ultimately constituted of homogeneous material particles occurring in dynamic interrelation with one another, which in their spatio-temporally persisting configurations comprise the realm of primary and secondary qualities of sense perception) threatens constantly to adversely influence our thoughts about reality, and usually succeeds. Of course this view, with some of its aforementioned presuppositions, proved remarkably fruitful for viewing the universe solely in terms of its primary qualities; hence yielding such concepts as mass, velocity, etc., that in turn were inestimably propitious for revealing many formally specifiable relations amongst entities. Thus the enormous historical success of materialism undoubtedly persists in coloring our fundamental theories about reality.

But the great history of formal and natural scientific development seems to have importantly constrained theory construction in the psychological sciences, to cite but one area of human studies—a general area that appears never to have escaped in modern thought the negative or reductionistic influence of materialistic presuppositions. This is to say that, essentially, the theory of ultimate material particles in motion which function in dynamic interrelation with one another, regardless of the extent to which this view is elaborated, as in certain contemporary physical theories, possesses a presuppositional basis that is *in principle inappropriate* for systematically investigating *human conscious processes*. Let us not confuse the scientific study of conscious processes with that of physio-chemical processes. It is obvious that the most sophisticated physical-biological theories available should be consulted in investigating, for example, the structure of cerebral mechanisms and their various modes for energy transference. However, scientifically conceptualizing physio-chemical cerebral processes and, similarly, gross manifest human behavioral phenomena as strictly methodologically dictated by a Skinnerian behavioristic psychology is, in principle, different from systematically conceptualizing their subjectively accessible conscious correlates. Hence the view of mind propounded in the following chapters will be fundamentally an interactionism, a view designating two experientially distinct domains of phenomenal occurrence—i.e., phenomena perceptually ascertained through two mutually exclusive modes of perceptual presentation—one natural, and the other, ideational.

Conceived differently, it will be argued that from materialistic-mechanistic theories presently used for studying physio-chemical processes, it is in principle impossible to deduce logically any information about their correlative mental process if this is attempted from strictly a physical and/or biological scientific frame of reference. To persist in attempting to accomplish this necessarily places such investigators in the position of committing what is typically defined as an "unwarranted scientific reductionism."

Furthermore, the factual perceptual deliverances constituting our personal experience do not suggest an exclusively physical, biological, or even behavioristic approach to studying human behavior.

1. Even with our extraordinary knowledge of natural and biological phenomena, we are nevertheless quite ignorant of the ultimate character of the microcosmic entities comprising nature. This is true, at least to the extent that the tenet "The universe is constituted of ultimate homogeneous material particles occurring in dynamic configurational relations with one another, thereby collectively uniting into what individual human beings directly experience as reality" (e.g., primary and secondary qualities as they portray nature and inner bodily experience) must at this time remain an open question. In fact, twentieth-century physical scientific inquiry has shown materialistic presuppositions to be of diminishing importance in yielding fruitful investigation.

2. Since most of our knowledge of the microcosm proceeds from theoretically postulated concepts, representative of independently existing entities, and, equally important, because the validity and reliability of these theoretical constructs are ultimately determined from direct external bodily sense perception, it seems evident that we ought to practice what has so often been preached and thereby place optimum confidence in our direct perceptual deliverances. In principle our awareness of reality must ultimately be understood in terms of our direct perceptions of it, regardless of how abstractly theoretical are the explanations that we offer to systematically comprehend phenomenal occurrence or how intellectually removed our hypothetical devices become, in terms of being subject to direct perceptual verification. It is obvious that the writer is ascribing an ideational ontological status to theoretical formulations, and hence, regarding as untenable any position advocating that theoretical constructs can somehow transcend the testimonies of concrete perceptual experience and thereby comprehend the ultimate structure of nature.

3. In attributing an ideational ontological status to theoretical formulations and all symbolic thought (conceived as a causally efficacious class of human behavioral determinants that cannot be exhaustively intersubjectively directly ascertained through external scrutiny, and thereby must be regarded as an *inferred* class of *intervening* variables

capable of significantly influencing human behavioral modes), predominate emphasis should not be placed upon external bodily sense perception, a view generally unpopular in contemporary, scientific, and philosophic circles. The theory propounded here proceeds from an expanded concept of perceptual experience. Emphasis will be placed upon inner bodily perception regardless of the fact that these percepta are not available to direct intersubjective verification, in contrast with external bodily sense perception. Our personally accessible internal bodily perceptions are considerably more numerous, and hence, proportionately causally efficacious as components of human behavior, than perception contributed from the natural world through external bodily sensory modes. Without adequate systematic attention to the structure subjectively introduced to symbolic, predominately linguistic, behavior, human behavioral research is seriously impaired. In ultimately verifying these bold assertions, the reader will be repeatedly required to reflect on the content of his direct perceptual experience, for it is essentially from this frame of reference that all conscious thought must proceed.

To formulate a comprehensive concept of mind for the behavioral sciences that is concordant with the direct (perceptual) facts of concrete experience, two theories representing the major trends in modern psychology, namely, psychoanalysis and behaviorism should be considered briefly. Each view is fundamentally subject to the criticism of effecting an "unwarranted scientific reductionism"; that is, of theorizing that for the purpose of science mental processes can be exhaustively explained in terms of their correlative physio-chemical process, or their manifest behavior as it is directly accessible to scientific observers via their external bodily senses. Both theories are based on materialistic presuppositions, and hence contain the ultimate erroneous conception that scientific theoretical entities, such as atoms, alleged to be ultimately constituted of configurations of homogeneous material particles in motion, actually embody the intrinsic structure of their independently existing correlative objects. Conversely, the formal and natural sciences yield extraordinarily precise knowledge of the mathematically, statistically, and geometrically ascertained relations among hypothetically postulated scientific entities. Further, this knowledge of relations yields relatively little information about the intrinsic nature of their independently existing correlates that constitute the natural world. Due to the unavailability of any relevant direct external bodily sense perception, we have no way of knowing at this time whether atoms really consist of material subparticles, or if light really travels in wavelike trains of material particles. In pursuing this mode of inquiry, it is easy to miss the fact that hypothetical constructs are used instrumentally to facilitate the establishment of more determinate formal relations among theoretically postulated entities.

Let us now further analyze the claim that psychoanalysis and behaviorism are epiphenomenalistic theories.

1. Both psychological theories can be regarded as unwarrantedly reductionistic, in that mental events are conceived as causally inefficacious by-products of correlative (underlying) physio-chemical processes which, in fact, wholly determine the nature of mental processes and overt behavior. It is necessary to maintain, from an epiphenomenalism, that ideas constituting human thought do not move men or determine their intelligent behavioral modes. Rather, it must be held that all human behavior results from a functional interaction between a human organism's physio-chemical and manifest-behavioral states at a given time as they interpenetratively relate with correlative external environmental conditions.

2. Psychoanalysis conceptualizes human behavior as primarily motivated by unconscious drives, the specific modes of which are established physiologically and in early childhood, and which determine resulting behavior throughout the lives of individuals.

3. The contemporary behavioristic viewpoint of B. F. Skinner emphasizes the theoretical concept of conditioned reflex as being the fundamental human behavioral response unit. Therefore it is maintained that the nature of human behavior can exhaustively be explained by regarding behavior as an exact function of externally located antecedent environmental stimulus-events and resultantly activated manifest response-events, with a theoretical reflex arc mechanism representing the physiological intermediary between the stimulus and response events. In this way, it is alleged, all causally significant variables in producing human behavior can, in principle, be ascertained, utilizing methods and procedures entirely intersubjectively verifiable.

4. Client-centered theories of psychotherapy, which diligently attempt to avoid epiphenomenalism and thereby accentuate the causal efficacy of individual consciously reflective behavior, are primarily deficient in that they do not define theoretical constructs and operational procedures in terms that facilitate rigorous scientific inquiry. Conversely, behavioristic experimental procedures are, methodologically speaking, much more commensurate with those of contemporary natural sciences. Behaviorism, apart from certain theoretical constructs that can be subjected to severe criticism, emphasizes a rigorously specified methodological approach for studying behavioral phenomena, derived from the

highly developed natural sciences. In this important sense, behaviorism is, methodologically, a more suitable approach to studying human behavior than through psychoanalytic or client-centered methods.

5. Both psychoanalysis and behaviorism de-emphasize the role of consciously reflective behavior as a causally efficacious factor in determining human behavioral responses.

6. Although this point is less evident in psychoanalysis, its presuppositional basis necessarily implies an epiphenomenalism. This follows because manifest verbal content is interpreted as being symbolically representative of a real underlying, unconsciously motivated, sexual drive or libido. Libido, however, has its source of origin in physio-chemical processes, Freud argues, and therefore, any aspect of subjective conscious meaning is necessarily a mere symbolic reflection of a more valid unconscious content that ultimately has its ground in atomic materialistic process. This latter point is readily evident since Freud was importantly influenced by Hegelian dialectical materialism.

7. Behaviorism commits a similar unwarranted reductionism in maintaining that all causally significant variables determining human behavior, whether occurring in an organism's external natural environment or manifest behavior, or as a physiological process, can be ascertained through the external bodily senses of scientific observers. This necessarily implies that the only causally efficacious variables that directly intervene between intersubjectively accessible stimulus conditions and subsequent response behaviors are physio-chemical processes, and thus render inner mental states epiphenomenal.

8. It is from a basic disagreement regarding the theoretical adequacy of behaviorism in providing a complete account of human behavior, that this alternate theory of human behavior has been developed to supplement an "enlightened" behavioristic position. It will be argued that human behavior can be theoretically conceptualized in a mechanistic model, though one omitting materialistic presuppositions. An attempt will be made to show the inadequacy of the construct reflex arc, and consequently, demonstrate that it is precisely the phenomenon of symbolic conscious reflection that distinguishes human organisms as importantly unique from other objects of scientific scrutiny. Therefore, novel theoretical constructs are required to characterize this aspect of human behavior in a nonreductionist manner and subsequently promote fruitful systematic study. It will also be shown that behavioristic viewpoints are methodologically prohibited from directly investigating the fact of conscious reflective behavior as causally efficacious in determining many human behavioral responses to stimulation. This results from the influence of materialistically defined presuppositions and from

their overly narrow verificational criteria that lead to the exclusion of inner mental phenomena as legitimate factual data.

9. A basic problem for a behavioral science purporting to offer a complete systematic understanding of human behavior is that a theoretical model for investigating this class of phenomena must be postulated which provides due emphasis on both the involuntary and the voluntary dimensions of behavior as they are efficacious in determining various modes of individual and group behavior, while adhering to the strict methodological policies of the more exact sciences. Further, a theory is needed that is sufficiently comprehensive to include the global, integrated nature of human behavior as it occurs in a multiplicity of environments.

Currently renewed speculations on the nature of mind are being seriously constrained by an excessive adherence to the highly admirable achievements of the natural and biological sciences. Theorists who endeavor to conceptualize mind generally are misled in contemplating mind exclusively in terms of the theoretically postulated entities devised for the exact sciences. The bare fact of the matter is that, regardless of the great experimental utility of these theoretical entities and their auxiliary concepts, they are in principle directly unobservable and thereby must be regarded as abstract ideas constructed by the minds of men. Hence they possess, ontologically speaking, ideational existence. This unwarranted reductionistic trend achieves its extreme form in those contemporary schools of psychology and philosophy professing, basically, materialistic, mechanistic and epiphenomenalistic views of mental processes.

These cognitively well-habituated but erroneous reductionistic views can be ultimately understood to issue from, perhaps, an unwitting acceptance of certain presuppositions leading one to regard the ultimate entities, of which the universe is often alleged to be comprised, as being intrinsically materialistic.

Systematic speculation on the nature of mind requires a careful examination of the characteristic features and modes of occurrence of directly ascertained human perception, both external and internal. It is in direct perception of reality that the distinctive character of mind and its relation to nature is to be understood. From this analysis, it will be seen that concepts (i.e., theoretical constructs) not having directly verifiable external natural world perceptual correlates must be attributed a purely hypothetical, and therefore, ideational status.

But in order, psychologically speaking, to conceive of ideas and, more generally, mind as having an intrinsically different type of actual-

ity from natural world objects, many of which they symbolically represent, it is necessary to formulate a notion of ideas as legitimate entities,
and further, to show how they may determinately influence the behavior of men and thus provide a reasonable theoretical alternative to
the absurd conclusions of epiphenomenalism.

A satisfactory conceptualization of ideational entities will necessarily
demand that all materialistic presuppositions be purged from our formulations, though in a way not inconsistent with mechanistic explanation.
It is to this task that we shall now proceed.

PART ONE

Chapter one / A criticism of contemporary behaviorism

This book will be concerned with the general problem of theoretically conceptualizing human behavior so that in maintaining scientific definitional rigor we do not commit the error of adopting a behavioral model which neglects to comprehend causally efficacious aspects of human behavior. It has been said that of the three major approaches for systematically investigating human behavior within counseling and psychotherapeutic contexts for example, psychoanalytic and behavioristic schools are, on logical grounds, unwarrantedly reductionistic in their comprehension of behavioral phenomena, and client-centered therapies frequently define their theoretical constructs in terms inappropriate for rigorous scientific investigation. This latter criticism may also be directed at psychoanalytic schools, over and above the criticism of untenable reductionism. Therefore, the fundamental problem to be considered throughout this volume is that a new, comprehensive model for scientifically comprehending human behavior must be devised, retaining tenable features of current theories, while, on the other hand, introducing novel constructs which will include causally important behavioral phenomena heretofore methodologically excluded from experimentation by both former and current theories because of their materialistic and/or mechanistic presuppositional bases and hypothetical constructs.

It seems reasonable that an appropriate model should, ideally at least, be predicated upon the standards established by the three following criteria:

1. The constructs comprising the model should be logically consistent with one another.

1

2. The model should be sufficiently comprehensive so as to include all the relevant factors which could possibly enter into any scientific explanation of human behavior.

3. The hypothetical constructs of the model should be defined in terms readily amenable to precise scientific investigation.

Kurt Gödel has shown that, logically speaking, the first two criteria are ultimately irreconcilable with one another. However, they are used here as postulated ideals toward which a developing science may aspire as it undergoes theoretical revision.(1)

With the above criteria in mind it would be absurd for any theoretician to assume that his formulations could qualify as the final word in such an ambitious endeavor. This text is primarily meant to provoke critical reflection in those individuals who, perhaps unwittingly, regard their cherished theories as adequate for yielding an exhaustive explanation of important human behavioral phenomena. Considering the present level of development of the behavioral sciences, dogmatism is wholly unwarranted. This is not to discourage the practice of carrying out long-term programs of research stimulated from any given theoretical frameworks. However, researchers should be willing to entertain and critically reflect upon presuppositions and theoretical constructs of diverse viewpoints, including their own, in an effort to suggest, if not synthesize, new modes for conceptualizing theoretical and experimental procedures.

The text is also intended to explicate and systematically comprehend various important dimensions of human behavior which have been obscured heretofore by reductionistic psychological and philosophical theories. Specifically, now that the influence of logical positivism is generally beginning to wane in many disciplines, the highly perplexing and historically problematic nature of "private" or directly accessible mental states is again being seriously studied by some philosophers and psychologists.(2), (3) In line with this renewed interest, attention will be given to formulating a theory for comprehending the subjective psychological form in which mental processes occur. This shift in emphasis in contemporary psychology from a more strictly behavioristic position seems justified for two reasons. First, behavioristic views appear to be adequately conceptualizing what may be termed the manifest, intersubjectively directly accessible aspect of human behavior. Thus, there seems to be little need to suggest any dramatic methodological revisions in this approach, for current practices are being steadily refined. Secondly, contemporary behavioristic efforts in the last forty to fifty years, under the influence of logical positivism, were devoted to placing psychology on a firm scientific foundation, thereby creating a discipline capable of formulating knowledge claims based upon evidence obtained from intersubjectively valid and reliable procedures for verification. In this endeavor a clearly defined methodological approach for studying behavior was introduced that admitted as its evidential grounds only those behavioral phenomena available for direct intersubjective confirmation. A major problem with this procedure is that there are other causally efficacious human behavioral phenomena which must necessarily be excluded from behavioristic methodologies for they are not subject to direct public confirmation. These phenomena fall into the class of mental events. Mental events are perceptually accessible only to individual persons who directly experience them. External observers can, however, have indirect access to these states if individuals who directly experience the mental phenomena wish to symbolically, usually through linguistic expression, describe their character.

Behavioristic thinkers, and specifically B. F. Skinner, would argue that such directly accessible mental states, while genuinely real phenoma, are actually epiphenomena, and thus extraneous to scientific inquiry for they do not qualify as causal behavioral determinants.(4) This brings us to what is probably the central problem: mental events do, in fact, have a causal status as human behavioral determinants, and if this can be proven, behavioristic methodological formulations must necessarily be regarded on logical grounds as overly limiting, for they must, in principle, exclude that class of causally efficacious factual phenomena called mental events. Further, it must be granted logically from such a proof that while behaviorism can yield very important contributions to the scientific explanation of human behavior, it can never provide a full explanation for its methodological stipulation that all factual data must be amenable to direct intersubjective confirmation excludes the entire domain of personally accessible mental events which are incapable of direct public ascertainment. Therefore, working on the assumption that the above criticism against behaviorism can be substantiated, it is legitimate to theorize about the logical form of private mental behavior which could then be subjected to scientific experimental analysis and verification. This subjective psychological viewpoint is by no means a new one for its origin can be traced to the introspective methods of Titchner (5) and thereafter to the Gestalt (6) and phenomenological schools of psychology.(7) In this work, however, an attempt will be made to reconcile the objective and subjective psychological viewpoints which, in themselves, are insufficiently comprehensive to effect a complete explanation of human behavior.

Wilfrid Sellars, a highly respected contemporary logician and philosopher of science, regards the mind-body problem in the following way:

The traditional mind-body problem is . . . a veritable tangle of tangles. At first sight but one of the problems of philosophy, it soon turns out, as one picks at it, to be nothing more nor less than the philosophical enterprise as a whole. Yet if, to the close-up view of the philosopher at work, it soon becomes a bewildering crisscross of threads leading in all directions, it is possible to discern, on standing off, a number of distinguishable regions which, although but vaguely defined, provide relatively independent access to the whole. (8)

In considering the mind-body problem, one embarks upon a tradition of inquiry which many have undertaken during the long history of philosophical thought. Traditionally, the results of these numerous inquiries have been, at best, highly illuminating, though subject to incessant criticism. At worst, however, the whole issue of mind and body has been periodically discredited as a pseudo-problem and hence repressed. This latter attitude has predominated during the last forty years, particularly in positivistically oriented philosophies and psychologies. One of the increasing number of current testimonies to the fact that the mind-body problem is still highly problematic is that the Minnesota Center for Philosophy of Science devoted an entire volume, entitled *Concepts, Theories, and the Mind-Body Problem,* to studying this issue, with some of the most highly respected philosophers and scientists of our time as contributors. Interestingly enough, several of these men in past years were closely associated with the famed Vienna circle, but more recently have found it necessary to modify their positions, in varying degrees, as philosophical positivism has become an increasingly untenable position to maintain. Obviously, men of great ability—men who formerly regarded the mind-body problem as a pseudo-issue—in response to valid criticism, now find the problem to be a genuinely substantive one.

The reader may wonder why such an abstruse philosophical problem is so important for the behavioral sciences. The answer, to a great extent, is that applied disciplines such as counseling and psychotherapy, for example, are specifically the areas in which the full, pragmatic implications of philosophical and psychological theories of mind are tested in terms of their practical utility. Practitioners in these areas have an excellent opportunity for careful observation of concrete behavioral phenomena. In an effort to explicate and unite relevant facts into a theoretical scheme to explain the causal conditions underlying various important behavioral phenomena, one has abundant opportunity to subject theoretical formulations, many of which are philosophical derivations, to empirical tests. Therefore, acute and sensitive practitioners are in a prime position to generate, and thereby contribute to, the construction of intelligent theories, as well as to evaluate their operational adequacy. Further, now that the sciences of human behavior are developed sufficiently to begin seriously dealing in systematic behavior modification, the mind-body problem is certainly no longer a purely speculative or discursive matter. It is, conversely, imperative that intelligent thinkers again reflect without prejudice upon the innumerable difficult and illusive aspects of behavioral phenomena in order to avoid accepting reductionistic formulations or terms so metaphorical that they are rendered inexpedient for scientific inquiry. We must heed the words of the great mathematician and philosopher, Alfred North Whitehead, who has said:

In order to discover some of the major categories under which we can classify the infinitely various components of experience, we must appeal to evidence relating to every variety of occasion. Nothing can be omitted, experience drunk and experience sober, experience sleeping and experience waking, experience drowsy and experience wide awake, experience self-conscious and experience self-forgetful, experience intellectual and experience physical, experience religious and experience skeptical, experience anxious and experience carefree, experience anticipatory and experience retrospective, experience happy and experience grieving, experience dominated by emotion and experience under self restraint, experience in light and experience in the dark, experience normal and experience abnormal.(9)

Of the many things implicit within this quotation, one of the most important is that in our direct concrete experience of both nature and our personal bodily states, there exist, if only we are sufficiently precise in our reflective awareness to discern them, innumerable instances of stubborn fact, primordially presented to us as perceptions, delivered through the internal and external sensory modes. Potentially implicit within these primitive facts, if relevant and penetrating reflective cognition is brought to bear upon them, are the possibilities for indeterminately expanding our human mentality as it endeavors to understand the reality of which it is a part. But if we commit the error, termed by Whitehead as "misplaced concreteness," whereby deceptively abstract concepts are erroneously regarded as concrete matters of fact, then the full richness of concrete reality as it is disclosed in direct experience is largely overlooked, thus prompting us down the path of ultimate contradiction, for our reasonings lack concordance with the structure of reality. Experience and error are merely two of the ideas contained within the writings of Whitehead that we shall have occasion to utilize.

Although in the *Introduction* it was indicated that there are generally three schools of thought that dominate applied psychology—psychoanalytic (developmental), client-centered (perceptual-structural) and behavioristic (bio-mechanistic)—only the latter will be specifically considered; the others will be indirectly implicated.

In beginning with a critical analysis of the highly influential be-havioristic thinker, B. F. Skinner, it is imperative to become clear as to the essential elements of Skinner's methodological approach to studying human behavior, a methodology which he does not regard as theoreti-cally based. Let us consider the methodological position of Professor Skinner's behaviorism, which can be regarded as an adequately repre-sentative version of the divergent schools of behaviorism. Skinner maintains that human behavior can, in principle, be completely "de-scribed" in terms of direct, publicly observable, and thereby operation-ally specifiable, stimulus and response functional relationships.(4) It is, according to Skinner, in this alleged possibility that a genuinely objective, exact science of human behavior can be established. This is the basic presupposition upon which all other propositions are predicated. An-other fundamental tenet is that all human behavior occurs from an inter-penetrative relationship between organism and environment. More specifically, this means that behavior can be completely comprehended in terms of a functional interaction between specified environmental conditions at a given point in time as they determine, through provid-ing reinforcement, the behavior of an organism whose response capacities at that time are limited to the previously conditioned repertoire of behavioral predispositions developed in the organism as a result of its antecedent experiential interaction with corresponding environments. Organismic predispositional capacities, conceived separately from actual learned behaviors, are ultimately governed by genetic inheri-tance. Thus a practical consequent of the former methodological princi-ples, with respect to actually experimentally verifying basic behavior-istic postulations, is that

both behavior and environment may be broken into parts which may be referred to by name and that these parts will retain their identity from ex-periment to experiment. If this assumption were not in some sense justified, a science of human behavior would be impossible.(10)

Let us look more closely at the concepts of stimulus and response and focus upon some of their necessary implications. Stimulus and response are regarded as events and not properties of given objects. Considering response-events, Skinner holds that

given a particular part of the behavior of an organism . . . the investigator seeks out antecedent [environmental] changes with which the activity is correlated and establishes the conditions of the correlation. This is the reflex nature of the behavior.

We may define a reflex as an observed correlation of a stimulus and a re-sponse . . . Once given a specific stimulus-response correlation, we may, of course, investigate the physiological facts of its mediation. The information there revealed will supplement our definition, but it will not affect the status of the reflex as a correlation.(10)

Thus by reflex, Skinner is positing a theoretical category of overt behavioral activity which serves as the empirical basis for investigators' bare observations of stimulus and response. The observed correlation between two spatially discrete phenomena has also led to the inference of a series of unobserved intervening physiological events which establish a causal connection between the directly observed stimulus and response events. The construct defined as "reflex arc," from the point of view of Skinnerian psychology, represents these unobserved, hence hypothetically postulated, series of events. This leads to a distinction between reflex physiology and a psychological science of human behavior whose differences are seen primarily in the immediate purposes of each discipline. That is, reflex physiology seeks description of reflex in terms of physio-chemical events. Therefore the term "synapse" is used instead of "reflex arc." At a more macroscopic level of inquiry, a psychological science seeks to describe behavior in terms of reflex. Here, also, as in the case of the term "synapse," reflex arc is a hypothetical construct which is in principle not observable. Rather, both terms are theoretical instruments used to interpret and thereby facilitate experimental inquiry dealing with observable phenomena such as physio-chemical process and reflexive behavior.

The term "behavior" must include the total publicly manifest activity of an organism at a given time—the functioning of all the behavioral components in their interrelationships with one another. Behaviorists are primarily interested in the activity of an organism within a strictly controlled experimental situation. This, of course, must also ultimately include any inferred internal changes subsumed under the reflex arc construct, which produce an observable, causally significant effect upon what is generally regarded as publicly observable macroscopic behavior. Moreover, the task of a behavioral science is to describe events not only in their isolated particularity, but also in their relationship with other events. It is in this that a science can achieve substantially valid and reliable "explanatory and predictive power."

Contemporary science maintains a more humble position with regard to explanation and causation. Explanation is reduced to description, and the notion of function is substituted for causation. Therefore, a full description of an event is regarded to provide a description of its functional relationship with antecedent events. In the description of behavior we are interested in the relationship within a regressive series [observed response] to those energy changes at the periphery which we designate as stimuli. The two end events, the behavior and the stimulus, have a particular importance because they alone are directly observable in an intact organism, and because they limit the series [they provide the "cut-off points" for an event so that it can be called a particular event]. With the relationship of these two end terms the description of behavior is chiefly concerned.(10)

Skinner again effectively demonstrates the concept of reflex when he states:

The reflex is important in the description of behavior because it is by definition a statement of the necessity of this [stimulus-response] relationship. The demonstration of the necessity is ultimately a matter of observation: a given response is observed invariably to follow a given stimulus. The more general statement, the hypothesis "the behavior of an organism is an exact function of the forces acting upon the organism" states the correlation of a stimulus and a response. It is, in this sense, the broadest possible statement of a reflex, but it is not an observed correlation and is therefore a hypothesis only.(10)

In the next statement, Skinner justifiably tempers the immediately preceding view as a result of the practical limitations of actual experimental situations when he says:

It is, nevertheless, solely the fault of our method that we cannot deal directly with this single correlation between behavior as a whole and all the forces acting upon an organism stated in the hypothesis. Quantitative statements of both stimulus and response and a statistical demonstration of the correlation are theoretically possible but would be wholly unmanageable. We are led, for lack of a better approach, to investigate the correlation of parts of the stimulus with parts of the response. For the sake of greater facility of description, we turn to analysis.(10)

This last quotation is an excellent statement of Professor Skinner's position with respect to the problem of privately accessible mental events which he regards as the middle, though causally inefficacious epiphenomenalistic, link intervening between stimulus and response.

The objection to inner states is not that they do not exist, but that they are not relevant in a functional analysis. We cannot account for the behavior of any system while staying wholly inside it; eventually we must turn to forces operating upon the organism from without. Unless there is a weak point in our causal chain so that the second link is not lawfully determined by the first, or that the third by the second, then the first and the third links must be lawfully related. If we must always go back beyond the second link for prediction and control, we may avoid many tiresome and exhausting digressions by examining the third link as a function of the first. Valid information about the second link may throw light upon this relationship but it can in no way alter it.(4)

The above quotations contain the essential elements of Professor Skinner's position in respect to those basic principles upon which his more comprehensive theory of human behavior rests.

John Dewey, a man who possessed great faith in the explanatory powers of science as it enhances the well-being of mankind, held views that are in certain respects markedly similar to Skinner's. He wrote at a time when various mentalistic psychologies were still influential, and thus most of his writing contains numerous explicitly and implicitly stated criticisms of such obscurant schools of psychology and philosophy. However, careful notice should be taken of the serious confounding of "physicalistic" and "mentalistic" terminology pervading many of the excerpts from his writings cited below. This is odd, because Dewey's concept of behavioral scientific method is assuredly intended to be "behavioristic," for one of his primary philosophical missions was to emphasize the importance of instrumental thinking. There is no intention to denigrate the many valuable philosophical contributions of Dewey. His analysis of thought processes, contemplated as an action-oriented, instrumental class of behavior which if properly disciplined could yield progressively increased intelligent action, was a profound contribution to the ongoing study of human behavior. But in systematically explaining this intricate process, Skinner is careful to purge his works of mentalistic terminology and this is not the case with Dewey. Therefore, many of his writings are marred by ambiguity. However, paradoxically, it is precisely due to this persistent undercurrent of terminological confounding that Dewey becomes a highly appropriate transitional figure from strict Skinnerian behaviorism to the theory which is the basis of this text. Dewey, while having a profound commitment to clarifying and promoting scientific inquiry, was primarily concerned with explicating the full implication of personal human experience, and therefore was not overly reductionistic in his characterization of man. Dewey was not preoccupied with explaining human behavioral phenomena in strictly physio-chemical or otherwise naïvely mechanistic terms. It will be seen that many concepts in the general theory of mind subsequently to be proposed are very much implicit in the writings of Dewey, although it is unlikely that he would have strictly subscribed to them as they will be formulated. A case in point is the mutual admiration of Whitehead and Dewey. Many philosophers, particularly positivistic thinkers, have been highly critical of the strong metaphysical sentiments of Whitehead, while on the other hand regarding Dewey as a champion of rigidly empirical views. However, there are numerous similarities between Whitehead's "liberal" realism and Dewey's instrumentalism.

Dewey's position on thinking-behavior is that thought is a dynamic functional process, inextricably a part of the human organism's total behavior, and thus cannot be a distinct consideration apart from physical behavior. To separate thinking from physical behavior is to necessarily commit an indefensible mind-body dualism. Behavior is an interpenetrative process where organism first acts upon environment and experiences the reciprocal environmental effects of both random and premeditated action, and then makes appropriate behavioral adjustments to increase future behavioral efficacy. Since this problem-solving, reflectively disciplined behavior is what Dewey conceives as intelligent activity facilitative to further growth, it can be concluded that all human behavioral phenomena, although qualitatively variable, can be systematically comprehended in functional relationships involving organisms and their environment. In this, the organism must effectively adjust to the environment or modify its environment to fulfill organismic needs in order for the species to survive and prosper. Skinner, of course, would agree wholeheartedly with this general view. The important differences between the two thinkers occurs merely in their ultimate purposes and in their methods of theoretically describing behavioral functional relationships. Stated simply, it appears evident that any significant differences in conceiving thinking-behavior are due to the fact that Skinner is a behavioral scientist and Dewey is a philosopher.

In one place Dewey defines thinking as

the intentional endeavor to discover specific connections between something which we do and the consequences which result, so that the two become continuous. Their isolation, and consequently their purely arbitrary going together, is cancelled; a unified developing situation takes its place.(11)

It is obvious that this definition contains many provocative implications. Clearly the definition is antithetical to the notion of merely random behavior. Dewey's definition of thinking—intelligent thinking in this case—is a statement about uniquely human behavior with "consciously intentional" and "reflectively conscious" causal factors implicit. Moreover, it is a specification of a particular behavioral mode, one quite distinct from other possible modes. Let us investigate how this proposed form of intelligent behavior differs intrinsically from other types such as sheer habitual behavior, or those which could be explained in mechanistic terms. Dewey defines habitual behavior as follows:

Habit means that an individual undergoes a modification through an experience, which modification forms a predisposition to easier and more effective action in a like direction in the future. Thus, it also has the function of making one experience available in subsequent experiences. Within certain limits, it performs this function successfully. But habit, apart from knowledge, does not make allowance for change of conditions, for novelty. Provision for change is not part of its scope, for habit assumes the essential likeness of the new situation with the old.(11)

For Dewey, habitual behavior occurs, to use Skinnerian terms, when the organism has discriminated among only a narrow class of stimuli and as a result can merely evoke a correspondingly narrow group of responses. The organism cannot adequately respond to novel stimuli; thus established habituation will persist until a new class of behavioral operants become effectively habituated through proper reinforcement and thereby integrated into the organism's behavioral repertoire. This, of course, entails the maintenance of appropriate corresponding schedules of reinforcement to firmly establish given operant behaviors. In any case, for Dewey, behaviors termed "negative habituation" are those in which human beings cannot readily break out of their established behavioral routines as they necessarily arise as a function of certain corresponding familiar stimuli. The implication is, therefore, that individuals cannot often adequately cope spontaneously with novel problematic circumstances. To grow beyond this constraining situation, Dewey proposes that greater knowledge is required for effective problem-solving. Here "knowledge" has a highly determinate meaning.

While the content of knowledge is what has happened, what is taken as finished and hence settled and sure, the reference of knowledge is future or prospective. For knowledge furnishes the means of understanding or giving meaning to what is still going on and is to be done.(11)

Thus knowledge is what is generally agreed upon as scientifically ascertained fact at a given period of time. However, because of the incessantly changing nature of reality and the acquisition of increased knowledge, previously established facts must also undergo commensurate revision. Otherwise a resultant lag in knowledge would occur, thus impairing future progress. An effective way to achieve this constant revision of factual information is to intelligently utilize presently established facts as a frame of reference, hence as instruments for both suggesting and conducting future scientific investigations. But this raises a problem. Is Dewey merely advocating that, in order to transcend habitual patterns of behavior, one has only to provide a given individual with a greater quantity of facts? Certainly not. This bring us to the crucial dimension of this problem, namely, the factor of reflective thinking which is the essence of Dewey's well-known five-stage characterization of the logical form of intelligent thinking-behavior. Dewey says, "While all thinking results in knowledge, ultimately the value of knowledge is subordinate to its use in thinking."(11)

This quotation contains the fundamental maxim of instrumentalism: thinking for its own sake is of limited value, but thinking as a means to promote more thinking is the basis of a utilitarian attitude toward life whereby human organisms can make more effective reconciliations between environmental demands and organismic needs. Reflective thinking is our most potent means of realizing the instrumentalists' ideal, for when intelligently engaged in contemplating the nature of an unfamiliar event, for example:

We respond to its connections [with other facts that are already known] and not simply to the immediate occurrence. Thus, our attitude to it is much freer. We may approach it, so to speak, from any one of the angles provided by its connections. We can bring into play, as we deem wise, any one of the connections. Thus we get at a new event indirectly instead of immediately—by invention, ingenuity, resourcefulness. An ideally perfect knowledge would represent such a network of interconnections that any past experience would offer a point of advantage from which to get at the problem presented in a new experience. In fine, while a habit apart from knowledge supplies us with a single fixed method of attack, knowledge means that selection may be made from a much wider range of habits.(11)

Reflective behavior, then, involves a disciplined, habitual (in the positive sense) attitude and method for effectively coping with problematic, novel situations. Initially, we comprehend a problem in terms of its particular dimensions with which we already have some factual familiarity. We understand a given problematic occasion in terms of what our past knowledge has predisposed us to comprehend in the present occasion. Then, by means of reflection, more numerous cognitive associations are made until we have established a program for further analysis guided by tentatively formulated hypotheses, subject to revision as further factual information is experimentally obtained. Frequently during this reflective stage, overt, action-orientated behavior is postponed until an intelligently determined program for analysis can be formulated. Therefore, perhaps the most important factor Dewey stresses is that when we confront a problem we are not compelled merely to contemplate those data immediately manifested by the problem. Rather, over and above the "immediately" given data there is a backlog of relevant wisdom that has been gradually learned and incorporated as positive behavioral habits. This wisdom has been acquired through having intelligently reflected upon a multitude of past experience. Consequently, much of this previously learned information can be fruitfully

brought to bear upon currently available perceptual data to enhance
their meaning by suggesting novel modes for constructive inquiry. This
is an extremely important point.

This cursory account of Dewey's concept of intelligent thinking-
behavior provides the basis for our next step, in which this same topic is
conceived by Dewey from a somewhat different perspective. He presents an analysis in terms that may more appropriately be regarded as
mentalistic than "behavioristic" or, for that matter, not even philosophi-
cally precise. Dewey, in effecting this slight shift in analytical perspective, enables us, in a sense to more clearly understand his conception of
consciousness, a notion, it will be argued, about which he is unclear.

Here Dewey is again discussing the nature of intelligent problem-
solving behavior.

Action with a purpose is deliberate; it involves a consciously foreseen end
and a mental weighing of considerations pro and con. It also involves a
conscious state of longing or desire for the end. The deliberate choice of an
aim and of a settled disposition of the desire takes time. During this time
complete overt action is suspended. A person who does not have his mind
suspended does not know what to do. Consequently he postpones definite
action so far as possible. . . . During the time in which a single overt line
of action is in suspense, his activities are confined to such redistributions of
energy within the organism as will prepare a determinate course of action.
. . . All this means an accentuation of consciousness; it means a turning in
upon the individual's own attitudes, powers, wishes, etc.

Obviously, however, this surging up of personal factors into conscious recognition is a part of the whole activity in its temporal development. There is
not first a purely psychical process, followed abruptly by a radically different physical one. There is one continuous behavior, proceeding from a more
uncertain, divided, hesitating state to a more overt, determinate, or complete
state. The activity at first consists mainly of certain tensions and adjustments
within the organism; as these are coordinated into a unified attitude, the
organism as a whole acts—some definite act is undertaken. We may distinguish,
of course, the more explicitly conscious phase of the continuous activity as
mental or psychical. But that only identifies the mental or psychical to mean
the indeterminate, formative state of an activity which in its fullness involves
putting forth of overt energy to modify the environment.

Our conscious thoughts, observations, wishes, adversions are important because they represent inchoate, nascent activities. They fulfill their destiny in
issuing, later on, into specific and perceptible acts. And these inchoate,
budding organic readjustments are important because they are our sole
escape from the dominion of routine habits and blind impulse. They are
activities having a new meaning in process of development. Hence, normally
there is an accentuation of personal consciousness whenever our instincts and

ready formed habits find themselves blocked by novel conditions. Then we are thrown back upon ourselves to reorganize our own attitude before proceeding to a definite and irretrievable course of action. Unless we drive our way through by sheer brute force, we must modify our organic resources to adapt them to the specific features of the situation in which we find ourselves. The conscious deliberating and desiring which precede overt actions are then methods of personal readjustment implied in activity in uncertain situations.(11)

Dewey has been quoted at length for the preceding statements are a powerfully imaginative, succinctly comprehensive expression of his conception of holistic organismic behavior, an integral part of which is thinking-behavior. However, the quotations also contain a clear indication of a serious error, one which is clearly evident throughout Dewey's voluminous writings, that thinking-behavior can be entirely explained in terms of directly observable, intersubjectively valid, scientific functional relationships.* (12) It will be subsequently argued that privately accessible phenomena cannot be accounted for in this analytical or objective psychological framework. An important distinction to be made at this point is that there are two general classes of phenomena of which human organisms can become aware through direct perceptual acquaintance. First, there is our experience of the natural world, that region presented through the external bodily senses. Perceptions occurring in this category of awareness will be hereafter defined as natural event-components. The components are also directly accessible to other human organisms and therefore qualify as intersubjectively verifiable event-components. Secondly, there is another category of event-components not experienced via the external bodily senses, and yet we individually have direct experiential or perceptual access to them. These will hereafter be referred to as internal bodily event-components. The unique quality of these event-components is that they are directly accessible to only the individual human organism who experiences them. Hence, in principle, they are incapable of direct intersubjective verification. They can, however, be made partially intersubjectively verifiable via the possible modes of overt symbolic expression, but internal bodily event-components are nevertheless only indirectly accessible to other human organisms.(13) A further crucial distinction should be made between the objective and subjective psychological forms in which behavior can be systematically and scientifically comprehended. Briefly stated, the objective psychologi-

---

* Here it seems that the term "functional" must possess a meaning similar to that of Skinner's, whereby "descriptions" or explanations for understanding given observed behavioral phenomena are provided by specifying those antecedent observable environmental conditions which correlate with resultant observed behaviors, hereafter referred to as a physical 1 form of explanation. This issue is discussed in greater detail by Herbert Feigl (13) and Ernest Nagel.(14)

cal form for explaining human behavior is that imprecisely articulated as Skinnerian behaviorism, for example. The subjective psychological form, conversely, systematically deals with the intrinsic structure of private mental events and their coherent and continuous relations with one another as they occur in individual human organisms. This formal characterization of human behavior will be presented in moderate detail in *Part Three* of this volume. Both psychological modes of conceptualization are necessary for an ideally complete explanation of human behavior, and further, the internal bodily event-components to which the subjective psychological form refers must be presupposed *a priori* in order to have any kind of intelligible interpersonal, or intrapersonal communication at all!

In the previous quotation, upon which much of the immediately ensuing argumentation will be based, Dewey talks as though all of that which he has stated could be fully translated into observable, scientific terms. Perhaps, he would have even argued that a science of human behavior, such as Skinner's, could have fulfilled this scientific end.

In the following paragraphs, Dewey elucidates the organic mechanisms underlying consciously directed intelligent behavior.

But in fact the nervous system is only a specialized mechanism for keeping all bodily activities working together. Instead of being isolated from them, as an organ of knowing from organs of motor response, it is the organ by which they interact responsively with one another. The brain is essentially an organ for effecting the reciprocal adjustment to each other of the stimuli received from the environment and responses directed upon it. Note that the judging is reciprocal; the brain not only enables organic activity to be brought to bear upon any object of the environment in response to a sensory stimulation, but this response also determines what the next stimulus will be.

. . . the brain is the machinery for a constant reorganization of activity so as to maintain its continuity; that is to say, to make such modifications in future action as are required because of what has already been done.

What makes it [any given purposive activity] continuous, consecutive, or concentrated is that each earlier act prepares the way for later acts, while these take account of or reckon with the results already attained—the basis of all responsibility. No one who has realized the full force of the facts of the connection of knowing with the nervous system and of the nervous system with the readjusting of activity continuously to meet new conditions, will doubt that knowing has to do with reorganizing activity, instead of being something isolated from old activity, complete on its own account.

The development of biology clinches this lesson, with its discovery of evolution. For the philosophic significance of the doctrine of evolution lies precisely in its emphasis upon continuity of simpler and more complex organic forms until we reach man. The development of organic forms begins with stimulus where the adjustment of environment and organism is obvious, and where anything which can be called mind is at a minimum. As activity becomes more complex, coordinating a greater number of factors in space and time, intelligence plays a more and more marked role, for it has a larger span of the future to forecast and plan for. The effect upon the theory of knowing is to displace the notion that it is an activity of a mere onlooker or spectator of the world, the notion which goes with the idea of knowing as something complete in itself. For the doctrine of organic development means that the living creature is part of the world, sharing its vicissitudes and fortunes, and making itself secure in its precarious dependence only as it intellectually identifies itself with the things about it, and forecasting the future consequences of what is going on, shapes its own activities accordingly. If the living, experiencing being is an intimate participant in the activities of the world to which it belongs, then knowledge is a mode of participation, valuable in the degree in which it is effective; it cannot be the idle view of an unconcerned spectator.(11)

Dewey presents us with a highly perspicacious analysis of organic processes as they have relevance for intelligent behavior, an adjustive, interpenetrative process occurring between organisms and their environments. Equally important is the fact that human organisms reflect the most highly sophisticated manifestations of what Whitehead characterizes as "concrescent" synthesis of organic functional mechanisms. These quotations from Dewey contain the implicit assumption that all human behavior can be fully explained in terms of scientific functional analysis. This tenet, as we have seen, is explicitly proposed in the writings of Skinner. There is the further complication in Dewey's writings, as has been suggested, that he utilizes many mentalistic terms—terms that refer to behavioral states which could never be scientifically verified through direct public observation—to explain his "wholly objective" scientific theory for analyzing human thinking-behavior. This criticism can be applied to Skinner as well.

With the above in mind, we can proceed with a detailed criticism of Skinner's "pure" behaviorism and Dewey's "alleged" behaviorism, endeavoring to reveal some of the philosophical difficulties of these "methodological" proposals for building a theoretically complete, exact science of human behavior. The question can be raised whether it is possible, in principle, to give a full explanation, or "description," as Skinner would say of human behavior without referring to subjective psychological event-components as being, at least in some sense, causally efficacious in producing publicly manifest behavioral responses to antecedent environmental stimuli. For example, a writer at work manifests relatively neutral overt behavior. If a group of behaviorists were observing and describing the writer's behavior, they would make such determinations as: "eyelids are blinking," "chest is heaving," "subject is verbally mute," "subject is sitting quietly in a chair," and so on. From their observational perspective they could not take direct empirical cognizance of the fact that subjective psychological, causally efficacious thinking-behavior of a highly complex nature was occurring within the organism before their eyes. They could make educated inferences about the nature of what was being silently thought by directly observing the various reference books on the desk near the writer, but nevertheless, this procedure could yield little information about the specific thoughts occurring within the head of the writer to which he has direct perceptual access. Furthermore, inferential statements about matters of privately accessible factual occurrence are poor alternatives for facts that can be indirectly ascertained merely by asking the subject in question to verbally report on the nature of his inner or private states.

It must be realized, however, that in this line of discussion we are criticizing the position of an outdated and extreme form of behaviorism, namely that of Watson—one admitting as valid factual data only concrete motor behavior, in "describing" the relationship between stimulus and passively executed response events. Today, there are more tempered positions, such as those of Skinner and Hull, which admit as legitimate factual data such behavioral phenomena as verbal reports, but strictly deny that these reports refer to corresponding trains of inner, privately accessible events. These philosophies reject psychological parallelism, a valid rejection because when one is talking aloud before a group of people, for example, one is assuredly not thinking concomitantly of an inner train of corresponding private events. This example is not analogous to the situation where the subject in question was publicly demonstrating neutral behavior, though, in addition, was also experiencing a class of behavior—one of utmost importance—in principle directly inaccessible to the behavioristicly predisposed onlookers. It is this latter, profoundly typical and uniquely human phenomenon which must be carefully scrutinized, for it is from this type of behavior that such creative enterprises as writing poetry, building bridges, and even planning and executing bank robberies, issue. These products of human intelligence are intrinsically different from behavior issuing from mechanistically "blind" sequences of conditioned reflexes in which mental events have no significant causal role.* For this reason we should care-

* Behaviorists cannot logically use nonmechanistic terms like "mental weighing" or "deliberating", for any phenomena in any way referring to conscious or reflectively conscious states would necessarily have to be regarded as mental phenomena, and thereby be considered as causal factors intervening between publicly accessible stimulus conditions and response behaviors. Since such causal factors are not per-

fully analyze a methodological viewpoint whose logical consequences necessitate that the conditioned reflex and reflex arc constructs be substituted for what has been traditionally regarded as a causally efficacious mind.

The situation has been illustrated of a writer whose behavior was being scrutinized by a group of behavioristic psychologists. It was said that the observers could make intersubjectively valid and reliable direct-determinations about their subject's behavior, defined as neutral, from their observational or objective viewpoints. But the difficulty in this analysis was that the subject had been silently engaging in complex thinking-behavior, the precise nature of which was in no way publicly determinable. Now private thinking of this sort is undeniably a distinctive form of human behavior, and beyond this fact there is also the fact that the subject in question was determining the mode of his thinking. He was causing, in the sense of imposing a personally determined direction, the nature of his thought to be what it was. It was not the result of any stimulus factors that could have been specified as existing within the immediately antecedent environment. This illustration accentuates the central problem to be faced by a psychological viewpoint which purports to be able, in principle, to completely explain, in intersubjectively verifiable language and procedure, human behavior as an exact function of operationally defined antecedent environmental conditions as they are observationally and statistically correlated with given behavioral responses. It does not increase the tenability of a behaviorism to admit verbal reports as an additional source of publicly verifiable factual data, for the central logical confusion to be reconciled does not involve this issue.

Professor Skinner's argument for a behaviorism can be stated as follows:

1. For example, if one wants to explain why a man is suffering from anxiety—if we want to get to the cause of the anxiety—it does no good to seek causes in mental or inner states.

2. Causes are to be found in immediately antecedent environmental conditions (that is, in stimulus-objects having publicly ascertainable anxiety-producing characteristics) and not in inner mental states.

3. Anxiety is a directly observable behavioral phenomenon; the

---

ceptually accessible for direct intersubjective scrutiny, their admittance into scientific explanation would mean a violation of the basic behavioristic methodological maxim that all publicly verifiable behavioral responses are, in principle, an exact function of immediately antecedent environmental conditions and previously learned behavioral predispositions whose stimulus conditions are also, in principle, capable of direct intersubjective confirmation.

inner state of anxiety is not directly observable. Therefore it is an inferred event, one that is of little value to a behaviorism.

4. Thus, if the inner state is inferential and if the cause of the anxiety is not to be found among inner states, but, rather, in antecedent environmental conditions which correlate significantly with manifest anxiety, then knowing about inner states is of no value at all in explaining the causes of behavior.(4)

Obviously, Skinner is arguing that it is not one's own private, directly accessible, psychologically meaningful state of anxiety that causes the anxious manifestations (trembling, wavering of voice, etc.) directly perceivable by onlookers. Rather it is a publicly verifiable stimulus-object, such as a snake that is placed before a subject's eyes, that causes him to tremble. From this, Skinner maintains that we can purge our scientific explanations of inner causes. But supposing a psychologist were to present a snake to a subject who, although extremely fearful of snakes, is fast asleep. The behaviorist would find, of course, that no manifest trembling would ensue; but if the subject were awakened, trembling-behavior would result. What is the issue here? It is that in the former case the subject was not consciously aware of the snake's presence, but in the latter instance he was consciously aware. In conscious awareness, the stimulus-object had subjective psychological meaning for the subject. This is a much different situation from the case of a thermostat designed to control an automatic heating system, operating necessarily as a direct, mathematically ascertainable function of temperature variation. We would regard it as odd to ask the thermostat if it was fearful of an anticipated temperature drop. The illustration, although bordering upon absurdity, crudely embodies the distinction between scientific objects of physics and chemistry, for example, and those of the behavioral sciences. At this point it must, at least, be conceded that involuntary behavioral responses of objects of psychological concern differ markedly from those of the more exact sciences because of the causal presence of the nebulously understood phenomenon of consciousness. This statement refers to the snake and thermostat illustrations.

Let us consider the issue at hand from an exact scientific perspective. Assume from the point of view of an extraordinarily sophisticated neurophysiology that it were possible to specify all the physio-chemical conditions, stated in appropriate scientific language, underlying an individual's subjective psychological state of anger. This feat is of course at present a mere science fiction, although in principle it is an eventual possibility. Here it would have to be conceded that there are two logically distinct types of meaningful statements inherent in this illustration, namely, a scientifically meaningful one, and a subjective psychological one. The former statement, in its admittedly complex and more refined form, does not analytically imply the latter type of statement, and vice versa. Rather, the correlation of the two categories of meaning is necessarily a synthetic one. Stated differently, by knowing that chemicals C_1, C_2, and C_3, for example, were somewhat deficient in the blood of a given subject, we could never infer strictly from this evidence that he was directly experiencing the subjective psychological phenomenon of thirst, for example. This connection could, in the most precise sense, only be established by asking the subject to report on his private bodily states as variables C_1, C_2, and C_3 were systematically manipulated. Skinner could quickly reply that we would not need this type of subjective report for making the determination because the subject's manifest behavior could be directly observed, that is, thirst-behavior would be manifested by him. This is true to a degree as in the cases of grossly overt states like excessive happiness or sadness, but it must be remembered that logically speaking the human phenomenon of thirst, for example, is a subjective psychological state which must necessarily have been directly experienced by some individual at some time to have become meaningful at all, for the intrinsic meaning of thirst issues from, and thereby presupposes, a personal experiential basis. We do not scientifically analyze the human physiology to formulate a meaning defined as thirst. Rather, all individual human beings have experienced the private event of thirst, but only at a much later stage in the development of man's mentality did some men become cognizant of the fact that the private or subjectively accessible phenomenon, thirst, had a physio-chemical basis. From this it can be more generally stated that in order to have a science of any kind, one must presuppose *a priori* that private experiential events are factual occurrences. The reader may question the significance of the writer having proven what most intelligent people take for granted. The issue is this: if we must presuppose *a priori* that all modes of intersubjectively verifiable symbolic expression, encompassing knowledge claims of varying degrees of certitude as well as opinion, we must necessarily presuppose direct individual perception of both the natural world and inner bodily states. Then it must also be concluded that all humanly experienced events and those in principle capable of being experienced—some of which possess intersubjective as well as merely subjective grounds for verification—are privately experienced. This is to maintain no more than the simple fact that if there are phenomena capable of occurring as components of human experience, then an individual mind must directly experience them. But if this is true, what are we to conclude about the frequently maintained distinction between public and private events—that public events refer to those natural objects and their relations available for direct apprehension by all human beings via their external bodily senses, and that private events refer to those psychological states and relations occurring within individual human beings, capable in principle of direct apprehension only by those individuals within whose organism the events occur? This distinction between public (physical) and private (mental) events, offered for argumentative reasons, contains a fundamental epistemological vagueness which, although subtle, has an extremely pronounced effect on our theories about the nature of the human mind. Positivists and behaviorists are frequent proponents of this highly questionable distinction, which in one way or another has been historically made in various schools of empirical philosophy. The mental-physical dichotomy has been recently articulated by Herbert Feigl in a most illuminating article on the mind-body problem, but here again, it seems that Feigl's view embodies the same epistemological vagueness suggested above.(13) Nevertheless, Feigl offers a fine argument supporting the view that physio-chemical states have only an empirically ascertainable identity with mental states, not an analytically ascertainable one.

What is this alleged epistemological vagueness? This is difficult to answer for we are habitually predisposed to make the mental-physical dichotomy, or even more typically, the mind-body distinction, in our contemplation of human behavior. It has been briefly intimated earlier that we could consistently conceive of at least two ways of comprehending statements of meaning with respect to characterizing human behavioral phenomena. One category of statements includes those embodying scientific knowledge claims, with their various criteria for certitude: that evidence in support of theoretical formulations be available for direct intersubjective verification to establish the validity and reliability of knowledge claims; that the principle of noncontradiction be observed; and that hypothetical-deductive explanations be effected in terms of axioms, postulates, and laws—preferably as formalized statements— whenever possible. Another category of meaningful statements includes those whose primary function is to characterize the subjective psychological, phenomenological states of individual behavior; that is, the effects of both natural world and physio-chemical bodily phenomena ingressing into personal consciousness as directly accessible components of consciousness. This is the experiential perspective from which the quotation from Whitehead characterizing experience was predicated. This second category of statements, referring to bodily feelings, emotions, and ideational states, is required to coherently explicate the phenomenological contents of individual minds as those contents are continually modified by external natural processes and personally accumulated, integrated learnings. A major point to be made about the intrinsic nature of statements in this category of meaning, whether silently thought via language or symbolically expressed for intersubjective comprehension, is that coherence in expression, occurring as silent thinking or manifest communication, is a basic operational criterion. These statements partially reflect individual experience as it is during each moment of occurrence. They are ridden with unfactual as well as factual assertions, value judgments, highly charged emotional reports, and so on. Here the obvious distinction to be made is that in the latter category of human articulation the criterion of coherent expression is the one to which we all adhere spontaneously. But in the former category, however, beyond mere coherence there is a highly determined, conscious effort made by scientists and logicians who are seriously and systematically engaging in generating statements characteristic of this category to construct propositions demonstrating maximal epistemological certitude. These statements result from a procedure entailing continual logical clarification of rules governing the processes of deduction and inference from which theories and facts are both affirmed and related. The rules also designate and facilitate a multitude of other complex, difficult, constructive operations. Therefore, as can be seen, a considerably greater amount of disciplined thinking is involved in generating scientific statements in distinction from those categorically regarded as subjective psychological.

Having distinguished between two separate categories of meaningful statements, we must consider the frames of reference from which the two categories of statements are predicated. It may be noted here that scientific statements are intended to be "value free" in their exposition of fact and theory, while subjective psychological statements contain references to directly accessible inner states including value judgments. It is often said that scientific statements, including those of the formal as well as empirical sciences, have "public" grounds for expression and verification, but those that are subjective or subjective psychological have only "private" grounds, and thereby must be regarded as inappropriate scientific knowledge claims for they require direct intersubjective confirmation of evidential phenomena. We have seen that Professor Skinner has emphatically urged that statements about inner psychological, allegedly causal, events be omitted from scientific psychology for methodological reasons; namely, that they are irrelevant to an exact science for they refer to causally inefficacious epiphenomena and they are incapable of appropriate validation. But it may be asked what is the specific nature of the epistemological grounds which have so reverently been regarded as public, and those apparently disavowed grounds termed private or subjective? In analyzing this problem, the central confusion of the public-private issue can be resolved. It may initially seem as though there are two distinct frames of reference for perceiving and hence making determinations about phenomenal occurrences: one public and one private. In a sense this is correct. Individuals have direct access to their own inner states while others have only indirect, thereby inferential, access to them. On the other hand, there are natural world phenomena directly available to all persons via their external bodily senses. But in acknowledging this concrete factual distinction, another very important one often goes unnoticed, and hence is not critically evaluated for its epistemological significance.

It can be readily granted, on one hand, that a public or scientific view of natural phenomena does not have as its frame of reference some type of universal world soul having a facility for viewing natural world objects in themselves. Obviously public events are those natural world phenomena intersubjectively apprehended directly through individuals' external bodily senses. This is a point that has been repeatedly made. But is it possible to perceive a natural phenomenon without a human mind to do the perceiving? Unless we are to admit a world soul or a Cartesian god, the answer must be emphatically negative, for only mind-perceptions are suitable for subjective psychological statements of meaning, or those statements of meaning appropriate as knowledge claims, empirical or otherwise. One may object to this line of reasoning and demand that the definitionally vague term 'mind' be omitted from the discussion for other types of objectively precise hypothetical constructs, such as reflex arc or cerebral structures, may be used as more suitable alternates. To this anticipated objection, critics are reminded of the snake illustration where conscious awareness was an unavoidable, hence causal, consideration in yielding trembling-behavior from the hypothetical subject. Thus for those still unconvinced of the necessity for using the term "mind," it can be maintained that "mind" can be equated with conscious and reflective conscious behavior, though this will undoubtedly be construed by some as replacing one vagary with another.

On the other hand, it would be equally as absurd to speak of having direct perceptual acquaintance with inner private occurrences without presupposing a mind which perceives the phenomena. Thus the common factor which must be presupposed *a priori* in both the cases of public and private perceptions is an individual mind which directly perceives those perceptual phenomena. It can thus be concluded that all possible humanly experienceable events are private events in that they are all experienced through direct acquaintance by individual minds. Apart from these considerations it is meaningless, logically and subjective psychologically, to speak of other types of events that could not in principle enter into our experiential domain.

It should be emphasized that the basis for a human behavioral model has been suggested; that is, of conceiving 'mind' as standing over against perceptual occurrences, whether the perceptions are directly perceived through the external bodily senses or directly perceived via internal bodily modes. Stated differently, specifically with regard to linguistic behavior, it is the notion of the wisdom of the past, occurring as predispositioned symbolic learning, coming synthetically to bear upon contemporary perceptual phenomena, whether issuing from external natural or internal bodily modes so that the subjective psychologically meaningful present is in great part interpretively determined by prior learning. But before beginning to systematically explicate this view, there is much to be said with respect to the former line of argumentation. The view has a highly elaborate metaphysical basis in the writings of Alfred North Whitehead and is one frequently suggested in the writings of various philosophers throughout history.(15) Oddly enough, it is a view espoused, at least implicitly, by Skinner, although with the crucially important difference that he would omit as causally irrelevant what the concept of 'mind' standing over against percepta.

Now that it has been shown that 'mind', a factor that must be necessarily presupposed *a priori* in order to have subjective psychological experience, and in turn, objective knowledge, must be assumed to stand over against all directly apprehended perception whether originating from external natural sources or internal bodily sources, what sense is to be made of the public-private dichotomy? The answer is that all events are private to the extent that human awareness of their occurrence is contingent upon an individual human mind to entertain them. For example, seeing red flames, hearing melodious tones, or feeling the roughness of asphalt, and on the other hand, feeling a pain, thinking of a novel solution for a problem, or feeling despondent, all necessarily presuppose that individual minds directly experience these occurrences, for the phenomena cannot meaningfully be understood as they are apart from individual human beings to directly experience them. The whole concept of an event has to be more carefully analyzed to determine what individuals, in fact, experience when they experience natural inner perceptual phenomena. There are many ramifications to this issue, but at this point it is relevant to draw upon the aforementioned categorical distinction between subjective psychological and scientific statements. These two categories of statements are made with reference to two distinct classes of perceptual phenomena: natural world phenomena and internal bodily phenomena. Therefore, there is a crucial difference in the two

statements, "I see the tree" and "I feel a pain," in that the location of the
stimulus-object in the former case is in the external natural world, and
in the latter case the location of the stimulus-object is in the internal
organism of the subject articulating the statement of pain. The following
conclusions can be drawn.

1. In both categorical cases the perceptual phenomena were known
via direct acquaintance.

2. In both categorical cases an individual mind must be admitted to
have had the perceptions; therefore, all events are private in that they
are directly experienced by individual human minds. Also there is the
obvious sense of privacy, in that no other individual human being can
experience one's personal experiences at their particular time and place
of occurrence.

3. The basic issue of the public-private dichotomy is to be resolved
in determining the location of the stimulus-object which gives rise to the
perception (hence defined as the stimulus-object effect) whose source
of origin must necessarily be either from the external natural environment or a percipient's internal physical organism.

4. Therefore in the logical definition of an event there is necessarily
implied a twofold consideration: a mind that perceives perceptions and
the location of the source of a perception coming to mind.

Thus in the two statements, "I see the tree," and "I feel a pain," there
are at least two factors in common for each of these distinctly different
events: an I (i.e., a mind) that perceives the pain and tree phenomena;
and a stimulus-object location from which the phenomena issue (the
stimulus-object tree located in the natural world, and the stimulus-
object physio-chemical states giving rise to the pain-perception located
within the bodily organism of the individual directly experiencing the
pain).

5. The resolution of the public-private problem can be achieved by
saying that with respect to all perceptions of which human beings can
ever, in principle, become aware it must necessarily be presupposed
a priori that an individual human mind directly perceived them. Therefore, it is necessary to conclude that all these events are private or mental
events and that there are at least two factors to be considered in our
concept of mental or private events: a mind is required to perceive (or
stand over against) perceptions, and the perceptions are a (causal) result
of stimulus-objects located either in the natural world or in the organism
of the percipient whose mind entertains the perceptions. From this, we
can conclude that the concepts of public and private verification must
necessarily refer to the location of the stimulus-objects which yield
event-components. These components by definition do not comprise a

complete mental event, for this would be to exclude reference to the
individual mind which directly experiences the event-components or
perceptions. Thus the concept of event necessarily implies a mental
event in that a mind must stand over against percepta or stimulus-
object effects that arise from stimulus-objects residing in either the
natural world or the internal body of the percipient.

With the above argumentation in mind, we are now in a position to
criticize Skinner's "methodological" viewpoint.

1. Skinner wants to omit statements alleged to refer to events
having components whose stimulus-object location is said to be within
the subject's own organism so that only the subject himself has access to
the causal state ("My sadness caused my irresponsible behavior").
He also wishes to methodologically omit those statements referring to
causal agents which, in principle, by their intrinsic theoretical nature
are not directly accessible to either subjects or observers, although
trained observers can come to understand the effects of these causal
entities indirectly (ids, egos, etc.). In each case, Skinner would maintain, the alleged causal agents are, in principle, not directly accessible to
behavioristic observers. Hence they are inappropriate subject matter for
a behavioral science which must ultimately resort to evidence capable of
direct intersubjective verification for suitable knowledge claims. Skinner
regards such subjective psychological states as sadness, desire, anxiety,
thoughts, etc., as epiphenomena which are directly accessible to the
subject in question, but are of little value to a behavioristic psychology
as causal agents, for they are not directly verifiable. Since all human
behavior is an exact function of stimulus and response—both of which
are intersubjectively verifiable classes of states—intervening mental
states can be omitted from functional analysis. This is to say that causes
for manifest irresponsible behavior, for example, are to be found in the
immediately antecedent natural environmental conditions preceding the
irresponsible response-behavior. The data collected from these antecedent causal conditions must, of course, be interpreted in light of the
subject's history of relevant learned behavioral and reflexive predispositions with respect to given stimuli.

2. This methodological approach to investigating human behavior
can legitimately be undertaken, apart from the unwarranted theoretical
conclusion that mental events are causally inefficacious epiphenomena,
and it can be defined as a scientific objective (as distinct from subjective)
psychological approach to studying human behavior.

3. But to say that private events are to be omitted from a behavioristic psychology on the grounds of being causally inefficacious elements
in human behavior is wholly untenable for this is to confuse the logical

meaning of private event. Private events must be presupposed *a priori* to involve human thinking-behavior, whether thinking occurs as subjective psychological states consisting of personal values, feelings, biases, or emotions, or in the considerably more disciplined subjective psychological form out of which scientific statements, possessing intersubjective confirmability, are generated.

4. Thus it cannot be said that private events are not causally efficacious, although it has not been demonstrated at this point how they function causally, for the phenomenon for intelligent human behavior itself, for example, is a creative product of disciplined private-event processes.

5. Specifically, Skinner is advocating an objective psychological science of human behavior that admits into its behavioral descriptions only those statements referring to private events of individual behavioristic observers containing directly experienced event-components resulting from natural world stimulus-objects which, contemplated from the relative perspective of each behavioristic observer, become part of the category of natural world phenomena that are intersubjectively confirmable. In propounding this methodological viewpoint, Skinner is necessarily admitting only those statements articulated by individual behavioristic observers that refer to each observer's own private events having components (perceptions) resulting from natural world stimulus-objects, for example, a subject's verbal expression, the subjective psychological meaning of which referred to a stimulus-object not directly perceivable by that behaviorist. A heard verbalization can be admitted as scientific evidence, but not the causal entity to which the verbalization is alleged to refer (i.e., the inner state, anxiety).

6. Therefore, although Skinner can legitimately banish all references made by subjects to inner causes and retain reference to only their manifest behavior, he cannot, in principle, conclude from this that private events are causally inefficacious, for the very possibility of even making behavioristic determinations about someone else's manifest behavior presupposes *a priori* the possibility of individual behaviorists having mental events, in that a mind must stand over against individual behaviorists' perceptions of their subject's behavior perceived as natural world phenomena because the location of the stimulus-object in question is located outside the behaviorists' bodies. To neglect this line of argumentation, thereby falling into a purely epiphenomenalistic view of mental events, would be to necessarily regard human behavior as entirely reflexive, and therefore, to contemplate behavioral processes in a manner similar to seventeenth-century materialistic determinism.

7. Another crucially important conclusion follows. From the bare

behavioristic observation of eyes blinking, hands trembling, etc., the interpretive inference going beyond the bare factually perceptual given, that there is manifest anxious behavior, does not analytically follow! Rather, it is a synthetic judgment which presupposes ultimately that logically one individual human being, at least, had the direct subjective psychological experience of anxiety, and took the liberty of reporting the phenomenon to others.

The inquiry thus far has been difficult and involuted, but at least two things are conspicuously evident as a result. First, as is so often the case, considerations which seem to be initially straightforward frequently contain numerous, subtle implications that, if overlooked, can give rise to very perplexing antinomies, as in the case of the mind-body problem. This admonition is merely to reaffirm what has been frequently proven throughout an ageless backlog of philosophical criticism. Secondly, it can be seen in retrospect that the logical difficulties inherent to behaviorism are closely related to, if not an actual embodiment of, the problem of philosophical relativity. The difficulties are revealed when individual minds begin to systematically reflect upon the phenomenon of minds taking account of other minds as well as of natural objects.

In the interest of terminological clarification, hereafter, we shall designate objects capable of direct intersubjective verification, such as objects and their properties and relations located in the natural world, as public event-components as distinct from the misleading term, "public events," and those objects with their properties and relations not capable of direct intersubjective confirmation, such as inner subjective psychological states, as private event-components. The term "private event," as we have seen to some moderate extent, is far more inclusive than "private event-component." In the statement, "I feel happy," the bare feeling of happiness would be a private event-component in the sense that a particular individual at a particular time and place is directly experiencing a feeling of happiness in such a way that no other human being can have precisely that experience to which reference is being made. On the other hand, the individual when uttering the statement, "I feel happy," is understanding considerably more than merely taking specific account of a happy feeling. This is to say that the literal words, "I feel happy" are a great linguistic oversimplification of what the individual at the exact time of experiencing the happy feeling was in fact experiencing. Beyond the clearly articulated recognition of a happy feeling private event-component, there are a multitude of progressively more subtle event-components; that is, pure affective and vague symbolic elements less clearly recognized by the subject of the experience such as a concept of "I," "a concept of what it means to have a feeling," "a concept of qualitatively different feelings," etc., as well as a host of other ramifications that are intrinsic to any given moment of subjective psychological experience. This stipulation with respect to the more inclusive, far-reaching implications associated with the newly defined concept of private event, because of its complex, predominately linguistic structure is rarely emphasized by psychologists and philosophers. But it is herein that a penetrating understanding of the logical form of subjective psychological experience is to be discovered.

The more general term "stimulus-object" will be used for the causal agent giving rise to or providing the necessary condition for the perceptual occurrence of public and private event-components, or what we have also termed stimulus-object effects.

It is possible to schematically represent some of our previous analysis of subjective psychological events and their various possible modes for disciplined thought-behavior in the following hierarchical way:

Level$_N$	Formal scientific statements (e.g., mathematical and symbolic logical) with their definitional assertions and procedures subject to the principle of noncontradiction
Level$_{N-1}$	Rigorously empirically verified statements with theoretical constructs subject to the principle of noncontradiction, and intersubjectively validated experimental evidence
•	
•	
•	
Level$_2$	Opinion statements about various matters based on personal, pragmatic conclusions resulting from nonmethodological acquaintance with reality
Level$_1$	Statements reporting on subjective psychological states, e.g., feelings, desires, values; any phenomenologically "given" states

Figure 1. A hierarchy of symbolic discipline

The entire area within the rectangular chart would represent all the possible kinds of assertions that could be made from any particular person's subjective psychological experience at a given time, as private events which must be presupposed *a priori* in order to have any type of thinking behavior at all. Those modes of thought at the lower levels on the hierarchy are characterized by their lack of cognitive disciplining, while those at progressively higher levels are distinctly characterized by their rigorous cognitive discipline, with respect to specified procedural rules, evidential confirmability, etc.

The foregoing sequence of argumentation is not intended to be an act of epistemological subterfuge whereby mind has been deceitfully smuggled, once again, back into psychology and some philosophical camps. Rather it is an argument that mind, as an active, constructive agent, functions causally in each of us during every conscious moment of experience throughout our lives. The fact of its causally efficacious role, as it is disclosed in our concrete subjective psychological experience of the natural and internal bodily environments, is frequently overlooked and obscured by certain schools of psychology and philosophy. In subsequent chapters we shall endeavor to isolate the categories of perceptual facts testifying to the causal efficacity of mind, and hence, formulate a theory of mind whereby these facts, occurring as concrete experience, can be shown to embody the logical form common to all possible subjective psychological experience. If this end can be accomplished, then the principles of a subjective psychology will in great part be provided, thus revealing more clearly certain lawlike relations in human behavior, in addition to suggesting many novel possibilities for experimental research.

PART TWO

The General Behavioral Model

Chapter two / Criticism of behaviorism reconsidered

Essentially the basic argument of *Part One* was as follows:

1. We cannot exclude private or mental events from the realm of scientific behavioral analysis either in an objective or subjective psychology, and therefore conclude that all behavior is ultimately blindly (mechanically) reflexive in the sense that resultant human behavioral responses are an exact function of antecedent environmental conditions. Such an exclusion would render inner mental states epiphenomenalistic, for the very possibility of any methodological and, moreover, rationally coherent enterprise must presuppose *a priori* the causal efficacity of mental states.

2. Mind was metaphorically conceived as standing over against perceptual phenomena capable of occurring in two categorically distinct ways: as perceptions occurring subjective psychologically as stimulus-object effects issuing from stimulus-objects located in the external natural world; and as perceptions occurring subjective psychologically as stimulus-object effects issuing from stimulus-objects located in the internal organism of the individual percipient himself.

3. This amounts to saying that to conceive of an individual having perceptions, and hence executing complex intelligent behavioral operations without a consciousness to stand over against the perceptions—that is, to directly apprehend them—leads to complete absurdity.

4. More specifically, mind has been defined as conscious awareness and reflective conscious awareness, which is thought critically taking

account of previously experienced thought, entailing the utilization of
former symbolically disciplined experience to constructively enhance the
meaning of contemporary thinking. To deny the efficacious role of consciousness and reflective consciousness, in the sense that they are
necessary factors intervening between antecedent stimulus conditions
and resultant behavioral responses, is to lead to logical contradiction.
However, Skinnerian behaviorism demands that manifest human behavioral responses be regarded, in principle, as an exact function of
intersubjectively verifiable antecedent environmental conditions. What
are regarded as inner mental events are causally inefficacious by-products
or epiphenomena resulting from stimulus-response actualizations. In this
way it is alleged that an entirely objective behavioral science can be
established, for all stimulus and response phenomena are intersubjectively verifiable. But since human conscious and reflective conscious
awareness are not directly intersubjectively ascertainable, and yet
their causal efficacity in the production of human behavior cannot be
denied, it follows that Skinnerian behaviorism, on methodological
grounds, must and does purge statements referring to inner states from its
scientific domain. However, contrary to its conclusions, it can thereby
provide only a partial account of human behavior. The conclusive refutation, then, of the possibility for Skinnerian behaviorism (and hence
all behaviorisms) to provide, in principle, a complete scientific exposition of human behavior lies in the fact that a mind must be presupposed
a priori to stand over against percepts originating from stimulus-objects
located in either the external natural or internal bodily environments.
Behaviorists cannot, however, in principle, incorporate statements into
their system referring to percepta originating from internal bodily regions for these data are not directly available for intersubjective
verification. But the obvious fact of the matter is that internal percepta,
capable of direct verification only by those individual percipients
within whose organism the perceptions arise, include such indubitably
existing phenomena as bodily feeling, emotions, and most important,
ideational processes. Behaviorisms attempt to avoid this difficulty by
restating such alleged internal phenomena in terms of operational
definitions whose evidential grounds are consistent with their
methodology.

However, the limitations of this endeavor can be easily exposed by
pointing out that statements referring to subjective psychological experiential states cannot be analytically deduced from their operationally
defined, intersubjectively directly verifiable counterparts. Thus, on logical grounds this is to establish the certainty of two distinct psychological
domains: one which manifests itself in the same way as any natural

phenomena and is thereby available for direct intersubjective scrutiny; and the other which refers to phenomenal states directly accessible only to those individuals within whose bodies the perceptual phenomena occur. The final conclusion to be drawn from the lack of analytical equivalence between the two behavioral domains is that, since subjective psychological behavior is in great part thinking-behavior, it must be conceded that behaviorism—if we are to regard it as a product of intelligent, reflective thinking—must itself presuppose *a priori* those subjective psychological states which it wishes to purge from its inquiries in order to be an active scientific enterprise; unless, of course, behaviorists are willing to also maintain that their experimentally derived fruits are products of mere unconscious, reflexively executed behavioral efforts.

The distinction has also been made between the possibility of an objective and a subjective scientific psychology. The former, which is the currently established discipline of behaviorism, deals with human behavior purely as it directly appears or is phenomenally given as external bodily perceptions of individual behavioristic observers. Therefore, in this methodological but, in fact, theoretical scheme, reference to inner, not directly perceivable causes must be omitted from their behavioral analyses. But such inner causes do, in fact, influence resultant behavior. The argument underlying this position is essentially that even a logically possible, complete physio-chemical explanation, stated in appropriate scientific terms, of a particular neurological state cannot, in principle, analytically contain the concept, "I feel angry," which is a directly accessible subjective psychological state, because the logical meaning of the two states of affairs involves a synthetic leap. They are not logically identical with one another because one statement contains different information from the other. Therefore the correlation to be established by an extremely advanced neurophysiology must be established empirically. Feigl argues to the same conclusion, only from a different frame of reference.(13)

Stated differently, Dewey's and, without question, Skinner's explanation of thinking-behavior basically yields natural cause-effect, functional explanations. However, this category of cause-effect explanations does not explain the intrinsic nature of subjective psychological meaning directly experienced by given individuals in any given spatio-temporal region who demonstrate manifest behavior to behaviorists. This holds true even if we consider a less extreme illustration than the hypothetical one of a writer directly observed by a team of behaviorists who had direct access to his manifest behavior, but not to his silent thinking-behavior. To know what a given thought was a function of (stated in appropriate physio-chemical scientific terms) does not explain the intrinsic subjective psychological meaning of the thought phenomenon. It only explains how a thought can physically occur as it does and not the subjective meaning of the thought phenomenon itself. Granted, a trained behavioristic observer can hear and understand to some degree, and in many cases even better than the individual experiencing the private state, the verbalization about the subjectively experienced particular state, but the observer cannot, in principle, have the personally experienced state. Even if the functional analysis is considerably more complex and systematic than the subject's own description of his inner state, it is, nevertheless, not logically identical with the subjective psychological meaning that is directly accessible to the subject experiencing it. It goes without saying that the very possibility of human consciousness is contingent upon an extraordinarily large number of integrated biochemical processes which, in effect, physically provide the necessary conditions for conscious and consciously reflective behavior. Medical science explores the organic basis of pains, for example, ultimately because there are subjective psychological states of pain directly experienced by individual human beings. Thus the occurrence of human pain prompted the development of the science of medicine. Furthermore, the science of medicine was created by intelligent, consciously reflective, and aware individuals whose knowledge, because it was in disciplined or systematic symbolic form, could be personally utilized and intersubjectively understood and therefore shared. Hence awareness must be presupposed *a priori* for any thinking behavior at all. All this was not a result of purely blind, reflexive behavior—a position which Skinner must necessarily maintain if we are to understand his words for their exact meaning. Rather, another factor has entered the causal scene, namely, conscious reflection. Thus if consciously reflective behavior is necessary for the very possibility of high-ordered thinking behavior, then this behavioral realm must be opened to scientific investigation even though consciously reflective behavioral processes are not directly available for scientific intersubjective scrutinization, but are directly accessible to the subjects which can be used for controlled experimentation. Therefore behavioral scientists will have to formulate hypothetical constructs designed to represent the form in which subjective psychological events occur, and then utilize various mathematical and statistical procedures with specially designed experiments, whose evidential basis is available to direct intersubjective verification, for proving or disproving given theoretical constructs. It is in this type of procedure that a subjective psychological science can be grounded. The objection may be raised that this procedure would seem methodologically inappropriate because of the logical impossibility of direct intersubjective accessibility of inner states by observational scientists, for behaviorism does not operate under this limitation. But we must recall that the science of physics, for example, is not by any means a behavioristic one in that there are numerous hypothetical constructs (e.g., light waves, atoms, etc.) which are operationally used with extraordinary utility without ever having been directly intersubjectively observed. In fact, a subjective psychological science has the advantage that its objects of scientific inquiry can provide direct testimony to their dynamic internal states when subjected to controlled experimental conditions, an advantage that is not possible in all other natural and biological sciences.

The task at this point is to outline a general nonreductionistic, mechanistic model suitable for meeting the immediate needs of both an objective and a subjective psychology. Many of the features of the model to be proposed are suggested in the writings of Whitehead, Ernst Cassirer, Dewey and Skinner. We will begin to develop the constructs of this model by initially analyzing the concepts of consciousness and, particularly, the mechanism of reflective consciousness; and then work progressively toward a comprehensive behavioral model for conceiving individual and, if the principles are extended, group behavior as it occurs within given environmental contexts.

It should be kept in mind that theoretical definitions will gradually acquire increasingly precise meaning as "key" terms are successively qualified. The overall context in which the terms are used will additionally suggest by implication their more universal meanings at increasing levels of abstraction. This is precisely the case with the concepts of consciousness and reflective consciousness. Some moderate attempt at defining these terms has been made, in roughly equating them with 'mind,' and the attempt will be made to render their meaning more precise and comprehensive. In any case, the meaning of technical concepts must be pondered within the contextual framework of the final model to be proposed, even though they will be defined essentially in mechanistic terms.

Chapter three / Consciousness and conscious reflection

Let us begin by maintaining that consciousness must at least be equated with awareness. Awareness is a phenomenon having many degrees of subjective intensity. For example, one can momentarily be aware of the presence of a tree and then turn one's attention to some other matter, hence forgetting the experience of ever having seen the tree. On the other hand, we have profound, lasting awarenesses. For example, there are the complex experiences of "feeling fully reconciled with life"; "a deep satisfaction resulting from the way that one is leading one's life" (a transitory awareness to be sure), or even the higher-ordered awareness of the "I-thou," articulated by Buber.(16) In any case, intensity of awareness can be comprehended as occurring on a continuum, whereby the intensity of understanding a given stimulus-condition indicates the degree of an individual's subjective psychological awareness of a given object of concern. Thus if awareness is to be roughly equivalent with consciousness, it can be said that consciousness ranges in its level of understanding from bare sensory perception to having insight into, for example, the Platonic Good. Usually, however, we think of consciousness as merely taking account of something. For purposes of argument at this point, awareness or consciousness will be defined as taking minimal cognitive account of an object's perceptual presence. The perceptions in this case are event-components, keeping in mind the twofold way of characterizing all possible humanly perceivable events. There is a *something* of which an individual is conscious or aware (an event-component) that issues from a stimulus-object. This is a necessary assumption that must be posited in order to have science at all. On the other hand, there is a mind (a consciousness) that it must be admitted has the perception. It will be recalled that stimulus-objects, of which we directly experience the effects as perceptions, have two possible sources of location: the external natural world, and the internal organism of the perceiver. It is crucial to note that we directly experience the effects of stimulus-objects, which are event-components in our consciousness, for to directly experience a stimulus-object in itself would necessitate that the percipient must be that stimulus-object, a logical absurdity. Furthermore, the concept of stimulus-object is not constrained to tangible and intangible objects as such. It may also characterize properties of and relations among entities which we directly experience through internal or external perceptual modes, such as the redness of a rose, an object becoming warmer, one object passing another, or an intensifying emotional state. The above distinctions serve as an introduction to a more comprehensive analysis that will be subsequently presented.

Therefore, if consciousness generally refers to the psychological act of merely taking account of something, this must be regarded as entailing some minimal amount of thought-behavior. From this, the concept of reflective consciousness follows, defined as the phenomenon of thought critically analyzing formerly experienced thought. Thought, as it has intrinsic meaning from a subjective psychological perspective, one that is logically distinct from behavioristically observing or listening to any manifest expression of subjective psychological thinking-behavior, or from a content analysis of a verbal report articulated by a given subject, is the cumulative synthetic product, at any given point in time, of a long-termed, antecedently initiated, reflectively disciplined process involving innumerable learned ideational associations integrated into an overall, instrumentally operative cognitive system capable of being activated by a large number of qualitatively diverse stimulus-conditions. Thus the production of a given thought at a particular time is, in a very definite sense, an embodiment of formerly acquired relevant wisdom. This is to say that an indefinitely large number of previously learned associations can be, in a very short time, synthetically brought to bear upon any given contemporary stimulus-occasion. Some of the associations we recall through a deliberate conscious reflective effort, while the majority are reflexively conjured to consciousness, in the sense that they have been so thoroughly habitually learned that they arise spontaneously in response to a stimulus-object. In this, we often cannot recall the original experiential circumstances in which these early learnings occurred, except in some cases through hypnosis. Characteristically, many of the learnings we undoubtedly found originally difficult can with increased maturity become spontaneously executable. An entire synthetic configuration of ideational propensities, possessing a profound operational interrelationship with one another, can often be reflexively delivered to a contemporary occasion at a moment's notice. Therefore, for example, a man's contemporary, spoken comment on the theory of rela-

tivity—an action requiring considerable antecedent educational preparation—embodies within it, as subjective psychological meaning, at the
moment of expression, perhaps years of accumulated, integrated wisdom
explicitly and implicitly delivered within the comparatively small number of linguistic symbols required to verbally express the comment. This
is truly a remarkable phenomenon, but one executed with ease by
typically intelligent human beings. It is in this way that three time dimensions are synthetically actualized in one present temporal occasion.
The wisdom of the past is embodied within a contemporary verbal
utterance, for example, and in this verbalization lies the predispositional
groundwork for the future, successive verbal symbol to be articulated by
the same person. It is only in the phenomenon of mind that such an
ontological possibility can be repeatedly actualized with ease. It is this
phenomenon that we shall subject to intensive analysis throughout the
remainder of this book, for such issues are the rightful subject matter
for a subjective psychology.

Heretofore several implications inherent to the concept of consciousness have been explored. The phenomenon of reflective consciousness,
over and above that of consciousness, involves the process of thought
critically analyzing formerly experienced thought. This notion suggests
many more ramifications in the light of the brief discussion on how the
wisdom of the past can be brought constructively to bear upon present
occasions in producing ideational states, thereby preparing the way for
future cognitive activity. Reflective conscious thinking, then, is the
phenomenon of thought turning analytically upon itself in an attempt
to generate novel, more profound understanding. The terms used to
introduce the concepts of consciousness and reflective consciousness have
occasionally been metaphorical, for we have not yet pursued our investigation in sufficient depth to have developed more precise terminology. This task will be a major objective in our analysis of mind. The
definitional terms used to achieve this end must be cybernetic in scope
because of the vast number of physio-chemical processes, organic mechanisms, and hence mental processes involved in producing human
behavior. A quotation from W. Ross Ashby illustrates this point when he
says:

. . . [cybernetics] offers a single set of concepts suitable for representing
the most diverse types of systems. Until recently, any attempt to relate the
many facts known about, say, servo-mechanisms to what was known about
the cerebellum was made unnecessarily difficult by the fact that the propensities of servo-mechanisms were described in words redolent of the automatic pilot, or the radio set, or the hydraulic brake, while those of the
cerebellum were described in words redolent of the dissecting room and the

bedside—aspects that are irrelevant to the similarities between a servo-mechanism and a cerebellar reflex. Cybernetics offers one set of concepts that, by having exact correspondences with each branch of science, can thereby bring them into exact relation with one another.

The second peculiar virtue of cybernetics is that it offers a method for the scientific treatment of the systems in which complexity is outstanding and too important to be ignored. Such systems are, as we well know, only too common in the biological world!(17)

Thus we will have occasion to develop a small number of theoretical terms carefully defined to portray the similarities in functioning among indeterminately numerous and complex human organic processes, processes which can in principle be explained in mechanistic biological terms. In this connection, see Nagel's arguments for mechanism in biology.(14)

Again, it can be said that the ideational product of reflective thought process is an intrinsically subjective psychological one, therefore potentially revealing itself as directly accessible in its entirety only to the individual engaged in reflecting. This directly accessible meaning can be rendered intersubjectively verifiable only when it is manifestly expressed in a symbolic mode, such as spoken verbalizations, written words, mathematics, art, or music. Frequently, what has been defined as subjective psychological meaning has many accompanying objective psychological manifestations. As a result of these lines of argumentation there is no reason for concluding that silent reflective thinking is to be regarded as what Gilbert Ryle has termed "ghost-in-a-machine" phenomena.(18) It is perfectly consistent to maintain that silent reflection occurs via the same linguistic symbolic medium as does thinking-out-loud, which is, conversely, largely intersubjectively directly verifiable.

A basic principle involved in the concepts of consciousness and reflectively conscious thinking-behavior can be diagrammatically represented. See Fig. 2.

Event A (necessarily representing both a perceptual event-component and a mind which has the perception) at time$_1$ represents an immediate consciously experienced event, the nonreflective behavior of an individual who has just had a subjective psychological thought. The organic structure of the human organism is such that it enables the organism to have conscious awarenesses and, more remarkably, the organism can recall having had former awarenesses. Even beyond this, the organism can synthetically utilize previously acquired wisdom (a term implying constructive cognitive integration) in conjunction with present perceptual awarenesses to successively transcend contemporary

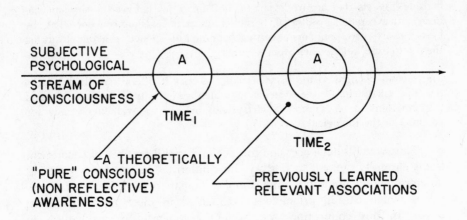

Figure 2. The form of conscious reflection

levels of understanding. Therefore, event A at time$_1$ represents a temporally antecedent condition of mere conscious awareness, and the successive condition, at time$_2$, is that of reflective consciousness. In the latter cognitive act, where the organism is constructively recalling having directly experienced event A at time$_1$, more complex organic and thereby ideational processes are involved, for it entails at time$_2$ bringing to bear many previously learned relevant associations upon the event-component being contemplated, event A actualized at time$_1$. This is essentially the reflective process: gradually developed thinking-behavior is instrumentally implemented to analyze the implications of more specific, previously experienced thinking-behavior. The diagram is meant merely to demonstrate the principle of reflection in its barest form, and not as an exhaustive exposition of the phenomenon.

A major tenet of this book is that any mode of intersubjective communication, and thereby any knowledge-claim statement, regardless of how rudimentary or sophisticated its form, must necessarily be contemplated as having its ultimate basis in the subjective psychological individual human organisms. This is to be presupposed *a priori* for the very possibility of any kind of human thinking at all. This position is difficult to present in simple terms for our distinctions have been subtle in order to dispel firmly ingrained philosophical and psychological misnomers that have tenaciously persisted in Western thought. Once this groundwork has been completed, however, the subjective psychological theory can be expressed in simpler form. The reason for raising this issue again is that we must reconsider the necessity and *function* of symbolism as a means for executing both *inter*subjective and *intra*subjective thought. In communicating with others, we rely upon symbolic media, and similarly, when communicating with ourselves, its possibility is also grounded in symbolism, the most common form of which is language. Meaningful thinking of any kind is ultimately grounded in individually actualized symbolic thought, regardless of whether the symbols are embodied in mind or matter. Libraries are repositories for symbols embodied in matter, symbols which have no meaning whatsoever until a human mind is brought to bear upon them. This involves both imputing subjective psychological meaning to the symbols, and reciprocally having meaningful ideational associations stimulated by the materially embodied symbols. In this latter interaction, the symbols function as stimulus-objects, but from the standpoint of subjective psychological experience, they are experienced as stimulus-object effects or event-components. But oddly enough, brains like libraries in a very broad sense are material objects, and similarly, have a capacity for storing symbols. However, brains think and libraries do not. We may wonder therefore, apart from obvious structural differences, what unique modes of behavior are demonstrated by minds that render them distinct entities from libraries. An extremely important initial distinction is that the very concept of library, for example, is unthinkable without human minds to initially conceive of it as a conceptual entity and then proceed to provide the concept with a physical or existential counterpart. In any case, symbolic behavior is the essence of subjective psychologically meaningful behavior, and consequently, must be subsumed to careful analysis.

In formulating a concept of mind we place primary emphasis upon analyzing the subjective psychological structure of linguistic symbols. However, the theory to be propounded appears generally applicable to all types of symbolic expression. The questions, What do symbols represent? What is the intrinsic nature of symbols?, must be considered in some detail. These questions yield highly speculative answers, for little has been offered by interested theorists that could qualify as even a minimally satisfactory, comprehensive theory of linguistic behavior. The theory most consistent with a subjective psychology is that presented in the writings of the late Ernst Cassirer.(19), (20) Cassirer's work on this subject is unusually penetrating, both in scholarly presentation and imaginative development. However, interpretation of some of these writings in light of the general theory of human behavior now being developed, will subject Cassirer's views to a certain amount of modification.

Since the ability to use linguistic symbols is essentially developed at a relatively early age, the theory to be presented refers primarily to the early childhood years. Although there are many empirically verified studies on symbolic development, facts alone are relatively meaningless unless associated within a comprehensive theoretical framework. Actually one may legitimately argue that abstract facts considered in themselves have little utility unless empirically ascertained within the context of a clearly specified theory. Further, an indefinite number of theories can logically fit given groups of facts. Particularly with respect to various theories of linguistic development and usage, it seems evident that nearly all of those presently regarded as being useful are essentially founded upon rather naïve, mechanically reductionistic epistemological grounds such as associationism and operant conditioning. This point can be easily comprehended by reading Cassirer's chapter on language in his book, *An Essay on Man*.(19) This whole issue is also masterfully made evident in the first chapter of his earlier penetrating work, *Substance and Function*.(21) As a result of the current sterility of most theories on the nature of language, a philosophical outline of a general theory of symbolic behavioral development is in order. Moreover, after the logical possibility of a subjective psychological science is revealed, new theoretical constructs about symbolic thought are needed both to accentuate the plausability of such an enterprise and to serve as operational instruments for methodological inquiry.

Chapter four / A theory of
symbolic development

In considering the questions, What do symbols represent? What is the intrinsic nature of symbols?, it should be stated that language, and all symbolic expression, develops initially out of early adjustive behaviors executed by individual human organisms as they learn to meet the demands of their environments, and later, through actively exploring various comprehensible dimensions of these environments. From a subjective psychological perspective, at early stages of behavioral development this amounts to saying that human organisms, because of their organic or physio-chemical structural nature, are able to organize and clarify, by subjecting personal behavioral modes to functional discipline, and later, to communicate symbolically the nature of primordial and intensely felt emergent emotional feelings. At progressively later stages in infantile cognitive development, there is a gradual shift in emphasis in which organisms organize, clarify, and symbolically represent as direct communication, clearly experienced and qualitatively more sophisticated emergent ideational states, while correspondingly less behavior is executed representing the nature of vague internal emotional percepta. This is a phenomenon which, it will be seen, has both positive and negative implications for the well-being of human organisms. In this process of cognitive or symbolic development, human organisms increase their survival capacities by more effectively maintaining what is essentially an interpenetrative relationship between organism and environment. At higher levels of development, the human organism adopts a progressively more active approach to learning efficacious behavioral modes for increasing the frequency of qualitatively more desirable subjective psychological experience. Intellectual maturation consists, obviously, of linguistic acquisition, and is utilized facilitatively as a principal means for promoting human intelligence. Words are learned behaviors—behaviors that become thoroughly habituated, that, in effect, "tag" those stimulus-object effects issuing from internal or external environmental locations whose nature has been represented by particular linguistic universals. Ultimately the meaning and significance of language is grounded in individual subjective psychological experience; similarly at very early ages, presymbolic behavior issues directly from organic bodily and undisciplined emotional feelings. At this level, bare symbolically undisciplined consciousness is being-as-it-is-comprehensively and undifferentiatedly felt, both as emotion and as organic bodily feeling. Stated differently, consciousness is that dimly illuminated, subjectively experienced focal point into which the relevant effects of inner and outer environments enter, hence gaining unique actualization as unsymbolized subjective psychological experience within the personal organism of human beings. All more sophisticated conscious experience, including the supreme achievement of reflective conscious thinking, entails an extraordinarily complex, lengthy program of progressively imposing symbolic discipline, involving the learning of words, modes of conceptual thinking, and grammatical rules, upon unwieldy, sporadic emotional feeling. Human behavior is rendered intelligent by proceeding through the stages of higher-grade emotional feeling, then of conscious ideation, and finally to the paramount level of reflectively conscious ideation where, ideally, a delicate synthetic balance is achieved between high-grade emotional and ideational feeling. In this, highly flexible symbolic units demonstrating a sophisticated rational structure, (and in their inextricably related felt relationship yielding a commensurately profound quality of subjective psychological meaning) are capable of accurately representing subtle features of complex reality as they emerge in human organisms in the form of mature perceptual symbolic experience. The many ramifications of the subjective psychological phenomenon of experience, many aspects of which are capable of symbolic representation by critically reflecting upon its distinguishable dimensions, are, paradoxically enough, rendered more determinate, and yet, are obscured by the explicative device that permits the possibility of their elucidation in thought. This is to say that symbols, primarily linguistic, stand between man and the immediately revealed external natural and internal bodily worlds as a filtrative screen representing and thereby accentuating direct experience in terms of those elements that are of greatest relevance to the percipient, while the extensive concrete subtlety of the fleeting present moment is lost. Therefore, even the most potently meaningful symbolic representations cannot communicate the full richness of qualitatively mature, direct experience. At best, deceptively complex immediate experience can only be partially expressed by those human individuals whose organisms entertain such occurrences. For example, even in the relatively typical experience of consuming a steak, who would attempt to exhaustively linguistically characterize the many intimately pleasurable ramifications of this experience and think, as a result, that the verbal description of the experience adequately portrayed the subjective quality of the original occasion?

This theory of symbolic development, then, regards intelligent thinking as a very high-ordered behavioral process that gradually emerges out of originally unorganized, randomly occurring emotional feelings that are thereafter progressively transformed into symbolically rational behavior. The function of language in all this, as well as in other modes of more primitive symbolism, is to gradually organize and explicate the significance of primordially occurring internal and external perceptions by assigning to their many directly accessible aspects, intersubjectively agreed upon linguistic symbols in order to render those meaningful experiential components determinate, and hence, available for future reference in instrumental usage.

Chapter five / Evidence for a theory of symbolic development

Now that we have outlined a general theory of symbolic development, let us consider some of the evidence that would seem to be compatible with such a theory, making primary reference to the relevant works of Ernst Cassirer which contain a wealth of empirical studies regarding this matter.(19), (20), (21)

We will begin our evidential inquiries by considering a quotation from Cassirer in which his general impression of contemporary psychology is expressed.

Few modern psychologists would admit or recommend a mere method of introspection. In general they tell us that such a method is very precarious. They are convinced that a strictly objective behavioristic attitude is the only possible approach to a scientific psychology. But a consistent and radical behaviorism fails to attain its end. It can warn us of possible methodological errors, but it cannot solve all the problems of human psychology. We may criticize or suspect the purely introspective view, but we cannot suppress or eliminate it. Without introspection, without an immediate awareness of feelings, emotions, perceptions, thoughts, we could not even define the field of human psychology. Yet it must be admitted that by following this way alone we can never arrive at a comprehensive view of human nature. Introspection reveals to us only that small sector of human life which is accessible to our individual experience. It can never cover the whole field of human phenomena. Even if we should succeed in collecting and combining all the data, we should still have a very meager and fragmentary picture—a mere torso—of human nature.(19)

It can be seen at the outset that in terms of a basic philosophic outlook, Cassirer's view of empirical psychological methodology is concordant with this writer's view; i.e., that a strict behaviorism which, although capable of yielding a great deal of useful information about human behavior, cannot provide a comprehensive explanation of it. Hence, reports of introspectively accessible states, where stimulus-objects are located within individuals in such a way that only the individuals themselves are in a position to have direct access to the effects, and which are obtained under experimentally controlled conditions, must also qualify as an acceptable class of data if a complete psychological understanding of man is to be, in principle, ascertained.

Cassirer reminds us of an extremely important admonition originally articulated by Socrates—one that was perhaps fundamental to the entire Socratic philosophy.

We cannot discover the nature of man in the same way that we can detect the nature of physical things. Physical things may be described in terms of their objective properties, but man may be described and defined only in terms of his consciousness. This fact poses an entirely new problem which cannot be solved by our usual modes of investigation. Empirical observation and logical analysis, in the sense in which these terms were used in pre-Socratic philosophy, here proved inefficient and inadequate. For it is only in our immediate intercourse with human beings that we have insight into the character of man. We must actually confront man, we must meet him squarely face to face, in order to understand him. Hence it is not a new objective content, but a new activity and function of thought which is the distinctive feature of the philosophy of Socrates.(19)

This statement, in its proper context, makes reference to the philosophical dialogical method of inquiry propounded by Socrates, indicating that the problem of how to properly study the nature of man, complicated by the unique status of man's intellect, was one given careful consideration many centuries ago.

The following is a summary of Cassirer's view of the present situation regarding the methodological study of man.

No former age was ever in such a favorable position with regard to the sources of our knowledge of human nature. Psychology, ethnology, anthropology, and history have amassed an astoundingly rich and constantly increasing body of facts. Our technical instruments for observation and experimentation have been immensely improved, and our analyses have become sharper and more penetrating. We appear, nevertheless, not yet to have found a method for the mastery and organization of this material. When compared with our own abundance the past may seem very poor. But our wealth of facts is not necessarily a wealth of thoughts. Unless we succeed in finding a clue of Ariadne to lead us out of this labyrinth, we can have no real insight into the general character of human culture; we shall remain lost in a mass of disconnected and disintegrated data which seems to lack all conceptual unity.(19)

The theory of symbolic development previously outlined placed great emphasis upon the notion that the origin of symbolic behavior was intimately related to the primordial bodily feelings, and particularly, the spontaneous emotional responses of infantile human organisms to changes in their internal bodily and external natural environments. Further it was maintained that the essential utility of symbolism, in its gradual mode of personalized development, is that it is the instrument by which vague, amorphous emotional feeling acquires successive discipline, thereby resulting in commensurately higher-ordered intelligent behavioral manifestations Jacques Maritain, a contemporary neo-Thomistic philosopher who was importantly influenced by Henri Bergson's subjective realism(22), characterizes the subjective psychological view on symbolic behavior in the following profound, nearly poetic, fashion:

The fathomless abyss of personal freedom of the personal thirst and striving for knowing and seeing, grasping and expressing—I should call them the preconscious of the spirit in man. For reason does not consist only of its conscious logical tools and manifestations nor does the will consist only of its deliberate conscious determinations. Far beneath the apparent surface of explicit concepts and judgments, of words and expressed resolutions or movements of the will, are the sources of knowledge and poetry, of love and truly human desires, hidden in the spiritual darkness of the intimate vitality of the soul. Before being formed and expressed in concepts and judgments, intellectual knowledge is at first a beginning of insight, still unformulated, which proceeds from the impact of the illuminating activity of the intellect on the world of images and emotions and which is but a humble and trembling movement, yet invaluable, toward an intelligible content to be grasped.(23)

More specifically with respect to the causal role of symbolism, the following quotations from Cassirer embody the fundamental elements of his views on the nature and role of symbolism as a causally influential factor in determining individual behavior. It is necessary to quote Cassirer at length in order to appreciate his profound theory.

. . . in the human world we find a new characteristic which appears to be the distinctive mark of human life. The functional circle of man is not only quantitatively enlarged; it has also undergone a qualitative change. Man has, as it were, discovered a new method of adapting himself to his environment. Between the receptor system and the effector system [in the domain which Skinner would regard as the reflex arc], which are to be found in all animal species, we find in man a third link which we may describe as the symbolic system. This new acquisition transforms the whole of human life. As compared with the other animals man lives not merely in a broader reality; he lives, so to speak, in a new dimension of reality. There is an unmistakable difference between organic reactions and human responses. In the first case a direct and immediate answer is given to an outward stimulus; in the second case the answer is delayed. It is interrupted and retarded by a slow and complicated process of thought.

Man cannot escape from his own achievement. He cannot but adapt the conditions of his own life. No longer in a merely physical universe, man lives in a symbolic universe. Language, myth, art, and religion are parts of the universe. They are the varied threads which weave the symbolic net, the tangled web of human experience. All human progress in thought and experience refines upon and strengthens this net. No longer can man confront reality immediately; he cannot see it, as it were, face to face. Physical reality seems to recede in proportion as man's symbolic activity advances. Instead of dealing with the things themselves man is in a sense constantly conversing with himself. He has so enveloped himself in linguistic forms, in artistic images, in mythical symbols or religious rites that he cannot see or know anything except by the interposition of this artificial medium. His situation is the same in the theoretical as in the practical sphere. Even here man does not live in the midst of imaginary emotions, in hopes and fears, in illusions and disillusions, in his fantasies and dreams. "What disturbs and alarms man," said Epictetus, "are not the things, but his opinions and fancies about the things."

From the point of view at which we have just arrived we may correct and enlarge the classical definition of man. In spite of all the efforts of modern irrationalism this definition of man as an *animal rationale* has not lost its force. Rationality is indeed an inherent feature of all human activities. . . . Language has often been identified with reason, or with the very source of reason. But it is easy to see that this definition fails to cover the whole field. It is a *pars pro toto;* it offers us a part for the whole. For side by side with conceptual language there is an emotional language; side by side with logical or scientific language there is a language of poetic imagination. Primarily language does not express thoughts or ideas, but feelings and affections. And even a religion "within the limits of pure reason" as conceived and worked out by Kant is no more than a mere abstraction. It conveys only the ideal shape, only the shadow, of what a genuine and concrete religious life is. The great thinkers who have defined man as an *animal rationale* were not empiricists, nor did they ever intend to give an empirical account of human nature. By this definition they were expressing a rather fundamental moral imperative. Reason is a very inadequate term with which to comprehend the forms of man's cultural life in all their richness and variety. But all these forms are symbolic forms. Hence, instead of defining man as an *animal rationale,* we should define him as an *animal symbolicum.* By doing so we can designate his specific difference, and we can understand the new way open to man—the way to civilization. (19)

The implications of these passages for the type of theoretical formulations which we have been developing is obvious.

Next, we begin to focus upon the precise nature of language and its various modes of usage.

But instead of giving a ready-made definition of speech, it would be better perhaps to proceed along tentative lines. Speech is not a simple and uniform phenomenon. It consists of different elements which, both biologically and systematically, are not on the same level. We must try to find the order and interrelationships of the constituent elements; we must, as it were, distinguish the various geological strata of speech. The first and most fundamental stratum is evidently the language of emotions. A great portion of all human utterance still belongs to this stratum. But there is a form of speech that shows us a quite different type. Here the word is by no means a mere interjection; it is not an involuntary expression of feeling, but a part of a sentence which has a definite syntactical and logical structure.[4] * It is true that even in highly developed theoretical language the connection with the first element is not entirely broken off. Scarcely a sentence can be found—except perhaps the pure formal sentences of mathematics—without a certain affective or emotional tinge.[5] Analogies and parallels to emotional language may be found in abundance in the animal world. As regards chimpanzees Wolfgang Koehler states that they achieve a considerable degree of expression by means of gesture. Rage, terror, despair, grief, pleading, desire, playfulness, and pleasure are readily expressed in this manner. Nevertheless one element, which is characteristic of and indispensable to all human language, is missing: we find no signs which have an objective reference or meaning. "It may be taken as positively proved," says Koehler, that their gamut of phonetics is entirely "subjective," and can only express emotion, never designate or describe objects. But they have so many phonetic elements which are also common to human language, that their lack of articulate speech cannot be ascribed to secondary (glosso-labial) limitations. Their gestures too, of face and body like their expression in sound, never designate or "describe" objects (Bühler).

Here we touch upon the crucial point in our whole problem. The difference between propositional language and emotional language is the real landmark between the human and the animal world. All the theories and observations concerning animal language are wide of the mark if they fail to recognize this fundamental difference.

For the sake of a clear statement of the problem we must carefully distinguish between signs and symbols. That we find rather complex systems of signs and signals in animal behavior seems to be an ascertained fact. We may even say that some animals, especially domesticated animals, are extremely susceptible to signs.[12] A dog will react to the slightest changes in the behavior of his master; he will even distinguish the expression of a human face or the modulation of a human voice.[13] But it is a far cry from these phenomena to an understanding of symbolic and human speech. The famous experiments of Pavlov prove only that animals can easily be trained to react not merely to direct stimuli but to all sorts of mediate or representative stimuli. A bell, for example, may become a "sign for dinner," and

* Superscript reference numbers which appear in this and the following extracts apply to Cassirer(19).

an animal may be trained not to touch its food when this sign is absent. But from this we learn only that the experimenter, in this case, has succeeded in changing the food-situation of the animal. He has complicated the situation by voluntarily introducing to it a new element. All the phenomena which are primarily described as conditioned reflexes are not merely very far from but even opposed to the essential character of human symbolic thought. Symbols—in the proper sense of this term—cannot be reduced to mere signals. Signals and symbols belong to two very different universes of discourse: a signal is a part of the physical world of being; a symbol is part of the human world of meaning. Signals are "operators"; symbols are "designators." [14] Signals, even when understood and used as such, have nevertheless a sort of physical or substantial being; symbols have only a functional value.

Some psychologists and psychobiologists have flatly refused to speak of the intelligence of animals. In all animal behavior they saw only the play of a certain automatism. This thesis had behind it the authority of Descartes; yet it has been reasserted in modern psychology. "The animal," says E. L. Thorndike in his work on animal intelligence, "does not think one is like the other, nor does it, as it is so often said, mistake one for the other. It just does not think about it at all; it just thinks it. . . . The idea that animals react to a particular and absolutely defined and realized sense-impression, and that a similar reaction to a sense-impression which varies from the first proves an association by similarity, is a myth." [15] Later and more exact observation led to a different conclusion. In the case of the higher animals it had become clear that they were able to solve rather difficult problems and that these solutions were not brought about in a merely mechanical way, by trial and error. As Koehler points out, the most striking difference exists between a mere chance solution and a genuine solution, so that the one can be easily distinguished from the other. That at least some of the reactions of the higher animals are not merely a product of chance but are guided by insight appears to be incontestable.[16] If by intelligence we understand either adjustment to the immediate environment or adaptive modifications of environment, we must certainly ascribe to animals a comparatively highly developed intelligence. It must also be conceded that not all animal actions are governed by the presence of an immediate stimulus. The animal is capable of all sorts of detours in its reactions. It may learn not only to use implements but even to invent tools for its purposes. Hence some psychobiologists do not hesitate to speak of a creative or constructive imagination in animals.[17] But neither this intelligence nor this imagination is of the specifically human type. In short, we may say that the animal possesses a practical imagination and intelligence whereas man alone has developed a new form: a symbolic imagination and intelligence.(19)

For Cassirer, symbolic imagination and intelligence have two crucially important developmental stages. He relies heavily upon an illustration drawn from the early life of Helen Keller to dramatically portray, as a "key" experiment, this two-stage process, necessarily involved in acquiring symbolic imagination and thereby intelligence.

Helen Keller had previously learned to combine a certain thing or event with a certain sign of the manual alphabet. A fixed association had been established between these things and certain tactile impressions. But such a series of associations, even if they are repeated and amplified, still does not imply an understanding of what human speech is and means. In order to arrive at such an understanding the child had to make a new and more significant discovery. It had to understand that everything had a name—that the symbolic function is not restricted to particular cases but is a principle of universal applicability which encompasses the whole field of human thought.

The principle of symbolism, with its universality, validity, and general applicability, is the magic word, the Open Sesame! giving access to the specifically human world, to the world of human culture. Once man is in possession of this magic his further progress is assured. Such progress is evidently not obstructed or made impossible by any lack in the sense material. The case of Helen Keller, who reached a very high degree of mental development and intellectual culture, shows us clearly and irrefutably that a human being in the construction of his human world is not dependent upon the quality of his sense material. If the theories of sensationalism were right, if every idea were nothing but a faint copy of an original sense impression, then the condition of a blind, deaf, and dumb child would indeed be desperate. For it would be deprived of the very sources of human knowledge; it would be, as it were, an exile from reality. But if we study Helen Keller's autobiography we are at once aware that this is untrue and at the same time we understand why it is untrue. Human culture derives its specific character and its intellectual and moral values, not from the material of which it consists, but from its form, its architectural structure. And this form may be expressed in any sense material.

The thing of vital importance is not the individual bricks and stones but their general function as architectural form. In the realm of speech it is their general symbolic function which vivifies the material signs and "makes them speak." Without this vivifying principle the human world would indeed remain deaf and mute. With this principle, even the world of a deaf, dumb, and blind child can become incomparably broader and richer than the world of the most highly developed animal.

Universal applicability, owing to the fact that everything has a name, is one of the greatest prerogatives of human symbolism. But it is not the only one. There is still another characteristic of symbols which accompanies and complements this one and forms its necessary correlate. A symbol is not only universal but extremely variable. I can express the same meaning in various languages; and even within the limits of a single language a single thought or idea may be expressed in quite different terms. A sign or signal is related to the thing to which it refers in a fixed and unique way. One concrete and individual sign refers to a certain individual thing. In Pavlov's experiments the dogs could easily be trained to reach for food only upon being given special signs; they would not eat until they heard a particular sound which could be chosen at the discretion of the experimenter. But this bears no analogy, as it has often been interpreted, to human symbolism; on the contrary, it is opposite to symbolism. A genuine human symbol is characterized not by its uniformity but by its versatility. It is not rigid or inflexible but mobile. It is true that full awareness of this mobility seems to be a rather late achievement in man's intellectual and cultural development. In primitive mentality this awareness is very seldom attained. Here the symbol is still regarded as a property of the thing like other physical properties. In mythical thought the name of a god is an integral part of the nature of a god. If I do not call the god by its right name, then the spell or prayer becomes ineffective. The same holds good for symbolic actions. A religious rite, a sacrifice, must always be performed in the same invariable way and in the same order if it is to have its effect.[21] Children are often greatly confused when they first learn that not every name of an object is a "proper name," that the same thing may have quite different names in different languages. They tend to think that it "is" what it is called. But this is only the first step. Every normal child will very soon learn that it can use various symbols to express the same wish or thought. For this variability and mobility there is apparently no parallel in the animal world.[22] Long before Laura Bridgman had learned to speak, she had developed a very curious mode of expression, a language of her own. This language did not consist of articulated sounds but only of various noises, which are described as "emotional noises." She was in the habit of uttering these sounds in the presence of certain persons. Thus they became entirely individualized; every person in her environment was greeted by a special noise. "Whenever she met unexpectedly an acquaintance," writes Dr. Lieber, "I found that she repeatedly uttered the word for that person before she began to speak. It was the utterance of pleasurable recognition." [23] But when by means of the finger alphabet the child had grasped the meaning of human language the case was altered. Now the sound really became a name: and this name was not bound to an individual person but could be changed if the circumstances seemed to require it.

Another important aspect of our general problem now emerges—the problem of the dependence of relational thought upon symbolic thought. Without a complex system of symbols relational thought cannot arise at all, much less reach its full development. It would not be correct to say that the mere awareness of relations presupposes an intellectual act, an act of logical or abstract thought. Such an awareness is necessary even in elementary acts of perception. The sensationalist's theories used to describe perception as a mosaic of simple sense data. Thinkers of this persuasion constantly overlooked the fact that sensation itself is by no means a mere aggregate or bundle of isolated impressions. Modern Gestalt psychology has corrected this view. It has shown that the very simplest perceptual processes imply fundamental structural elements, certain patterns or configurations. This principle holds for both the human and the animal world. Even in comparatively low stages of animal life the presence of these structural elements—especially of spatial and optical structures—has been experimentally proved.[25] The mere awareness of relations cannot, therefore, be regarded as a specific feature of human consciousness. We do find, however, in man a special type of relational thought which has no parallel in the animal world. In man an ability to isolate relations—to consider them in their abstract meaning—has developed. In order to grasp this meaning man is no longer dependent upon concrete sense data, upon visual, auditory, tactile, kinesthetic data. He considers these relations "in themselves". . . . Geometry is the classic example of this turning point in man's intellectual life. Even in elementary geometry we are not bound to the apprehension of concrete individual figures. We are not concerned with physical things or perceptual objects, for we are studying universal spatial relations for whose expression we have an adequate symbolism. Without the preliminary step of human language such an achievement would not be possible. (19)

The following quotations suggest how we may conceive of primitive and infantile minds as they comprehend reality in early life. It is clearly seen that the vague undifferentiated complexity of emotional consciousness is the predominate characteristic of this type of mentality.

To be sure all attempts to intellectualize myth—to explain it as an allegorical expression of a theoretical or moral truth—have completely failed. They ignore the fundamental facts of mythical experience. The real substratum of myth is not a substratum of thought but of feeling. Myth and primitive religion are by no means entirely incoherent, they are not bereft of sense or reason. But their coherence depends much more upon unity of feeling than upon logical rules. This unity is one of the strongest and most profound impulses of primitive thought. If scientific thought wishes to describe and explain reality it is bound to use its general method, which is that of classification and systematization. Life is divided into separate provinces that are sharply distinguished from each other. The boundaries between the kingdoms of plants, of animals, of men—the differences between species, families, genera—are fundamental and ineffaceable. But the primitive mind ignores and rejects them all. Its view of life is a synthetic, not an analytic one. Life is not divided into classes and subclasses. It is felt as an unbroken continuous whole which does not admit of any clean-cut and trenchant distinctions. The limits between the different spheres are not insurmountable barriers; they are fluent and fluctuating. There is no specific difference between the various realms of life. Nothing has a definite, invariable, static shape. By a sudden metamorphosis everything may be turned into everything. If there is any characteristic and outstanding feature of the mythical world, any law by which it is governed—it is this law of metamorphosis. Even so we can scarcely explain the instability of the mythical world by the incapacity of primitive man to grasp the empirical differences of things. In this regard the savage very often proves his superiority to the civilized man. He is susceptible to many distinctive features that escape our attention. The animal drawings and paintings that we find in the lowest stages of human culture, in paleo-lithic art, have often been admired for their naturalistic character. They show an astounding knowledge of all sorts of animal forms. The whole existence of primitive man depends in great part upon his gifts of observation and discrimination. If he is a hunter he must be familiar with the smallest de-tails of animal life; he must be able to distinguish the traces of various animals. All this is scarcely in keeping with the assumptions that the primi-tive mind, by its very nature and essence, is undifferentiated or confused, a prelogical or mystical mind.

What is characteristic of primitive mentality is not its logic but its gen-eral sentiment of life. Primitive man does not look at nature with the eyes of a naturalist who wishes to classify things in order to satisfy an intellectual curiosity. He does not approach it with merely pragmatic or technical in-terest. It is for him neither a mere object of knowledge nor the field of his immediate practical needs. We are in the habit of dividing our lives into the two spheres of practical and theoretical activity. In this division we are prone to forget that there is a lower stratum beneath them both. Primitive man is not liable to such forgetfulness. All his thoughts and his feelings are still embedded in this lower original stratum. His view of nature is neither merely theoretical nor merely practical; it is sympathetic. If we miss this point we cannot find the approach to the mythical world. The most fundamental feature of myth is not its special direction of thought or special direction of human imagination. Myth is the offspring of emotion and its emotional background imbues all its productions with its own specific color.

Long before a child learns to talk it has discovered other and simpler means of communicating with other persons. The cries of discomfort, of pain and hunger, of fear or fright, which we find throughout the organic world begin to assume a new shape. They are no longer simple instinctive reactions, for they are employed in a more conscious and deliberate way. When left alone the child demands by more or less articulate sounds the presence of its nurse or mother, and it becomes aware that these demands have the desired effect. Primitive man transfers this first elementary social experience to the totality of nature. To him nature and society are not only interconnected by the closest bonds; they form a coherent and indistinguishable whole. No clear-cut line of demarcation separates the two realms. Nature itself is nothing but a great society—the society of life.

The "hunger" for names which at a certain age appears in every child and which has been described by all students of child psychology [39] . . . reminds us that we are here confronted with a quite different problem. By learning to name things a child does not simply add a list of artificial signs to his previous knowledge of ready-made empirical objects. He learns rather to form the concepts of these objects, to come to terms with the objective world. Henceforth the child stands on firmer ground. His vague, uncertain, fluctuating perceptions and his dim feelings begin to assume a new shape. They may be said to crystallize around the name as a fixed center, a focus of thought. Without the help of the name every new advance made in the process of objectification would always run the risk of being lost again in the next moment. The first names of which a child makes conscious use may be compared to a stick by the aid of which a blind man gropes his way. And language, taken as a whole, becomes the gateway to a new world. All progress here opens a new perspective and widens and enriches our concrete experience. Eagerness and enthusiasm to talk do not originate in a mere desire for learning or using names; they mark the desire for the detection and conquest of an objective world.[40]

The name of an object lays no claim upon its nature; it is not intended to . . . give us the truth of a thing. The function of a name is always limited to emphasizing a particular aspect of a thing, and it is precisely this restriction and limitation upon which the value of the name depends. It is not the function of a name to refer exhaustively to a concrete situation, but merely to single out and dwell upon a certain aspect. This isolation of this aspect is not a negative but a positive act. For in the act of denomination we select, out of the multiplicity and diffusion of our sense data, certain fixed centers of perception. These centers are not the same as in logical or scientific thought. The terms of ordinary speech are not to be measured by the same standards as those in which we express scientific concepts. As compared with scientific terminology the words of common speech always exhibit a certain vagueness; almost without exception they are so indistinct and ill-defined as not to stand the test of logical analysis. But notwithstanding this unavoidable and inherent defect our everyday terms and names are the milestones on the road which leads to scientific concepts; it is in these terms that we receive our first objective or theoretical view of the world. Such a view is not simply "given"; it is the result of a constructive intellectual effort which without the constant assistance of language could not attain its end. (19)

Cassirer, a notable philosopher in his own right, amassed an extraordinary wealth of empirical and historical research on the subject of symbolic development. His exactitude and clarity of expression are difficult to surpass. In the light of his thoughts on symbolic development we shall attempt to elaborate, in an increasingly precise and scientifically propitious manner, the theory of symbolic development originally proposed.

Chapter six / Analysis of stages of symbolic development

Let us endeavor at this point to clearly and systematically formulate a theory of symbolic development appropriate for a subjective psychology. Three very general categorical stages of development can be said to encompass this phenomenon, namely, the familiar divisions of infancy-childhood, childhood-adolescence, and adolescence-adulthood. Since the most important and dramatic developments in symbolic behavior occur during the first stage, preponderant analytical attention will be devoted to this period.

INFANCY-CHILDHOOD STAGE

1. At the immediate outset of a child's life (i.e., prenatal and shortly thereafter) anything that could be regarded as mind (defined merely as conscious awareness) is minimal. There is probably in evidence a bare subjective world of undifferentiated, highly vague organic-feeling percepta. At this level, it seems tenable to say that the perceptual world of the infant is greatly introverted in that felt percepta arise from internal organismic locations as well as from the natural world. Of course no such distinction between these two distinct realms is realized by an infant mentality, for such an understanding is itself contingent upon some amount of symbolic facility. This period appears to be dominated primarily by pleasure-pain feelings whose intensity and hence distinctness from one another would seem to increase as the organism matures both physiologically and mentally.

2. Next it would appear that qualitatively more sophisticated states of emotion, beyond a minimal awareness of painful and pleasurable feelings, would develop merely as a result of physiological growth, and in

varying degrees, to low-ordered presymbolic learnings. Thus, vaguely aware experiences like feeling the consumption of food and mother's warmth, for example, could be progressively differentiated, still, however, as predominantly introverted experience.

3. The vague subjective emotional state of anticipation seems to be the next significant development. Here we assume that after a back-log of important experiences has been "neurologically recorded" (a mode of acquiring very basic information that is presymbolic and does not rely upon considerably more sophisticated causal factors such as conscious intentionality, but rather, involves automatic reflexive behavior developed through various modes of reinforcement that require minimal conscious entertainment of previously learned information), a primordial form of memory or wisdom would be coming to bear upon the infant's ever-emerging present perceptual awareness, so that the present subjective psychological or conscious occasion would be constructively qualified to some extent by the integrated learnings from past experience. Thus the emotional states resulting from experiencing food and motherly caressing would, in a very minimal way, be consciously anticipated by the infant human organism. Pleasurable reactions would also be somewhat more intense due to the newly achieved state of anticipation. Reflective recognition of anticipated experience would still remain introverted in that the pleasurable experience would be acknowledged as such during its actual occurrence, but not recalled after the fact, or recognized to have resulted from the external stimulus-objects, food or mother.

4. We now move to the phenomenon of projecting emotion whereby the infant becomes aware that there is an external world possessing an independent existence that is capable of influencing his experience. This corresponds to the outset of Cassirer's sign stage. This is simply to say that "something [mother] yields warmth," "something [food] is pleasurable," "something [fear] is the absence of something [a comforting mother]," and so on. Out of these vaguely conscious discriminations, the infant begins to respond to external stimulus-objects by projecting his emotional states at those objects, thereby demonstrating a more consciously active character as opposed to former reflexive, passive behavioral qualities. This is manifested through crying, biting, touching and by other types of spontaneous emotional expression that promote an increased frequency of crude exploratory behaviors as a result of their pleasurably reinforcing consequences.

5. A result of being aware of an external world and actively responding to it the primordial emotion represented by the term "power" arises. The infant becomes vaguely cognizant of the fact that certain behaviors

that he executes tend to increase the number of emotionally satisfying subjective states, while minimizing the frequency of those experienced as unpleasant. For example, the act of crying when an infant organism has feelings of hunger often results in the appearance of a something [mother] which relieves the discomforting state. The words used for certain phenomena such as the hypothesized "feeling of power," merely by the fact that they are words, used to designate and explain the phenomenon, greatly overstate the subjectively understood infantile meaning undoubtedly characteristic of such vague, amorphous experiential occasions. However unsuitable this kind of explanation may be, some attempt at designating developmental stages must be made to accentuate the distinctive, and hence, psychologically necessary conditions that must be developmentally achieved for early symbolic, and later consciously reflective, behavior.

Thus in this way infants have some determination in increasing the frequency of pleasurable states and minimizing the unpleasant ones; this is the bare experience of power. This whole developmental process resembles the notion of a computer having data programmed into its memory to be used for future operations. However, the limitations of the computer analogy—and consequently a basic reason for analyzing with precision the nature of directly experienced organic feelings, bodily emotions, as well as consciousness and reflective consciousness—is that the concept of programming does not emphasize or even logically imply the unique synthetic power of brain neurology. The profoundly characteristic phenomenon of relevant past experience coming constructively to bear upon immediately delivered internal and external perceptions, thereby enhancing their subjective psychological meaning, is not implicit in the computer illustration. This is to say that disciplined felt awareness is not a causally efficacious intervening variable in mechanical intelligence. It is imperative to understand that the acquisition of felt wisdom is crucial to human mentality. Data from past experience are not merely passively stored and blindly mechanically utilized. They are, rather, consciously entertained and hence actively contemplated in their utilization as instrumental stimulus-objects for making additional future consciously intelligent behavioral responses to consciously understood problematic circumstances. This does not mean, however, that intelligent behavior somehow exceeds, or is incomprehensible within, systematically determinable cause-effect relationships.

6. At this level, Cassirer's sign stage is more clearly evident. Infants attempt to imitate the verbally articulated sounds of an attentive other person, initially to acquire and hence sustain the emotional pleasure of gaining attention and affection. Consequently, infant responses are imi-

tative without any meaningful understanding of the uttered linguistic symbols. The interpersonal exchanges in themselves are highly gratifying for infants even though their inner states are essentially emotional. At higher levels of emotional discipline infant gratification results, in addition, from active reality testing prompted by primordial curiosity.

7. But after prolonged, consistent exposure to the sign mode of behavior, what Cassirer defines as the symbol stage emerges. This is the crucially important one for human organisms. Here, we are presented with the phenomenon of a mother who, for example, after having repeatedly spoken the word "mama" while concomitantly making self-referential gestures, discovers that the child is beginning to emit verbal mama-responses when he perceptually apprehends her presence or he desires her attention. In this, the child becomes vaguely aware of the fact that his entire relevant experiential backlog referring to mother-stimulus-object effect, derived from a multitude of vaguely recalled, but powerfully felt, previous experiences, is projected at mother-stimulus-object by expressing the word "mama." The relevant past has been constructively brought to bear upon the present occasion, hence meaning fully transcending the bare implication of the external perceptual apprehension delivered in the contemporary circumstance. The highly vague and indeterminate emotional configuration of mama-experiences are united and, hence, intentionally projected, merely by speaking the word "mama." After this process has been frequently repeated, using other words as well, the child begins to understand that verbally articulated sounds are more than merely sounds expressed to attract and maintain adult attention. Rather, words represent universal categories of relevant emotional experience with respect to given familiar stimulus-objects. Pleasurable and painful experiences can be differentiated by subsuming them to the inclusive, and thereby unifying, category of emotional meaning represented by an appropriate word. This excites a feeling of power in young children; they have discovered a means for organizing and clarifying their world of concrete emotional experience. As a repertoire of words is accumulated, the precondition for the still higher-ordered phenomenon of subjective psychological symbolic meaning is progressively provided. Words are found to not only comprehend categories of emotional experience. By expressing them in certain sequences, emotional categories of experience can be manipulated; and more exciting, one can project this process of word manipulation to others and thereby establish reciprocal communication! Here we are at the very heart of the primordial nature of subjective psychological meaning. If words encompass determinate categories of feeling and emotional experience,

one has the power of retrieving, in a rapid and succinct way, many pleasurable mama-experiences. It is a way of concentrating the feeling of formerly experienced pleasure by merely saying "mama." This is certainly an extraordinary power; therefore, there is considerable motivation for children to develop this verbal capacity when they are initially learning to talk. Further, as the number of emotionally qualifying symbols increases, enabling past experience to be re-enjoyed, although less vividly, simply by expressing the appropriate linguistic symbol, and further, by manipulating ordered sequences of symbols, the phenomenon of meaning-as-directly-felt-relatedness develops. This is the experience of feeling the meaningful unity of symbols which represents objects in a vague but psychologically satisfying way. Symbols not only represent global emotional configurations of important past experience and provide a means for retrieving and hence rendering aspects of the past relatively permanent, also they are a means for reducing the intensity of anxiety resulting from indeterminate, felt complexity of a given experiential occasion. Thus a symbol can simplify complex and otherwise unwieldy emotional experience so that the more prominent aspects of experience can be cognitively retained while the remaining portions either entirely escape or fade from conscious recognition. In the process, then, of organizing clearly determinate symbols into a definite order, diverse aspects of emotional experience can be brought into novel relationships. By their characteristic nature the symbols are devices for simplifying and rendering permanent important features of original concrete experience, so that they may become intelligible instruments for thinking-behavior. Hence they have denotative aspects in that they can be clearly and easily brought to mind, and thus manipulated with reference to other symbols. But, in addition, they have a connotative dimension which refers to the vastly complex network of rich emotionality, directly felt with greatest intensity particularly in infantile concrete experience, that cannot, in all its ramifications, be brought clearly to consciousness due to the very fact of its subtle complexity, and also, because much of the original intensity quickly fades from consciousness. Nevertheless, some of this vague connotative dimension is neurologically recorded as it occurs as highly concrete, unified, barely conscious emotional experience, in addition, of course, to those denotative aspects which have been intentionally symbolically qualified. Thus when the activity of symbolic thinking is engaged in, symbols are clearly present in mind, specifically relating various cognitive factors with one another. However, there is also the concomitantly occurring, vague connotative dimension which is experientially implicit in all thought by being vaguely and comprehensively suggested within the specific, clearly apprehendable symbols, as well as clusters of symbols, intended to embody complete thoughts. The connotative elements comprising complete symbolic thought, considered as they are synthetically united within the actual concrete activity of thinking, is what is meant here by the phenomenon of meaning-as-directly-felt-relatedness. This is, perhaps, the most profoundly complicated of all humanly perceivable behavioral phenomena. Yet, it occurs as a typical and vital constituent of all human thought, as a necessary result of individual human organisms possessing a neurological system containing mechanisms capable of synthesizing massive quantities of sensory data progressively obtained from experience and stored in millions of brain cells. Meaning-as-directly-felt-relatedness is the learned product, then, of developed symbolic behavioral capacities in a class of highly ordered organisms, in which the symbols are used to simplify the profound complexities of the directly experienced effects from inner and outer environments. After having symbolically "tagged" a small number of the objects, properties, and their unifying relations, functioning as stimulus objects, in these environments the organism has, in effect, imposed some small degree of discipline upon his formerly vague, amorphous organic and emotional feeling. The symbolic "tagging" is a behavioral act made possible through a gradually emerging process in which a substratum of emotional feeling is subsumed to symbolic discipline. This is of course a slowly acquired ability, hence yielding to individual organisms, as subjective psychological experience, a commensurate amount reinforcing confidence, at least until the organism reaches a high level of behavioral sophistication, that is proportionate to the rate of symbolic mastery. Symbolic acquisition is also a source of great motivation for promoting further and more precise comprehension of reality. The form which this process of symbolic discipline acquires seems to be determined by the very objects, properties, and relations that are directly experienced as unified in their occurrence as perceptions resulting from internally and externally located configurations of stimulus-objects. In any case, meaning-as-directly-felt-relatedness, at least in early stages of symbolic development, is the way that organisms have experientially felt being, both as organic bodily and emotional feeling. The term "mama," for example, is heavily laden with connotative meaning. The barren, clearly conceived, spoken term occurs as merely a single component of subjective psychological experiential meaning, in contrast to the accompanying emergence of connotatively vague, emotionally charged, symbolically undisciplined felt meaning. At the other extreme, however, that of highly developed adult symbolic intelligence, the converse situation is in evidence. We can consciously entertain many clearly understandable symbols both in silent thought and in intersubjectively manifest behaviors. To maintain that the substance of thought is highly disciplined emotional feeling made possible through gradual symbolic development is, indeed, to express a very peculiar view at face value, and one repugnant to contemporary philosophy and psychology. The rationale for this position, although somewhat implicit in our previous discussion on symbolic development, will be subsequently presented in greater detail. Suffice it to say that at higher stages of intelligence, myriad symbols are acquired, hence internalized, and so profoundly interrelated that they can be reflexively conjured to characterize experience with such great facility that the original connotative, emotionally felt aspect of experience is sublimated. As a result of this phenomenon philosophers have come to define thought in many diverse ways. Aristotle has characterized thought as pure form that can accept any perceptual matter.(24) Descartes considered thought as extentionless substance or images.(25) Ryle conceptualizes thought as entirely manifest behavior resulting from given stimulus and reinforcing environmental conditions, considering any recourse to inner states as an unwarranted regression to seventeenth-century ghost-in-a-machine naïveté; and similarly with Skinner, the problem of thought is resolved by short-circuiting over the whole issue via the concept of reflex arc. As it is the case with all theories of mind, the view herein espoused is also subject to criticism as well because of the very difficult problem of attempting to define and explicate the experiential as well as the structural nature of thought as it is revealed in direct subjective psychological experience, hence raising subjective psychological phenomena to a factual status if properly conceived within an appropriate theoretical framework. The basic justification for this complicated theoretical viewpoint is that it seems precisely characteristic of our immediate concrete experience of reality.

The purpose of the deviation from our attempt to define the conspicuous features of the developmental stages of symbolic acquisition manifested in the infant-childhood period has been to introduce the crucially important concept of meaning-as-directly-felt-relatedness, and to demonstrate, in some minimal way, its relationship to adult symbolic intelligence.

We have at this point indicated the final developmental substage of the infant-childhood period. As it has been said the most important stage, by far, with respect to symbolic intelligence, is this entire first stage for most of the fundamental aspects of symbolic behavior have been basically mastered, with the exception of purely abstract symbolic intelligence.

CHILDHOOD-ADOLESCENCE STAGE

For the purposes of this book, let us simply say that this period is primarily involved in acquiring symbolic sophistication in characterizing stimulus-object effects, including the properties, and the relations demonstrated by entities in relative change with one another, and in developing an operational facility in the active, instrumental usage of symbols. Also, there is the development of symbolic abstractive intelligence, embodied in such behaviors as developing generalizations about phenomenal occurrences which have properties in common, such as in developing inductive-deductive reasoning powers, characteristic of the mathematical and geometrical scientific reasoning.

ADOLESCENCE-ADULTHOOD STAGE

Similarly, for the purposes of this book, this period can be said to involve a final major development in refining symbolic intelligence, and in exploiting this ability, in some cases, to its optimal limits.

It can be generally concluded from this discussion on symbolic development that the phenomenon initially arises from an organism's ability to subjectively experience qualitatively different types of organic bodily and emotional feeling. Because of the organism's intrinsic bodily structure, it actively proceeds to increase the frequency of states experienced as pleasurable and from this to progressively organizing and clarifying vague, primordial, sporadic organic and emotional feelings via symbols. Habits also originate in the same way, in principle. However both processes are greatly accelerated through interpenetrative relationships with other human organisms already possessing a mature symbolic facility, who function as agents capable of yielding feedback responses to symbolically unsophisticated organisms actively endeavoring to increase the frequency of their qualitatively pleasurable subjective psychological experiences. The rational structural form through which symbols acquire coherence and qualitatively variable subjective psychological meaning also arises from the organism's gradual understanding of the directly experienced structure of reality. Reality is revealed concretely in re-occurring configurations of percepta as these percepta and their modes of occurrence are progressively attributed specificity through precise symbolic representation, hence, testifying to the predictable and distinctive features of inner and outer experience. Truly, then, the situation is as Cassirer has conceived it:

Man has, as it were, discovered a new method of adapting himself to his environment. Between the reception and the effector system, which we find in all animal species, we find in man a third link which we may describe as the symbolic system. This new acquisition transforms the whole of human life. As compared with other animals man lives not merely in a broader reality; he lives, so to speak, in a new dimension of reality. There is an unmistakable difference between organic reactions and human responses. In the first case a direct and immediate answer is given to an outward stimulus; in the second case the answer is delayed. It is interrupted and retarded by a slow and complicated process of thought.

No longer can man confront reality immediately; he cannot see it, as it were, face to face. Physical reality seems to recede in proportion as man's symbolic activity advances. Instead of dealing with the things themselves man is in a sense constantly conversing with himself.

. . . side by side with conceptual language there is an emotional language; side by side with logical or scientific language there is a language of poetic imagination. Primarily language does not express thoughts or ideas, but feelings and affections.(19)

Here we can clearly determine the difference between Cassirer's concept of human behavior and that of Skinner's. The foregoing has, in effect, been a series of arguments criticizing the behavioristic conception of human behavior, showing it to be highly useful as a methodological way of investigating the class of human behavior which is directly apparent to external observers but never capable of providing, in principle, a complete exposition of all causally efficacious variables that determine behavior, for all subjective psychological factors are methodologically purged from a behaviorism. The way is now clear to devote our attention to developing a systematic concept of human behavior issuing from subjective psychological experience having much in common with the views of Cassirer and Whitehead, and in this way, laying the foundation for a second, independent, and in effect, general theory for conceiving human behavior. Thus, both an objective and a subjective psychological approach to studying human behavior can, in principle, yield a full systematic account of this phenomenon.

Chapter seven / A general
mechanistic model of human behavior

The preceding discussion on the theories of conscious and consciously reflective behavior and the development of symbolic behavior was presented in terms capable of more precise definition. A discussion of this sort is the raw material out of which more precise formulations can be developed, for meticulous, less formalized analysis is generally more in accordance with the vast subtlety of concrete, immediate experience—a source of indeterminate suggestibility for theoretical construction. To remain exclusively within the domain of formal abstraction or stricter operational definition is to purge from one's thoughts the very elements that frequently stimulate novel, experimentally fruitful cognitive associations. Particularly when devising constructs to systematically characterize human behavior, great care should be exercised to avoid the frequent error of developing a concept of man that includes only those aspects of his behavior which he shares in common with lower-ordered organisms and mechanical or electronic computing devices, while omitting many dimensions that are uniquely distinctive to the human organism, under the guise of being rigorously scientific. Concrete human experience as it is perceived through direct acquaintance provides us with an abundance of fundamental factual data. The key to understanding this type of complex information is in developing testable hypothetical constructs designed specifically to elucidate the unique character of concrete human experience as it reveals itself perceptually in reoccurring ways. Man should not be studied as though he were a consciousless physical entity whose behavioral manifestations could be understood solely in terms of natural and biological scientific concepts, for this is to exclude the causal efficacity of mental events as a powerful class of uniquely human behavioral determinants.

Proceeding from this analytical groundwork, an abstract, comprehensive theoretical model for human behavior can be developed which is suitable for systematic scientific investigation, but carefully designed to avoid the error of unwarranted scientific reductionism through the methodological omission of important causally efficacious aspects of human behavior. The terms to be used in defining the model are intended to possess cybernetic universality in comprehending the physio-chemical processes involved in activated human organic bodily mechanisms. Hence there should be no serious incompatibility between the methodological procedures used and those demonstrated by W. Ross Ashby in his *Design for a Brain* (26) and *Introduction to Cybernetics*.(17) The uniquely human behavioral phenomena formerly discussed and analyzed in nontechnical terms, i.e., conscious and reflective conscious symbolic behavior, have in principle empirically ascertainable equivalent or correlative physio-chemical processes that can be theoretically comprehended in their dynamic states by the general mechanistic model to be proposed. This cybernetic model, then, will represent the physio-chemical processes that are empirically identical with correlative mental processes and show the relationship of mental events, defined as subjective psychological emergent phenomena, to their underlying physio-chemical processes. This is not to say, however, that the cybernetic model to be presented is in itself sufficient for a complete explanation of human behavior; rather, it is a necessary theoretical instrument for such an endeavor.

In previous discussions we have begun the analysis of new topics by initially considering some of their intuitively obvious dimensions, and then gradually working toward clarifying them by carefully analyzing their basic presuppositions to explicate their more subtle intrinsic implications. This reflective, critical and constructive process seems characteristic of intelligent behavior in general. Speaking metaphorically, this analytical activity is the process of moving from vague awareness in understanding to clear understanding. However, stated in this manner, there is the erroneous implication that clear understanding is to be equated with final understanding. Rather, the process of achieving clear conception is a cyclical one, for in having attained clarity of understanding at a given point in time, part of the triumph entails coming to realize the extraordinary symbolic interrelation among concepts; hence, the paradox that clarity also perpetuates vagueness. Clear understanding can be evaluated, as such, only in reference to one's former state of vague understanding, but once an issue has been clearly understood, we often concomitantly become aware of our limited comprehension of a topic of concern. To be unable to accept the fact of the relatedness among things is to degenerate into dogmatism, for this ontological fact demands that we incessantly subject our most cherished theories to intensive, persistent critical examination. We must be ready to strip away their outmoded and/or contradictory aspects, and more important, to contemplate them from continually novel perspectives in an effort to derive fresh meaning from concepts. If this general view of intelligent behavior is substantially valid, then a critical evaluation of conventional techniques for measuring intelligence seems warranted, as well as the theories upon which they are predicated. These theories generally tend to de-emphasize the relatedness among concepts. The connotative implications that intrinsically define these ideational entities are not given sufficient consideration, in terms of their instrumental function in producing meaningful thought, while erroneously stressing so-called determinate factual information. Empirical factual knowledge is not simply hard and fast; its very possibility for synthetic expansion, as is similarly the case with even analytical knowledge, issues from the relatedness amongst things. The logical meaning of the term "human intelligence" will, then, be worthy of further attention in future discussion, for our present inquiries will shortly lead us to the essence of subjective psychological meaning in its various qualitative manifestations, arising as a function of given stimulus-occasions. But for the present, the basic reason for raising the issue of vague-to-clear understanding and the accompanying concept of relatedness is that they are intrinsic to the cybernetic model to be developed in the sense that these notions, beyond the fact that they have relevance for human conscious processes, signify also, on a physio-chemical level, the synthetic character of the organic processes that underlie mental events. We shall now proceed to develop the model.

Human beings are constantly exposed, at any point in time, to an incessant flow of stimulus-object effects, issuing from both the external natural world and their internal bodily organisms. Not only are we constantly bombarded, for example, by myriad details of manifest macrocosmic environments, but also those of the physical microcosm. There are colors, pains, desires, sounds, concepts, perceptions of solidity, and relations among these entities, as well as cosmic rays, ultrasonic sounds, and electromagnetic forces—to mention but a few of the many diverse stimulus-object effects that persistently affect our entire organism in varying ways throughout time. On the other hand, in our matter-of-fact daily activities, our worlds seem to be tolerably comprehensible and well ordered. Trees are trees, duties are duties, love is love, and so on. Thus amid the enormous concrete complexity of physical and conscious processes and modes of interaction among these processes, the human mind comprehends daily affairs in a greatly simplified manner; particularly attending to those factors of importance, while innumerable other equally as conspicuous factors are left unnoticed as they appear as potential stimulus-object effects. The point to be made is that we selectively perceive, and hence think about, stimulus-object effects. We consciously dwell upon that which is important to us, for whatever reason. More specifically, even apart from considering the many hypothetically postulated phenomena alleged to exist in our environments which are not directly perceivable by us, and are thereby regarded as theoretical constructs, such as light waves, ids, egos, and gravity, our sensory apparatus does enable us to potentially perceive considerably more perceptions than we ordinarily in fact do. For example, while an author is engaged in writing, there may be many sounds of automobiles passing; yet they are not consciously heard by the writer. Certainly the organic mechanisms involved in hearing are operating, but conscious attention is focused upon another matter of greater importance, thereby gaining precedence over concomitantly occurring stimulus-object effects. There are many diverse manifestations of this selective-perceptual phenomenon. Frequently, for example, during psychotherapy, a patient will exhibit certain manifest behaviors without being aware of this fact until the counselor makes specific reference to the occurrences. An illustration of this is when a patient's hands tremble while he talks. Another example of selective perception is the case of a student who has carefully read a poem and is quite confident that he has mastered its meanings, but is surprised when in class the instructor reveals an obvious, important consideration well within the student's realm of understanding that he had completely overlooked. We have cited three rather distinct and progressively complicated illustrations of the familiar phenomenon of selective perception, varying primarily with respect to the level of complexity of the potentially perceivable ideational component omitted from the cognitions that were consciously entertained. In the first instance, the perceptions of external natural sounds did not emerge as important components of consciousness. The second case involved a patient who was not aware of the fact that his hands were trembling, a behavior no doubt accompanied by a vaguely experienced concomitant subjective psychological feeling of anxiety that subtly plagued him during his reflective efforts. And third, there was the student who unwittingly failed to consider a particular poetic interpretation that he had repeatedly entertained in prior reflections; while on the other hand, he was able to consciously generate several other equally as complex interpretations. In all three cases something potentially capable of perceptual or intellectual apprehension had been excluded from conscious awareness until either personally reflectively brought to attention at a later time, or ascertained with the aid of another person. Then the previously overlooked factors were spontaneously understood by the subjects in question. These manifestations of unintentional perceptual omission could be regarded as resulting from the gradual development of preconscious and conscious modes of habituation. The writer, when overlooking insignificant external sounds, did not consciously and deliberately say to himself, "I am now going to write, therefore I will not admit external sounds into my conscious recognition." Nor did the patient deliberately decide not to be aware of the fact that his hands were trembling while he spoke. Similarly, the student certainly did not decide to overlook an obvious interpretation of an assigned poem to be analyzed. From this, we may generalize that human behavior includes a vast number of similar habitual modes. Hence, even though we could potentially respond differently than we, in fact, do in almost any circumstance, such is typically not the case, for over the years human organisms gradually develop complex and interrelated patterns of both reflexive and conscious habitual modes of behavior in response to frequently and typically reoccurring stimulus-object effects. For example, we see the color, red, or the object, table, and we reflexively linguistically characterize them as such; hence infusing our perceptions of these entities with subjective psychological meaning and rendering them personally intelligible. Similarly, we speak in linguistically coherent sequences, perform mathematically sophisticated calculations, and experience personally meaningful human relationships, largely from the possibility of having developed innumerable constitutive cognitive habituations, in principle determinable as resulting from specific, reoccurring stimulus-object effects. However, the first two selective-perception illustrations, and particularly the latter one, cannot be exclusively analyzed in terms of reflexive phenomena. Rather, as we have seen, conscious awareness is a necessary consideration in such an analysis.

The point being made is that although a scientific psychology must, of course, view behavior in cause-effect relationships, our notions of what may qualify as causally efficacious agents must be expanded to include not only natural factors, but ideational factors as well. This basic habituative character of human behavior will hereafter be expressed in the following technical manner: human organisms develop preconscious and *conscious ideational propensities* for responding to given correlative stimulus-object effects. Further, it is reasonable to assume that physiochemical conditions underlie all possible mental events. A consciousness stands over against percepta or stimulus-object effects, the latter components issuing from stimulus-objects located in either the concomitantly perceived natural world or personal bodily organism of the percipient himself. Therefore we can, in principle, even maintain a more general position in theoretically conceptualizing human behavior, namely: human organisms develop determinate organic propensities for responding to given correlative stimulus-object effects or stimulus conditions; propensities, then, can manifest themselves as unconscious, preconscious, and conscious classes of behavior. In this last refinement, we have extended our principle to include both physio-chemical and conscious organismic processes. The term "propensity," whether physiochemical, preconscious, or conscious, as used above, is of course attributed a meaning beyond that conventionally intended. The definition will be extended to characterize the actual ontologically occurring physiochemical, preconscious and conscious processes themselves in their predispositioned mode of occurrence. Thus the three basic classes of propensities or behavioral habituations can be designated as follows. A physio-chemical or organic propensity from a subjective psychological perspective would be, for example, the actual secretional process of a given bodily organ as it occurs as a function of given determinate stimulus-conditions. A preconscious propensity would be a reflexive behavior as in the case, for example, of a given word which is spontaneously spoken without any significant amount of consciously deliberate effort. A conscious propensity is a behavior principally contingent upon conscious and reflective conscious awareness, or what has been termed denotative and connotative symbolic meaning, as when a person responds to the stimulus-object, "Hello," by saying, "I'm fine, how are you?", or in the more sophisticated situation where one's political contentions (often based on habitual, naïve bias rather than careful reflective analysis) predisposes one to give stereotyped responses to typical questions (the former occurring as stimulus-object effects). These distinctions acquire more precise meaning as the propensity-mechanism concept is contemplated within the complete context of the comprehensive theory of human behavior being presented.

Of course it should be reiterated at this point that since individual human organisms can be affected by stimulus-objects both on a sensational level where the mode of sensory stimulation is not consciously perceivable as subjective psychology experience and on a perceptual level, as in a subjective psychological experience, a complete scientifically specified account of these effects is, for all practical purposes, impossible, although important progress can be made in this endeavor by the conjoint efforts of an objective and subjective psychology. Further, the many potentially ascertainable stimulus-object effects would also have to be systematically conceived in conjunction with a specification of an organism's predispositional modes for responding to given correlative stimulus-conditions. This would be a task equally as difficult as precisely

specifying how an organism is affected by given stimulus-conditions.
Thus in view of these very difficult concrete methodological problems,
we must conclude that our usage of theoretical terms such as "stimulus-
object effects," and "propensities" is portraying the human organism's
functional states as they are ideally conceptualized to occur within a
complete, unified organismic system existing within a determinate environment. What we shall often describe, therefore, in future discussion
as seemingly evident relationships demonstrated by organismic mechanisms are only dimly understood at present in terms of satisfactory experimental verification. For example, complex functional relations among
dynamic physio-chemical processes underlying organisms' behavior can,
at best, be comprehended only in probability terms. In fact, there are
many researchers who feel that the possibility of expressing human behavior in exact scientific terms is sheer folly. This issue is discussed in
Ernest Nagel's book, *The Structure of Science.*(14) However, for our
purposes of philosophical analysis, and an attempt to better understand
the nature and interrelations among causal determinants of human
behavior, this paradigm model will be of great theoretical value. Moreover its utilitarian value will provide a practical instrument for formulating hypotheses facilitative of empirical inquiry.

Implicit within the bare theoretical statement, "Human organisms
develop determinate organic propensities for responding to given correlative stimulus-object effects or stimulus-conditions," is the fact, of
course, that a vast multitude of integrated organic functional processes,
occurring logically prior to emergent conscious and reflective conscious
mental events as temporally concomitant unconscious processes, are presupposed as necessary conditions for the possibility of such high-ordered
emergent phenomenal manifestations. Therefore, as Skinner has partially
suggested, for different reasons however, it seems plausible to assume
that in principle the physio-chemical conditions underlying all types of
mental events are a direct causal function of both temporally and
logically antecedent organic functional processes whose origin could
conceivably be traced ultimately to the effects of the stimulus-conditions
that had originally stimulated the resultant processes. Hence, let us think
of a very long chain of physio-chemical functional reactions that begin
with the initial effects of any given stimulus-condition and frequently
culminate as extraordinarily high-ordered physio-chemical conditions directly underlying correlative mental events. Typical illustrations of this
theoretically possible emergent culmination are the subjective psychological states to which the following statements refer: "I burned my
finger," "The tree is brown," "My thoughts about this issue are . . ."
However, there are also a great number of organic reactions to stimulus-

conditions never reaching the level of consciousness, such as homostatical processes. Changes in these states are obviously not directly accessible as conscious perception in the same way that we perceive pains or thoughts.

We may say that when a human organism responds to the effect of a given stimulus-condition, the organism must necessarily bring to bear all of its relevant organic propensities upon the corresponding stimulus-condition affecting the organism at that time. In effect, the stimulus-objects are demanding the most sophisticated response of which the organism is capable at that time, and the relevant brain neurology and other physio-chemical mechanisms are functionally activated to meet the demands posed. Here we are stressing the physio-chemical, mechanistic aspect of human behavioral response phenomena and omitting any reference to conscious causality and its relationship to physio-chemical processes. It should be noted that this mode of analysis is valid for it is being conducted from an empirical identity frame of reference; we are maintaining that mental events have physio-chemical correlates that are in principle ascertainable through empirical procedures, and thereby arguing as if this information were available. There is a close resemblance to the operation of a computer, although obviously a computer does not have anything like subjective psychological states, in that one could equate, in a very general way, what has been defined as stimulus-object effects, appearing as contemporaneously delivered data, with data cards fed into the already programmed computer. The programmed form or memory could be roughly equated to what we are defining as percepta representing the cerebrally stored affective and symbolic wisdom of the past. Thus when the computer is activated, it necessarily executes its prescribed modes for processing the input data; it does not consciously hesitate—choose not to perform its task, etc. The output information is a resultant product of both the input data and the program. Similarly with respect to certain manifestations of human perception and thought, we frequently perceive and think in a spontaneously meaningful way. A critic of this view could, in protest, close his eyes, for example, or refuse to think for a short period of time.

One may ask at this point, in reference to the three earlier illustrations, if the writer was capable of hearing the sound of passing automobiles, and if the patient was capable of perceiving his trembling hands, and if the student was capable of understanding the interpretation he did not recall, why did they not do so? The answer to this question, as it relates to neurological blocking of some processes and admittance of others, is ultimately a matter to be empirically resolved and cannot be answered by mere logical analysis. However, the phenomenon does suggest an important hypothetical construct, one which we shall define as perceptual field. In the three examples, even though the subjects in question were entirely capable of comprehending the overlooked considerations, the fact of the matter was that they did not do so while responding to the original stimulus-conditions. We may interpret this by saying, again speaking with a mechanistic emphasis, that the stimulus-conditions did not activate those organic propensities (i.e., all those relevant physio-chemical mechanisms and processes activated by appropriate correlative stimulus-object effects) corresponding to the unactualized mental event-components (i.e., "sounds from automobiles," "awareness of trembling," "realization of an interpretation characterizing the poem as . . ."). Whether this was a result of the insufficient intensity of the original stimulus-object effects affecting the organism, or of neurological blocking mechanisms, or both, is not an issue that can be settled here. At the present state of scientific knowledge with respect to complex problems of this type, it would be very difficult to provide even a tentative answer for this empirical question. We can better comprehend the problem in terms of the construct defined as perceptual field. It has been said that this construct refers to the predisposition of organisms for selective perception. If human organisms responded to all the stimulus-object effects which they are capable of perceptually or consciously entertaining, great dysfunctioning would result. However, because of their selective perception capacities, only those organic resources are needed that tend to facilitate efficacious behavioral modes, or promote those behaviors deemed personally important. Thus, in the three previous examples of selective perception it was seen that all subjects executed behaviors of which they were consciously aware. In the first two examples subjects demonstrated behaviors of which they were unaware during the time in question, and in the third example, cognitive associations that the student was capable of making without additional learning were overlooked. Therefore the stimulus-object effects involved in stimulating each subject activated organic propensities that in all cases culminated in mental event-components, and other propensities that did not reach this level of occurrence. The ones that did become mental event-components, precisely because the subjects did have conscious and reflective conscious perceptual access to them, were available as personally accessible stimulus-objects capable of causally influencing the subjects' behavior. But the propensities not emerging as event-components were not available to the subjects as causally effective ideational instruments. Although this is an abstract way of stating the matter, it concretely amounts to saying the following: the patient, having conscious and reflective conscious awareness of the thoughts occurring within his head concomitant with other relevant internal and external perceptions, could causally influence his behavioral responses to the counselor on the basis of these ideational and natural perceptual data. He was not aware of his trembling, and hence continued to tremble without realizing it. However, if the counselor verbally informed the patient of his trembling behavior, the latter would have made a determined effort to terminate the behavior. The new information, because of the patient's conscious awareness of it, would function as a stimulus-object capable of directly influencing his subsequent behavior. The trembling had, no doubt, developed over a long period of time as a preconscious habitual or reflexive response to a particular correlative stimulus-condition. It originally had, perhaps, conscious, clearly ascertainable anxious dimensions whose specificity diminished with the passage of time, leaving as behavioral remnants only a negative habituation of trembling and a pervasive though vague subjective psychological feeling of anxiety. The illustration of the student exemplifies an instance of conscious habituation that the student may have gradually developed, for example, a relatively stereotyped method for analyzing poetry, without making a determined, reflective effort to broaden or render more profound his mode of analysis. Here we have instances of only negative habituation. There are also many typical examples of positive habituation in daily behavior, such as speech, perceptual interpretations, thought modes, and walking. It can be seen from this that thought, as we know it through direct acquaintance, could not be possible at all without well-established positive habituations. The concept of perceptual field, then, refers to those stimulus-object effects which emerge into our consciousness as perceptions and thereby become potentially efficacious as behavioral determinants. On the other hand, as portrayed in the examples on selective perception, there are those stimulus-object effects that we do not consciously entertain and hence reflect upon, thereby effectively constraining our behavioral responses to well-established preconscious and conscious habituations. To transcend the adverse influence of negative habitual behaviors, their efficacious occurrence as behavioral determinants must be made perceptually evident to the subject executing the undesirable behaviors, thus enabling the subject to become aware of the negative effects with sufficient conscious clarity that this recognition will act as a stimulus-object to initiate a more suitable program for relearning an alternate pattern of response-behaviors. In one sense a new stimulus-object, capable of producing more desirable behavioral responses, has entered into a subjective's perceptual field.

Here we are very close to the essential function and method of productive psychotherapy and teaching, both of which are presently

moderately systematic endeavors to facilitate the development of qualitatively more suitable responses to given problematic or unfamiliar
stimulus-object effects. Both fundamentally involve broadening an organism's perceptual field so that newly developed responses to novel
stimulus-object effects are more precisely discriminative of the distinctive
nature of given stimulus-object effects and the relationships among unfamiliar stimulus-object effects with those that are already relatively
familiar to the subject. By broadening an individual's perceptual field,
given stimulus-object effects conjure an increased, and often qualitatively
better integrated, number of organic propensities to consciousness, thereby
increasing the number of ideational stimulus-objects that can, in
turn, conjure other relevant information. This amounts to saying that
with a broadened perceptual field, given stimulus-object effects can
conjure more relevant wisdom constructively to bear upon the effect,
hence promoting greater interrelatedness between relevant aspects of
the present occasion and previously integrated learnings. In psychotherapy, the most difficult task is often that of clearly revealing to the
patient the precise nature of adverse stimulus-object effects, and more
important, in assisting him to become sufficiently cognitively clear about
the negative effect to reflectively initiate his own program for effective
relearning. Typical learning, however, differs from psychotherapy in that
less effort is required for transcending negative modes of habituation,
established prior to subsequent constructive learning or relearning.
Rather, the major emphasis in novel learning is on increasing the amount
of relevant wisdom that can be conjured to any given stimulus-object
effect, that is, increasing the amount of integrated, operationally instrumental information that can be brought to bear upon a given problematic situation. Therefore, when a perceptual field is broadened,
there is an increase in the number of qualitatively subtle ideational
stimulus-object effects that a subject can consciously perceive in a given
stimulus-situation. The stimulus-object effect activates a greater number
of organic propensities that, in turn, emerge into consciousness as an
increased amount of wisdom available to the subject for more profoundly comprehending the stimulus-object effects. In progressively
broadening perceptual fields, quantitatively more potential ideational
causal factors can enter into decision-making or problem-solving, hence
generally, qualitatively enhancing resultant decisions or solutions, for
more variables are considered. This view is a restatement in contemporary terms of the Socratic-Platonic adage, "Knowledge is Virtue." The
fact frequently overlooked in this view is that knowledge is not merely
regarded as an accumulation of unrelated facts. Rather, the concepts of
relatedness and harmonious integration of behavioral processes are in-

trinsic to this ancient Greek concept. In short, the notion of wisdom is the only suitable way to characterize the quality of information gradually acquired and carefully reflectively analyzed to insure maximal integration of cognitive factors in a way concordant with concrete experience. Similarly the term "virtue"—defined in the Aristotelian sense as doing something and doing it well—accurately characterizes the functional nature of the high-grade consciously reflective processes and their underlying physio-chemical correlates, involved in executing intelligent response-behaviors; i.e., through making effective synthetic usage of contemporary stimulus-object effects and previously acquired relevant wisdom. As we become more familiar with the unified behavioral model being developed, it will be seen that these classical concepts are an inextricable part of the configuration of theoretical constructs designed to comprehend the logical form of human behavior as it is contemplated by a subjective psychology.

With reference to the perceptual field construct, it is extremely important for psychologists and educators to understand that broadening individuals' perceptual fields is only the initial phase of a two-phase process of education or re-education. First, formerly inexperienced or novel stimulus-object effects should be gradually and systematically introduced to an individual's perceptual field to increase the number of ideational stimulus-objects that are personally accessible for promoting cognitive interrelation among relevant perceptual components. This predisposes the individual to yield qualitatively better responses. Clearly, however, the mere introduction of novel stimulus-object effects into an individual's perceptual field does not always guarantee that these effects will be harmoniously integrated with an organism's previously established configurations of propensities. In fact, it more frequently results in promoting behavioral dysfunctioning. Therefore, it is absolutely imperative that the experiential integrative efforts exercised by an organism be conducted under the careful guidance of trained personnel. The latter can facilitate this process by capitalizing upon the constructive efforts of the individuals who are experientially involved in gradually attempting to coherently and consistently synthesize newly acquired information with previously established wisdom, to promote more virtuous behavioral functioning. Thus in conjunction with the subjects' personally initiated efforts, observers must be careful to see that these integrated measures are achieved in a suitable developmental sequence with no important phases omitted. Instead of introducing merely disruptive stimulus-object effects into an individual's perceptual field and hence increasing the probability that many negative habituations will be formed in attempting to cope with sources of novel stress, it is necessary to see that appropriate propensities are developed to reconcile these unique factors with the organism's established wisdom in order that maximal functional virtue be behaviorally achieved. When attempting to modify preconscious reflexive behavioral modes, it will be found that engineered programs for systematically introducing stimulus-object effects into subjects' perceptual field will be more successful in changing behavior, because at this primitive level of conscious awareness the mechanism of reflective consciousness is often not a causally potent instrument for changing spontaneously occurring, reflexive behaviors. This type of problem methodologically lends itself well to the conditioning procedures of an objective psychology. In any case, whether systematic behavior modification entails the predominate usage of the subject's reflective capacities, conditioning techniques, or a combination of both approaches, undoubtedly the most important consideration is that the subject be deeply experientially involved as an *active instrument* of his behavioral change. Similarly, professional persons facilitating this change should also be personally and vicariously or empathically involved. However, the ultimate locus of cognitive integration resides within the experiential efforts of the subject desiring behavioral change.

It should be noted, before extending our investigations to formulating additional constructs, that in much of what has been said the metaphorical characterization of intelligent behavioral growth as being a cyclical process of moving from vague-to-clear understanding was pervasively implicit. Most of the preceding discussion of constructs for the behavioral model has been intended primarily as an introduction to a more elaborate and precise ensuing exposition. The reader must, in fact, make a significantly important conceptual shift in contemplating human behavior, away from the established views of most current behavioral theories. This difficult task is further complicated by the fact that a position such as the one presently being propounded cannot satisfactorily be understood until the system is pondered at length in its entirety, and then compared with other theories.

When a human organism is affected by an internal or external environmental change, or experiences the ingression of stimulus-object effects, all relevant physio-chemical mechanisms or organic propensities react to the change or are brought to bear upon the stimulus-object effects. Involved in this phenomenon are an almost incomprehensibly large number of physio-chemical sensory and neurological processes, in addition to a multiude of relevant supportive organic mechanisms and processes not directly involved with high-ordered emotional and ideational activity. In the sequential execution of these organic processes, beginning with the original stimulus-condition, we may in principle conceive of relevant organic mechanisms whose threshold for activation has been exceeded, hence causing their unique function to be executed, which in turn provides the necessary condition for activating other subsequently related mechanisms, and so on. Here we begin to appreciate the cybernetic character of a massive, highly integrated or interconnected organic-functional system comprised of physio-chemical mechanisms existing in crucial proximity with one another, each mechanism conceived as operating individually and with a society of similar mechanisms in executing a specific task, given the appropriate stimulus-conditions. Also, in turn, each of the society of mechanisms, upon having performed the task, yields stimulus-object effects or notification of completed tasks ingressing as stimulus-conditions into the constitution of consecutive relevant mechanisms and societies of mechanisms, hence promoting sequential activation. In all this, there are the implicit notions of transmitted activation and hence progressive propagation of physio-chemical processes that synthetically coalesce to various stages of unconscious integration and then to a preconscious reflexive stage marking the novel ontological emergence of vaguely conscious organic bodily and emotional feeling, and finally to the two highest-ordered stages of clear consciousness and conscious reflection. This developmental, coalescent, negative entropic process will hereafter be technically defined as concrescence.(9), (27) The phenomenon could be described cybernetically as the concrescence of organic propensities in response to the ingressed effects of stimulus-objects. This characterization represents a terminologically simple, yet highly flexible and precise, way of comprehending in principle vastly numerous and complex organic processes. Implied within this novel descriptive mode are such central scientific objects and constructs of physiology and mechanistic biology as threshold, binary "go or no go" cerebral mechanisms, such organic mechanisms as cells and other vital bodily organs, neurons, synapses, and so on. Further, since it is presupposed that the nature of these entities and their relational processes can be exhaustively explained in mechanistic biological terms, they are hence rendered amenable to mathematical and statistical modes of formal relation. However, the theoretical model here proposed, while defined in terms concordant with and complementary to traditional mechanistic, though clearly not materialistic, scientific theories, is by no means completely explicable in terms of these theories.

When organic concrescence reaches the level of development where primitive emotional feeling occurs, the first necessary condition has been satisfied for the resultant organization of what has been generally described as emergent mental processes. This initial emergent stage, as well as those higher-ordered succeeding stages, provide us with striking evidential proof of an ontologically unique realm of phenomenal being. Mental phenomena are the emergent, felt products of an indeterminately complex human physiology, subsequently disciplined into potent causal agents through interpenetrative relationships with inner and outer environments.

When it is said that a highly complex, integrated human physiology generates an ontologically distinct class of phenomena, we are in a sense led to an interactionistic viewpoint of the relation between mind and body, but one of a special type. When considering a single mind we may think of a single train of physio-chemical processes occurring in a brain, but it is a series of processes, functioning as stimulus-objects, yielding effects that are directly perceived through two logically distinct modes of perception, both of which are necessarily grounded in what has been defined as mental or private events. First there is the inter-subjectively verifiable way of observing natural neurophysiological phenomena, through the external bodily senses. Secondly there is the direct mode of perceptual apprehension available only to the subject within whose head the neural processes occur. He consciously perceives his own mental states as they emerge as stimulus-object effects from the neurophysiological processes occurring in his head. However, as has been repeatedly argued, both perspectives are ultimately contingent upon a mind for their very possibility as intelligible percepta. Hence, the causal presence of mind must be an *a priori* presupposition in any discourse on the matter. The further conclusion to be drawn from this is that all humanly perceivable events must, in principle, be private events. Thus the statements, "This is the electroencephalograph wave pattern representing those physio-chemical states empirically correlating with subject A's feeling of sadness" and "I (subject A) feel sad" are both statements that refer to two distinct categories of event-components, both of which necessarily presuppose an individual mind for the possibility of their perceptual apprehension. Again, the first category refers to directly perceivable phenomena which are intersubjectively verifiable. The second category, however, can be directly verified only by the subject within whose physiology the event occurs. But the ontologically existing train of physio-chemical occurrences to which both categories of statements ultimately refer are those transpiring within subject A's brain neurology. In saying this, we will not have to submit to the difficulties of solipsism or idealism for reasons to be introduced subsequently.

Returning to the discussion on emergent, infantile, primordial mental states, let us say that these undisciplined emotional feelings are indicative of an organism's primary reaction to given stimulus-object effects issuing from internal and external environmental regions. These feelings are spontaneous, symbolically unclarified in their original mode of occurrence, and not generated by or contingent upon thought. Included in this lowest emotional stratum are such primitive phenomena as pleasure, fear, and fight-or-flight states. We might speculate that feelings on this level are the amorphous psychological states constituting the vague, sporadic emotional consciousness of infants.

The next level of spontaneous emotional reactions, at least when experienced by symbolically mature mentalities, is progressively influenced by former intelligently comprehended experience, retained as memory. For example, our initial immediate reaction to a loved one presupposes a multitude of prior learning, including a knowledge of the loved one's personality, the meaning of the term "love," the concrete experiential information derived from prolonged interaction with the loved person, and so on. A very high-grade manifestation of this form of spontaneous emotional-intellectual experience would be in aesthetic intuition, or the I-Thou experience about which Martin Buber speaks. But at less sophisticated levels, spontaneous emotional reactions are generally, though vaguely, indicative of the way our entire unconscious-to-conscious relevant organism responds to a given stimulus-object effect. Throughout our conscious and reflectively conscious awarenesses, these emotional reactions concomitantly accompany all ingressed stimulus-object effects. Their topology is highly variable. Most frequently, our emotional reactions to stimulus-conditions as they present themselves in daily life are relatively incapricious. However, as in the case of fight-or-flight, intense intellectual involvement with a matter of great interest, romantic experience, and so on, there is considerable topological variability in emotional substrata. In most cases, it is important to note, the emotional dimension of experience, subtly persisting throughout conscious and consciously reflective events, remains unscrutinized. The previous example demonstrating selective perception, where the writer was unaware of the sounds of passing automobiles, is somewhat analogous to our typically infrequent reflective examination of subtle emotional event-components concomitantly accompanying ideational activity, although the former example dealt with natural world perception as distinct from internal bodily affective percepta. Some psychotherapists emphasize that both counselor and patient scrutinize their personally occurring emotional-intellectual reactions to reciprocal stimulation while in therapy as an extremely valuable practice. That is, it is hypothesized that in developing a personal facility for accurately discriminating among dynamically emerging emotional states, in their intense

spontaneous occurrence as a direct causal function of both predetermined and undetermined stimulus-object effects, individuals can progressively better understand their modes of preconscious and conscious
habituation. Thus from making these reflective discriminations, many
formerly unnoticed or unclarified stimulus-object effects, to which
possibly undesirable responses were unwittingly habitually made, are
raised to the level of conscious experience, thereby broadening the
individual's perceptual field. Beyond this, with additional innovative
reflection, more appropriate, harmoniously integrated and personally
fulfilling behavioral responses can be developed with respect to given
stimulus-object effects.

A logical and empirical implication in the notion of spontaneous,
primordial, symbolically undisciplined emotional feelings is the subjective psychological view that these primitive mental emergents are the
synthetic culmination of an organic concrescent, almost instantaneously
reflexive process, beginning with the effects of stimulus-objects which
activate relevant organic sensory mechanisms. The mechanisms in turn
transform the effects into physio-chemical equivalents or analogues
which are then synthetically united, in an extraordinarily complex concrescent process, with physio-chemically stored wisdom. As a result,
the synthetic product emerges as a consciously experienced perceptual
event-component. It is nearly impossible to conceive of an organism
whose structure is so complex and integrated that it can yield emergent
mental phenomena. This is in addition to the striking fact that years
of affective-cognitive disciplining are required for developing the functional harmony among organic mechanisms, to the degree that their
collective functional interrelation acquires sufficient discipline to produce
high-grade, intelligent, innovative mental events, to say nothing of the
millennia required for the human organism to have developed to this
level of perfection.

Through exercising conscious reflection, we can to a great extent
linguistically explicate the directly perceived experiential nature of our
subjective psychological states. In light of this possibility let us specify
some of the universal characteristics intrinsic to the emotional substrata of our personal, inner, ideational experience. Essentially four major attributes can be determined.

First, it may be said that emotional feeling is the base medium for
the eventual development of higher-ordered cognitive processes in that
sophisticated ideational experience is disciplined emotional feeling
symbolically subdivided and thereby greatly sublimated.

Second, emotional feelings considered in their own right are
essentially vague and undisciplined, although they can be gradually

symbolically disciplined, defined, organized and clarified, via the mechanism of conscious reflection.

Third, feelings are the consciously vague manifestations of an organism's spontaneous reaction to stimulus-object effects. Implicit in this statement are some very important indications of an organism's functional virtue as this is demonstrated by the kind of qualitative response elicited from a human being as a result of given stimulus-object effects. An individual's immediate emotional reaction to certain types of stimulus-object effects is often indicative of the "best" and "worst" organic, preconscious, and conscious propensities that are habitually brought to bear upon given stimulus-occasions. The reaction provides an index of the overall functional efficacity of the organism's harmonious response-capacity. From this, psychologists and educators can make determinations about the breadth of a person's perceptual field. They can conclude on many occasions that an individual's perceptual field is insensitive to certain determinate stimulus-object effects, whose probable ingressional influence, if properly incorporated into the individual's relevant scheme of positive behavioral habituations, would increase his overall behavioral efficacy in solving problems. Hence, specific schedules for stimulus-object ingression could be planned that would, in effect, increase the perceptual sensitivity, with respect to specified predetermined effects, of the individual's perceptual field. As a result of being better able to discriminate amongst various relevant stimulus-object effects, the subject in question is rendered more capable, with a determined reflective effort, of reconciling novel and perhaps, initially, functionally disruptive stimulus-object effects, for he now possesses an increased conscious awareness of those factors formerly adversely controlling his behavior without his realization.

Fourth, feelings are the initial manifestations of any phenomena that could be minimally defined as mind. This designation would also apply to lower-ordered organisms, which are said to experience similar primordial emotional states. However, the view must be essentially inferential for we have no way of directly verifying such a claim.

Let us consider, once again, the nature of habits. Our conception of habits and their formative development has much in common with John Dewey's view of habituative behavior. In certain quotations from Dewey's writing it was seen that he argued that reflective thinking occurs when previously established behavioral habits are no longer adequate to meet the demands of novel stimulus-conditions. For example, a factory worker who has repetitiously performed a particular task for several years generally experiences some initial difficulty when required to work at a completely different job. He must, in effect, develop an importantly different set of preconscious and conscious habituations to effectively perform the new task. Another example, on a much more sophisticated level, is the case of Immanuel Kant, the eighteenth-century German philosopher, who remarked that the basis for his having written the monumental *Critique of Pure Reason* was the fact that after having persistently contemplated the major philosophical problems of his time in a relatively conventional manner, he suddenly as a result of formulating a novel approach to conceptualizing the various problematic issues (of course, in consequence of prolonged, intensive reflection on these matters) was able to transcend what he regarded as his "dogmatic slumber."(28) Kant was able, from his novel perspective, to contemplate traditionally conceived philosophical problems within a dramatically new theoretical framework, thereby transcending the constraining cognitive habituations of his less innovative philosophic contemporaries and casting new light on enduring issues. These illustrations accentuate our view that as new stimulus-object effects enter into an individual's perceptual field, in varying degrees disrupting his habitual response efficacy, conscious reflection must be invoked in order to supersede formerly established, but presently dysfunctional, modes of habituation. Contemporary problematic circumstances require that expanded, more efficacious modes for satisfactorily meeting the demands of present stimulus-occasions be developed as correspondingly new, positive habituations, in order to maximize functional virtue. Dewey argued that if it were not for an organism's capacity to synthesize novel cognitive associations, intelligent thinking-behavior could not advance to increasingly higher levels of understanding.

With reference to the behavioral model being developed, it can be said that all conscious thought has its origins ultimately in vague, amorphous emotional feeling, and that over a long period of symbolic, primarily linguistic disciplining, the originally unorganized, sporadically intense emotional experiential character of primitive mentality is lost or dissipated merely because experiential recollection fades as a function of temporal passage. More important, the experiential intensity is gradually sublimated, essentially for the reason stressed by Cassirer.

No longer can man confront reality immediately; he cannot see it, as it were, face to face. Physical reality seems to recede in proportion as man's symbolic activity advances. Instead of dealing with things themselves man is in a sense constantly conversing with himself.(19)

To use the metaphysical terminology of Aristotle, symbols impose form on primordial, unorganized experience corresponding to matter.

Thus as ideational development proceeds, there is a marked increase in the sheer number of forms or symbols, and hence in linguistic sophistication, because a necessary condition for meaning-as-directly-felt-relatedness, namely, consciously understood symbolic relatedness, is progressively being fulfilled. The web of linguistic interconnections is rendered increasingly elaborate as unrestrained, raw emotional experience is steadily subsumed to symbolic discipline. This means that in mature intelligent behavior, our thoughts are constituted by predominately linguistic symbolic forms which can be clearly consciously conceived. The "pure matter," or originally unorganized perceptual experience, has been long forgotten. In fact, it could never be clearly recalled for symbolic disciplining is a necessary prerequisite for clear comprehension and hence recall. But in a very definite sense the form-matter distinction still applies to human experience regardless of how symbolically sophisticated our experience may become. Regardless of the extent to which our experience may undergo formalization and thus emotional sublimation, unsymbolized emotional elements or matter will still be experientially present in ideational processes. This is to say that all private or mental events are directly experienced unities. The basic fact of private events is that all their possible event-components are experienced in their uniquely felt, vague relatedness as well as in clearly perceived symbolic relationships with one another. Among other relevant ramifications of this point to be developed, the preceding conclusion indicates that many of these event-components can be readily linguistically comprehended, while other more subtle and inextricably unified emotional components cannot be adequately symbolized due to their nebulous conscious, affective nature. This fact was made clear in a previous illustration demonstrating that regardless of the precision and eloquence exercised in one's attempt to fully characterize the experience of savoring a fine steak, the verbal characterization of the pleasurable direct experience could not be as concretely informative as the actual experience of consuming the steak itself. This illustrates the applicability of the form-matter distinction in that in any private experience, particularly a highly complex one, there are many aspects that can be symbolically or formally comprehended, but also there are other dimensions which because of their emotional primitiveness and intuitively unitary nature are perceivable only as direct, vague ephemeral experience. These latter dimensions, through exercising a subtly concrete, emotional understanding of affective event-components, can occasionally, though inadequately, be linguistically clarified.

There is also a less nebulous symbolic aspect to human experience occurring as the connotative symbolic meaning implicit within linguis-

tic symbols used instrumentally to reflectively clarify and discipline our
experience at all levels of development. Both the purely emotional and
vague symbolic aspects of mental events embody those portions of
human experience demonstrating the quality of consciously pervasive,
though nebulously profound, familiarity of one's intimate relation with
components of reality; this has been technically defined as meaning-as-
directly-felt-relatedness. The latter is an extremely important portion
of the matter of human experience. Beyond the fact that this dimension
of linguistic symbols introduces the substantive experientially meaningful
quality to subjective psychological awareness, in distinction from denotatively clear symbolic components, it provides a vast resource for
suggesting novel modes of thought that can be ascertained and hence
elaborated through reflective analysis. The point of this discussion is
that both presymbolic emotional and vague symbolic experience, considered together, comprise those aspects of subjective psychologically
meaningful linguistic symbols formerly defined as connotative symbolic
components or meaning-as-directly-felt-relatedness. Further, this synthetically compounded domain contains all the relevant learned wisdom of
the past as it has been permanently recorded in given cerebral mechanisms, awaiting conjuration to a contemporary conscious occasion
whereupon it will constructively unite with denotative symbolic elements
in meaningfully characterizing the occasion. Thus the development of
complex symbolic phenomena, with their extraordinary capacity for
meaningfully enhancing the intrinsically barren perceptual deliverances
of the ever-emerging present through synthetically introducing the
symbolically embodied wisdom of the past, leads precisely to the condition Cassirer had portrayed when he said, "No longer can we confront
reality immediately. . . . Instead of dealing with the things themselves
man is in a sense constantly conversing with himself."(19)

It may be asked what sort of cognitive resources do we have to draw
upon when we engage in reflective thinking in our effort to effectively
engage in problem-solving? One certainly does not always analyze
primordial emotional feelings when engaging in reflection. Let us say, to
begin with, that our responses to stimulus-conditions can obviously be
of variable quality in terms of effective problem-solving. It has been said
that there are unconscious, preconscious, and conscious modes of habituation, only the last of which we typically regard as including conscious
and reflectively conscious thinking. Conscious habituations involve, it
will be recalled, generally stereotyped thought modes in response to
familiar stimulus-object effects, such as the usage of linguistic symbols
in spontaneously executed verbalizations, and in such standard expressions as "Good morning," "My name is. . . ," "Republicans comply to the

sentiments of big business while Democrats attend to the needs of the common man," "Negroes are naturally inferior to Whites," or "The Pythagorean formula is $a^2 + b^2 = c^2$." In short, conscious habituations are standard repetitive ideational responses, conjured by frequently reoccurring stimulus-object effects, that individuals have learned to spontaneously execute. Usually, people produce these responses without seriously subjecting their often naïvely conceived, deceptively profound, or erroneous implications to critical reflection.

Beyond the domain of conscious habituation there is the general, qualitatively variable realm of consciously reflective habituation. An example of this is in the case of many academicians who comprehend their areas of intellectual inquiry in terms of set theoretical viewpoints year after year without ever seriously questioning the presuppositional grounds upon which their cherished theory is predicated, or seriously considering the logically compelling features of other competing theories addressed to similar areas of concern. Granted, these individuals frequently consult relevant journals to remain technically up to date, engage in discussions of appropriate didactic issues, and often have access to considerable factual information which can be quickly conjured to vindicate personal intellectual biases, but nevertheless, there remains a basic disinterest in submitting fundamental personal views to critical, reflective examination. The situation is basically similar in disciplines where individuals work according to well-defined "mental sets" which delineate areas to be studied and the methodological manner in which problems are to be resolved, while theoretical and methodological presuppositions, or the far-reaching implications of the area of work on human affairs generally, remain reflectively unanalyzed. This is not to imply that this type of high-ordered habituation is necessarily, or even frequently, perverse. Actually, a substantial portion of all intelligent human productivity can be subsumed to this category of habituation. It is one unquestionably involving intelligent thinking, in that the implications of already established principles are systematically and pragmatically carried out in innumerable fruitful and tangible ways. It is, in effect, an "engineering" level of intelligence.

There is still a higher, optimally productive level of intelligence in which the human mind explores and exercises the depths of its intellectual resources in order to increase its understanding of the fundamental features of perceptually disclosed aspects of reality. This most advanced level of understanding is one where the human mind adopts a habitually critical, constructively reflective attitude toward problem-solving. Here, great reflective sensitivity is demonstrated in attempting to understand the precise implications of subjective psychological ex-

periential deliverance. The mind, with extraordinary exactitude, is able
in reflection to symbolically discriminate between those concepts which
precisely characterize given aspects of reality, and those that only
partially describe or even seriously misrepresent existential phenomena.
Of course, in explaining phenomenal occurrences in terms of functional
relationships, we quickly transcend the cognitive act of mere description; explicitly stated theories are, in most cases, utilized to interpretively
account for concretely perceived facts, while, in addition, presenting
various types of acceptable evidence to support interpretative explanations of observational reports. Finally, in describing mental activity at its
highest level of perspicacity, it can be said that the mind has achieved
an aesthetically satisfying reconciliation between pregnant connotative
symbolic meaning and that which is concomitantly denotatively clear
and distinct, as the two modes of perception synthetically unite in producing fully actualized linguistic symbols and configurations of symbols,
for accurately interpreting given directly perceived and hypothetically
postulated aspects of reality. An absolutely minimal number of relevant
data are sacrificed in the resultant symbolic representation. The rich
suggestibility of emotional feeling in its initial spontaneous response
to a problematic circumstance, and later, its final function as a psychologically primitive criterio-logical basis for evaluating the adequacy of
conceptual interpretations of significant phenomena provide an extraordinarily fruitful, though subtle, resource for developing subsequent
hypotheses and explanations. Our intuitive feelings vaguely inform us of
how well or badly given formulations fit the facts. At this primordial
level of spontaneous reaction to the effects of given stimulus-objects, the
"best" wisdom an organism can bring to bear upon the stimulus-occasion
is concrescently delivered to conscious awareness, in all its unclarified,
difficult, and indeterminately rich nuances of subtle emotional meaning.
Next, synthetically unified, connotatively symbolic meaning-as-directly-
felt relatedness, the most eminently relevant aspects of which are
some of the ephemeral potential significance of highly refined, disciplined emotional feeling in order to cognitively grasp implications capable of emerging into consciousness as clear, distinct symbolic formulations. From this synthetic process, concepts are generated, interpreting
with precision directly perceived aspects of reality—experienced directly
in their inextricable unity as stimulus-object effects. In this creative
process maximal organismic functional virtue is in evidence. Concrescence reaches its highest transcendent stages, as innumerable relevant
organic propensities synthetically unite to meet the challenging demands
of stimulus-occasions. The initial consciously perceivable testimonies of
this process spontaneously emerge as richly suggestive, amorphous,

comprehensive emotional feelings, followed by connotative or vague symbolic meaning, manifesting the distinctive quality of profoundly felt relatedness, the most eminently relevant aspects of which are simplified and hence projected into clear consciousness as clear and distinct denotative event-components. Little of this perhaps incomprehensibly complex process is directly governed by conscious determination, or at the other extreme, is directly ascertained through conscious reflection. The entire process can, however, be given important direction by mental or private events which function as ideational stimulus-objects. The multitudinous organic mechanisms of the human organism have been subjected through unconscious, preconscious, and conscious modes of causal determination to gradual disciplining. And, fundamentally, it is the unconscious physio-chemical constitution of the human organism that provides the operational foundation for the extraordinary functional harmony intrinsic to high-grade human behavior, hence providing the ultimate basis for generating novel, powerfully efficacious entities that emerge into consciousness as linguistic symbols. Perhaps the most recent, dramatically important example of intelligence being reflectively brought to bear upon foundational presuppositions, while maintaining an acute sensitivity to the precise deliverances of concrete perceptual experience, and intuitively emotionally felt contradiction or conceptual departure from experiential facts, is the revolution that occurred in theoretical physics during the first quarter of the twentieth century. The period that George Gamov has described as "the thirty years that shook physics" began with the theory of relativity, and later, the development of quantum theory. These theoretical innovations required a fundamental change in long-established "mental sets."

In positing the four very generally characteristic levels of cognitive functioning, the primary intention was to accentuate the distinctive features of each categorical level of habitual thinking-behavior. In terms of individual behavior, most human organisms typically execute the first two levels of habituation, while a smaller percentage, upon occasion, behave at the third level. Only an extremely small percentage of human beings ever demonstrate all four levels of habituation with any significant frequency.

It is important to mention, from a psychotherapeutic and educational point of view, that habitual and high-level reflective cognition (stages three and four) seem importantly contingent upon how free an organism is in its capacity to respond to stimulus-conditions. "Freedom," as it is used here, has a mechanistic implication in that the term refers to freedom from personal anxiety, that is, organically speaking, a factor that is functionally disruptive to the execution of instrumentally virtuous response-behaviors. Similarly the constraining influence of dogma, convention, mental sets, situations promoting bureaucratic efficiency, many outdated cultural mores, and so on, subtly impose varying amounts of closure upon perceptual fields. Freedom, more specifically, characterizes the degree of functional virtue an organism can achieve in attempting to spontaneously and harmoniously conjure relevant, concrescent organic propensities to given stimulus-object effects or stimulus-occasions. This process involves, among other things, the functional virtue of intrarelated components of particular organic mechanisms as they operate unitarily in executing their unique task, as well as interrelational functional virtue manifested among societies of mechanisms. As has been said, functional virtue is defined in the classical Aristotelian sense of "doing something and doing it well."

Beyond unconscious and preconscious functional virtue in their relation to the operation of an organism's constitutive organic mechanisms, assuming the possibilities for freedom are maximal, there is, in addition, a degree of reflective virtue which an organism can exercise in explicating the vast possibilities implicitly contained within emotional feeling and vague symbolic meaning for perceiving novel ideational suggestions for future inquiry. Certainly this cognitive ability is greatly contingent upon unconscious physio-chemical processes, with respect to the reflexive functional virtue of organic mechanisms, but beyond this, reflective virtue is significantly determined by the quantitative and qualitative acquisition and hence integration of positive ideational habituations which an organism has developed in the process of symbolic discipline or education. Positive habituations, behaviors that were given important consideration in the writings of Plato, Aristotle, Dewey, Whitehead, and others, play a crucial role in the overall functional virtue or harmony demonstrated in individual behavior. When this global attribute is developed to a high degree, the organism can both spontaneously and habitually conjure its unconscious organic resources, as well as its habituated discriminative powers of reflection to given stimulus-occasions. All the potentially efficacious organic and conscious resources an organism possesses for meeting the demands of a stimulus-occasion harmoniously join as consciously clear and distinct denotative components of symbolic clarity, concomitantly accompanied by an ideationally profound and richly suggestive periphery of consciously vague symbolic and emotionally felt meaning.

Much of what has been previously said was stated in definitionally universal concepts, applying to human behavior and to some extent that of lower organisms, hence rendering them necessarily abstract and, no doubt, difficult to comprehend. Although there are too many possible ramifications to be inferred from the former constructs to cite concrete examples of each, let us consider several that embody some of the more conspicuous principles of the general theory being developed.

Initially, we shall turn our attention to the concept of perceptual field. Figure 3 represents two instances, T_1 and T_2, in a time series. In each case there is an object of perception, a stimulus-object, the effects of which are the subjective psychological perceptions of the object, and a percipient. The cross-hatched section of the percipient-symbol represents the "width" of the subject's perceptual field with respect to the number and integrated quality of ideational associations conjured to consciousness resulting from the effects of stimulus-condition S_1, as measured by a special achievement test, crude as this instrument may be for the purpose of determining the nature of this phenomenon. Let us further assume that during the temporal interval transpiring between T_1 and T_2, the subject was exposed to a particular short-term, well-specified program of education, and later retested at T_2 by a highly reliable alternate form of the test originally administered at T_1, with the results showing that the subject's perceptual field had broadened or

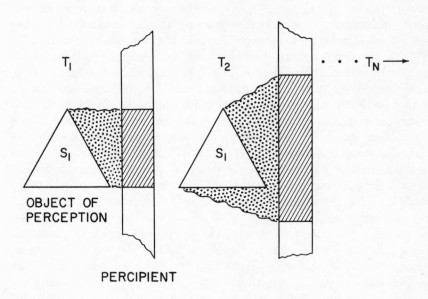

Figure 3. Perceptual field

increased in both cognitive and emotional sensitivity. We could validly conclude from this that at T_1 the subject was less perceptually sensitive than at T_2, as measured by our psychometric device. Now the question can be raised as to what the possible organic difference might be, with respect to the functional virtue of the organism's physio-chemical mechanisms are activated by stimulus-object S_1 at T_2 than at T_1, or that the physio-chemical terms about this manifest change in behavioral development, so in the present discussion we shall avoid difficult and scientifically indeterminate neurophysiological problems. However, it seems perfectly tenable to suggest that, in principle, either more organic mechanisms are activated by stimulus-object S_1 at T_2 than at T_1, or that the organic processes activated were more complex or integrated, or that it is a combination of the two, which is most probable. If this view is generally correct, and it is ultimately an issue to be empirically verified, we may inferentially conclude that the increased width of the subject's perceptual field at T_2 represents a quantitative and qualitative increase of integrated learning. This conclusion of course would rely heavily upon well-conceived experiments designed to measure cerebral changes as a function of improved instrumental learning demonstrated in concrete problem-solving, as opposed to mere diverse and nonutilitarian factual recall. That is, at T_2 the subject's consciously reflective behavior was being influenced by quantitatively more and/or qualitatively better integrated organic, and hence, ideational stimulus-objects than at T_1. Finally, and this is a more speculative but, in principle, possible fact, we can infer that a higher degree of organic concrescent synthesis is in evidence at T_2 than at T_1. This is to say that at T_1 the organism brought his best relevant organic propensities to bear upon the stimulus-object effects, but at T_2, primarily as a result of the intervening period of formal instruction which, in effect, gave the subject a greater resource of directly accessible consciously integrated ideational stimulus-objects hence increasing his power of conscious reflection, additional disciplined organic propensities were available. This enabled concrescence to be more complex, integrated, and, thus, of a higher order.

Let us consider another example of the varying width of an organism's perceptual field as determined by response-behaviors resulting from the taking in of stimulus-object effects into the organic conscious constitution. The following illustration involves, to some extent, the preconscious as well as the consciously accessible phases of many behavioral responses. The reduction of environmental temperature yields a stimulus-object effect that can conjure qualitatively different reponse-behaviors from various individuals, each response potentially demonstrating different levels of intelligence or consciously reflective deliberation. At the lowest level, perhaps, all individuals share in common the fact that their physiology automatically, apart from conscious considerations, responds to a drop in temperature by an increased rate of blood circulation. This is manifested overtly in shivering or rapid movement of limbs. Another more complex possible response is that in sensing the temperature drop, the organism may merely put on a coat and not give the matter of a reduced environmental temperature any further thought. If, however, the experienced temperature drop has impressed an organism as unusually important, assuming that all the individuals experience the same temperature drop under similar circumstances, he may, after having taken short-term measures to insulate his body from the cold, appropriate time to cut firewood for the anticipated winter. A still higher-ordered response may be elicited from a more ingenious person who, as a result of having been caught off-guard by the sudden, unexpected drop in temperature, decides to develop long-range, carefully formulated plans as an elaborate preventative measure against reoccurring instances of uncomfortable temperature variation. This man thus contrives a plan entailing the procurement of various necessary commercially made automatic heating system components such as thermostats, motors, a blower, high-limit temperature controls, etc. Beyond this, he investigates elementary considerations on heat-loss, proper distribution and location of registers, and so on, in an effort to gather the necessary information needed to design an efficient and economical heating system for his home. Finally, he utilizes the relevant information, materials, and final plan for construction and actively proceeds to fabricate the conceptualized heating system. These four examples of qualitatively different responses to a given stimulus-condition illustrate the profoundly variable subjective psychological significance that a given stimulus-object effect can have upon individually unique minds, as determined by the number and quality of relevant connotatively meaningful perceptions conjured to consciousness when the original stimulus-object effect entered the individual's perceptual field. They also demonstrate the variable temporal influence that the conjured connotatively meaningful perceptions, functioning later in reflective consciousness as ideational stimulus-objects, had upon resultant behavioral programs for action. In the first two examples only very short-term measures were taken in responding to the temperature drop, and then the problematic occurrence was promptly forgotten. But in the latter two examples, moderate-to-extensive long-term measures were taken as preventives against future unexpected drops in temperature. The last illustration portrays an admirable utilization of previously learned positive habituations as they were sequentially and harmoniously implemented, in accordance with a premeditated plan, as relevant emotional and ideational resources for solving, over a long period of time, a problem whose origin occurred with the original sudden drop in temperature.

A simple example will be given next to demonstrate the hypothetical process of progressively higher-ordered or transcendent concrescent synthesis. We shall refer to the psychotherapeutic technique of reciprocal inhibition as illustrative of concrescence, although the originators of the procedure would not interpret it theoretically as such. Reciprocal inhibition is a methodological procedure for modifying human behavior recently adopted by behavioristic researchers, having diverse and occasionally unsavory historical roots. Albert Bandura describes desensitization, a specific version of this general procedure, as follows:

On the basis of historical information, interview data, and psychological test response, the therapist constructs an anxiety hierarchy, a ranked list of stimuli to which the patient reacts with anxiety. In the case of desensitization based on relaxation, the patient is hypnotized and given relaxation suggestions. He is then asked to imagine a scene representing the weakest item on the anxiety hierarchy and, if the relaxation is unimpaired, this is followed by having the patient imagine the next item on the list, and so on. Thus, the anxiety cues are gradually increased from session to session until the last phobic stimulus can be presented without impairing the relaxed state. Through this procedure, relaxation responses eventually come to be attached to the anxiety evoking stimuli. (29)

Wolpe, one of the most recent proponents of this therapeutic technique, would interpret theoretically the dynamics allegedly underlying the manifestly observable behavior involved in this process by using the behavioristic learning theory propounded by Ivan Pavlov, as distinct from the operant conditioning theory of Skinner, which, as has been shown, is erroneously purported to deal exclusively with manifestly observable or wholly intersubjectively directly confirmable phenomena.(30) Moreover, there are critics of behavior modification techniques who would interpret manifest behavioral processes within a theoretical framework whose presuppositional basis, and hence constructs, differ markedly from those of Bandura and Wolpe.(31) The point to be made is that in the seemingly simple concrete process of desensitization, for example, there are innumerable behavioral phenomena manifested by both client and counselor that could be causally efficacious in psychotherapy. In fact, there are so many directly perceivable phenomena in evidence that if researchers attempted to deal with them simultaneously, mere confusion would result. Therefore, in order to isolate only those phenomena fundamentally relevant in bringing about positive behavioral change, an instrument entitled "theory" is introduced to eventually reveal which phenomena are causally operative, in contrast to those alleged to be irrelevant for experimental purposes. A theory, then, enables researchers to methodologically select appropriate phenomena for scientific investigation, and therein establish carefully controlled conditions for valid and reliable research procedures. But though this appears to be a rather straightforward methodological format, serious confusion and practical difficulty frequently arise in experimental inquiry, for in dealing with phenomena, we must select some phenomena for investigational and evidential purposes and reject others as irrelevant, and theoretical constructs, devised for explanatory purposes, are in most cases in principle incapable of direct intersubjective verification. Further, those directly ascertainable phenomena alleged to serve as empirical evidence for confirming given theoretical formulations are nearly always subjected to interpretation which can be here defined as an intellectual contribution to overt sensory perceptions not directly confirmable via direct external sensory experience. Thus with regard to our former consideration of desensitization, Bandura and Wolpe would maintain that permanent positive behavioral change, brought about as a function of using a stimulus hierarchy, or merely an appropriate reinforcement schedule as the therapeutic program would be conceived by Skinner, is achieved through the removal of anxious behavioral symptoms that are capable of direct intersubjective confirmation by observers. The removal of manifest adverse symptoms would serve as the evidential grounds for confirming their theoretical formulations. Such other theorists as psychoanalysts, however, would interpret the same behavioral phenomena within different theoretical frameworks yielding vastly different conceptions of basic problems and procedures for constructive reconciliation. It is easily seen that many deceptively profound and difficult philosophical and methodological problems are inherent within the seemingly obvious distinction between facts and theories. We have done little more at this point than merely suggest that the fact-theory dichotomy has many problematic ramifications. This writer would propound the somewhat extreme view that the interpretive symbolic contribution of mind is inextricably associated with the fact-theory distinction. Therefore, before the latter problem can be resolved, scientists and philosophers need a clear concept of mind.

Bandura's description of a particular technique of reciprocal inhibition has been used for it clearly illustrates, on a rather elementary level, the principle of systematically introducing stimulus-object effects into a subject's perceptual field in order to increase the subject's consciously reflective discriminative sensitivity to those effects. Consequently, from increased perceptual sensitivity, which enables the organism to conjure qualitatively better connotative symbolic meaning or wisdom to an occasion, newly learned discriminations can be used by the individual for executing more effective behavioral responses to formerly problematic stimulus-object effects.

The theories here proposed are, of course, at odds with those of Wolpe and Bandura. Ultimately the grounds for dissent lie in the mind-body issues. However, although there is disagreement with the proponents of behaviorism on epistemological grounds, this is not to reject their concern for sound methodological procedure. The quotation from Bandura's writings is an excellent example of an area of agreement, insofar as his methodological practice is capable of scientifically precise specification.

More specifically, the process of desensitization would be interpreted from a subjective psychological viewpoint by saying, first, that the manifest anxious behavioral symptoms with their directly experienced subjective psychological affective counterparts are representative of a dysfunctional, unintegrated repertory of unconscious and preconscious habituations, activated by the effects of certain stimulus-conditions. Thus the subject cannot readily, through conscious reflection, alleviate the adverse perceptual experience of anxiety. He is unable to do so for the stimulus-object effects causing the undesirable anxious responses primordially enter into the subject's organism; that is, they stimulate organic mechanisms which are not under the direct control of conscious reflection. They are unconsciously and preconsciously reflexively activated. For example, an athelete who is attempting to perfect a particular sequence of bodily movements is confronted with the task of rendering constituent components of the comprehensive movement, habitual, and moreover, collectively habitual in a developmental order, as a precondition for spontaneously executing the ultimately desired comprehensive behavior. Similarly, in the case of the hypothetical anxious subject, certain previously learned behavioral responses to corresponding stimulus-conditions were initially improperly learned. At the time of origin, the negative responses no doubt had a consciously perplexing effect upon the subject in question, but as time passed, other competing stimulus-conditions demanded satisfaction, so that over a long period of time, the original environmental circumstances causing the dysfunctional response had been forgotten. However, the negative preconscious behavioral habituation still persisted in adversely influencing contemporary behavior. This particular behavioral analysis of the causal conditions underlying both the direct personal experience and symptomatic manifestations of anxiety does not differ significantly from various other interpretations that may be offered, even though they issue from importantly different theories. The area of significant discrepancy begins to appear as we carefully consider the therapeutic measures, i.e., programs for systematically introducing stimulus-objects into perceptual fields, whether as electric shocks or as emotionally charged verbalizations, used to alleviate anxious subjective psychological experience, or extinguish undesirable manifest symptoms. To define the cause of anxiety in psychoanalytic terms as resulting from an excessive dependence upon an improper maternal figure during the first year of life may accurately designate the original stimulus-condition causing the development of an early-life negative habituation. But if an inappropriately learned behavior still spontaneously arises as a function of a given stimulus-object effect that enters a subject's consciousness twenty or thirty years hence, it seems ludicrous to introduce a long dialogical program of linguistic stimulus-object effects, alleged to be therapeutic, corresponding to, for example, regressing to the original conflicting early-life state of affairs evidenced between infant and mother. These stimulus-object effects (as they assume the form of highly sophisticated and abstract linguistic symbols, whose meaning, at best, is typically very far removed from the contemporary concrete subjective psychological experience of anxiety, as well as its original source of provocation) are not at all identical with those causing anxious experiential and manifest symptomatic behavioral responses in later life. This point is stressed merely to reiterate, though from a different theoretical frame of reference, a criticism that Professor Skinner has vigorously advocated for many years.(4), (10)

What, then, is the specific nature of the contemporary stimulus-conditions yielding anxious responses? What are the causal dynamics involved in modifying the anxious behavior directly experienced and symptomatically manifested? It has been logically demonstrated that a strict behavioristic analysis, in which human behavior is regarded as purely reflexive and mental events are causally inefficacious epiphenomena, is untenable. This view fails to recognize that mind, defined minimally as consciousness and reflective consciousness, must be presupposed *a priori* in order to have any meaningful, intelligent thinking behavior at all. A mind must be supposed to have perceptions if anything resembling human behavior is to be in evidence. But how do we reconcile the fact that in circumstances where a subject is experiencing anxiety, he is both consciously and even reflectively aware that certain stimulus-object effects are causing his anxiety; yet on the other hand, he cannot, from his own subjective psychological frame of reference, actively nullify the efficacy of the undesirable effects? These disruptive effects are within his perceptual field and can be, therefore, reflectively analyzed. However, concomitantly on a more primordially efficacious level, there are preconscious, reflexive stimulus-object effects to which the individual's organism is responding that do not enter his perceptual field but which yield the feeling of anxiety, an uncomfortable state that cannot be positively modified merely through a reflective understanding of its causal conditions. How can it consistently be maintained that there are certain stimulus-object effects of which the subject is aware and therefore can consciously and determinately utilize as ideational stimulus-objects to influence future behavioral modes, while conversely, there are other effects that exceed his conscious control in that they influence his behavior despite his consciously determined efforts to control their adverse influence? First, it can be said that if conscious awareness were not a necessary condition in executing uniquely human behavior, no anxious experience and manifest symptoms, for example, would be possible at all. This is simply to reiterate that if a subject were not consciously aware of the effects of the stimulus-object "dog," no trembling behavior would transpire. Therefore we may conclude that on some occasion in the past, the subject had learned, although not intentionally, to be fearful of dogs as a result, perhaps, of a former unpleasant experience with a particular dog. Disregarding the appropriateness of the learned response, let us say that later as an adult, the phobic reaction to dogs is of such severity that it significantly impairs the subject's daily behavior. Moreover, in therapy, he is able to conclude rationally that the vast majority of dogs are not to be feared, and so on, yet when a dog stimulus-object effect enters his perceptual field, excessive anxiety and hence trembling results. It is clear that the example now embodies the condition defined by the two former questions. The subject has conscious control of some stimulus-object effects, but there are other effects, causing trembling and the subjective psychological state of fear, that are consciously uncontrollable. These latter responses can be defined as negative preconscious habituations, perhaps learned previously under fully conscious, determinable circumstances. But as time passed, the habituations with their directly experienced concomitant anxiety had remained efficacious, while recollection of the original experiential occasion had faded from memory. Now assuming that we subject him to the program of desensitization suggested by Bandura, what organismic behavioral changes can be expected, specifically, as this psychotherapeutic process is explained by the behavioral model being developed? The solution to the global problem of developing more harmoniously integrated, functionally virtuous positive habituations that supersede former dysfunctional habituations, involves developing systematic programs of stimulus-object effects that, over a period of time, sequentially enter the subject's organism in such a way that the subject can experientially feel his own organic mechanisms, through their preconscious and conscious effects, effectively meeting the demands of each stimulus-object effect as they are progressively introduced to his organism. It is in this way that relevant organic and ideational propensities can be disciplined to systematically and constructively come to bear upon stimulus-conditions so that increasingly high-ordered concrescent synthesis is achieved. This procedure is effectively utilized in the type of therapy portrayed by Bandura and Wolpe, for it is designed to help clients transcend the constraining influence of certain kinds of negative, primordially reflexive, habituation. It enables the organism to gradually relearn responses to given stimulus-object effects, previously uncontrollable consciously, by progressively introducing increasingly more intense stimulus-object effects in succession to immediately preceding, less intense effects that had been successfully behaviorally mastered. In this way, formerly problematic responses are gradually subsumed initially to unconscious, then to preconscious, and finally, at higher stages of concrescence, to linguistic symbolic functional discipline. When dissipating the influence of negative preconscious habituations, which are usually intrinsically presymbolic, emotional feelings are typically the phenomena to be therapeutically construed, and hence positively disciplined. Thus as an anxiety hierarchy is presented to the client, he must learn to discriminate carefully among the vague, amorphous feelings and emotions directly experienced as comprehensible and controllable from those that embody dysfunctional anxiety. In this way a gradual discipline is imposed upon the vaguely conscious substratum of primordially felt spontaneous emotional reactions to given stimulus-object effects. As these feelings are more precisely symbolically comprehended and experientially accepted as "legitimate human" responses, they successively emerge with increased disciplined clarity into the subject's perceptual field. When this precondition has been fulfilled, the formerly vague, dysfunctional anxious feelings can be constructively reconciled with the organism's relevant comprehensive mode of behavior, and furthermore, acquire the status of stimulus-objects capable of functioning efficaciously as behavioral determinants.

Psychotherapists, when attempting to modify higher-ordered levels of negative habituation, may utilize increasingly more abstract linguistic stimulus-objects, in contrast to the concrete and even physically tangible stimulus-objects required for dealing with preconscious negative habituations, in order to generate effects that will enter the subject as novel, provocative direct experience, necessarily embodying complex emotional-intellectual perceptual components that can be subjected to his earnest, critical reflection. This therapeutically more frank and aggressive approach to behavior modification is considerably more affectively concrete and specific in its application than most traditional types of therapy. Such predetermined stimulus-object effects, communicated linguistically and in other manifestly perceivable ways as accurate empathy in understanding client responses, therapists' positive regard for their patients, the concreteness of therapists' communications to their patients, and so on, have been subjected to experimentation.(32) Many of the results issuing from these programs of investigation appear to possess numerous promising implications for understanding the process of therapeutic interaction, both in individual and in group situations. It seems that such implicitly embodied qualities in therapists' behavior as positive regard, concreteness, and therapist congruence, would effectively facilitate concrescent synthesis, particularly on the level of emotional awareness, and perhaps to a lesser degree on those levels corresponding to connotative and denotative symbolic meaning. Promoting increasingly high-ordered concrescence at these more advanced levels would appear to be largely a function of accurate empathy.

Traditionally, accurate empathy in psychotherapeutic circles has involved interpreting frequently confused and allegedly overtly deceptive verbalizations in an effort to reveal the essential meaning of the patient's fundamental sentiments about given matters of concern. It is an effort to expose what is "really" meant as opposed to accepting as factual mere naïvely manifest, literally stated verbalizations. This technique reaches its extreme, unrestrained form in psychoanalytic therapies. But we shall develop a less extreme conception of accurate empathy. Let us, with reference to our model, begin by saying that in any given counseling session many phenomena are directly in evidence. There are innumerable gestural and facial responses, bodily movements, and subtle reflexive behaviors to be considered in the actions of both the patient and the counselor. On a more sophisticated level, there are the highly complex implications of patient-counselor verbalizations, with their myriad connotatively meaningful nuances. In short, counselors are deluged with many data from which to formulate interpretive inferences about behavioral dynamics. The question becomes, then, what sort of theoretical guides or constructs should a counselor utilize in making these inferential determinations. With respect to the theory being developed, we can partially answer this question by saying that the multitude of phenomena manifested in the patient's global behavior enters the therapist's consciousness as mental event-components that are hence critically, through reflection, subsumed to the therapist's backlog of relevant wisdom. Thus the phenomena perceived as event-components are directly experienced in their unified mode of occurrence throughout given time spans. It is the cardinally important task of counselors to take this often complex unity of data, critically reflect upon the essential significance or factual character of the patient's complete behavior—whether it is overtly manifest, or at the other extreme, behaviorally covert; and finally, restate or indicate to the patient, concisely and clearly, the simplified, essential, perhaps concretely interpreted meaning of his unified behavioral response. This process can be defined as communicating accurate empathy. Simplifying must not be confused with unwarranted oversimplification. Simplification, properly conceived, is one of the most valuable products of reflective analysis, for it presupposes a profound and accurate understanding of the subject matter and involves the personal states of the therapist as well as those of the patient. Therefore, when a therapist has accurately and meaningfully informed the patient of a previously unknown, concretely relevant fact about his behavior, the accurately empathic, simplified communication is potentially capable of becoming a causally efficacious stimulus-object in the patient's perceptual field. The interpretive utterances of counselors can be utilized by their patients for conceptually understanding, and thereby better integrating, formerly ill-conceived dimensions of personal behavior. Vaguely comprehended and thus fearful and dysfunctional feelings can be harmoniously reconciled with overall behavior once they can be subsumed to linguistic and then ideational-emotional discipline.(33) There is also a more nebulous but characteristically human by-product resulting from having successfully engaged in therapeutic self-discipline. It is the profoundly humane aesthetic satisfaction derived from personally initiated (though usually with the aid of a counselor) behavioral integration. We may conclude by saying that an integrated understanding of formerly problematic feelings is a result of transcendent concrescent synthesis. Interpreted as subjective psychological experience, this corresponds to the gradually emerging awareness that uncontrollable, adverse feelings can be transformed into constructive sources of animation if they are allowed to manifest themselves with full conscious intensity under appropriate therapeutic circumstances, and then reflectively understood in terms of their essential factual significance. That is, from intense, frank therapeutic involvement, a patient can come to understand vague, fearful subjective psychological states through a cyclical process of experientially entertaining the full emotional impingement of dysfunctional feeling and, using this as a basis for departure, proceed to

reflectively explicate and hence subsume intelligible portions of primordial emotion to linguistic discipline. Continuing in this cyclical
manner, an individual can, with intimate conjunct assistance from a
therapist, systematically transmute his personal experience from a
state of oppressive anxiety to sentient autonomy. Perplexed emotional
feeling organically corresponds to conditions where important organic propensities are not synthetically integrated into higher-ordered
concrescent unification. Counseling and psychotherapy, therefore, become an enterprise designed to systematically provoke transcendent
concrescence by successively introducing stimulus-object effects into the
patient's perceptual field that will conjure moderately problematic emotional experience to consciousness for experiential entertainment, and
hence reflective discipline, in order to develop more efficacious propensity repertories in response to the effects. In all this, however, investigators must begin to pay much closer attention to the specific nature of
the stimulus-object effects that they, as therapists and educators, introduce into patients' and students' perceptual fields, for in many instances the effects are so diffuse, unspecified, or irrelevant, that they
have little effective cognitive impact upon the patients' behavior and,
perhaps frequently, have even a deleterious influence!(34)

A formal explication and systematical analysis of the psychotherapeutic process as it is comprehended by the model being developed,
would entail a major and lengthy effort. We can consider only the mere
unelaborated fundamentals of the therapeutic process as certain of its
phenomenal aspects have utility in meaningfully elucidating our primary
theoretical investigations. With this point in mind, we again devote our
attention to developing additional theoretical constructs.

Generally speaking, the human organism has heretofore been conceived as an extraordinarily complex system of harmoniously integrated
organic and subjective psychological functional mechanisms, capable of
responding to given stimulus-object effects whose categorical modes of
entry can, in principle, be only twofold: as effects from the external
natural world, and as effects arising from an organism's internal bodily
environment. At unconscious levels of entry, where effects initially appear as sensation, in contrast to consciously ascertainable direct
perception, an indefinitely large number of potentially specifiable response-processes, defined most generally as organic propensities, are
activated ultimately in response to initial reoccurring stimulus-object
effects. These response-processes are qualitatively contingent upon the
functional virtue, ultimately demonstrated among the constituent components of organic mechanisms operating as distinct cellular units, with
their molecular, atomic, and subatomic processes. The functionally

harmonious, progressively integrative, coalescent character of organic processes, arising purely from the intrinsic structure of cells as they exist in strategic proximity to one another within the domain of an individual organism living in a propitious environment, has been defined as concrescence. As propensities achieve greater organic synthesis, they in effect promote concrescence. When cerebral processes become synthetically conjoined with relatively uniformly enduring supportive organic processes, so that optimal levels of concrescence are approached, the sheer concomitant integration of multitudinous physio-chemical processes existing throughout given time spans, provides the necessary condition for an ontologically unique class of emergent phenomena that we have defined as subjective psychological or mental events. These emergent mental phenomena can be conceived to occur upon three distinctly perceivable experiential levels of sophistication: the lowest is organic bodily feeling, then emotional feeling, and the highest is ideational feeling. The latter two levels constitute the domain of symbolic behavior, rendering conscious and reflective conscious behavior possible. One fundamentally important implication of this fact is that original stimulus-object effects acquire as a result of concrescence, over and above their primitive unconscious occurrence as sensation, the ontologically superior status of perceptual experience, capable of intelligently aware acknowledgment of reality. Stimulus-object effects, entering as consciously determinable causal agents as distinct from unconscious physio-chemical causal conditions, can appear as external bodily perception originating from the natural world, and internal bodily perception occurring as organic feeling, emotional feeling and ideational feeling. Ideational feeling, as has been said, is a high-ordered symbolic derivative, resulting from gradually subsuming emotional feeling to discipline. Symbolic acquisition, the preponderance of which in mature intelligence is linguistic, permits and necessarily entails an extensive increase in the human organism's behavioral flexibility. Here the term "behavior" is used in a broad sense: as that, in principle, comprehensible by an objective and subjective psychological science. Concretely speaking, behavior includes manifest bodily movement and usually verbally emitted sound; and dynamic inner feeling, including organic bodily feeling, emotional and ideational states. Because of the human organism's greatly increased capacity for behavioral flexibility and adaptability, there rises the possibility for an indefinite elaboration of intelligence. Intellectual development is a function of conscious reflection. This ideational synthetic phenomenon involves first having consciously meaningful symbolic experience, and then attempting to logically explicate through reflection some of its indeterminately complex dimensions, using the necessary medium of linguistic symbols in order to render vaguely understood experience linguistically clear and distinct. Once a backlog of general information has been learned, mechanistically speaking, as propensities established among societies of cerebral physio-chemical mechanisms, vague undisciplined conscious experience is, in effect, transformed into meaning-as-directly-felt-relatedness. Reflection, defined as the learned capacity to bring formerly acquired relevant wisdom analytically to bear upon present experience, develops increased explicative potency as numerically more symbolically precise discriminations are ascertained within concrete experiential phenomena, and then integrated into the organism's spontaneously emerging conscious awareness. In this way, higher-ordered concrescence is achieved because of the greater information contained within the organism's reflective wisdom as it is exercised in problem-solving behavior, if the information is integrated perceptually as connotative meaning. Reflective powers develop cyclically. Experience is entertained, and hence critically pondered in the light of past wisdom in order to effect novel ideational synthesis. Then the twofold operation is repeated indefinitely. This cyclical developmental process, of course, commensurately broadens the individual's perceptual field. Transcendent concrescent synthesis, contemplated from a subjective psychological perspective, is the novel establishment of cognitive relations among concepts whose former, vaguely understood conscious character rendered them unassociated. It is the instrumental acquisition of novel ideational perception and, thereby, stimulus-objects which will be spontaneously embodied within the connotative symbolic meaning (wisdom) of future cognitive activity oriented at still higher-ordered concrescence. Implicit in this ideally postulated progression for intellectual growth are some important considerations that must now be more carefully contemplated.

In our recent line of argumentation it becomes evident that all conscious thoughts and their consciously intelligible modes of association or relation with one another emerge into awareness typically as linguistic symbols perceptually constituted of denotative and connotative components. The denotative component and the innumerable factors that collectively comprise the connotative symbolic component could each be regarded as consisting of ideational propensities. They are consciously ascertainable dimensions of what we have already defined as high-ordered organic propensities. Thus any possible complete, single idea is consciously entertained as a determinate configuration of inextricably unified denotative and connotative ideational propensities. The issue to be contemplated, then, is that ideas, including consciously perceived relations among ideas which, when novel, promote concrescence, emerge perceptually from highly complex, integrated empirically identical correlative organic propensities as subjective psychological or mental events. For example, at $time_1$ the subject is reflecting on a problem, endeavoring to discover its solution. But at $time_1$ he has no solution. The man is emotionally and intellectually involved with the problem, thereby bringing his best cognitive resources reflectively to bear upon the matter. Then at last, at $time_2$, the subject consciously discovers the solution to the problem! What were the considerations involved in this consciously intelligible novel awareness? We should explain the causal basis of a typical act of synthetic intelligence where an individual discovers a solution to a problematic circumstance, a solution that he had never before contemplated. We may begin by saying that consciousness and reflective conscious awareness were necessary conditions for the novel discovery, in that a mind is required to intelligently understand and hence entertain the problem. Further, reflective consciousness was required in order to analytically bring the organism's relevant emotional and ideational wisdom to bear upon the problem. However, the novel solution was actually synthesized initially on an unconscious physio-chemical level, the necessary conscious preconditions of which were established through a determinate reflective conscious act. Then, the uniquely synthesized unconscious products emerged into awareness as a consciously intelligible solution to a problem. As a result of a subjective psychologically determined reflective conscious effort, the necessary and sufficient conditions for initially unconscious physio-chemical concrescent synthesis of relevant organic propensities were provided. A reflective conscious mental event (a phenomenon which, in itself, presupposes a sufficient level of organic concrescence to yield the event) causes transcendent concrescent synthesis, in that reflection, as an ontologically existing subjective psychological phenomenon, is a prerequisite perceptual organizational condition for the establishment of propitious proximity among physio-chemical states so that they may unite in novel synthesis. Stated again, the sequence of emergence is as follows. First, conscious reflection, itself dependent upon sufficient organic concrescence to render the conscious act possible, involves bringing the stimulus-condition and relevant wisdom (embodied as connotative linguistic meaning, including vaguely conscious disciplined concepts and emotional feeling) concomitantly into a consciously intelligible ideational proximity. This intelligent behavioral act, on an underlying physio-chemical correlative level, has the net unconscious effect of conjuring relevant organic propensities to come synthetically to bear upon those organic propensities which correlate with the consciously ascertainable stimulus-occasion. Then, when this necessary precondition is fulfilled, novel organic concrescent synthesis can occur. Last, when transcendent concrescence has unconsciously occurred, its subjective psychological correlate emerges into conscious experience, thereby constituting a component of conscious experience, as an intelligible solution to a problem.

We may conclude that the phenomena of consciousness and reflective consciousness are emergent resultants from preconditioned organic concrescence, and yet reciprocally, transcendent organic concrescent synthesis is necessarily contingent upon reflective consciousness for its continued promotion. Transcendent concrescence is a three-stage cyclical process. Most of this extraordinarily complex synthetic process occurs at an unconscious level, one which is in principle inaccessible to direct reflective consciousness. This is merely to say that we cannot, for example, directly experience, as subjective psychological perception, a localized neural synthesis functioning as a stimulus-object yielding conscious percepta. Rather we can only experience the resultant stimulus-object effects of this physio-chemical synthesis as it provides the preconditional grounds for an emergent perceptual component of a subjective psychological event. Private or mental events are themselves a unique class of ontological phenomena in that they are emergents of synthetic concrescence. Stated in more concrete terms, mental events are subjective, psychologically direct perceptual experiences of given, enormously complex configurations of integrated cerebral states, concomitantly activated throughout given temporal durations. They are, in existentially being, those physio-chemical states in their actualized unity, a unity so profoundly complex and integrated that an ontologically unique class of phenomena emerge, termed subjective psychological experience. Mental events, in their inextricable perceptual unity, are all that we can ever mean by the notion of a thing in itself. In this sense, every reflectively conscious human being is a thing in itself that directly and privately has an awareness of some of its own behavioral states by being those behavioral states.

The essential issue we are considering is how private, subjective psychological events can cause transcendent organic physio-chemical concrescence, while concomitantly being emergent products of the physio-chemical organismic system which it is to transcendently modify. It has been said that mental events function causally in the sense that they bring stimulus-objects or conditions into a clearly conscious, intelligible focus. These conditions are directly experienced, over and above barren or meaningless external natural or internally felt perceptual deliverance, as symbolically elaborated and hence subjective psychologically meaningful problems, ontologically existing as clearly intelligible, linguistically disciplined thought. What is the intrinsic nature of a clearly conscious, intelligible focus that can cause organic synthesis? Here we are seeking a notion of causal efficacy similar in form to the proposition, for example, that when chemical element X is combined with element Y, a resultant synthesis of the two elements occurs, producing a unique compound, Z. Of course recognition of the factual phenomenon does not presuppose an ability to theoretically explain its basis for synthesis. Rather it merely entails an understanding of contingent relations. It can be concluded that, loosely defining "cause" in terms of contingent relations as distinct from "creatively bring into being," the introduction of X to Y caused the resultant compound, Z. However, a subjective psychological thought is not generally regarded as a tangible causal agent similar to that of chemical X or a physical object transmitting force. Therefore, how can mental event M_N, comprised of the directly perceivable event-components, denotative and connotative symbolic meaning and stimulus-object effects, cause in the sense of contingent relations the transcendent concrescent occasion C_N? If it is concluded that the innumerable mental-event components constituting the conscious and reflective conscious dimensions of mental event M_N have physio-chemical correlates, then it can be said that these correlates comprise a substantial portion of the relevant organic propensities participating in concrescence C_N. Further, it has formerly been proven that we must presuppose a priori the causal efficacity of mental events in order to have, in principle, any kind of logically and subjective psychologically meaningful discourse at all. It was proven that linguistic reports referring to directly experienced subjective psychological phenomena are not logically equivalent to, in principle, possible scientific statements of physio-chemical correlative underlying conditions. Rather, this correlative determination must be established empirically, thereby yielding synthetic knowledge. This is to say that since an analytical identity cannot be established between statements referring to directly perceived subjective psychological experience and scientific statements referring to its underlying physio-chemical correlates, we must admit the existence of two logically and hence ontologically distinct domains of phenomenal occurrence, one physio-chemical or natural and the other, mental. Concretely speaking, this means that what each human being directly perceives as inextricably unified subjective psychological experience is a phenomenon whose intrinsically meaningful nature could not possibly be logically deduced from an analysis of the meaning of scientific statements referring to its physio-chemical correlates, and vice versa. From these considerations, we have been led to conclude that mental events are an ontologically unique class of phenomena, emergents of high-ordered concrescent physio-chemical processes. Since these private mental events embody the intrinsic general property, feeling, with its three modes of occurrence—organic feeling, emotional feeling, and ideational feeling—symbolically disciplined emotional-ideational feeling is in fact an ontologically unique class of phenomena, gradually developed by individuals in accordance with the aforementioned theory of symbolic development, that intervene as intelligent conscious awareness in what otherwise would be an entirely unconscious relationship between a perceptionless organism and its immediate environment, the stimulus-object effects of which would enter the organism as bare meaningless sensation. In this latter sense, the subhuman organism would be operating on a level of reciprocal ingression among stimulus-objects, similar, for example, to that of chemical elements engaged in synthesis, a phenomenon hardly to be regarded as involving conscious awareness. Moreover, this intervening symbolic domain, as we have seen, acquires a highly determinate causally efficacious status in influencing the behavior of human organisms. This is to say that nonphysio-chemical as well as typical physio-chemical factors causally operate between sensation and manifest bodily behavior. Nonphysio-chemical factors are what we have designated as complete, usually linguistic symbols, synthesized from denotative and connotative symbolic components that are concomitantly united as inextricably unified moments of private subjective psychologically meaningful experience. These disciplined units of meaningful experience embody the power to symbolically represent innumerable stimulus-object effects, generally perceived as entities, properties, and static and dynamic relations among entities and their properties. Therefore, intervening mental phenomena, while on one hand emerging from correlative physio-chemical states, can also concomitantly promote transcendent organic concrescence through conscious reflective efforts. Specifically, this means that since all mental events have empirically identical correlative states, from which no statements of corresponding subjective psychological experience could ever in principle be deduced from scientific statements of physio-chemical correlates, it must be concluded that not only do mental events constitute an ontologically unique class of phenomena, but also, they denote, similarly, a unique domain of causality, in principle distinct from physio-chemical causality. A great part of subjective psychological experience occurs as connotative and denotative symbolic meaning which is concomitantly actualized with other contributed perception as complete, inextricably related mental events. These are, then, the disciplined products of a long process in which purely amorphous infantile emotional feeling (itself a primordial emergent from enormously complex and integrated cerebral mechanisms and processes) is gradually transformed into intelligent conscious awareness, or mental events. Mental events have numerous event-components participating in consciousness as natural and internal bodily stimulus-object effects. Since a large portion of these subjective psychologically experienced effects are symbolic, indicating that the relevant wisdom of the past, symbolically stored as memory, can constructively enter contemporary occasions as the connotative meaning necessarily accompanying denotatively clear event-components, ever-emerging contemporary natural world and internally felt perceptual occasions are not merely unintelligible. Rather these percepta are rendered subjective psychologically meaningful. Thus within the inextricably related domain of mental events, incessantly emerging reality can be intelligently understood, a phenomenon capable of being generated only by individual human minds. Mental events, then, are ontologically unique causal domains in the sense that, although event-components are emergents from underlying physio-chemical conditions, their concomitant collective emergence as inextricably related perceptual unities embodying intelligent conscious and reflective conscious awareness, in effect, are ontologically unique frames of reference from which ideational stimulus-objects may be symbolically synthesized, and thereby utilized as conscious causal behavioral determinants. To consciously manipulate intelligently meaningful symbols is also to concomitantly manipulate their underlying correlative physio-chemical states. Since physio-chemical states can be manipulated from a perspective or intelligent consciousness, novel proximate relations can be established among organic propensities, demonstrating that mental events can causally promote transcendent organic concrescence. The extraordinary emergent, spontaneously meaningful unity—culminating with denotatively clear perception—intrinsically characteristic of mental events, occurring in contrast during reflection with its massively complex and numerous connotatively meaningful implications, suggests innumerable possibilities for symbolic combination and thereby innovation. Ensuing cognitive synthesis, as transcendent concrescence, then emerges as consciously intelligible conceived objects and perceived relations among given objects of concern. It is in this way, psychologically speaking, that human thought is rendered constructive. It is in this way that "mind can move matter."

Although the problem of ideational causality is, without question, very difficult to comprehend theoretically, in contrast to natural causality, in the sense of demonstrating contingent relations, it is truly a remarkable and profound phenomenon. That stimulus-object effects initially enter an organism as sensation, and then concresce to the level where they emerge as conscious percepta, participating thereby as private event-components which denote a small, personally relevant aspect of reality that has been consciously illuminated through becoming intelligible, is remarkable to say the least. Even more astounding is the phenomenon of conscious reflection, again in contrast to natural causal processes, whereby consciously intelligible stimulus-object effects function within the unity of mental events to conjure relevant, previously learned wisdom to enhance the present perceptual occasion by rendering it subjective psychologically meaningful. In this, conscious reflection provides the necessary preconditions for emergent, ideational objects and relations, which can later function as stimulus-objects to establish additional unique cognitive objects and relations. It is in this manner that conscious reflection can be understood as the principal mechanism for intellectual development.

Another cybernetic generalization that could be inferred from the previous discussion is that the human organism can be conceived, theoretically, as an immensely complex, integrated organic functional system, predisposed because of its intrinsically interconnected physical structure to maintain physio-chemical equilibrium amongst its organic mechanisms despite the continually disruptive influence of stimulus-object effects entering its constitution via external and internal perceptual modes. Here, of course, the notion of disruptive types of stimulation must be expanded to include consciously provocative stimulus-conditions as well as natural conditions. The term "disruptive" is not used here with its negative connotation. We mean by disruptive stimulus-object effects those capable of provoking changes of state—whether physio-chemical or subjective psychological—relative to former antecedent states.

The intrinsic structure of the human organism renders it capable of reconciling its constitutive states, physio-chemical or ideational, with reasonably normal external and internal stimulus-object effects. Such modes of behavioral reconciliation regularly entail degrees of complexity ranging from executing unconscious organic mechanistic functions, to consciously reflexive behaviors, to long-range, highly intelligent, reflectively constructed programs of purposive behavior. It follows, however, that those stimulus-object effects not reconciled with overall organismic functional harmony yield a dysfunctional influence upon behavior. In this situation, assuming that the adverse stimulus-object effect determinately enters an organism's perceptual field, the organism attempts to coexist with the difficulty until a resolution can be effected, either by dissipation of disruptive experiential reaction merely through temporal passage, or as a result of reflective resolution. Therefore, when problematic stimulus-object effects, or those for which no previously established habitual repertory is suitable, enter organisms, all relevant organic propensities come to bear upon them. Reflective consciousness, in its most effective manner, persistently endeavors to establish facilitative conditions for transcendent concrescence in an effort to synthesize a novel, more efficacious habituation. If none is forthcoming, the organism must coexist with the problem, and if functional harmony becomes seriously impaired, psychotherapeutic assistance may be needed in an effort to restore behavioral integration. However, from the viewpoint of educational methodology and learning theories, some amount of functional disruption is necessary for motivational purposes. But obviously this means that sufficient dysfunction is required to have a stimulus-object effect appear in a subject's perceptual field with adequate intensity to provoke constructive reflection. The affective-cognitive impact should be commensurate with an individual's intellectual and emotional capacities for disruption.

Although many additional constructs could be fruitfully added, only those theoretical instruments have been introduced which specifically enhance our understanding of a subjective psychology and the mind-body problem as they have relevance for scientific psychology. Regardless of how unrelated the constructs of divergent schools of psychology may appear when initially subjected to scrutiny, it is necessary upon more careful analysis that they be consistent, whether explicitly or by implicaton, with the scheme presently being developed, which consistently reconciles mind with body.

Figure 4 schematically represents the bare mechanistic structure of the theory here presented. However, the schematization can be more of a hindrance to careful understanding than a facilitative instrument if the difficult preparational work for its comprehenson, entailing a careful reflective consideration of each successive argument as they collectively constitute a unified human behavioral theory, is neglected.

In concluding this part of the discussion of the mind-body problem an important position articulated by Herbert Feigl, one of the foremost authorities on this issue, must be critically analyzed in terms of the subjective psychological theory. His view is relevant for both theories yield a fundamentally common conclusion, namely, that mental events are identical with correlative physio-chemical states only to the extent that the identity is ascertained through empirical means. This conclusion is called the "identity theory of mind and body." (35)

Professor Feigl, who has written a penetrating, comprehensive article on the mind-body problem, has concluded that the resolution of this issue which contains many difficult ramifications, must ultimately follow from the tenet that mental or "raw feel" (Feigl's term) events and

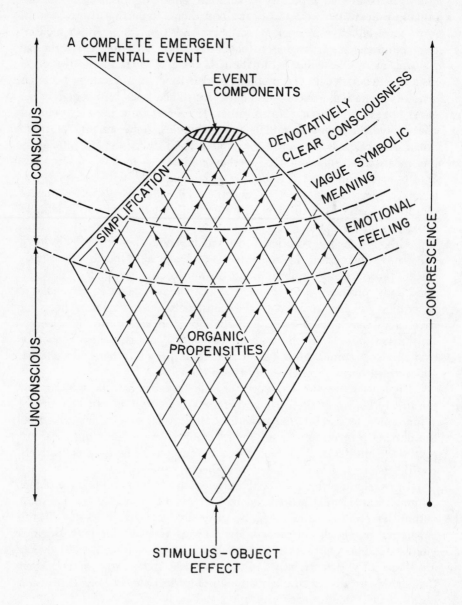

Figure 4. A general mechanistic model

physical events refer to the same process. This means that there are two distinct ways of studying mental phenomena: we may investigate the cerebral states underlying given mental events, and the person who directly experiences the mental states may provide verbal reports about his inner states for scrutiny by researchers. From this, Feigl concludes that there is an empirical identity between mind phenomena contemplated on one hand as physio-chemical states, and on the other experienced through direct acquaintance by individuals themselves.(13) This is to say, as we have argued, that the mental state, "I feel sad," is not logically or analytically identical to its corresponding physio-chemical states S_1, S_2, S_3, . . . S_N. Further, Feigl argues that mental events are causally efficacious behavioral determinants:

Any solution of the mind-body problem worth consideration should render an adequate account of the efficacy of mental states, events, and processes in the behavior of human (and also some subhuman) organisms. It is not tender-mindedness or metaphysical confusion, I trust, which impels this repudiation of a materialistically oriented epiphenomenalism. Admittedly, the testimony of direct experience and of introspection is fallible. But to maintain that planning, deliberation, preference, choice, volition, pleasure, pain, displeasure, love, hatred, attention, vigilance, enthusiasm, grief, indignation, expectations, remembrances, hopes, wishes, etc., are not among the causal factors which determine human behavior is to fly in the face of the commonest of experience, or else to deviate in a strange and unjustified way from the ordinary use of language. The task is neither to repudiate these obvious facts, nor to rule out this manner of describing them. The task is rather to analyze the logical status of this sort of description in its relation to behavioral and/or neurophysiological descriptions. In the pursuit of this objective it will of course be necessary to avoid both interactionism and epiphenomenalism; and it will moreover be desirable to formulate the solution in such a way that it does not presuppose emergentism. . . ; although the door to a scientifically formulated emergentism need not be closed.

In this same connection justice should be rendered to what is meaningful and scientifically defensible in the notion of free will and choice. If our personality-as-it-is at the moment of choice experiences itself in the choice made; if our choices accord with our most deeply felt desires, e.g., if they are not imposed upon us by some sort of compulsion, coercion, or constraints such as by brute physical force, by other persons (or even only by components of our personality we do not acknowledge as the "core" deemed centrally our "self"), then we are "free" in the sense that we are the doers of our deeds, the choosers of our choices, the makers of our decisions. In other words, it is in this case that our central personality structure is a link in the causal chain of our behavior, predominately, even if not exclusively, effective in the determination of our conduct. This sort of freedom (in the superb formulation of R. E. Hobart-Dickinson Miller) "involves determinism and [is] inconceivable without it." (13)

The general view suggested by this quotation is representative of an unusually well-balanced philosophical position on the mind-body problem. Generally speaking, the view heretofore developed does not seriously contradict that of Feigl. Even the concept of concrescent synthesis is reasonably consistent with what Feigl regards as a "scientifically formulated emergentism." This is not to say that Feigl would be enthusiastic about the general theory being proposed herein, for his overall philosophical outlook seems considerably more in accord with an objective psychology rather than with a subjective psychological science, which Feigl might characterize as unwarrantedly speculative, and hence vague. On the other hand, Feigl could be criticized for not referring to any scientifically appropriate theoretical formulations satisfactorily demonstrating, in detail, how subjective psychological states could function in a causally efficacious manner, although he does regard the relevant constructs of contemporary psychological theories as suitable for investigating human behavior, a point with which one could take issue. Most current psychological theories persist in avoiding the problem of mind and its causal efficacity in relation to correlative physio-chemical process, a limitation which subjective psychological theory can reconcile.

Let us now briefly examine some of the more important areas of difference between Feigl's identity theory and that propounded here. Generally stated, though Feigl maintains that we must acknowledge the necessity for an empirical equivalence between mental and physical events, this view can be extended by arguing that physio-chemical states, in addition to providing the necessary conditions for mental events, can also be modified by their mental emergents. Because of the intrinsic structure of mental events (defined now as inextricably related units of perceptual components, portraying reality throughout given temporal durations, having relevance for and hence actualized as consciousness and reflective consciousness within individuals during particular occasions), inner and outer environments can be consciously felt in such a way that progressively higher-ordered concrescence is achieved. In fact, it is contradictory to conceive of any type of subjective psychological or logically meaningful discourse without necessarily presupposing *a priori* this ontologically unique mode of disciplined feeling as its causal basis. To feel reality in the technical way here defined is to engage in what is normally, though unclearly, conceived as thinking-behavior. But to characterize the process, for the moment, as feeling reality is to suggest a considerably more comprehensive way of contemplating the profound complexity of ordinary concrete experience.

Disciplined feeling is the medium through which stimulus-object effects can be meaningfully felt in their full, clear, intimately related, symbolically represented character. It involves the active process of the relevant symbolically characterized past coming constructively to bear upon present perceptual deliverance, so that the formerly learned wisdom causes the barren perceptually contributed present to be intelligently interpreted as subjective psychologically meaningful. Thus, in its fully actualized state, disciplined feeling consists of the denotatively and connotatively felt symbolic components as they synthetically unite to render a natural or internal bodily stimulus-object effect intelligible. In any case, private mental events are individual human organisms' ever-emerging spatio-temporally successive understanding of relevant reality, which undergoes revision and development primarily as a function of accumulated wisdom.

Therefore, although an empirical identity between mental and physical states can be established, both categories of phenomena, as they are conceived as subjective psychologically and/or logically meaningful, are grounded in private mental events in that mental events must be necessarily presupposed *a priori* in order to have any intelligible discourse about either category of discourse. Thus the ultimate basis for the distinction between mental and physical, it will be recalled, was in determining the location of stimulus-objects yielding what we directly perceive as perceptual event-components. Finally, the characterization of mind (in the narrow sense of denotative and connotative feeling, united as complete symbols) concomitantly standing over against percepta was used to portray the human organism's relation to stimulus-objects.

The difference between the two identity theories can be somewhat more rigorously demonstrated in the following way:

Feigl

1. Feigl argues for an empirical identity between "raw feels" and their underlying correlative physio-chemical processes.

2. Raw feels are mental events or the referents which are symbolically characterizable; those phenomena which are the direct intersubjectively inaccessible objects of verbal reports (e.g., pains, etc.).

3. Therefore, mental events can be systematically studied from a neurophysiological viewpoint and/or that of a psychology admitting as suitable evidence verbal reports referring to directly accessible inner states occurring within individual subjects.

4. Feigl, then, admits individual verbal testimonies referring to inner, intersubjectively inferred states as legitimate evidence for scientific psychology providing such data are gathered under rigorously specified, experimentally controlled conditions.

5. Feigl also maintains that current molar psychological constructs (ego, self, operant conditioning, etc.) are suitable theoretical devices for systematically understanding raw feel phenomena by establishing operational definitions and statements of relation to represent correlative mental events or raw feels.

Quill

1. An empirical identity is wholly satisfactory for correlating mental events with their underlying physio-chemical processes. See also Zener's article.(36)

2. However, in Feigl's distinction between "mental" and "physical," the fact that a mind (loosely defined as denotative and connotative symbolic meaning) must be presupposed *a priori* to stand over against both raw feels and physical (what Feigl defines as intersubjectively directly perceivable states, but here defined as external natural stimulus-object effects) event-components is not clearly evident from his arguments. It is highly questionable whether he would admit to the dipolar notion of mind standing over against percepta at all. Therefore Feigl's mental-physical distinction suffers from the same epistemological vagueness as the problematic 'public-private' dichotomy.

3. Further, since Feigl does not mention how mental states may function in a causally efficacious manner, and moreover, since current psychological theories appear to be vague, to simply avoid, or to resort to an unwarranted reductionism when confronted with this problem, it appears that he would still like to ultimately maintain that all human behavioral states can be most satisfactorily understood and hence modified through dealing with physio-chemical or manifestly apparent behavioral states; and that mental-event reports are merely psychologically expedient as evidential checkpoints for conventional theories, or as sources of data in neurophysiological experimentation.

4. Therefore, it appears that although Feigl has effectively argued in support of an empirical identity thesis, the serious difficulties cited above impose important limitations upon his position.

The essential cogency of subjective psychological theory may be importantly enhanced, beyond the realm of strictly philosophical-psychological analysis, if we refer to responsible speculations on the nature and function of mind as conceived from a fundamentally empirical discipline. Such a measure may be comforting to those who still wonder if the issues being considered are genuinely problematic or mere philosophical sham. Therefore, as an additional source of evidential support, we quote some unusually imaginative comments of J. A. V. Butler, an eminent contemporary biochemist, taken from the sixteenth chapter of

The Life of the Cell.(37) Of interest, also, is his *Science and Human Life.*(38)

Initially, with reference to the fundamental theoretical constructs of our enlightened mechanistic model, let us consider the following passages.

The most important characteristics of the brains of humans and similar animals is the ability to receive a composite message from a large number of sensory nerves. The part of the message received carried by a single nerve or even by a small group of nerves means nothing by itself.

Into the brain comes most of the nerves from sense organs and out of it go most of the nerves which control the muscles. Can we discover what happens in between what paths are taken by the impulses which enter the brain through excited nerves, and how a coherent pattern is constructed from the messages arriving down many nerves?

Millions of brain cells may thus be concerned with receiving a single visual impression. How do they cooperate to produce the total instantaneous impression?

There is undoubtedly a great deal of electrical activity going on in the brain at all times. . . . With this instrument [an electroencephalograph] an overall rhythm of electrical activity can be detected. This must be due to many circuits between neurons oscillating in unison. The reason for this is not clearly known. The oscillations may be similar to a "carrier wave" on which the sensory imput produces modulations. The character of the oscillations varies with the mental state.

The brain deals with the innumerable sense impressions by producing a "picture" which we perceive—for example in the use of our visual sensations, this is the "picture" we are aware of when we look at our surroundings.

This "picture" which we perceive is not like a photograph—a mere projection of what we are looking at. It is itself an interpretation of the actual visual experience, which involves our previous knowledge and therefore our memories of similar scenes. . . . Infants also learn to interpret their visual impressions similarly and only slowly build up an understanding of the sensory information which reaches them.

The visual information which is received at any one time is therefore not interpretable by itself. The "picture" we make of it is an amalgam of the present and past experience.

. . . the sensory impressions of the moment take their place with the memories of those which have previously been interpreted, and have become part of our store of knowledge. They become part of a record which has been continuously built up since birth.

But the main purpose of memory is not the recollection of the past, but the recognition of the present. Memory is used mainly to recognize and identify the images of our present experience and for this purpose it is usually sufficient only to notice the salient features, unless there are some details of urgent interest.

We might ask ourselves how the composite amalgam of sense data and the memory data . . . is presented as the "picture" or perception we become aware of. It is possible that the whole matrix of impulses from the sense organs, now united with and interpreted by comparison with the memory record, pass into a further echelon of cells in which the perception we are aware of is produced, i.e., it enters our consciousness. This level is very selective in its ability to attend to certain parts of the whole sensory input and to ignore others. This is probably achieved by lowering the critical barrier necessary for the passage of impulses for some groups of sensations and raising it for others.

Next, Dr. Butler deals with the problem that we have described as emergent consciousness and conscious reflection.

It is . . . possible to give some sort of account of the physical events which produce sensations, but what are the sensations themselves? We could say that this is how the physical events are experienced, but we must ask then, experienced by what and what is the nature of experience? The perceptions themselves are not capable of being described in physical terms. Thus we cannot describe our experience when we see a green object in, say, physical terms. It cannot be described in physical quantities like length, velocity, force, orbit, wave length, temperature or even in the language of the quantum theory. Our only knowledge of it comes from our own experience, or from the description of others of their experience. Must we discuss it as an illusion and pseudo-phenomenon, which has no reality because it is only a description of how things appear to us subjectively and not as they are?

I think perceptions ought to be related to the rest of scientific knowledge, but we have no means, other than investigating the physical background, of dealing with them and this only tells us how they are produced and not what they are.

As I have said above, the [sensory] information is organized into a kind of picture, which includes both the present experiences and those remembered from the past. But how is this picture used in producing actions? There must be a stage at which all the information is reviewed in light of past experience and decisions are reached to act or not to act, and orders are then issued to the muscles.

Much of this [nervous] activity is entirely unconscious. All we are aware of is an intention to perform a certain action and the brain and central nervous system do the rest.

The important feature of voluntary actions is that the necessary muscle oper-

ations have to be learnt. We are not born with the ability to perform complicated voluntary actions.

So we see from all this that the connections in the brain between sensory
information and the muscles is not direct. The sensory information is built
up into a continuing record of sensation and experience.

All that is required for the whole sequence to be "triggered off" is a stimulus
or order from the higher level of cells in the brain whose decisions are made
and it appears to be at this level that the connections between the "sensory
picture" and the muscular stimulation are made.

The last sequence of quotations will deal with Butler's concept of
symbolic behavior.

What are the characteristic features of human intelligence? There is undoubtedly a greatly increased power of discriminating, remembering and interpreting
sense impressions. The human being connects his immediate sensations to a
much greater extent with his past experience, and the result is an enormous
structure of experience accumulated throughout life. His "intelligence" is a
measure of the skill and ability with which he uses the accumulated
experience.

But this is not all—or even the most characteristic feature of human
life, which is the ability to replace the sensory experiences themselves by
symbolic equivalents which can be manipulated in the mind. This involves
associating one kind of experience with something totally different in character.

Some physiologists and psychologists find in the conditioned reflex a sufficient
explanation of all kinds of behavior which are not completely instinctive.
. . . This may be so in some sense, but it overlooks the enormous amount of
experience and its organization which human beings bring to the task of
discrimination.

The important characteristic of human beings, which is almost completely
lacking in all other animals, is the fact that accumulated experience (=
knowledge) is organized and stored mainly in the form of symbolic equivalents. This can be supposed to be a consequence of the case with which the
human brain makes associations between even unlike things. This has given
rise, for example, to human language, which is the necessary basis of human
society. In language there is an association between particular experiences
and particular uttered sounds. The sounds are produced by muscular movements in the chest and throat, and like all other complex movement, have to
be learnt. . . . There is nothing necessary about these associations—in many
cases the sound has little in common with the experience it represents—it is
purely conventional association. But in one way or another particular sounds
have come to mean, for groups of people, specific types of experience.

The ability to replace actual experiences by symbolic spoken equivalents
has led to all the features which distinguish human life from that of higher

animals, because when experiences have been converted into spoken (and later, written) equivalents they can be communicated from one person to another and they often acquire a greater amount of permanence than the actual memory of experience, because it is often easier to recall the symbolic expression of an experience (in words) than the experience itself. It is easier to remember that you were tired on a certain occasion than to remember just what being tired felt like.

In this way it came about that besides their rather fragmentary simple memory of events, human beings have a memory of their symbolic expression. The latter is easily communicated from one individual and provides a means of sharing experiences, which can never or only rarely be shared directly, except by the actual participants. Human knowledge is in fact the shared experience of the community, expressed symbolically.

These quotations, extracted from Butler's writings, serve as a highly appropriate, intuitively intelligible summary, generally concordant with the philosophical-psychological position being developed.

PART THREE

Subjective Psychological Theory

Chapter eight / Recapitulation of previous argument

A brief recapitulation of our developing train of argumentation will facilitate a comprehension of the major problem to be considered in this chapter. In simplified fashion, our investigations heretofore may be essentially stated as follows:

1. In the *Introduction* it was argued that both psychoanalysis and behaviorism had to resort to explaining human behavior in terms that were unwarrantedly reductionistic. That is, in both cases, the theoretical systems logically reduced to a materialistic-mechanistic epiphenomenism. Thus each theory comprehends man in terms of those dimensions shared in common with lower-ordered substance and organisms, hence relegating mental events to a causally inefficacious status. Perceptual psychological theories, on the other hand, tended to place excessive emphasis upon the uniquely human dimensions of man, or his stream-of-consciousness, thereby devoting insufficient attention to the mechanistic aspects of human behavior. More important, however, is that their theoretical constructs tend to be definitionally vague, and therefore relatively problematic for rigorous scientific investigation. This criticism also applies to psychoanalytic theories.

2. Part One dealt with a more precise analysis of behaviorism, conceived as a methodological enterprise. We discovered that its reductionistic proclivity resulted from an epistemological vagueness, in effect,

discounting—even avoiding—mind as a necessary causal factor in any humanly conscious or reflective conscious behavior. However, in our critical analysis of behaviorism, it was seen that with regard to all human perceptions, both of internal bodily phenomena and of external natural phenomena, mind must be necessarily presupposed *a priori* as a causally efficacious factor in human behavior, or what has been more rigorously defined as subjective psychological experience.

3. Dewey's concept of intelligent behavior was also briefly considered in Part One, and it was discovered that he frequently wrote as if he had behavioristic inclinations but, actually, much of his terminology contained innumerable mentalistic connotations. Thus Dewey, for our purposes, became something of a transitional figure in that we capitalized upon his highly important instrumentalistic and mentalistic views, later incorporating some of these concepts into a more comprehensive and logically adequate or, model for human behavior. In this way we were able to incorporate several of Skinner's and Dewey's methodological and theoretical concepts into our model.

4. Part Two, beyond introducing an enlightened mechanistic model for human behavior, dealt with the crucially important problem of symbolism as a uniquely human class of causally efficacious behavioral determinants, facilitating organisms' interpenetrative relationships with their coexisting environments. Here, for a partial theoretical framework, we drew upon the penetrating wisdom of Ernst Cassirer. Cassirer clearly maintains that the human capacity to symbolize essentially introduces a new dimension to reality in that man no longer deals directly with his environment; rather a symbolic screen intervenes and hence interpretively organizes our perceptual experience so that man becomes, to a great extent, conversant with himself through a personally innovated version of the internal and external worlds. Since the view propounded here is concordant with a scientific emergentism (specifically with regard to the emergents, consciousness and the higher-ordered mechanism conscious reflection, causally operating as factors in human behavioral determination), it appeared quite conceivable that Cassirer's basic philosophical orientation was not seriously at odds with it. At least it seemed that Cassirer's thoughts on the development and function of symbolism could have great relevance for the theory being developed. Working upon this assumption, we proceeded to demonstrate how it was possible, from a subjective psychological theoretical viewpoint, to explain the development of thought (defined generally as ideational feeling) from emergent, originally undisciplined emotional feeling; phenomena which, with their higher-ordered disciplined

cognitive derivatives, must be assigned factual status in the scientific psychological study of human behavior.

5. This brings us up to date in that we must devise a scheme—a theoretical model—which permits us to attribute a factual status to causally efficacious mental or subjective psychological phenomena. We will argue that it is impossible to isolate what may ideally be regarded as a pure or uninterpreted fact, for the concept of fact necessarily implies a configuration of explicitly specified or implicitly present interpretive information, thereby confounding bare perceptually given fact with a cognitive element not directly implicit or revealed in the independent phenomenal given. In essence, this is a difficulty whose problematic basis resides in the same confusion we encountered with respect to the logically contradictory notion of pure percepta. It was proven, in this former case, that it is illogical to conceive of pure percepta without a mind which stands over against them. There is an additional necessary concomitant factor which must synthetically accompany the pure perceptual given, namely the element of symbolic meaning—an entirely subjective psychological phenomenon intrinsic to human cognition of any kind. With respect to the problem of facts and theories, the interpretive element is the meaning which cognitively illuminates the bare given percepta. Here, meaning is definitionally understood to be the subjective psychological symbolic element necessarily presupposed *a priori* in all possible factual assertions. The point to be made at this time, however, is that the subjective psychologically meaningful or interpretive element concomitantly, hence synthetically uniting with contributed external and internal perceptual deliverance, is what we mean by mind. Therefore the central problem to be comprehended and resolved is to precisely define the intrinsic nature of mind, and to rigorously designate its function as a necessary condition for human experience of any kind.

Chapter nine / An elaboration of the theory of symbolic development

Thus far we have defined mind in a rather indistinct way, but one adequate for argumentative purposes. This tactic was used to differentiate clearly between the two major divisions intrinsic to the process of intellectually understanding anything whatsoever: mind as an entity which generates subjective psychologically meaningful interpretations, and that which is subject to interpretation—percepta or the given. This division was emphasized to reveal the vital importance of what is generally regarded as awareness, or consciousness and reflective consciousness in that they are indicative of causally distinctive mind functions and, more generally, refer to the structure of ontologically unique, emergent ideational feeling. Ideational feeling is a general term referring to a particular class of disciplined emergents within the more comprehensive domain of emotional feeling. Emotional, and thereby, ideational feeling are the directly experienced stimulus-object effects of underlying or correlative physio-chemical mechanisms, functioning as stimulus objects, which yield these unique ontological emergents. Finally, the mind standing over against percepta distinction was used to critically evaluate those theoretical systems methodologically predisposed to an unwarranted scientific reductionism because of their materialistic presuppositional bases.

In our constructive theoretical endeavors we have laid a firm foundation, but one in need of considerable elaboration in order to develop a definitionally precise system of theoretical instruments suitable for highlighting and embodying the logical form in which subjective psychological experience can be scientifically comprehended. In effect, then, the task before us is to develop a theoretical model which can universally characterize the form in which mind comes constructively to bear upon percepta. Such a scheme must define the entities, mind and percepta, as well as demonstrate their relationship to one another. This enterprise may seem far more problematic and difficult than it, in fact, actually will be when pondering the matter in retrospect. The chief merit of the theory to be presented—one which is in varying degrees a modified and elaborated version of that articulated by Whitehead—is its resultant far-reaching simplicity.(15) More specifically, it is the view that concrete experience is the ultimate ground from which all cognitive entities and their modes of synthetic relation are essentially derived. The task, then, becomes one of designating the logical form intrinsic to our subjective psychological experience of the natural world and our bodily organism, so that it will be appropriate for a subjective psychology.

We shall again briefly reconsider the preparational measures previously elaborated, so that additional constructs may be resultantly developed to characterize mind. At the outset, an important definitional modification must be made. Mind has been loosely defined as that which stands over against percepta. It has been said that mind and percepta must necessarily occur concomitantly in a synthetic union. When subjected to careful critical analysis, the vagueness of these distinctions becomes readily evident. First, one is legitimately tempted to ask about the nature of that which stands over against percepta. Also, one may rightly argue that the original formulation implies that there should be a more comprehensive term which includes both components of the synthetic union. These anticipated criticisms demand a revision in our former definition of mind, to wit: mind is that subjective psychological process in which percepta come to bear upon other percepta, so that a concomitant synthetic union is achieved. At face value this definition may appear more problematic than the one it was designed to replace; therefore, further explication is needed to render it logically tenable. First it will be seen that the definition of mind has been renovated to include both dimensions of the two-aspect process of percepta coming to bear upon other percepta. But now we ask, is it not tautological to speak of percepta coming to bear upon percepta? This criticism may be countered by saying that implicit within the definition is the possibility for four distinct classes of percepta. In the discussion on symbolism it was said that there are three separate aspects of the psychological meaning of every linguistic symbol. For example, with respect to the symbol "red," there is first the clear and distinct word "red," in its bare particularity as a verbally uttered sound. Second, there is the less determinate level of subjective psychological meaning when we contemplate the vaguely conscious though powerfully efficacious substantive linguistic symbols, which

in their relatedness, add flesh to the bare-boned symbol, "red." The
concepts of color, sight, light wave, and hue, might concomitantly be
implicit in our notion of "red." Third, it will be recalled, there is an
even more vaguely conscious emotional periphery of subjective psychological meaning embodied within linguistic symbols. It is possible
that contained within the concept "red," for example, are such highly
unspecific primordial affective recollections as "a particularly pleasing
experience of having perceived a special red object," "the warm red
glow of a fire on a winter evening," and so on. These last two levels of
meaning are what we have defined as meaning-as-directly-felt-relatedness. Therefore, even in an apparently simple symbol such as "red,"
there are three levels of stored experience, ranging from that which has
been highly symbolically disciplined to that which was emotionally
grasped in a comprehensive but symbolically unclear manner during
past experience. These levels of subjective psychological meaning occur
concomitantly when we think the thought, "red," for example. This
is the uniquely human phenomenon defined as subjective psychological
experience. Consequently, with respect to our most recent definition of
mind as percepta coming to bear upon other percepta, we may contemplate the event "I see red," as the subjective psychological act of
consciously seeing red, and moreover, being aware of the red-seeing.
Here there is a subject-object dichotomization equivalent to the idea
of percepta coming to bear upon other percepta. Hence the first class of
percepta would include what we have defined as meaning-as-directly-
felt-relatedness and the denotative symbolic component, "red," while
the second class of percepta would include the natural world stimulus-
object effect, the direct perception of a red color. Therefore, our most
recent conception of mind now possesses considerably more cogency.

It is evident from our preceding discussion on developing an
adequate conception of mind that symbolic thought constitutes a predominate portion of what can be understood by the concept of mind.
This fact is manifestly clear in our previous deceptively simple example, "I see red." It was seen that through meaning-as-directly-felt-
relatedness with its denotatively clear symbolic focal point, the complete intelligible symbol "red" came constructively to bear upon the
perception "a red color" to the extent that it caused the subjective
psychologically *meaningful* experience, "I see red." This important
phenomenon we shall subsequently subject to careful scrutiny. It is
precisely what is meant by "the wisdom of the past coming constructively to bear upon the present, hence rendering the present occasion
personally meaningful." But before we proceed to develop this basic
notion, a further clarification must be made.

In Part Two of this book a somewhat speculative theory of symbolic development was presented. Beyond constituting a moderately determinate analysis of the developmental stages that a human organism undergoes in learning linguistic behavior, the presentation was also intended as an argument demonstrating the possibility that emotional feeling can be subjected to such extensive discipline that it is gradually transformed, through learning, into what we subjectively experience as human thought or ideational feeling. More specifically, it was maintained that the psychological development of symbolism can be explained as the individual human organism's endeavor, made possible by the intrinsic structure of the organism, to actively organize and clarify originally primordial, directly experienced, undisciplined emotional states. Therefore as a consequence of such an extraordinary program of discipline, a program greatly facilitated by interpenetrative relationships with other human organisms already capable of executing symbolic behavior, phenomena defined as ideational feeling are generated. It was further argued that these ideational states, whose intrinsic substantive nature is disciplined, and hence sublimated, emotional feeling, possess a unique ontological status among other types of being. The unique ontological emergent, ideational feeling is an extraordinarily sophisticated emergent product of an organism whose physiochemical structure manifests indeterminate complexity and integration among its numerous organic mechanisms. Nevertheless, there seems to be no evidence to suggest that in principle the phenomenon of ideational feeling should not be regarded as a scientifically determinate emergent occurrence. The intrinsic substantive nature of ideational feeling seems to indicate that its originally undisciplined, vague experiential quality is gradually sublimated to the extent that a clearly conscious symbolic precision results. Former spontaneously arising, unwieldy, highly vague emotional states undergo subsequent symbolic atomization so that primordial emotional states, essentially characterized as primitive urges, progressively become symbolically characterized. As a result, many precise, hence simplified, distinctions among experienced entities, their properties, and their relations evolve as their perceived effects enter our subjective psychological awareness and are actualized as concrete unified experience. Where once personal experience consisted merely of chaotic, undifferentiated externally delivered perceptual flux, coexistent with sporadic emotional feeling, there later arises, after considerable disciplining, a vastly complex system of symbols, transforming personal experience from amorphous percepta into succinct, highly flexible, meaningful ideational forms. These denotative, clearly conscious forms have two additional concomitant levels of meaning, together termed meaning-as-directly-felt-relatedness, containing both vaguely understood linguistic symbols and relevant highly subtle emotion. These later two realms of meaning embody the wisdom of the past. Therefore symbolic development necessarily means that the individual can no longer respond to internally or externally located stimulus-objects with the full uninhibited and comprehensive emotional vigor characteristic of primitive intellect. Rather, he must respond to, and now actively approach, his environments within the breadth and limits of his symbolic capacity—a power that, in effect, defines the intelligible domain of his species. We have only to recall the penetrating words of Cassirer to understand the revolutionary effect that symbolic acquisition has had on the mentality of mankind. It is impossible to overstate the significance of this achievement, especially in an age in which preponderant systematic attention is devoted to the logical coherence and physical properties of symbolic expression, distinct from the subjective psychologically meaningful basis whereby the former gain their existential possibility in the mind of individual human beings. It is now one of our primary objectives to systematically investigate, in some depth, the intrinsic nature and function of symbols, particularly linguistic symbols, for, as we have seen, symbols constitute a major portion of mind, conceived as a coherent and continuous subjective psychological process.

Before beginning a systematic development of theoretical constructs for comprehending the logical form of subjective psychological experience, an additional topic on symbolism must be considered in order to accentuate the great constructive power of meaning-as-directly-felt-relatedness in its capacity for illuminating both the emotional and the intellectual dimensions of our directly perceived, and hence reflectively clarified, experience.

1. In previous discussion on the developmental process of symbolic acquisition, it was seen that at the presign state, infants' initial experience of reality (and this, of course, is quite hypothetical) seems to be primarily introverted. Neurological processes necessary for organizing percepta have not yet been sufficiently integrated. An indication of this would be the incapacity to differentiate between internal and external environments, for consciousness would, undoubtedly, be constituted of vague or imprecisely discernible perception, whether occurring via external or internal bodily senses. Thus it appears that the most conspicuously comprehensible states would be internal bodily pleasure and pain in their gross, sporadic deliverance. These states would be transitorily entertained by the organisms within their durational occurrences, but nothing like the higher-ordered phenomena of recollection or anticipation

would yet be in evidence. Similarly, infant awareness that states of pleasure or pain are attributable to causal factors will also be absent. During
the particular experiential occasion of actually consuming food, for example, an infantile consciousness includes many pleasurable perceptions.
However, the infant will not yet realize that it is the "mother appearance" that causes the deliverance of food, which in turn, causes the
pleasurable internal experience. It is unlikely that infants, at this stage,
could adequately discriminate amongst visually perceived objects
with sufficient accuracy to have established a recollection of a visual
mother-image. Probably, primordial recollections of formerly experienced states would originate from being physically held and affection-
ately comforted. In this, the emphasis would be upon highly concrete
physical interaction with a substantial externality. These types of perceptual experiences have immediate bearing upon infant emotional
states as they occur in great frequency.

2. Next it was said that, as a result of increased neurological integration and storage of new experiential data, infant mentality develops to
a point where a vague emotional understanding of the fact that there is an
"out there," a domain that is independent of a more personal region, is
achieved. This issues from an active concrete interpenetrative relationship with a tangible world of solidity that can be bitten, grasped, etc.,
with reciprocal correlative effects consisting of pains, tastes, etc., all of
which are emotionally realized to have a consciously enduring, coherent
perceptual nexus in a peculiarly intimate region becoming progressively
more clearly understood as a self. Further, there is the realization that
externality does have a very real quality of indeterminacy, in that merely
because the personal urge for satiation or pleasure may be projected to
the exterior realm, commensurate gratification does not necessarily follow.
An infantile notion of causality can develop out of such concrete experiences as "mother-warmth," "mother-pain reliever," mother-food provider,"
"food-pleasure," etc. From these bare emotional, recognitional predispositions, the higher-ordered behavior of projecting emotion arises in relation
to an entity residing in an external region. Similarly such behaviors as
anticipation, for example, emerge out of former variable conditions of
satiation and deprivation.

3. The next important advance that was stressed occurs when the
infant develops the primordial sense of power, discovering that his
internal experiential states are not wholly contingent upon the whims of
externality. During early infancy, cries issued spontaneously from painful or importantly uncomfortable experiences. But later, after a gradual,
vague, reflective recognition that personal vocal outbursts frequently
brought motherly attention, some moderate element of premeditation

begins to operate regularly as a causally efficacious infant behavioral determinant, facilitated by such causal factors as recently acquired emotional predispositions for a sense of the internal and external, a sense of projection, a sense of causal relationship, etc. The wisdom from an experientially recorded past is now beginning to causally determine the organism's responses to stimulus-object effects in a way transcending mere mechanicality. Meaningfully intelligible, consciously reflective awareness is beginning to appear as a minimally disciplined emergent, succeeding former emotional urges whose causal potentiality remained unused for lack of concentrated, disciplined conscious specificity. Thus the nebulous recognition of power is one of the first manifestations of an organism's ingenious or innovative ability for actively dealing with reality.

4. The sign stage makes its appearance from children's desire to, perhaps initially, secure the attention of other human beings, thereby yielding the primitive subjective psychological experience of security. For example, in the development of speech, a child will reflexively mimic the vocal sounds expressed by a mother, not out of an intellectual understanding of the rational meaning and power of verbalizations, but rather, out of the concrete fact of being given attention, and as a matter of curiosity, a factor crucial for promoting a discriminatory attitude toward perceptual deliverance.

5. As the sign stage persists, during which a rich backlog of prerational experience is acquired, including learning to duplicate sounds and learning to exchange sounds with other human beings, children gradually develop the realization that spoken sounds represent external entities. This marks the onset of the symbol stage. Whereas at the outset of perceptual recognition, the word "mama" was merely meaninglessly repeated, slowly, as a result of highly subtle bits of learned information, a child comes to understand, i.e., to make emotional associations between previously established recollections and newly ascertained information, that the spoken word represents all of his mama-experience. Hence an entire backlog of infantile experiences with mother can be concisely conjured and subsumed to the sound, "mama." Moreover, in this, all of the vaguely felt emotional affection, issuing from an urge to immediately and comprehensively communicate a history of intense but highly amorphous emotional meaning, can be projected at the externally located mother-entity. In fact, apart from the physical presence of mother, the spoken word "mama" is a powerfully concise way of promoting self-initiated, consciously pleasurable experience, for the verbal utterance is a means for re-enjoying the relevant past.

6. Once this power has been recognized, the process is frequently repeated with different verbal symbols, thus building up a verbal rep-

ertoire representing categories of vivid emotional experience. From this, children derive the enormously gratifying recognition that the strange world of experience can be understood and symbolically retained for future reference, by characterizing objects with spoken words.

7. Finally children make their last triumphant linguistic discovery, namely, that spoken words can be related to one another, thus providing the possibility for arranging sequences of words into desired rational configurations, a condition necessary for coherent thinking. Now, upon having attained the symbol stage, a basic understanding of the relatedness of things is achieved. Not only are words used as instruments for organizing, and storing for future reference, similar categories of personal emotional experience with respect to particular external objects of importance and curiosity, in addition to being means for satisfying basic urges and desires, also they become devices for enabling personal ideational experience to characterize changing relational states as they are perceptually apprehended. Even more important, at a higher level, symbolically defined entities and principal modes of relationship among entities can be ideationally synthesized into many personally desired configurations! These sophisticated levels of operation are made possible through conscious reflection. Since the symbol stage enables dynamic experience to be characterized, whether it occurs as natural or ideationally synthesized phenomena, the important elements of original experience, as symbolically simplified, can be recalled at a later time with relative ease. Here a fundamental difficulty in evidence at the sign stage is effectively transcended. That is, that some words concisely represented a large number of accumulated, emotionally vague recollections like "mama," for example, but ones whose original experiential qualities lacked symbolic discipline and precision, and thus were therefore forgotten because of the organism's inability to clearly symbolize important attributes of those occasions.

8. Thus as more words are learned and integrated into an increasingly complex symbolic framework (a cognitive structure whose intrinsic quality is interrelatedness amongst linguistic symbols), language, and hence ideational feeling, becomes correspondingly less emotionally charged and steadily acquires a more disciplined quality. The experiential nature of sophisticated thought or ideational feeling is steadily transformed into mature meaning-as-directly-felt-relatedness. Here primordial emotional experience has undergone extensive symbolic atomization, thereby dissipating its intense somatic quality through its numerous subsequent symbolic qualifications. To illustrate this point, we need only compare the behavior of a young child when confronted with

severe disappointment with that of a mature adult encountering equivalent disappointment. In the former case, intense emotional feeling arises within the child's organism, followed by an uncontrollable period of crying. The adult, however, although similarly experiencing intense emotion, frequently dissipates this felt state through symbolic meaningful expression, consequently retaining his rational composure.

Symbolic proficiency also promotes an increased awareness of the infinite detail manifested by the natural world, therefore stimulating a desire to symbolically characterize this detail. This detail consists essentially of objects, both the static and dynamic relationships among objects, and the properties of objects.

Finally, internally experienced objects and relations are symbolically designated. At this higher level of development, consciousness consists, primarily, of sophisticated systems of symbols, the linguistic forms of which are clearly comprehensible because of their disciplined denotative quality. Therefore these can be fashioned into quite precise and unique patterns. At this stage, the unsymbolized periphery of emotion, intrinsic to every linguistic symbol, has been exiled to, at best, a status of infrequent and already obscure comprehension. However, vague as its character may be, it is this element in symbolic thought that provides the basic substance of consciousness. This is demonstrated by the fact that human organisms have a secure feeling about the orderliness and consistency of things; they feel at home in the world community; they feel that life can be meaningful; they feel primitive urges, compulsions, drives motivating them to establish determinate programs of action, very often proceeding well into the future; and finally, at their highest levels, a profound, acutely sensitive aesthetic feeling is experienced, as harmonious functional virtue is achieved when an organism's symbolic and emotional resources have been efficaciously embodied within creative, action-oriented behavior.

9. This particular argument is a concise restatement of the theory of symbolic development advocated previously. There are three reasons for having done this:

It is important to refamiliarize the reader with the fundamental complexity of concrete experience; a complexity so subtle that its philosophical and scientific implications are easily overlooked in an age when our mentality is constantly exposed to symbolic abstractions, very often mistakenly construed as concrete fact.

The discussion of early-life symbolic acquisition stimulates a sensitivity to the great inadequacy of naïve mechanistic theoretical constructs for revealing and elucidating causal behavioral determinants, because of the intrinsic disparity between the realms of materialistic mechanism and conscious experience.

Finally, the argument provides an introductory basis for illustrating the bewildering complexity of even simple learning tasks—tasks which, for a typical adult mentality, can be executed with such ease that their accomplishment goes completely unnoticed. The significance of this illustration will be in demonstrating the enormous symbolic qualificational power of what we have defined as meaning-as-directly-felt-relatedness as this symbolically and emotionally vague domain comes constructively and concomitantly to bear upon denotatively symbolized perception, thus actualizing what we directly experience as subjective psychological meaning.

10. A forceful example, meeting the conditions specified above, is the process in which an individual assigns a symbol to represent a given phenomenon. Therefore, we shall face the problem of how an individual symbolically characterizes a particular perception. Rather than make any pretense of capturing the experiential fullness of a particular real-life circumstance, let us merely elucidate several essential factors that would seem to be involved in such a task, during at least some occasions in early life. Of course, in mature life, the phenomenon that will be analyzed is executed with great ease because numerous ideational propensities or habits that were not available in early life are automatically invoked almost as soon as stimulus-object effects enter the human organism as sensation. A large number of these habits are so well established that they are unconsciously and preconsciously or reflexively implemented, for their functional virtue has been promoted over the years.

11. It has repeatedly been said that all symbols, in varying degrees, have a connotative and denotative, directly experienced aspect. The connotative aspect is defined as meaning-as-directly-felt-relatedness, containing a highly vague, but powerfully significant, concretely emotional dimension. It also has an implicit symbolic periphery that contains the entire relevant network or web of ideational relationships which any given individual has incorporated into his verbal repertory. Thus this vague symbolic relatedness, with its even more consciously remote emotional substratum, as they concomitantly appear with their clear and distinct conscious focal point of organization, is the essence of human intelligence. It is from this highly complex symbolic unit that conscious reflection is rendered possible. In reflection, necessarily using a clearly conscious unity of perceptual experience as an initial frame of reference, the myriad elements of relevant past wisdom, concomitantly implicit in the clearly conscious perceptual unity as meaning-as-directly-

felt-relatedness, can be, metaphorically speaking, traced out in successive temporal durations and resynthesized as novel ideational configurations of symbolic meaning. It is in this tracing-out process that the full potentiality or creatively synthetic possibilities of human cognition can be appreciated. Out of this, novel modes for suggesting future ideational synthesis emerge from primordial, unconscious organic concrescence. An individual human organism can intellectually and emotionally prepare himself for the emergence of ideational suggestions for novel modes for cognitive synthesis. This creative phenomenon is not as mysterious as it may appear. A consciously reflective human organism can increase his functional virtue through a moderate-to-great deliberate effort to succeed at a given task of interest. This entails a determined effort to acutely familiarize one's self with as many relevant ramifications of an issue as possible, therefore increasing the amount of wisdom that can be brought to bear upon the stimulus-occasion at any point in time, if the information is gradually integrated into one's understanding through a careful reflective effort. It can be seen that the process is not merely determinable in terms of blind, unconscious mechanistic determinism, for a state of reflective consciousness—an ontologically unique mode of existence—must necessarily be presupposed *a priori* in order to have the intellectual circumstances intelligible at all. Hence an intrinsically different type of mechanism is involved. We are not discussing a process which somehow transcends the realm of causal relationships amongst entities, but rather we must conceive the intrinsic nature of the entities and their properties and relations differently. Since meaning-as-directly-felt-relatedness and its denotative concomitant are subjective psychological experience in its mature form, we are provided the necessary conditions for a consciously reflective frame of reference from which the implications of symbolic ideational states can be traced out. Assuming that a high degree of functional virtue has enhanced the potency of this reflective process, then conscious intention has done its utmost in establishing fruitful ideational preconditions for ideational innovation. Beyond this, any suggested modes for novel ideational synthesis that may emerge into consciousness will be synthesized in organic physio-chemical regions as high-ordered novel concrescence. It can be said that this highly valued mode of behavior does not transcend, in principle, causally determinable formulations, but rather, that the variables capable of possibly entering into such phenomenal occurrences are so numerous and, very often, only vaguely accessible to direct reflection that any attempt to specify the causal conditions giving rise to particular classes of behavior will encompass only a small number of the potentially efficacious variables. However, on the other hand, if large quantities of data can be collected in these investigations, together with appropriate statistical procedures and electronic computing devices for rigorously processing the data, the situation need not seem experimentally dismal, by any means.

12. Thus when mind comes to bear upon an object of concern, all its relevant emotional, vague symbolic, and clear symbolic resources are being conjured by the demands of the stimulus-occasion, in their full synthetic potentiality. The simplified, denotative symbolic component clearly consciously represents the perceived object as its intelligible nature is synthesized from the resources of symbolic connotation, those realms which symbolically enhance the barren denotative clarity with a substance of meaningful feeling.

13. Let us consider an example of a single component of this substance of meaningful feeling which, when compounded with a multitude of other contributed components, thus producing the feeling of relatedness, would comprise the experiential substance of subjective psychological meaning. Some of the pertinent implications of the simple act of perceiving a table and understanding it as such are the following. We are dealing, here, primarily with linguistic symbols.

Linguistic symbols, logically separated from their subjective psychologically meaningful; i.e., their connotative context, are generally particular spoken sounds, or particular ideational feelings, occurring in private thought.

Learning symbols is contingent upon perceptions delivered through at least one mode of external bodily perception, if they are to possess an intersubjective basis for communication. (Note the case of Helen Keller.) Usually, bare denotative symbols, apart from connotative symbolic meaning, can be perceived in another person by observing movements of lips, feeling the vibrations in a throat, as well as hearing the particular linguistic sound. Although seemingly trivial, these uncommon ways of coming to understand symbolic expression are, in fact, typically utilized data occurring often as preconscious perception and, therefore in a subtle way, comprise a portion of the domain termed meaning-as-directly-felt-relatedness.

In learning a symbol there are roughly three stages to the process. First, the raw perception—the barren, uninterpreted stimulus-object effect, as it is independently contributed to the consciousness of an organism from a stimulus-object residing in the individual's own organism or located in the natural world—must be concretely experienced by a conscious individual. For example, the table must be seen and/or felt.

Next, the word "table" as typically heard from another, and hence personally articulated, including the internally felt vibrations of the sound, the felt muscular movements, hearing one's own voice, and so on, constitute important substantive data for learned symbolic acquisition.

Finally there is the stage, expressed in the writings of Dewey, where we come to understand an unfamiliar experience including, for our purposes, the perception, but primarily the symbol.

We respond to its connections [with other facts that are already known] and not simply to the immediate occurrence. Thus our attitude to it is much freer. We may approach it, so to speak, from any one of the angles provided by its connections. We can bring into play, as we deem wise, any one of the connections. Thus we get at a new event indirectly instead of immediately—by invention, ingenuity, resourcefulness. An ideally perfect knowledge would represent such a network of interconnection that any past experience would offer a point of advantage from which to get at the problem presented in a new experience. (11)

The previous three stages of symbolic acquisition as they are embodied in the example of characterizing the perception (or stimulus-object effect) of a table could be partially schematized as follows:

Stage 1: The basic perception as seen and the basic tactile perception

SEEN

    various patches of color in their fixed relationships

    the forms which define the color patches

    the observed texture of surfaces

    the unified object of concern as it exists in relation to other contiguous objects

    the unique shape of the table as it is perceived from the observer's perspective

TACTILE

    the felt smooth surfaces

    the felt straightness of its exterior edges

    the felt flatness of its surfaces

    the feeling of solidity

Stage 2: The concrete experience of learning the symbol, "table"

the uniquely heard articulation of the word "table" spoken by another

the sound of hearing one's own voice as the word "table" is spoken

the feeling of the muscular activity in one's own body in expressing the word "table"

the experienced difficulty in correctly formulating the sound "table"

the subtle emotional excitation that is felt when attempting new learnings and also the urge to learn

Stage 3: The establishment of cognitive relations.

the profoundly subtle experience of realizing that previously learned information is synthetically coming to bear upon the present occasion

the felt power of being able to rationally understand a problem as such, and hence the ability to execute a solution
the feeling of meaning-as-directly-felt-relatedness
the felt power of imposing direction upon one's thought processes
the enjoyment experienced in
synthesizing ideas into novel configurations
the experienced excitement of discovery
the feeling (and strange experience) of thinking, in that thoughts are felt to occur in one's head

Thus the significance of presenting the above schematization is in explicating a few of the explicit and implicit constituent factors (i.e., ideational propensities) that are typically contained within concrete subjective psychological events. These qualities or percepta are, no doubt, consciously more clearly in evidence during symbolically less mature stages of life, for many basic cognitive functions are then being developed and refined, thus occurring in subjective psychological experience as relatively difficult learning tasks. However, immature minds rarely, if ever, reflectively take account of these phenomena. Hence it is only later that they can be rendered subject matter for psychologists and epistemologists who can, through a determined reflective effort, recall these earlier experiences or recognize them in a more mature form in their personal contemporary ideational states.

We now approach an issue of crucial importance. These often subtle aspects of subjective psychological experience, primarily embodied in meaning-as-directly-felt-relatedness as the acquired wisdom of the past coming constructively to bear upon present occasions, thus meaningfully enhancing an understanding of their nature, have, in principle, physio-chemical correlates. This is one of the many important implications of an empirical identity thesis as it pertains to the mind-body problem. Specifically, it must be understood that considerable amounts of sensation and perception have been and will continue to be stored by appropriate physio-chemical mechanisms in the brain. A great many phenomena occurring as entities with their many characteristic qualities and relations among entities, issuing from both internal organismic and external environments, have been physio-chemically stored or recorded within the constitution of human organisms as the effects of these stimulus-objects have entered as sensation and perception. It is from this fact that concrete experience can be said to possess an indeterminate profundity. Further, because of this fact, no cognitive product can be cited which does not have its ultimate basis in concrete experience, whether it be the notion of causality, value, or modes of relationship. But the important point to be understood is that there are numerous perceived phenomena physio-chemically recorded which are not raised to clear conscious apprehension via critical reflection. In fact, our entire discussion in this book could be regarded as a modestly careful exposition of various relatively conspicuous dimensions of concrete experience. Whitehead's concept of misplaced concreteness is based precisely upon this issue. He argues that many philosophical and scientific theoretical errors can be attributed to an insufficient consideration of the perceptual deliverances of concrete experience. For example, his criticism of Hume was, in part, that if we critically reflect upon our perceptual apprehension of the external world it can be easily understood that sense-perception does not come to us in clear and distinct atomic units; this is an error resulting from having accepted a high intellectual abstraction as being a concrete fact of perception, thereby committing the error of misplaced concreteness.(15), (39)

Therefore, in our former example of a simple act of perceiving a table, our cursory analysis of this phenomenon revealed a multitude of experiential and theoretical ramifications of this apparently simple human act, an act expressed in its bare linguistic form as "I see the table." But in this simple statement, from a subjective psychological viewpoint, in addition to its denotative form, there is an accompanying extensive connotative realm that we have defined as meaning-as-directly-felt-relatedness which contains such implicit notions as "an individual identity," "an experiential and theoretical knowledge of natural world and innumerable personally learned notions about entities, properties, and their relations as they are collectively conceived as reality," as well as a multitude of additional relevant information. Anyone who reflects on this uniquely human cognitive phenomenon will begin to appreciate the profound significance and strangeness of ideation as an extraordinary ontological existent in contrast with other lower-ordered modes of being.

Before terminating this particular argument there are several other issues with respect to the process of symbolically characterizing perceptions to be considered. It has been said that symbolism—particularly linguistic, and surely mathematical symbolization—is a triumphant achievement of high-ordered intelligence, where the complex particularity of any single perceptual occasion can be greatly simplified by an appropriate word or sequence of words. This capacity enables human organisms to comprehend reality with great flexibility and precision; and moreover, to create their own ideational entities, many of which are translatable into physical environmental correlates. A large part of this ideationally creative process occurs in a way that is not in principle directly intersubjectively verifiable, namely as silent, private meditation.

Of course, almost everything that has been previously said in this discourse has had direct relevance to the process of thought, whether occurring in an intersubjectively determinate manner or in a silent, personally accessible mode. Topics such as the stages of symbolic development or the denotative and connotative elements of symbolic thought deal with the process and logical form of subjective psychological experience. But in the argument presently being developed, emphasis has been placed upon focusing specifically on certain logical and process dimensions of thinking-behavior in order to more fully appreciate the vast complexity of concrete experience, and particularly, the great significance of meaning-as-directly-felt-relatedness in contributing its necessary event-components to subjective psychological experience, thus rendering it phenomenally possible. In the preceding steps of this argument, we saw the vast complexity of processes involved in even the simple act of symbolically characterizing a familiar object in experience. From this we saw that considerable data are utilized by being synthetically converted into meaning-as-directly-felt-relatedness. Thus, many of these data are preconsciously implicit as vague yet powerfully efficacious connotative meaning as the wisdom of the past is brought constructively to bear upon present occasions to enhance their subjective psychological meaning. All this is rendered consciously lucid only through the prolonged and intense usage of analytical reflection. Therefore, in keeping with this emphasis upon specificity of exposition in explicating the nature of ideational phenomena, let us now focus more precisely upon the experiential characteristics of single, silently entertained thought components which, collectively considered, comprise complete units of symbolic thought. We have heretofore defined these ideational entities as highly disciplined emotional feelings whose original intensely somatic, primordial nature had been sublimated as a result of sophisticated symbolic atomization, leaving only a vaguely comprehensible emotional element—but one crucially important to the domain of meaning-as-directly-felt-relatedness. Linguistic symbols, as it has been seen, represent given perceptual occurrences via spoken words. But now a question is raised. In silent thought no sounds are uttered. Therefore, what is the experiential nature of that which remains as pure, particular thought-components? We most assuredly do not experience these event-components in the same way that we entertain throbbing bodily pains, for example. As the problem is posed, we are attempting to characterize the experiential nature of a particular silently entertained, highly disciplined thought-component within an ordered sequence of other symbols that collectively constitute a complete symbolic thought. In the complete thought-in-process, both the denotative and connotative aspects of symbolic experience can be, to a great extent, reflectively ascertained. But such is not the case in attempting to reflectively analyze the substantial experiential nature of a particular thought-component-in-process. Due to its ephemeral temporal duration, only its denotative element is reflectively accessible, although we must logically assume that its concomitant connotative components are present, for the denotative element, conceived by itself, is nevertheless meaningless. Therefore it can be said that at the specific time in which a particular thought-component occurs as silently executed ideational feeling, its intrinsic experiential, in-process nature possesses a symbolic form identical with its intersubjectively verifiable correlate, but obviously, the intersubjectively verifiable perceptual element is absent from the silently thought symbol. This fact, considered in conjunction with the additional fact that meaning-as-directly-felt-relatedness is generally a phenomenon only directly experienceable in a series of particular thought-components leaves us with a strange phenomenon indeed. We have as a remainder, it seems, the purest experiential manifestation of ideational feeling attainable, for it is devoid of any perceivable emotional feeling. It is a paradigm of cognitive clarity and distinctness-at-a-moment. This organismic capacity for producing such clear and distinct modes of ideational feeling—now conceived for expository reasons as logically separate from connotative elements—can be attributed to the extraordinarily sensitive physio-chemical perceptual recording mechanisms which record, with great fidelity, the perceptual deliverances from the internal and external modes of perception. As the physio-chemical recordings can be conjured to consciousness as correlative subjective psychological event-components, elements of past experience can be recalled in silent thought with remarkable fidelity. For example, most of us can silently think the various forms of pieces of music, of sounds of words, and of former experiences at given places, with often great reproductional exactitude. Of course these cognitive reproductions are experientially not as vivid as their original counterparts, but nevertheless, they are necessary for the possibility of any type of ideational process, regardless of its mode of occurrence. In fact, it seems obvious that it is this capacity to precisely reproduce certain former experiential elements in silent thought that importantly contributes to the essential structure of symbolic thought. If our organism was not capable of faithfully recording and then storing ideational copies of the perceptions of words, for example, as they are heard aloud, seen as lip movements, or felt through the tactile sense, then thinking as we know it would be impossible. Thus within the theoretical framework we have been develop-

ing, it can be said that the physio-chemical organic mechanisms for recording perceptual experience are so acutely sensitive to stimulation
that percepta initially occurring through external sensory modes are
occasionally recorded in their entirety, as in the cases of certain pieces
of music. More frequently, concise, simplified, symbolic representations
of original circumstances are physio-chemically stored as organic and
thereby ideational propensities. Once this has been achieved, their
original forms, as ideational reproductions symbolically represented or
situationally remembered, can be conjured to consciousness as manifestly expressed or silently entertained thought-components. For example, if an individual hears the word "perspicacity" for the first time,
he is able to silently think the word at a later time. However, if he could
not hear (or ultimately, have direct perceptual access to the sound of
vowels, etc.) the word, see the lip movements of another person pro-
nouncing the word, or have the word communicated to him through the
tactile sense, he could have no concept of the word or symbol to represent it for there would be no original physio-chemical recording of it.
If an individual had been both blind and deaf, the only remaining mode
for communicating with him would be through the tactile sense. We may
assume that in this way the person could silently entertain a thought-
component equivalent in meaning to the symbol "perspicacity," but a
symbol perceived as a direct experiential derivative from the sense of
touch. He would, in effect, silently think the tactile perception,
"perspicacity."

All of us have observed children playing various games in which
through voiced utterance they attempt to duplicate such natural world
sounds as gunshots, hoofbeats, and fisticuffs. This is an effort to recreate
a portion of formerly experienced reality. Brain mechanisms permit
recall of such natural world sounds with remarkable fidelity. We could
imagine a rude culture, perhaps having developed no system of sophisticated symbolism, effecting some minimal degree of communication
merely through articulating natural world sounds. But even in this, the
processes of abstraction and universalization would be achieved for even
a primitive mode of thought requires some degree of intentional rear-
rangement of voiced utterances, in effect, establishing those utterances
as universals. The illustration, apart from its inadequate elaboration,
demonstrates a principle also manifested in highly sophisticated linguistic thought. It is simply that the particularity of original occasions
fades quickly from our memory, but some elements of those occasions
remain with us as universals that can easily be recalled in reflection.
Instead of remaining within the realm of mimicking natural sounds, man
is physically capable of creating his own symbolic systems, expressible

as determinate sounds in the natural world yet remarkably transcendent of it.

This argument will be terminated by briefly drawing together some of the previously developed constructs. This last step is not intended to be a final statement on the nature of mind. Rather it will merely bring some of our formerly developed notions into a modestly clear proximity with one another in order to better prepare the way for future discussion, eventually concluding with constructs considerably more amenable to precise conceptualization.

Mind has been loosely defined as "percepta (class A) concomitantly coming constructively to bear upon other percepta (class B)." This definition was qualified, to avoid tautology, by indicating that class A percepta are phenomenally distinct from class B percepta. What is the intrinsic nature of these two classes of percepta? In effect, we are asking for a specification of the possible classes of mental event-components necessarily understood to constitute subjective psychological experience, or mind, in all its possible states! It has been generally stated throughout this discourse that there are components of our experience which are contributed to our consciousness, hence not created by individual consciousness, defined as stimulus-object effects. These effects can be classified as class B percepta in the following way: external bodily sense data, as colors, sounds, tastes, odors, tactile feels, and internal organic bodily feelings. The second class of percepta, class A percepta, which concomitantly come to bear upon class B percepta are ideational feelings made up of emotional feelings and symbolized ideational feelings, usually linguistic. This latter class (class A percepta) was defined to include the three basic levels of meaning intrinsic to linguistic symbols—namely, denotative meaning, and connotative meaning (meaning-as-directly-felt-relatedness, consisting of vaguely perceived symbols and emotional feeling).

Therefore, these two classes of percepta, as they are concomitantly synthetically united, are equivalent to the phenomenon of percepta concomitantly coming constructively to bear upon other percepta. This is to say that as stimulus-object effects enter a human organism's consciousness, the effects are rendered personally intelligible by being interpretively subsumed to disciplined linguistic symbols. It is important to mention, at this point, that the above schematization of class A and class B percepta is not sufficiently comprehensive to include the situation in which ideational feeling concomitantly comes to bear upon itself! This consideration has been omitted to prevent confusion, for additional constructs are needed to understand the phenomenon.

A major point to be understood at this time is that a concept of mind is being developed whereby the constitutive contents of subjective psychological states, which we designated as external sensory percepta, bodily feeling percepta, and ideational feeling percepts, are such that, in principle, an exhaustive understanding of the inextricably unified nature of mind, in any of its possible cognitive states, can be ascertained through carefully analyzing the nature of the contents of various particular mental states. In this way, it can be shown that mind is a phenomenon which by the nature and function of its perceptual contents can achieve organization and self-direction: the contents can achieve subjective psychological meaning! This is obviously a complex and difficult statement to comprehend. An attempt will now be made to elucidate its meaning.

Chapter ten / Experience, events, event-components, and space-time

Throughout our entire discussion, we have repeatedly referred to internal and external direct perceptual deliverances as the ultimate ground for verifying the theoretical constructs presented. The criticisms of various theoretical viewpoints with respect to the mind-body problem and, in general, the whole problem of scientifically investigating human behavior have had their evidential basis in the concrete perceptions comprising our conscious experience, sequentially appearing as unities of percepta. A fundamental assumption underlying this is that intelligent behavior arises from individuals having learned to understand, with progressively increased precision, the nature of entities and their relevant properties and relations as they are directly experienced as perceptual unities throughout spatio-temporal passage, specifically with regard to intrinsic properties and relations among properties of particular entities, as well as relevant extrinsic properties and relations among entities. This assumption is basic to the philosophy of Alfred North Whitehead and its far-reaching implications are developed in great detail in most of his works.

In our present discussion, we can only superficially elaborate upon several conspicuous dimensions of this profound assumption. The concepts to be introduced here are quite consistent with Whitehead's views although the terminology is not strictly interchangeable with his terminology. Where quotations are extracted from Whitehead's writings, the reader may legitimately contemplate them from the point of view being developed here.

The above assumption, that direct experience of the external natural world and our internal bodily phenomena consists of consciously apprehendable synthetic units of percepta, disclosing the inner and outer worlds in terms of entities, their properties, and the relations among these elements of experience, is one that clearly characterizes concrete awareness. Although stated as such, its meaning may not be intuitively clear to the reader and appropriate attention will be given to elucidating the assumption. The implications of this assumption permeate all areas of human endeavor, for human activity is experience and experience fundamentally consists of unitary configurations of inextricably related percepta occurring in relatively determinate temporal sequences. Keeping in mind that perceptual deliverances, disclosing the nature of entities, their properties, and the relations among these two factors, are to be regarded as the constitutive contents that are necessarily understood to occur within the logical form of subjective psychological experience, the conclusion can be drawn that as our theoretical constructs progressively approximate the logical form manifested in our subjective psychological experience our theories will acquire greater validity and reliability in explanation, for they are conforming more closely to the nature of concrete experience and hence fact. Our knowledge of external natural phenomena as well as subjective psychological phenomena will become more valid and reliable as our theories achieve greater fidelity with the indeterminately profound ramifications of concrete experience. In saying this, we are remaining strictly within the limits of mind defined as percepta concomitantly coming constructively to bear upon other percepta. If all possible percepta capable of constituting subjective psychological experience or mental events must occur as external bodily sense perception and internal bodily feeling, then all opinion and knowledge of any kind can be subjected to ultimate factual verification by consulting concrete experience, for it is from this ontological mode of existence that every factual and theoretical assertion arises. Hence error can be regarded ultimately as the degree to which knowledge claims deviate from our direct experience of reality. Here we must remember, of course, our unique definitions ascribed to the terms "event" and "event-component."

It will be our task, then, in postulating basic principles for a subjective psychology, to develop constructs that will best enable us to determine the logical form in which all subjective psychological experience must necessarily be conceived to occur. In doing this, we will be better able to understand the causal conditions that give rise to given particular modes of human behavior. Further, a greater understanding will be achieved for comprehending the methodological, logical, and evidential grounds upon which fact-theory distinctions are predicated, for our theory of mind will enable us to distinguish precisely those dimensions of knowledge claims referring to directly contributed natural world percepta and subjective psychological states from those ideational elements referring to the interpretative contributions of constructive mental activity over and above the former "bare" factual deliverance—if so strict a dichotomy as fact-theory can legitimately be made at all. Thoughout this particular inquiry it is imperative that the notion of mind as percepta concomitantly coming constructively to bear upon other percepta be kept clearly in view.

The ambiguous term "experience" has frequently been used without clarifying the meaning that it is to possess in order that certain crucial distinctions be made. Hence, we shall begin our analysis of the logical form of subjective psychological experience by initially establishing an exact concept of experience, or what has inadequately been defined as an event. Concrete experience is that which constitutes every consciously aware moment in our lives. It is that which fills out all subjective psychological awareness, regardless of its level of perspicacity. To better appreciate the profundity of this concept, we need only recall Whitehead's striking definition of experience.

In order to discover some of the major categories under which we can classify the infinitely various components of experience, we must appeal to evidence relating to every variety of occasion. Nothing can be omitted, experience drunk and experience sober, experience sleeping and experience waking, experience drowsy and experience wide awake, experience self-conscious and experience self-forgetful, experience intellectual and experience physical, experience religious and experience skeptical, experience anxious and experience carefree, experience anticipatory and experience retrospective, experience happy and experience grieving, experience dominated by emotion and experience under self-restraint, experience in the light and experience in the dark, experience normal and experience abnormal. (9)

This quotation within the framework of Whitehead's philosophical system has a rather precise meaning, but without engaging in an exposition of his views, we shall accept this definition of experience as it has been previously used.

Thus systematically speaking, experience includes all our awarenesses of the natural world as it is directly perceived through the external bodily senses, in addition to those directly perceived awarenesses of internal bodily states, including organic bodily feeling, emotional feeling, and ideational feeling. It is important to note that our concrete experience is directly apprehended as unified. This unity, most fundamentally, has its basis in the fact that the external and internal environments are disclosed to us as unified configurations of percepta or stimulus-object effects. The entities, their properties, and their relations with one another participate as ideational event-components in our consciousness so that their appearance as entities, properties, and relations is not created by mind. Rather, mind takes account of and hence records some of these phenomenal representations. There is, however, another dimension of the unity of experience which is caused by mind's active, synthetic role in apprehending unified perceptual deliverances from the external natural and internal bodily environments. This phenomenon was discussed in the previous analysis of perceptual field. It was seen that our understanding of any given stimulus-object effect was constrained, generally, to the meaning yielded as a result of the number of organic and thereby ideational propensities that could be conjured to a given stimulus-occasion, in addition to the extent to which the propensities were interrelated, thereby yielding even qualitatively greater meaning. The unity of individual experience at concrete levels is also (over and above the intrinsic unity of inner and outer environments, as they logically and empirically exist distinct from aware minds) in varying degrees determined by the extent to which the wisdom of the past comes constructively to bear on present occasions to enhance the meaning of those occasions. We have seen that in this latter way of conceptualizing experiential unity, much of the primordial complexity of intuitively apprehended experience eludes clear conscious understanding largely as a result of the human organism's ability to intellectually simplify the indeterminate complexity of immediate experience, hence achieving conscious symbolic clarity and precision in comprehending reality. The importance of this point cannot be overstated if we are to appreciate the magnificence and ontological peculiarity of meaning-as-directly-felt-relatedness. The extraordinary synthetic or interpretive power of mind is difficult to conceptualize unless one uses the extraordinary complexity of concrete experience as a basis for analysis. In this way it can be readily seen that ideational feeling represents a striking instance of ontological phenomenal transcendence beyond the bare given-ness of natural world representations and those occurring as bodily and emotional feeling. This unique emergence is nothing more nor less than the commensurate illumination of subjective psychology understanding as it steadily transcends the bare, intrinsically or subjective psychologically meaningless deliverances of stimulus-object effects conceived in-themselves.

On most occasions of which we are consciously aware, whether through mere conscious apprehension of percepta or in penetrating critical reflection, both modes of experiential unification are in evidence. The first level could be nearly experientially approximated in those rare moments when one's consciousness is filled predominately with sheer, immediately presented, unpondered configurations of percepta. In these fleeting moments, reflective thought is almost totally absent. In fact, this endeavor to perceive bare contributed percepta, and consequently achieve a connotative apprehension of the subtly enduring complexity of concrete experience, requires a deliberate intellectual effect. In this, we are attempting to achieve a state of affairs in which intellectual interpretation is at a minimal, thus entertaining a feeling of complex relatedness amongst mental event-components. It would seem that artists have developed this facility for directly apprehending concreteness with unusual exactitude. But the first level of unified conscious apprehension of internal or external concrete states is rarely attained, for in the vast majority of instances this primordially unified deliverance is concomitantly superseded in intellectual clarity by simplified, precise denotative understanding. A typical instance is when, during a given time span, one is concentrating upon reading a book, for example, while simultaneously the low murmur of voices and the quiet hum of a ventilating system can be heard, the solidity of the table and chair can be felt, the deliberate effort to focus attention on a page can be felt, the intellectual effort to comprehend printed symbolic meaning can be experienced, and so on. Thus, over and above the particular clearly conscious act of comprehending the printed content of a book, there are numerous other concomitantly occurring perceptions that are often, at best, only vaguely conscious. If this vast complex of perceptions can be conceived in their collective unity, then the full richness and multidimensionality of concrete experience will become more apparent. Stated differently, our concept of experience encompasses two levels of perceptual unification: primordially occurring as those continuous infusions of contributed percepta which are consciously recognized as entities, properties, and relations; and secondly, as the higher-ordered concomitant source of perceptual unification, simplified, clearly determinate interpretive cognition. It is these experientially integrated perceptual units, when occurring in their particular ontological sequences in the organisms of all individual conscious human beings, that constitute the conscious life or personality of men. Experience, then, has a far more inclusive character than that which any of us can exhaustively explain at a given time. For beyond the clear understanding of our thoughts at a particular time, there are the more primitive perceptual deliverances whose recognition in most cases is sacrificed in order to establish clear, simplified, linguistically meaningful organization, whether actualized as voiced expression or as silent thought. Here the point to be made is that concrete experience is far too subtle and intricate to be given complete symbolic explanation, for we live in the complex, ever-emerging, hence transitory, present. The future is upon us before we are done with its immediately preceding relevant occasions. So it is with human experience; our clear, conscious thoughts capture only the most conspicuous glitterings of fleeting present occasions. Thus linguistic universals serve as slender threads of continuity, regressing into a rich experiential history of learned wisdom that would be essentially lost from clear comprehension if it were not for these powerfully meaningful, enduring remnants of the past. Therefore, each unit of individual experience must be regarded as ultimate fact, for it truly embodies that which is the case. But since man's linguistic capacities enable him to only partially characterize those portions of immediate experience contemplated as personally important, those that are hence subjected to simplification, it is not difficult to understand that any notion of pure fact is necessarily relegated to the status of an ideal, for many elements of experience are denied precise conceptualization and are thereby lost forever. Moreover, the very act of linguistically characterizing a portion of experience entails abstracting this important element from its original experiential context. This, of course, becomes a source of much human error, even by the most acute mentalities. It can be easily seen that man's intellectual powers are greatly overshadowed by the profound structure of reality. We must come to this conclusion if our concept of experience is to be taken seriously, for it follows that experience logically demands the inclusion of every perceptual element of natural and internal bodily stimulus-object effects, regardless of their subtly and vaguely conscious status, collectively actualized as a temporal unit of subjective psychological experience. We may conclude by once again stressing the fact that experience, in its full comprehensiveness and deep compelling unity, is far broader than our intellectual capacity to symbolically characterize this human occurrence. Perhaps it is only through intuition, exercised by minds well disciplined in understanding the nature of what has been termed meaning-as-directly-felt-relatedness, that the indefinite pervasiveness of unfathomable perceptual complexity can be appreciated.

Now that the profoundly complex quality of human experience has been briefly contemplated, it is necessary to develop theoretical constructs which can provide the means of systematically comprehending this uniquely human phenomenon.

The concept of an event could, in a sense, be regarded as identical to our definition of experience, but the term "experience" seems to implicitly suggest an overly subjectivistic view of the world. As it has been said, the definition of an event demands a twofold distinction, namely, percepta concomitantly coming constructively to bear upon other percepta. However, when it is stated in this abstract manner, it is easy to forget the deep, intimate experiential quality of the percepta cited as definitionally polarized. With this in view, we can proceed to develop a specific definition of an event, emphatically incorporating the fact that powerfully informative concrete experiential factors are suggested by the theoretical construct. In defining an event we shall attempt to designate limits that will denote the domain of each possible particular event perceived by the mind of any given human being. Doing this makes possible a delineation of determinate individual atomic units of experience. Since mathematics is the exact science of establishing precise, universally valid relations among entities simultaneously occurring during instantaneous moments of time, it is possible to utilize mathematical and statistical techniques for ascertaining relations among experiential entities to be carefully defined as events. This theoretical approach for systematically comprehending phenomena was carefully explored and developed by Whitehead. In these inquiries his principal interest was in comprehending natural phenomena, but a similar approach is feasible for studying human behavior, for the theoretical viewpoint resulting from this mode of understanding is capable of encompassing a great number of subtle and transitory subjectively experienced phenomena.(40), (41), (42) Its chief advantage is precisely what is lacking in current psychological theories. It can utilize, in principle, every possible causally effective component of subjective psychological experience as factual evidence for evaluating given subjective psychological hypotheses, and this end can be accomplished within a definitionally precise framework not incompatible with mathematical, statistical, or geometrical modes of formalization. The ultimate criterion to which we shall adhere is that our constructs must remain concordant with the way that external and internal bodily percepta constitutively participate in our personal consciousness as ever-emerging, unique configurations of percepta, each in their unified totality being a directly experienced particular mental event.

Mind is an entity in the general sense that it is a something capable of being distinguished as intrinsically distinct in kind from other entities comprising the world. Hence mind gains ontological particularity. More specifically, individual minds are entities that stand in unique empirical relationships with their relevant coexistent natural world throughout given time periods, a process which is cognitively unidirectional. This suggests sophisticated organic concrescent processes yielding particular mental events, sequentially emerging within individual human organisms and manifesting an intrinsically intelligible meaning that persists throughout long series of these events. Thus particular events are a nexus of percepta or stimulus-object effects constituting the only valid and reliable factual representation of reality available to man. These percepta, in their unique, transitory patterns of deliverance, are the way that the relevant natural world enters the constitution of individuals, hence achieving an actualization of conscious experience within individual persons. As we have seen, the complexity of this synthesis is far broader than an individual mind's capacity to symbolically characterize the extraordinary phenomenal occasions defined as complete mental events. Determining the definitive limits of an event is wholly contingent upon an individual mind at a given time. Time elapses during acts of perceptual apprehension and thinking, regardless of their ephemerality. This is an unavoidable fact of concrete experience. Thus the time transpiring while thinking a complete thought designates the temporal limits of an event. Further, it is from the phenomenon of completeness that the notion of an atomic event is suggested. Our thoughts in the vast majority of instances occur as complete ideational units. This is merely to say that thoughts occur as "I see the red table," not "I see the;" or "That racing car accelerates more rapidly than its competitors," not "Accelerates more." Here we have a fundamental criterion for designating particular events. The ideational phenomena actualized throughout these time spans are unique entities, coexisting with innumerable other possible entities which simultaneously constitute reality throughout those durations. Therefore, their ontological status must be recognized as legitimate. This conclusion is particularly important for a subjective psychology whose principal thesis is that these ideational entities are in fact causally efficacious. The definition of the ontological particularity of events will be further developed in a subsequent analysis of space and time.

To understand the full importance of the view that consciousness is the actualized synthetic product of the way in which the internal and external environments affect individual organisms, we must recall the discussion of the unification of experience as it is perceived on the first level of presentation, which made the point that experiential events possess a highly sophisticated unity logically prior to the nearly automatic or reflexive functioning of mature intelligence at the second level of unification. It is imperative to understand that cognitive modes of thought have their primordial basis in properties of and relations among entities as their effects are experienced at the first level of unification. Stated differently, intelligent behavior arises from and hence acquires its ultimate discipline through primitive perceptual representation. For even the most immature intelligence, the world is not experienced as sheer, unfathomable perceptual flux for very long because physio-chemical storing mechanisms are operating considerably prior to the development of reflective consciousness. Wisdom is being accumulated without the organism's conscious realization at early stages of growth.

Amid the apparent kaleidoscopic perceptual flux is the overriding, but vague, recognition of 'permanence within perceptual processes, followed by the recognition that the permanence can be even more distinctly understood as entities manifesting certain characteristic properties. In fact, the essence of intelligent behavior is the ability to make these phenomenal distinctions and then incorporate the information into one's backlog of similarly acquired wisdom in order to increase one's behavioral efficacy. This is the power of establishing ideational relations among entities and their properties as they are in process. Relatedness is intrinsic to concrete experience at the first level of unification, and the second level is a way of extrapolating beyond the implications of the first level through the constructive, creative usage of symbolic reflective consciousness. We can know nothing beyond the appearance or effects of entities, properties, and relations as they enter consciousness from internally and externally located regions of reality. Yet there is the possibility for intellectually penetrating the mysteries of the microcosm and macrocosm. As Whitehead has said, the relations implicit in various given portions of our natural experience, for example, hold true for all entities throughout the universe even though the intrinsic nature of many of these entities can be only indirectly ascertained by using theoretical constructs. This principle, when comprehended within a scientifically rigorous spatio-temporal framework, is a cornerstone for the theory of relativity.

As we have seen, another extraordinary characteristic of mental events is that relevant past wisdom enters into every emergent, ontologically unique present occasion in such a way that it greatly increases the subjective psychologically meaningful comprehension of contemporary occasions. Not only the bare, intrinsically meaningless percepta of the printed words of a poem, for example, are seen but over and above this, a more powerful qualifying class of cognitive percepta infuse the manifest effects of the printed words with a deep meaning that reaches far into an individual's past experience, often stirring emotion and intellect at their primordial bases. From this, profound moments of indefinitely complex units of understanding fill out consciousness and provoke the limits of analytical reflection. Anyone who ponders the phenomenon of the past constructively entering into the fleeting present occasion, when both classes of percepta as synthetically united prepare the way for future novel cognitive emergence, cannot avoid recognizing the incredibility of this possibility. Mental events, in their inextricably unified perceptual atomicity during the ever-emerging present moment, in effect portray their relevant universe in an overly simple, representative and meaningful symbolic suspension, while the facts or causal conditions underlying this process can be reflectively and experimentally ascertained by the same individual mentalities rendering possible the former extraordinary action. What mechanistic scheme may we contrive to explain this extraordinary fact of experience? One such theory was proposed earlier, developed from the notion of concrescence as a physio-chemical synthetic coalescence of discrete, yet interdependent systems of organic mechanisms, each of which was necesssarily understood as a self-contained unit comprised of components whose functional presence are required for the organism to behave as a complete unit. In this view, our concept of organic bodily mechanisms leads us into the microcosm. For example, that discrete organs such as the heart are comprised of vastly complex systems of cells, that the cells in turn each have their own necessary components, that these latter components can be still subdivided further, and so on, demonstrates this pattern of regression. On the other hand, we may proceed up the scale of concrescence where organic mechanisms function as societies, and discrete societies interpenetrate with other relevant societies, and so on, so that holism becomes increasingly evident at progressively higher stages of organic concrescence. The optimum levels of concrescence culminate in consciousness and reflective consciousness where the organic, empirically ascertainable equivalents are those levels of concrescence providing the preconditions for cognitive emergence. It was said that this model seemed compatible with a scientific emergentism in that, for example, while mental states are not predictable *a priori* from their physio-chemical correlates, in principle they can be rendered scientifically determinate *a posteriori*. Feigl's identity theory, as we saw, affirms a similar view that mental events are not analytically derivable from their physio-chemical correlates.

In a different type of analysis, that of subjective psychological perceptual content, the phenomenon of past wisdom causally entering the present occasion was explained in terms of connotative and denotative symbolic meaning. This mode of explanation has its analogical grounds in mechanistic notions such as organic storing mechanisms which when activated in concrescent processes occur as organic propensities! Thus it can be seen that our mechanistic model is compatible with both an objective and a subjective psychological view of man, while our subjective psychological model, dealing with such notions as connotative and denotative symbolic meaning, can yield information about the subjective psychological aspect of human behavior, a dimension of human behavior that must be methodologically purged from a strict behaviorism, for example. A more basic fact, however, is that both psychological viewpoints must logically presuppose what has been defined as subjective psychological experience, and more specifically what we are presently defining as atomic mental events delivered and thereby perceived directly as concrete experience.

Our concept of mental events demonstrates that conscious life is primitively revealed as apparent perceptual permanence concomitantly contrasted with a backdrop of perceptual process. The conscious present is, moreover, invariably tinged by the presence of past wisdom, as contemporary moments incessantly slip into the future. The characterizational power of symbolism, particularly linguistic symbolism, obscures the transitory quality of experience arising as natural and bodily perceptual components and, hence, favors the selective recognition of enduring stability. This illusion is both facilitative and necessary for a full enjoyable life, but it is also a frequent source of important error as man's scientific inquiries proceed in understanding the lawful dimensions of reality. As we have seen, our immediate awareness of experiential events greatly exceeds our ability to symbolically characterize the full implication of experiential occasions. The ever-emerging present constantly fades from our cognitive grasp, leaving us only the opportunity to symbolically simplify those elements of experience that impress us with their importance. They resultantly become candidates for immediate contemplation and often for future recollection. The capacity to symbolically simplify our experience is, without question, a necessity for attaining conscious precision in understanding. This capacity is certainly sufficient reimbursement for the commensurate loss of experiential concreteness. But nevertheless, there is much variability in our precise characterization of things, although it is minimal in such disciplines as mathematics. For example, no two individuals agree exactly on how to achieve an enduring state of happiness or on a given phenomenon that they have both directly witnessed concomitantly. Discrepancy in understanding given matters results not only from differences in spatial or temporal perspectives of apprehension but, more importantly, from the great incongruence in the subjective psychological domains defined as connotative symbolic meaning or meaning-as-directly-felt-relatedness. This significant discrepancy can occur even though identical components of denotative symbolic meaning may be articulated. Two people observing a flower, and giving identical verbal testimonies to the fact, will have different conceptions of the flower if, let us say, one individual is a poet and the other a botanist. This illustration effectively portrays the distinction previously made between public and private events. It was maintained that all events were private or mental insofar as an individual human mind is necessarily presupposed *a priori* to stand over against perceptions of given phenomena. Otherwise the phenomena could not, in principle, enter into the domain of human experience. From this the conclusion followed that public events were actually mental events that contained event-components whose corresponding stimulus-object was located in the natural world; hence they were capable of direct intersubjective verification by other minds, as well. Similarly, subjective states were mental events containing event-components whose corresponding, scientifically inferred stimulus-object was *located* in the body of the individual experiencing the mental event. Hence, the event-component was capable of direct verification only by that individual, and occasionally capable of indirect detection by other individuals if there were manifest behavioral indications of the subjective state. Thus it is clear that only we as individuals can, in principle, experience what we do in fact experience, regardless of the location of the stimulus-objects under consideration. Therefore the important conclusion follows that objectivity, over and above the necessity that ultimate procedures and evidence be directly intersubjectively repeatable and confirmable, refers to the degree to which individuals can achieve concordance among their denotative and, more important, connotative domains of symbolic understanding, given that the percipients' spatio-temporal and environmental circumstances are sufficiently alike to yield such a similarity in understanding. This is the only concept of objectivity that we can have if we are to take into account, as we must, the ontological status of mind as a component of reality. Thus we are led to the abstract concept of mind as percepta concomitantly coming constructively to bear upon other percepta, presupposing all that has been said heretofore and all that will be said in future discussion, as implicit within this bare definition.

The most objectively valid and reliable knowledge is that stated in symbols possessing maximally determinate denotative and connotative domains. Stated more specifically, this type of knowledge has an experiential basis capable of such precise symbolic specification that the nature of its entities and particularly some of their relations can be rigorously conceived in formal terms. This statement appears to be verified by the exactitude achieved in mathematics and physics, for example. The former science is in great part a product of denotative ideational feeling as it derives its axioms and postulates ultimately from clearly perceived relations among objects in nature. Physics relies more heavily upon symbolically conceptualizing the nature of its natural and hypothetical entities, but the principal rigor is nevertheless derived from the ability to establish mathematical and statistical relations amongst its theoretically postulated entities. These are methodological disciplines where individuals, viewing the relevant universe from their

private, unique perspectives, can come to achieve relatively great concordance among their symbolic characterizations of those portions of
reality which they choose to scientifically scrutinize. Thus all events,
insofar as humans can know them, are necessarily private, for phenomena are directly perceived by individual minds. But, as we shall see
with increased specificity, this view by no means compels us to a
solipsism. It can be said at this point that since all our knowledge
about anything must, in principle, be grounded in mental events whose
components are delivered via the internal and external senses as
determinate experiential unities, any object of knowledge must necessarily enter into our subjective psychological experience as an event-
component, directly disclosing the object as an entity with properties
and knowable relations, or revealing at least some manifestation of the
object from which mathematical or statistical formulations may comprehend its relations with other entities and/or theoretical entities. In
this latter instance, scientists, in effect, take the data that are available for
any given object of concern, develop a theoretical model to fit the data,
establish formal statements of relations among relevant factors, and
finally, design key experiments to test the validity and reliability of
the model for explaining the phenomenal occurrence. In this way, deductive explanations can be given, proceeding from axioms, postulates,
etc., and finally demonstrating the lawful relations hypothesized to underlie the phenomena. This process is fundamental to rigorous scientific
explanation and hence prediction, achievements originally proceeding
from and ultimately verified in subjective psychological events.

We have seen that mental events, as atomic experiential unities
capable of being ascribed particularity in spatio-temporal coordinates, can
be indefinitely subdivided into event-components. These components
may occur as entities, properties of entities, or relations among properties
and entities. Further, entities, properties, and relations may represent
the natural, organic bodily feeling or ideational domains as they are
directly perceived through the inner and outer senses. The concrete
perception by mature minds of these myriad event-components in their
inextricable unity throughout given time spans or complete events is a
primordial and complex fact of reality for man. It is through this mode
of understanding that all possible knowledge of man and nature must
issue. The spatio-temporal components of mental events are the way in
which we experience, through direct acquaintance, the effects of stimulus-objects that participate in our being—at least those of which we can
become aware. Perhaps the most extraordinary fact is that these event-
components, collectively comprehended as events, and necessarily conceived as dipolar classes of percepta, can synthetically interact in such a

way that one class can impose discipline and hence direction on the other class. Out of this, subjective psychological experience gains its meaning and intellectual potency; man acquires a personal identity and the possibility for a creatively human life. Finally, to conclude our introductory analysis of the concept of mental event, let us generally say that these events can occur as experience in four distinct ways:

1. As intuitive immediately experienced subjective psychological events, where the stimulus-objects are organismically located in unconscious physio-chemical states, or are previously learned ideational feelings. Here, because of the immediacy of this type of phenomenon, conscious awareness is restricted primarily to connotative symbolic understanding while the denotative element is minimal.

2. As intuitive subjective psychological events, where the stimulus-objects are located in the natural world, ingressing into consciousness as external bodily sense perception. Here, because of the immediacy of this type of phenomenon, conscious awareness is restricted primarily to connotative symbolic understanding while the denotative element is minimal.

3. As subjective psychological events, where the stimulus-objects are organismically located in unconscious physio-chemical states, or are previously learned ideational feelings. Here, simplification has occurred, thus symbolically characterizing this type of phenomenon through both connotative and denotative symbolic means.

4. As subjective psychological experience, where stimulus-objects are located in the natural world, ingressing into consciousness as external bodily sense perception. Here, simplification has occurred, thus symbolically characterizing this type of phenomenon through both connotative and denotative symbolic means.

In our analysis of mind, it is becoming clear that the correct starting point for this inquiry is that of concrete experience because concrete experience is the fundamental medium for conscious life. We cannot transcend or otherwise escape concrete experience, except in such unconscious states as sleep or death. But it must be cautioned that the concrete facts of internal and external perception can be importantly distorted through careless cognitive interpretation that subtly and in an often unnoticed way unwarrantedly elaborates upon or deviates from our perception of stubborn facts. Well-known instances of erroneous determinations are, for example, the notion of sense data as intervening elements of clearly evident, atomic sensation between percipient and object, and the notion of substance as a substratum underlying and hence providing the basis of unity for perceived qualities of objects. Here we have examples of very high abstractions unwittingly accepted as concrete facts of experience, the results of which promoted many perplexities in philosophy. One never knows when one's own cognitive habituations are so well established that similarly erroneous misconceptions are unintentionally perpetuated. In any case, it is largely through prolonged, careful philosophical analysis that these problematic conceptions can be exposed. The fact, however, at the bottom of difficult errors of this sort is that ideational feeling introduced an interpretive element of cognition over and above that which is warranted by the contributed perceptual organizations delivered through the modes of external bodily perception, organic bodily feeling, and ideational feeling. Stimulus-object effects occur through these perceptual modes, symbolically characterized as entities, relations among entities, and the properties of entities. Therefore, it is from analyzing the percepta delivered via the three distinct modes of perception, as these percepta embody an intrinsic form logically independent from mind, that we can come to understand the subjective psychological form in concrete experience, and hence, ideational processes or mind. The task, then, is to achieve maximum fidelity between our theoretical constructs and concrete experiential deliverances, for their degree of discordance, resulting from unwarranted cognitive interpretation, will yield a commensurate amount of erroneous formulation. This does not mean, however, that all we are required to do is to represent pure perceptual fact purged of interpretation, for immediate experience is too broad for complete exposition by intellect. Thus mind simplifies certain important aspects of concrete, transitory experience through symbolic representations, and in so doing necessarily subsumes experience to interpretation, which in effect leads us to the conclusion that man is incapable of articulating pure factual statements, for this act would necessitate symbolically representing the complete original factual moment of experience. Consequently, man contents himself with the more humble endeavor of factually characterizing particular event-components that tend to recur throughout moments of human experience in a comparatively uniform way. But it must be understood, as we shall see, that even the apparently bare factual statment "The grass is green" is permeated with cognitive presuppositions and thereby interpretations!

Again to briefly recapitulate, it has been said that an ultimate, indubitable, and obvious fact of human existence is that mind is the consciously intelligible perceptual elements of individual concrete experience occurring in their inextricable unity and profound complexity. Also, it is from the contributed independent structure of concrete experience that mind essentially acquires its subjective psychological mode of understanding, ultimately derivable from the form of contributed perceptual deliverances, which eventually enables human organisms to meaningfully symbolically represent their perceptual experience, and at the highest levels of human understanding, to progressively develop an efficacious system of knowledge. This means that a class of natural organisms has achieved the symbolic capacity for intelligent reflective self-consciousness. To better understand the notion of subjective psychological experience, the theoretical concept of event was formulated for it emphasizes both the temporal or durational longevity of particular units of cognition, and also the far-reaching complexity of these experiential occasions. Thus "event" and similarly the term "experience" refer to the ontologically concrete mode of successive perceptual occurrence called process. From the perspective of sheer process, there is no possibility for delaying the temporal advance of phenomenal emergence in order that certain dimensions of reality may be subjected to reflective examination; rather, the mind must acquiesce to the relative permanence of its objects. The terms "event" and "experience," then, are also defined to comprehend the phenomenon of process, for implicit is the fact that reality is far broader than man's capacity to symbolically characterize even its momentary nature. Also the term "event," regarded as a particular spatio-temporal atomic perceptual epoch in the complete life of an individual human mind, is seen to include all possible ramifications of the concept of percepta concomitantly coming constructively to bear upon other percepta. And finally, as it has been frequently implied, the concept of event can be further analyzed into that of event-components, each of which is the perceptual effect of corresponding stimulus-objects. By means of symbolization, many of these event-components or stimulus-object effects can conversely be transformed into stimulus-objects, because of the causally efficacious symbolic nature of mind. Hence they provide a necessary condition for intelligent, innovative thinking.

Let us now proceed to a careful examination of the logical grounds upon which the relation of mind to the natural world and internal bodily states is based.

For argumentative reasons, the concept of event was originally loosely defined as having two aspects that were necessary in order for subjective psychological experience to occur at all: namely, percepta originating from external and internal environments, and a mind or conscious awareness that takes account of these percepta. This was later refined to the notion of percepta concomitantly coming constructively to bear upon other percepta. Although there are numerous ramifications to this latter definition, some of the more important ones are the following:

1. There is the implication of at least two distinct classes of percepta issuing from distinct perceptual modes as external bodily perception, internal bodily feeling, and ideational feeling, that are concomitantly actualized in a synthetic union, a union which emerges as subjective psychological states or events.

2. One class of percepta in this dipolar union must be regarded as uniquely contributed by the natural world as entities, properties, and relations (stimulus-object effects); and by the bodily organism as organic bodily feeling, occurring as entities, properties, and relations, and ideational feeling, occurring as symbolic entities, properties, and relations. But these ideational percepta must be contemplated as *previously* formulated ideas, thereby ingressing into the mind as the contributed component or stimulus-object effect of previously synthesized ideas that have acquired the status of stimulus-objects in the dipolar ideational synthesis. Although this phenomenon is easily executed in pure reflective thinking, an exposition of the logical grounds of this ideational occurrence is a difficult task, particularly without the appropriate constructs needed to effect an adequate explanation.

3. The other class of percepta in the dipolar union is that termed symbolic percepta, or disciplined ideational feeling. Symbolic percepta are comprised of denotative meaning and connotative meaning or meaning-as-directly-felt-relatedness, having two components: vague symbolic meaning and emotional feeling.

The above is a rough description of the logical form of subjective psychological experience at any possible moment. It indicates the logical form of mind, or an event throughout a given temporal duration. Of course, there are other discriminations that can be made with respect to logical form of mind, but they all basically follow from this essential formulation.

We will next consider the relation of mind to nature in the act of perception in order to enhance the epistemological clarity of our theory. Chapters 1 and 3 of Whitehead's *Concept of Nature* offer a more comprehensive and precise exposition of the theory to be presented but it should be noted that the position taken here differs slightly from that of Whitehead with respect to a somewhat greater emphasis upon the uniqueness of mind as a creative causally functional component of nature. It should also be noted that in *Concept of Nature*, Whitehead's arguments are generally delivered within a context that he defines as homogeneous thought:

Thus in a sense nature is independent of thought. By this statement no metaphysical pronouncement is intended. What I mean is that we can think about nature without thinking about thought. I shall say that then we are thinking "homogeneously" about nature.(41)

However, in this discourse we are not solely, as is the case with Whitehead, investigating the theoretical basis of the natural sciences. Our purposes are directly resultant from the objective of analyzing the nature of mind; thus we will be engaging primarily in what Whitehead has defined as heterogeneous thinking:

Of course it is possible to think of nature in conjunction with thought about the fact that nature is thought about. In such a case I shall say that we are thinking "heterogeneously" about nature.(41)

Nature can be defined as that externally located region directly perceived through the external bodily senses of individuals. The percepta derived from this region would comprise, during any given experiential event, one class of percepta involved in actualizing the phenomenon of conscious thought. These percepta could also be regarded as stimulus-object *effects*, although this is a concept which is more inclusive than merely encompassing natural percepta, and certainly as event-components. In external sense perception, as Whitehead has clearly indicated, we are aware of something that is not thought. If we carefully reflectively scrutinize our natural perceptual deliverances it is easily understood that human minds do not think into being the phenomena of trees, rocks, sounds, other human beings, sounds growing louder, cars passing one another, or felt increases in temperature. Rather, all possible natural stimulus-object effects are unique contributions to mind; hence they are logically and ontologically distinct from denotative and connotative event-components. But strictly speaking, this mode of characterization is suitable primarily for discursive purposes because it clearly portrays the notion of contribution. The concrete fact is that natural stimulus-object effects cannot be experientially separated from those percepta necessarily concomitant with them for this would violate the dipolar definition of mind while also being discordant with the factual nature of direct experience. Although it is possible for a mature individual to perceive a red object, for example, and not clearly consciously conceive the object as being red, the person cannot divorce himself from the fact that there is a vague connotative perception that could be characterized as red if he intended to clearly symbolically define the awareness. The point is that to be consciously aware at all necessarily means that vague symbolic connotation, or even more minimally, emotional feeling, is causally efficacious, for to be conscious or minimally aware at all logically demands the efficacy of these vague symbolic or presymbolic domains. In fact, in mature intelligence it is perhaps impossible to experientially divorce vague symbolic connotation from emotional feeling. This point will become more clear as we proceed.

A distinction to be clearly made at this point is that natural stimulus-object effects are event-components, and therefore, are elements of mind. The exact meaning of a stimulus-object effect can be defined as the way that the natural world affects us as perception; it is how the natural world, functioning as a stimulus-object capable of yielding perceptual effects, participates or ingresses into our individual consciousness. Effects are components of consciousness itself. This leads us to the equally important fact that, speaking first in terms of mind and then of the natural world, stimulus-object effects or contributions have as their termini, stimulus-objects. Termini are the entities that comprise the natural world. They exist independently from mind. Thus minds can know stimulus-objects only as they directly appear, hence participate perceptually, within consciousness. To reiterate, mind can only know stimulus-objects through their effects. Thus the concept of a stimulus-object as a thing-in-itself is, in all cases except those regarding individual human beings, a logical postulation facilitating a relativity spatio-temporal view of things. Hence, logically speaking, it is possible to say that we may participate in the purely subjective being of a rock, for example, if we were to crack the rock by striking it, just as rock is capable, as a stimulus-object effect, of participating in our being as an event-component. Participation, in an unconscious way, occurs in the example of a child who has swallowed a substance eventually having a disruptive effect on certain physio-chemical processes, although provoking no immediate subjectively ascertainable ill effects at the time of the assimilation. The possibility of this reciprocal ingression of stimulus-object effects among stimulus-objects does not sound nearly as absurd when the stimulus-objects are exclusively human beings engaged in complex discussion, for example! Thus the only thing-in-itself that any individual human being can experientially directly know is one's own conscious states; emergent phenomena made possible through the complex structure of one's physical organism. We may conclude, then, by saying that the nature of stimulus-objects cannot be intellectually conceived beyond the way in which they affect us, for any further understanding would demand that we somehow become those stimulus-objects, which leads to an absurd conclusion. However, this is no source for perplexity because stimulus-object effects reveal a great deal about the nature of stimulus-objects; namely, their occurrence as entities, having properties and internal and external relations with other entities.

We have briefly analyzed the way in which mind stands in relation to nature in the act of perception. The problem of the relation of a mind as a unified entity to its own purely ideational states, or event-components, has been postponed in order to introduce the issue with minimal confusion. Previously, the concept of experience has been defined and the term "event" introduced to provide the more exact notion of units of experience. Next, it was seen that units of experience can be further analyzed into elements defined as event-components.

It was said that the concept of an event was possible for it coincided with all conceivable concrete acts of human experience. This means that by reflecting upon how we conceptualize any given matter of concern, it can be seen that we think in atomic units or complete thoughts. The structure of linguistic expression demonstrates this fact since thoughts are expressed in complete sentences. However, this need not always be the case, for occasionally a mere spoken or silently thought word has the same effect upon us as an entire sentence. For example, the single utterance "Freedom" can yield an atomic unit of meaning whose implications can extend from a clear denotative, literal symbolic meaning to the compelling depths of our subjective emotional feeling. All this occurs merely in the single unitary moment required to express or silently entertain the concept. The stubborn fact of this illustration, as well as that of sentence structure, is mentioned to recognize the inextricable atomicity of events. The indefinitely subtle elements of these two types of occasions; i.e., complex sentences or single words, ontologically occur as a novel complex of ideational factors whose spontaneous mode of meaningful emergence is actualized as fact when the phenomenon occurs as it does, hence gaining particularity. All possible perceptual elements involved in each event must necessarily be classifiable into the dipolar form of percepta concomitantly coming constructively to bear upon other percepta. Thus the elements participating in these two events are technically defined as event-components. Over and above this is the important fact that the event-components are intrinsically bound to their unique mode of appearance during the original unitary event. This, as we have said, is the only type of phenomenal occurrence that could be conceived as pure fact of nature, for in the truest sense, it was that which was, or is, the case. The event of an individual expressing and hence experiencing the full implication of the utterance "Freedom" is the fact for that individual throughout *that* temporal duration and location of occurrence. However, from what has previously been said about the nature of fact, it was concluded that the sheer complexity and perceptual subtlety of any type of factual occasion is far broader than mind's capacity to symbolically grasp the comprehensive experiential moment. The problem is further compounded by the transitory character of nature. The present moment is perpetually perishing, never to be retrieved in its original particularity. Even in the act of reflecting upon the immediately preceding moment of thinking the concept "Freedom" the conditions have been met for defining the two cognitive acts as separate successive events. This is necessarily the case for the original atomicity of the antecedent occasion had been superseded by the subsequent ideational act of critically reflecting upon the immediately preceding concept of "Freedom" with its numerous meaningful ramifications. Therefore the notion of event-component is a theoretical device for facilitating analyses of atomic units of experience, or events. The point to be made is that it is logically impossible to directly experience an event-component in its particularity, for what we experience are events, unities comprised of event-components. Thus event-components are entities isolated through the usage of analytical reflection.

To illustrate the extensive implications of the event-component, let us consider the simple event, "I see the white bird flying." In this example we begin with the discrimination of a particular mind at a particular time and place directly perceiving or standing over against a particular configuration of natural stimulus-object effects entering into consciousness, corresponding to a particular natural-world stimulus-object. Next, there is the denotative symbolic characterization, "I see the white bird flying," considered in its barren literal form or contemplated as logically distinct from its connotative symbolic elements or event-components. Here the notion of denotative barrenness must be understood. Considered in itself as a mere natural world sound stripped of its connotative meaning similar to the heard articulation of an unfamiliar foreign language or nonsense syllables, the constitutive symbolic elements of a denotative assertion are event-components. It should be noted, however, that it is impossible for a mature intelligence to entirely divorce connotative meaning from its denotative element during a subjective psychological experiential act. The human mind reflexively attributes an inferential connotative meaning to every perception achieving the status of a denotative thought-component. This assertion can be affirmed apart from considering the accuracy or inaccuracy of conceptualized inferences. For example, a strange sound may enter our consciousness unexpectedly. Although we may not clearly symbolize the phenomenon as a bell ringing or branches cracking, two things can be said: the perception of a sound is apprehended by a percipient consciousness as an event-component and an individual's connotative symbolic resources are spontaneously and nonintentionally scanned to yield an appropriate denotative symbolic characterization of the sound, also event-components. From this, at least some minimal connotative subjective psychological meaning comes constructively to bear upon the distinguishable perception of a sound. We may conclude, then, that experientially speaking, it is impossible for a mind to entertain bare denotative meaning. Further, the extent to which the denotative expression simplifies the actual natural world perceptual deliverances of the original event is extraordinary. It has been said that contributed perceptions are known in their form as entities, properties of entities, relations among properties of entities, and relations among proximate entities as they are directly perceptually apprehended. The following partial analysis of the perceived phenomenon, placing emphasis upon the contributed element, gives some idea of the extent to which the verbalization "I see the white bird flying" actually simplifies the perceived occasion. The notion of an entity refers to anything—object, property, relation—that is perceived as a phenomenal unity. It is understood that the entity is perceived with sufficient clarity and distinctness to be at least minimally understood to be a something amid a consciously apprehendable contrasting background of perceptual otherness.

1. possible perceivable entities:
   the white form as distinct from a blue (sky) background
   the blue background streaked with (relatively) stable brownish-black lines (tree limbs, for example)
   innumerable shapes of objects
   brownish-black lines distinct from a blue background
2. possible perceivable properties of entities:
   whiteness
   blueness
   brownish-blackness
   texture of bird
   texture of trees
   texture of sky
3. possible perceivable relations among properties of entities:
   wings move in relation to body of bird
   head is smaller than body
   branches taper in shape
   branches are thinner than trunk
   branches fan out and upward in relation to trunk
4. possible perceivable relations among entities:
   bird moves, in relation to trees and sky
   trees are permanent in relation to bird's flight
   sky is permanent in relation to bird's flight

sky and tree are both relatively permanent in relation to bird's
flight

flapping wings are simultaneous with bird's flight

Without becoming tedious, this brief listing of possible entities,
properties, and relations provides us with some idea of the myriad
implications of the contributed perceptions in the phenomenon "I see the
white bird flying," and the considerable simplificational power of symbols. All these are, in effect, event-components. From this, it is not
difficult to understand that the elements of experiential events can be
far more numerous than the mind's capacity to symbolically represent
or fully comprehend them, although, conversely, much data is neurologically stored without the necessity of clear consciousness as a
precondition.

So far, we have presented a cursory analysis of the many possible
event-components implicitly suggested in denotative symbolic meaning
and the contributed natural world perception involved in the simple
conscious phenomenon "I see the white bird flying." We have yet to
mention the enormously greater number of possible event-components
that are concomitantly implicit within the realm of connotative meaning. Connotative meaning, as has been said, fills out the bare distinct
percepta of mental events with subjective psychological meaning, as
connotative percepta synthetically come to bear upon contributed and
denotative symbolic perception. One who has understood this synthetic process will have comprehended the logical and psychological
nature of subjective psychological experience or mind. A mere hint of
this extraordinary human phenomenon is contained in the following
brief exposition of the statement "I see the white bird flying":

1. All the learned associations implicit within the percipient's self-
concept as they are concentrated in the moment of time needed by the
percipient to meaningfully utter the word "I" as the initial word of the
entire sentence.

2. All the learned associations implicit within the percipient's
apprehension of the natural world phenomenon, "see the white bird
flying." This entails an active, operational understanding of a language
system which permits phenomenal components like those occurring in
our former analysis of the perceptual contributions of the natural
world to be nearly automatically symbolically characterized, and understood as subjective psychological meaning.

This analysis of the event, "I see the white bird flying," has demonstrated the incredible number of possible event-components in any single
mental event that are either explicitly discernible (the denotative symbols used to articulate the perceptual apprehension and those contrib-

uted percepta that are clearly consciously perceived) or implicitly present (the vast implicit symbolic domain necessary to fill out the denotative symbols with meaning-as-directly-felt-relatedness and the large number of unclearly apprehended contributed perceptions that are omitted by the simplified denotative utterance). This is in full concordance with the concept of mind as denotative and connotative symbolic percepta concomitantly coming constructively to bear upon contributed natural world and internal organismic percepta.

It has been repeatedly mentioned that ideational or symbolic event-components are a product of high-grade organic concrescence and transcendent concrescent synthesis. In this process primordial emotional feeling is subsumed to extensive discipline, the result being the development of a highly complex, interrelated symbolic system, each symbol of which possesses three peripheries of subjective psychological meaning: denotative meaning, connotative meaning, and subdivisions of the latter into vague symbolic meaning and vague emotional feeling. Through the acquisition of symbolic behavioral capacities the human organism is able to characterize innumerable entities, properties, and relations contributed from natural and internal bodily environmental states throughout time. Specifically with respect to internal bodily perceptual contributions, this says far more than the original statement literally implies because we have seen that the human organism can transcend mere organic bodily and higher-grade emotional feelings, for the acquisition of symbolic capacities necessarily implies, as Cassirer has said, that a new dimension of reality is achieved. This other dimension of reality is a novel causal domain which has been defined as subjective psychological experience. In this uniquely human domain, because of symbolic acquisition, conscious experience can attain denotative clarity, and therefore, cognitive precision. The basis for these capacities is the fact that the human organism's structure can experience perceptions and, moreover, percepta that are deemed personally important, whether in the primitive sense of mere contrast like the glitter of a trinket or in the most sophisticated form of aesthetic understanding, thereby submitting them to symbolically meaningful simplification, and frequently, erroneous oversimplification. But in conjunction with this view we must remember that simplification refers primarily to the denotative element of symbolic characterization while the simplified element is concomitantly constructively infused and thereby extraordinarily enhanced by the wisdom of the past occurring as meaning-as-directly-felt-relatedness. It is precisely for this reason that simplification must not be confused with oversimplification. The latter, in a sense, refers to what Whitehead has defined as misplaced concreteness where, in fact, a very high abstraction is erroneously regarded as a concrete fact of experience when it is ideationally utilized in characterizational or constructive thinking. The point to be made is that this other dimension of reality, disclosed as a class of event-components occurring in conjunction with contributed natural or organic bodily perceptions, or assuming the mode of contributed percepta (stimulus-object effects resulting from previously formulated ideas which acquire the status of stimulus-objects merely because they are past occurrents) concomitantly standing over against other symbolic percepta, is a truly unique realm distinct from natural world stimulus-object effects and those resulting from organic bodily states. Conscious awareness and reflective consciousness, with their intrinsic symbolic nature, are now causally efficacious behavioral determinants over and above brute materialism or reflexive epiphenomenalistic mechanism. Identity theory bears out this conclusion in that statements representative of the two latter theoretical positions cannot derive, analytically, statements designating the subjective psychological realm. In fact, statements of the subjective psychological domain must be presupposed *a priori* in order that discourse in the other two, or any meaningful, realms may ensue at all!

If event-components are perceived intrinsically as entities, properties, and relations contributed from the natural world and internal organic bodily stimulus-object effects that enter mental events and are subsequently symbolized, or unsymbolized in the sense that a person may experience an event-component without denotatively defining it as such; and if event-components may also include the entities, properties, and relations of ideational symbolic feeling occurring as contributed components from meaning-as-directly-felt-relatedness; it can be seen that we have a theoretical framework capable of yielding an exhaustive account of all possible combinations of percepta capable of constituting all possible mental events! An equally important conclusion follows: because of the definitional meaning of each category of percepta capable of being dipolarly actualized as a mental event, conditions that can be directly ascertained as components of concrete subjective psychological experience are such that mind can be seen as an incredibly complex, dynamic system of synthetically actualized percepta which, in their perceptual unification throughout time spans, can subsume themselves within the context of complete events to progressive discipline. This is a phenomenon which most of us understand intuitively although, perhaps, vaguely as the creative or innovative power of mind. Subjective psychological experience as a unique causal dimension of reality, over and above that posited by a materialistic mechanism, for example, means that contemporaneously occurring ideational event-components, as intrinsically nonphysical or natural entities not directly perceivable via the external bodily senses, which are symbolically representative of natural and organic bodily stimulus-object effects or percepta, in conjunction with previously synthesized pure symbolic ideational event-components that enter contemporary occasions of experience as stimulus-object effects, can both be intentionally utilized, particularly at mature levels of human development, for organizing and hence manipulating other symbolized components of experience. Human thinking is rendered possible precisely because of man's capacity to symbolically comprehend some of his experience and to subsequently elaborate upon the content and quality of subjective psychological experience in a way intrinsically transcending the mere perceptual deliverances of external and internal bodily and emotional modes—so that an extensive repertory of ontologically unique symbolic entities possessing unique properties and relations are constructed, given only the intrinsic nature of the event-components that can conceivably constitute mental events. It will be noted that the term "elaborate" was used advisedly to indicate the transcendent status of symbolic thinking, for even at this more sophisticated level of behavior, all symbolic entities, properties, and modes of symbolic relation are ultimately derived from the essential way that external bodily perception and internal bodily and emotional feeling enter as entities, properties, and relations. Thus human symbolic thinking can be described as the process of imposing form on the matter of experience. Stated more abstractly, it is the process of event-components necessarily occurring as atomic unities of human experience, and their intrinsic nature as such, acquiring self-discipline, and to some extent, self-direction throughout space-time. In this process a phenomenon gradually develops which is described by Cassirer in the following way:

Man cannot escape from his own achievement. He cannot but adopt the conditions of his own life. No longer in a mere physical universe, man lives in a symbolic universe. Language, myth, art, and religion are parts of the universe. They are the varied threads which weave the symbolic net, the tangled web of human experience. All human progress in thought and experience refines upon and strengthens this net. No longer can man confront reality immediately; he cannot see it, as it were, face to face. Physical reality seems to recede in proportion as man's symbolic activity advances. Instead of dealing with the things themselves man is in a sense constantly conversing with himself. He has so enveloped himself in linguistic forms . . . that he cannot see or know anything except by the interposition of this artificial medium.(19)

Every possible human event, necessarily private or mental in the sense that only we as individuals can directly experience the percepta that we in fact do experience, is an atomic, inextricably unified element in the dynamic composition of a particular individual at a particular place throughout a particular temporal duration. Only "I" can be the subject of "my" particular experience, which demands the conclusion that everything which we recognize as life, reality, etc., necessarily presupposes individual streams of consciousness. This is not to say, obviously, that the real world which exists independently of each of us is contingent on our particular consciousness for its existence. Further, each particular event can be partially reflectively analyzed into event-components through logical analysis (for we cannot directly experience isolated event-components, only atomic events). Even a partial summary of the manifold implications of these views would entail reiterating everything that has been propounded heretofore. Therefore, let us place primary emphasis upon the most important experiential aspects of these assertions. Our clearly determined experiences, acquiring symbolic precision because of the human organism's capacity to simplify important portions of events, are clarified as atomic ideational units. What each of us directly experiences throughout every particular conscious atomic moment of experience, only a portion of which is subject to symbolic specification, can theoretically be analyzed into event-components. Of course this theoretical advance is not concretely suggested in direct experience. A considerable reflective effort is required to formulate constructs from a backlog of concrete perceptual deliverance. Thus the notion of event-component arises only from a highly abstract conception of human experience. It demands a deliberate, prolonged reflective effort to theoretically contemplate our concrete experiential moments as synthesized from a comparatively small number of categorically distinct elements perceptually appearing and reappearing in both diverse and similar ontological modes. On one hand, the particular shade of green observed in a leaf, an entity possessing a determinate, distinctive form, can reappear in a green dress, an entity possessing a form and properties differing from those of a leaf, for example, during another event. But on the other hand, continuity and coherence in ideational processes are, in great part, rendered possible by the temporal endurance and recurring perception of particular entities. For example, the green leaf observed by an individual on two successive days was the same leaf in both occasions. Here we are bordering on difficult metaphysical issues that must be avoided for the purposes of this discourse. Our emphasis rests squarely upon formulating a subjective psychological theoretical comprehension of directly experienced mental events. The point being made is that it is conceivably theoretically fruitful to comprehend every possible experiential event as comprised of basic perceptual elements which occur and recur throughout space and time in both similar and different configurational modes. Let us use as an illustration a moment from an experience, which can be loosely defined as a single event in a psychotherapeutic interaction between a patient and a therapist. The more conspicuous event-components throughout the particular temporal duration were roughly the following: the vague awareness of books on shelves, manifesting a multitude of diverse shapes and colors; the vague awareness of the room as an enclosure; the vague awareness of furniture in the room with the many characteristic properties of each piece; the more clear awareness of the overt physical nature of the patient sitting before the therapist; a rather clear awareness of the exchanged verbalizations and their meanings, in addition to other closely associated behaviors such as the patient's head occasionally turning from side to side, the only occasionally achieved eye contact, etc.; a rather clear apprehension of dynamic patterns of emotional and ideational states directly accessible to the therapist as the patient-counselor interaction transpired, such as periodic feelings of dislike for the patient and feelings of anger; moments of reflective analysis of certain key phrases articulated by the patient; moments of reflective analysis on why the counselor had occasionally reacted angrily to certain responses; determined analytical efforts made by the therapist to clearly and concisely express certain concrete phenomenal occurrences manifested within the emerging therapeutic interaction, etc. These conscious recollections of a moment during a psychotherapeutic event constitute only a very small number of the myriad factual details of that brief occasion. The illustration readily demonstrates the profound complexity of human experience and the limited success of linguistic exposition in attempting to recapture the inextricable unity of a directly experienced factual event.

Yet even when confronted with the fact that language has obvious limitation in its usage as an instrument for symbolically portraying elements of previous human experience in their original complexity and animation, it is possible to present a schematization of all the possible categories of perceptual event-components capable of entering, in principle, into any individual's experiential events during any particular occasion. Such an exposition would be of great value to a subjective psychology in analyzing both the perceptual contents and the modes of ideational synthesis typically embodied within individual experience during problem-solving and other given types of behavior. The scientific importance of this categorical analysis may not be readily apparent at this point. Its significance must be pondered in light of additional constructs to be subsequently developed in order to appreciate some of the lawlike relations demonstrated in dynamic subjective psychological experience. Of course this inquiry must be governed by the constructs presently being developed for defining the logical form of mind. Therefore each experiential event, logically manifesting with *a priori* necessity the essential dipolar form of natural or internal bodily perceptual contributions as they are concomitantly and synthetically actualized with symbolic percepta, must necessarily be comprised, during any given event, of at least some of the following three Categories of event-components out of which all possible subjective psychological events must be constituted:

1. External bodily perceptions:
   vision
      entities
         spatial perceptual particularity as a localized unity
         form defining boundary of colors
      properties
         particular colors themselves
      relations
         spatial change among forms
         change in intensity of properties
   smell
      entities
         spatial perceptual particularity as a localized unity
      properties
         particular odors themselves
      relations
         change among odors
         change in intensity of properties
   sound
      entities
         spatial perceptual particularity as a localized unity
      properties
         particular sounds themselves
      relations
         change among sounds
         change in intensity of quality of properties
   taste
      entities
         tactually felt perceptual particularity as a localized unity
      properties
         particular tastes themselves
      relations

   change among tastes

   change in intensity or quality of properties

  touch

   entities

    tactually felt perceptual particularity as a localized unity

    form defining boundary of entity

   properties

    the particularity of perception: hot, cold, warm, coarse, smooth, etc.

   relations

    change among properties

    change in state of properties: solidity, flexibility, hot-to-cold, etc.

2. Organic bodily feeling perceptions:

 entities

  organically felt perceptual particularity as a localized unity

 properties

  particular internal feelings themselves

 relations

  change among properties

  change in intensity and quality of properties

3. Ideational feeling perceptions:

 emotion (vague, unsymbolized ideational feeling)

  entities

   emotionally felt perceptual particularity as a localized unity

  properties

   particular distinctive and/or qualitatively unique emotions themselves

   very vague, consciously felt quality

  relations

   change among properties or entities

   change in intensity and quality of properties

 connotative symbolic ideational feeling

  entities

   the particular vague symbolic unity that is thought

  properties

   the particular configuration of meaning-as-directly-felt-relatedness

   vaguely conscious emotionally felt quality

  relations

   change among properties

   change in intensity and quality of properties

denotative symbolic ideational feeling
    entities
        the particular usually linguistic symbol that is thought
    properties
        the particular clearly conscious symbol itself, logically distinct
        from the connotative symbolic elements
        pure sublimated feeling
    relations
        change among properties

The above schematization of the possible categories of event-components is intended to be an exhaustive specification of perceptual phenomena, in that all possible elements of subjective psychological experience can be comprehended within these categories. However, the specific subcategories contained under Entities, Properties, and Relations do appear to be susceptible to alternate modes of classification, and without question, the Categories are capable of further subclassification. The Categories are, in effect, an exposition of the possible types of matter that may receive form through subjective psychological experiential actualization through space-time.

In our discussion on theoretically comprehending the logical form of human experience, there is one final step to be considered. Thus far, beginning with a definition of the most inclusive term "experience," there has been a determined effort to progressively introduce constructs that demonstrate the universal structure of human experience in all its possible modes of concrete occurrences. Event, event-component, and finally, Categories have been defined. Here the basic principle upon which our inquiries have been based is that if an adequate concept of mind is to be developed, it is essential that that out of which mind is substantively comprised be clearly elucidated. For it is unsatisfactory to contemplate mind as merely a behavioral process capable of exhaustive functional comprehension solely through its manifest effects. As has been argued, this is to deny factual phenomena known to us through direct acquaintance as ideational states. Since consciousness and reflective consciousness are ideational states in process, necessarily having both objective and subjective psychological factual manifestations, it is a serious error to maintain that the nature of mind is entirely ascertainable by only an objective psychology or vice versa. Therefore, not only must a satisfactory concept of mind portray mind as process, but, in addition, it is imperative to define that, subjective psychologically speaking, which is in process, as well. An attempt is being made here to precisely define the form of that which is in process. Later we will proceed to partially demonstrate the relation of the universal logical form to the concrete spatio-temporal process of mind. This twofold analysis will yield a basic subjective psychological conceptualization of human experience from which experimental and philosophical inquiries may ensue. At this point, however, now that the elements of that which is in process have been designated, constructs must be developed showing the precise relationship among mental events, with their constitutive event-components, collectively comprising the process of mind. The constructs that can fulfill this requirement are space and time, utilized to define the theoretical limits of concrete experiential events both as instantaneously occurring spatial entities and during their concrete temporal evolvement.

Our views with regard to the concepts of space and time are essentially those articulated with great clarity and precision by Alfred North Whitehead. It is impossible to cite a single work of Whitehead's that deals exhaustively with his theory of these concepts. Nearly all his works contain a somewhat unique approach to expressing his basic thoughts on these problems. The books which we shall liberally quote are probably those most intelligible to readers unfamiliar with Whitehead's works. Also, at our present level of discussion, they have greatest relevance for the problem of mind conceived within our theoretical framework. Our consideration of Whitehead's conceptions of space and time is merely introductory. For those whose primary interest in our concept of mind is experimentally grounded, a more penetrating study of his concept of space-time is essential.

Whitehead maintains that there has been a prevailing misconception in philosophy and science subtly responsible for creating major theoretical problems in these disciplines by predisposing mentalities to an erroneous conception of the essential nature of the material world.

Thus the origin of the doctrine of matter is the outcome of uncritical acceptance of space and time as external conditions for natural existence. By this I do not mean that any doubt should be thrown on facts of space and time as ingredients in nature. What I do mean is "the unconscious presupposition of space and time as being that within which nature is set." This is exactly the sort of presupposition which tinges thought in any reaction against the subtlety of philosophical criticism. My theory of the formation of the scientific doctrine of matter is that first philosophy illegitimately transformed the bare entity [here the term "entity" has essentially the same meaning ascribed to it in our former discussions on event-components], which is simply an abstraction necessary for the method of thought, into the metaphysical substream of these factors in nature which in various senses are assigned to entities as their attributes; and that, as a second step, scientists (including philosophers who were scientists) in conscious or unconscious ignorance of philosophy presupposed this substratum, qua substratum for attributes, as nevertheless in time and space.

This is surely a muddle. The whole being of substance is as a substratum for attributes. Thus time and space should be attributes of the substance. This they palpably are not, if the matter be the substance of nature, since it is impossible to express spatio-temporal truths without having recourse to relations involving relata other than bits of matter. I waive this point, however, and come to another. It is not the substance which is in space, but the attributes. What we find in space are the red of the rose and the smell of the jasmine and the noise of cannon. We have all told our dentist where our toothache is. Thus space is not a relation between substances, but between attributes.

Thus even if you admit that the adherents of substance can be allowed to conceive substance as matter, it is a fraud to slip substance into space on the plea that space expresses relations between substances. On the face of it space has nothing to do with substances, but only with their attributes. What I mean is, that if you choose—as I think wrongly—to construe our experience of nature as an awareness of the attributes of substances, we are by this theory precluded from finding any analogous direct relations between substances as disclosed in our experience. What we do find are relations between the attributes of substances. Thus if matter is looked on as substance in space, the space in which it finds itself has very little to do with the space of our experience.(41)

It is clearly evident from the above quotation that the substratum view of the material world generates certain highly problematic issues; one of them embodying a concept of space that is seriously discordant with our concrete experiential perceptions of the natural world, for it overlooks the fact that our perceptions are actually of the natural world appearing to us as attributes or properties of and relations among entities. Also the substratum theory de-emphasizes the separative, prehensive, and modal characters of space-time:

Things are separated by space, and are separated by time: but they are also together in space, and together in time, even if they be not contemporaneous. I will call these characters the separative and the prehensive characters of space-time. There is yet a third character of space-time. Everything which is in space receives a definite limitation of some sort, so that in a sense it has just that shape which it does have and no other, also in the same sense it is just in this place and no other. Analogously for time, a thing endures during a certain period, and through no other period. I will call this the modal character of space-time. It is evident that the modal character taken by itself gives rise to the idea of simple location. But it must be conjoined with the separative and prehensive characters.(43)

But we are advancing a bit too rapidly in introducing the concept of time without yet having considered an extremely important error that has traditionally been made in philosophy and science with respect to the concept of time; an error that has extraordinary implications for conceiving, theoretically, subjective psychological experience, and a science thereof. Whitehead clearly and concisely delineates this error.

The eighteenth and nineteenth centuries accepted as their natural philosophy a certain circle of concepts which were as rigid and definite as those of the philosophy of the Middle Ages, and were accepted with as little critical research. I will call this natural philosophy "materialism." Not only were men of science materialists, but also adherents of all schools of philosophy. The idealists only differed from the philosophic materialists on the question of the alignment of nature in reference to mind. But no one had any doubt that the philosophy of nature considered in itself was of the type which I have called materialism. . . . It can be summarized as the belief that nature is an aggregate of material and that this material exists in some sense at each successive member of a one-dimensional series of extensionless instants of time. Furthermore the mutual relations of the material entities at each instant formed these entities into a spatial configuration in an unbounded space. It would seem that space—on this theory—would be as instantaneous as the instants, and that some explanation is required of the relations between the successive instantaneous spaces. The materialistic theory is however silent on this point; and the succession of instantaneous spaces is tacitly combined into one persistent space. This theory is a purely intellectual rendering of experience which has had the luck to get itself formulated at the dawn of scientific thought. It has dominated the language and the imagination of science since science flourished in Alexandria, with the result that it is now hardly possible to speak without appearing to assume its immediate obviousness.

But when it is distinctly formulated in the abstract terms in which I have just stated it, the theory is very far from obvious. The passing complex of factors which compose the fact which is the terminus of sense awareness [what we have defined as stimulus-object, hence yielding stimulus-object effects—a term roughly to be equated with Whitehead's sense awareness— contributed as perceptions participating as event-components in our conscious events] places before us nothing corresponding to the trinity of this natural materialism. This trinity is composed (i) of the temporal series of extensionless instants, (ii) of the aggregate of material entities, and (iii) of space which is the outcome of relations of matter.

There is a wide gap between these presuppositions of the intellectual theory of materialism and the immediate deliverances of sense awareness. I do not question that this materialistic trinity embodies important characters of nature. But it is necessary to express these characters in terms of the facts of experience . . . we have now come up against the question, Is there only one temporal series? The uniqueness of the temporal series is presupposed in the materialistic philosophy of nature. But that philosophy is merely a theory, like Aristolean scientific theories so firmly believed in the Middle Ages. If . . . I have in any way succeeded in getting behind the theory to the immediate facts, the answer is not nearly so certain. . . . On the materialistic theory the instantaneous present is the only field for the creative activity of nature. The past is gone and the future is not yet. Thus (on this theory) the immediacy of perception is of an instantaneous present, and the unique present is the outcome of the past and the promise of the future. But we deny this immediately given instantaneous present. There is no such thing to be found in nature. As an ultimate fact it is a nonentity. What is immediate for sense awareness is a duration. Now a duration has within itself a past and a future; and the temporal breadths of the immediate durations of sense awareness are very indeterminate and dependent on the individual percipient. Accordingly there is no unique factor in nature which for every percipient is preeminently and necessarily the present. The passage of nature leaves nothing between the past and future. What we perceive as present is the vivid fringe of memory tinged with anticipation. This vividness lights up the discriminated field within a duration. But no assurance can thereby be given that the happenings of nature cannot be assorted into other durations of alternative families. We cannot even know that the series of immediate durations posited by the sense-awareness of the one individual mind all necessarily belong to the same family of durations. There is not the slightest reason to believe that this is so. Indeed if my theory of nature be correct, it will not be the case.

The materialistic theory has all the completeness of the thought of the Middle Ages, which had a complete answer to everything, be it in heaven or in hell or in nature. There is a trimness about it, with its instantaneous present, its vanished past, its nonexistent future, and its inert matter. This trimness is very medieval and ill accords with brute fact.

The theory which I am urging admits a greater ultimate mystery and a deeper ignorance. The past and future meet and mingle in the ill-defined present. The passage of nature which is only another name for the creative force of existence has no narrow ledge of definite instantaneous present within which to operate. Its operative presence which is now urging nature forward must be sought for throughout the whole, in the remotest past as well as in the narrowest breadth of any present duration. Perhaps also in the unrealized future. Perhaps also in the future which might be as well as the actual future which will be. It is impossible to meditate on time and the mystery of the creative passage of nature without an overwhelming emotion at the limitations of human intelligence. (41)

This brilliant passage speaks for itself; hence we shall only briefly reiterate certain key concepts as they have particular relevance for our inquiries into the nature of mind, specifically with reference to the notion of time. First it should again be stressed that process or the incessant change of things, whether their perceptual effects come to us from internal or external environments, is a primordial fact of direct concrete experience. Some implications of this fact were explored in our discussions on symbolically characterizing individual experiential phenomena and the problems due to the vast multidimensionality of even a moment of experience.

But the most important aspect, for present purposes, of Whitehead's criticism of the materialistic concept of time is the error of, first, contemplating phenomenal reality as occurring within space and time, instead of understanding the notions of space and time as intellectually abstracted, derivative concepts formulated from having reflectively pondered concrete experience. Here is an admirable illustration of misplaced concreteness. Next, following from the preceding untenable materialistic presupposition, and specifically in regard to the above quotation, it can be seen that if one maintains the within-space-and-time view, it is a mere elementary, mathematically predisposed inference to assume that the one-dimensional time series intrinsic to the materialistic theory can be subdivided into an infinite number of mathematical points along the temporal continuum. This is to say that it is possible to logically conceive of an infinite number of cross-sectional slices of space extending along a temporal continuum, each representing an instantaneous, durationless moment of time at which the entire universe at an instant can in principle be mathematically defined in terms of ultimate particles and their mutual properties and relations. A major portion of Whitehead's criticism of traditional concepts of time is devoted precisely to this erroneous notion of instantaneous durations of time regarded as an ultimate fact of nature for it is clear that no such perceptual phenomenal occurrence is to be found in human experience. Rather, this concept is an idealized, abstract postulation that has uncritically been incorporated into scientific and philosophical systems. Curiously enough, the same criticism pertains to the Skinnerian notion of reflex arc. However, the criticism does not refer to instantized time spans but rather, to a different though related consideration. From the unwarranted concept of instantized time it would be necessary, if we were to validate this view in factual experience, to concretely experience an instantaneous event. But there is no such experiential occasion, although adherence to this erroneous view has predisposed many thinkers to devote insufficient attention to concrete experiential deliverance and, hence, the concrete evidential bases upon which factual and theoretical assertions must ultimately be predicated. Such assertions issuing from any empirical scientific inquiry must ultimately be evidentially verified through some direct perceptual mode. We need only recall the often tedious demand of strict positivists, to present the supporting data, to understand the importance of this epistemological requirement if knowledge claims are to be placed upon firm foundations. Thus the data to which Whitehead repeatedly refers are those of direct concrete experience, or stubborn facts. Since direct concrete experience yields no data testifying to the occurrence of instantaneous moments of time, what information about time is revealed in direct experience when the problem is reflectively analyzed? Our perceptions of any given occasion, in the most primitive sense, inform us concomitantly of permanence amidst change. This awareness does not require any epistemological deliberation when considering this low intuitive level of understanding. Therefore, if change is perceived amid permanence, in the manner, for example, that a perceived chair seems to temporally endure as a natural object within a backdrop of changing sounds or bodily states, the notion of succession arises. Conversely, at its highest levels of intellectually abstract formulation, the concept of succession may be that defined in various formal sciences, and far more profound than the concrete experiential recognition of time. At unsophisticated levels we merely understand that it takes time to construct a house, it takes time to read a book, it "takes time" to think a thought. It directly contradicts the concrete facts of individual human experience, in which conscious lives are lived and theories are verified, to formulate a concept of instantized time as a basic fact of nature, for the notion is entirely incompatible with the concept of individual experience. Individual human experience does not occur in instantaneous moments; rather it evolves as atomic entities throughout time spans. To conceptualize any portion of a human event as theoretically instantaneous is to sacrifice the factual character of the subjective psychological meaning intrinsic to mental events, for actualizing subjective psychological meaning requires concrete time. The assertion "I see the brown tree" requires time to subjectively understand and hence articulate. It is precisely this stubborn fact which demands that a mind be conceived as standing over against percepta, or more specifically, that percepta concomitantly come constructively to bear upon other percepta. If consciousness is not presupposed *a priori* in understanding any perceived phenomena, then the basic notion of understanding becomes meaningless. It is for this reason that it has been said that all events in principle available to human comprehension must necessarily be mental events. Similarly with respect to behaviorism, although it is obviously understood that time must elapse between a stimulus and a response, it becomes wholly untenable to regard a reflex arc as an entirely satisfactory construct for adequately explaining the intervening processes. It has been seen that mind, even minimally defined as awareness or consciousness and reflective consciousness, must necessarily be presupposed *a priori* in order to intel-

ligibly consider any matter of concern at all. This amounts to saying
with respect to behaviorism, that inner ideational states cannot be regarded as causally inefficacious or epiphenomenalistic, for behaviorism
must logically presuppose *a priori* the inner states whose reference it
must necessarily purge from its inquiries in order to be consistent with
its methodological pronouncements!

Our critical remarks on the concept of time can be summarized as
follows:

The thought "I see the brown tree," for example, requires time to
be meaningfully actualized, for subjective psychological events have a
necessary intrinsic perceptual atomicity which can only be realized in
temporal durations. The direct testimony of concrete experience necessitates that this view be held, for all thought or subjective psychologically meaningful experience necessarily occurs in atomic units. This
is merely to accentuate the obvious fact that we have such thoughts as
"I see the brown tree," and not "I see," "the brown," "see the," "brown
tree," etc. Moreover, even a single word possessing a unified meaning
for persons thinking or expressing it, and thereby qualifying as an
event, requires time for its actualization—brief as the duration may be.
But certainly there is no such event in direct human experience as an
instantaneous event; hence such a notion is an abstract innovation of
reflective consciousness. The notion of instantaneousness can be of great
value to the formal sciences, but must not be predicated from a materialistic viewpoint for it presupposes the erroneous within-space-and-
time implication. In the behavioral sciences materialism is the basis
for an unwarranted scientific reductionism when conscious processes
are considered logically identical with correlative physio-chemical process; epiphenomenalism is a typical erroneous consequent.

In the case of behavioristic theories, proponents obviously maintain
that time is required to establish stimulus-response bonds. The error
here, however, is that behaviorists deny the causal efficacity of inner
mental states, hence regarding them as epiphenomena. As it has been
said, absurd conclusions are reached in maintaining that all human
thinking is entirely reflexive to the extent of omitting the causal efficacy of consciousness for it is contradictory to conceive of human behavior without presupposing, *a priori*, consciousness and consciously
reflective behavior, phenomena that are not directly accessible to behaviorists, while on the other hand, phenomena which cannot be consistently regarded as causally inefficacious. Therefore, the conclusion
to be drawn is that behaviorisms cannot provide, in principle, a complete account of human behavior because of methodological narrowness.
This is to say that personal reports testifying to inner mental and bodily

states cannot be admitted as factual evidence. But contrary to this, it has been shown previously how such personal testimonies can acquire factual status if ascertained under appropriately controlled experimental conditions, and interpreted within a suitable theoretical framework.

Therefore, to remain consistent with the concrete facts of individual perceptual experience—that domain in which all epistemological certitude is ultimately grounded—it must be conceded that the ultimate basis for all intelligent thinking is in particular ideational events atomically evolving within temporal durations; durations in which components of subjective psychological experience develop into complete conscious thoughts.

What is immediate for sense awareness is a duration. Now a duration has within itself a past and a future; and the temporal breadths of the immediate durations of sense awareness are very indeterminate and dependent on the individual percipient. Accordingly there is no unique factor in nature [or subjective psychological experience, for that matter] which for every percipient is preeminently and necessarily the present. The passage of nature leaves nothing between the past and the future. What we do perceive as present is the vivid fringe of memory tinged with anticipation. This vividness lights up the discriminated field within a duration. But no assurance can thereby be assorted into other durations of alternative families. We cannot even know that the series of immediate durations posited by the sense-awareness of one individual mind all necessarily belong to the same family of durations. There is not the slightest reason to believe that this is so.(41)

It is from these ontologically unique subjective psychological occasions that a novel kind of causality is born unto the universe, for unconscious materialistic mechanism has been transcended. Intelligent conscious thinking does not causally result from the same comparatively simplistic basis as in the case of a thermostat operating as a function of temperature variation or an organic function that must occur as it does because of certain glandular secretions. Rather, the essence of conscious causality is in the phenomenon of denotative symbolic meaning and its profound concomitant, meaning-as-directly-felt-relatedness, occurring in their interpenetrative relationship with one another and hence providing an ontologically unique frame of reference from which modes of behavioral response may be influenced. In saying this, we still remain strictly within the realm of cause-effect functional relations, but relations as contemplated by a broader factual basis. A subjective psychology can systematically analyze a distinct experiential category of potentially causally efficacious factual phenomena that may influence human behavior, over and above those phenomena capable of determinate investigation by an objective psychology. Both methodological systems working in close conjunction with one another can, in principle, provide a complete account of human behavior.

Finally the basic problem with the notion of instantaneous temporal duration is that it is simply not reconcilable with the intrinsic nature of direct, concrete experiential events manifesting an inextricably unified atomicity absolutely essential to subjective psychologically meaningful thinking of any kind. Thus, to formally represent an instantaneously enduring spatial crosssection of a subjective psychological event, apart-from the technical impossibility of such a task, is to destroy an essential feature of mental events, namely, that in concrete experience time is required to think complete thoughts. The acknowledgment of this point is significant primarily for epistemological reasons, particularly with respect to the issue of verification. But the concept of time as necessarily grounded in experiential events will also have great importance for developing future constructs.

Since it takes time to formulate complete subjective psychologically meaningful thoughts, a more careful scrutiny of particular mental events will reveal that beyond their primordial character as process amid permanence there are developmental stages intrinsic to the emergent character of particular events. In effect, this is the wisdom of the relevant past constructively uniting synthetically with the present occasion, and preparing the way for future cognitive advance.

The past and the future meet and mingle in the ill-defined present. The passage of nature which is only another name for the creative force of existence has no narrow ledge of definite instantaneous present within which to operate. Its operative presence which is now urging nature forward must be sought for throughout the whole, in the remotest past as well as in the narrowest breadth of any present duration. Perhaps also in the unrealized future. Perhaps also in the future which might be as well as the actual future which will be.(41)

Thus mental events, considered in themselves, have stages of development capable of being reflectively and experimentally understood to some extent but are not subject to direct understanding, for an entire event is the minimal unit for our direct comprehension. An interval during the development of an event will be termed a "stage."

From this it can be readily understood that a spatio-temporal framework allowing for only instantaneous specification, which is a three-dimensional spatio-temporal system, must necessarily be inadequate for characterizing subjective psychological experience for it cannot comprehend the intrinsic durational quality of mental events. A spatio-temporal framework is needed which can, in principle, include all possible event-components as they are uniquely actualized throughout developing stages of particular events. To meet this requirement a four-dimensional spatio-temporal framework is needed. Again, our explorations of this mode for comprehending relations among entities will be repetitious of certain elementary principles already explored in depth by Whitehead.

In order to effectively introduce the concept of a four-dimensional spatio-temporal framework and properly emphasize the capacity of this geometrical device to attribute appropriate particularity to all possible event-components as they occur in concrete experience, it will be necessary to quote Whitehead at length. It is through his own words that the intrinsic wisdom of such a scheme becomes evident. The following quotations, although written in the first quarter of this century, still have great relevance for contemporary thinking, particularly for those working in the behavioral sciences, for in these areas the outmoded theories of materialistic-mechanism still remain powerfully efficacious in influencing the thinking of many researchers and theorists. Although only a small portion of the following quotations deals specifically with an explication of the geometrical properties of space and time per se, highly important introductory information is expressed and a basic rationale presupposed by a four-dimensional geometry is presented.

Here Whitehead concisely presents a brilliant analysis of issues of fundamental concern to scientific inquiry of any kind:

1. TRADITIONAL SCIENTIFIC CONCEPTS. 1.1 What is a physical explanation? The answer to this question, even when merely implicit in the scientific imagination, must profoundly affect the development of any science, and in an especial degree that of speculative physics. During the modern period the orthodox answer has invariably been couched in terms of Time (flowing equably in measurable lapses) and of Space (timeless, void of activity, Euclidean), and of Material in space (such as matter, ether, or electricity).

The governing principle underlying this scheme is that extension, namely extension in time or extension in space, expresses disconnection. This principle issues in the assumptions that the casual action between entities separated in time or space is impossible and that extension in space or unity of being are inconsistent. Thus the extended material (on this view) is essentially a multiplicity of entities which, as extended, are diverse and disconnected. This governing principle has to be limited in respect to extension in time. The same material exists at different times. This concession introduces the many perplexities centering round the notion of change which is derived from the comparison of various states of self-identical material at different times.

1.2. The ultimate fact embracing all nature is (in this traditional point of view) a distribution of material throughout all space at a durationless instant of time, and another such ultimate fact will be another distribution of the same material throughout the same space at another durationless instant of time. The difficulties of this extreme statement are evident and were pointed out even in classical times when the concept first took shape. Some modification is evidently necessary. No room has been left for velocity, acceleration, momentum, and kinetic energy, which certainly are essential physical quantities.

We must therefore in the ultimate fact, beyond which science ceases to analyze, include the notion of a state of change. But a state of change at a durationless instant is a very difficult conception. It is impossible to define velocity without some reference to the past and the future. Thus change is essentially the importation of the past and of the future into the immediate fact embodied in the durationless present instant.

This conclusion is destructive of the fundamental assumption that the ultimate facts of science are to be found at durationless instants of time.

1.3. The reciprocal causal action between materials A and B is the fact that their states of change are partly dependent on their relative locations and natures. The disconnection involved in spatial separation leads to reduction of such causal action and to the transmission of stress across the bounding surface of contiguous materials. But what is contact? No two points are in contact. Thus the stress across a surface necessarily acts on some bulk of the material enclosed inside. To say that stress acts on the immediately contiguous material is to assert infinitely small volumes. But there are no such things, only smaller and smaller volumes. Yet (with this point of view) it cannot be meant that the surface acts on the interior.

Certainly stress has some claim to be regarded as an essential physical quantity as have momentum and kinetic energy. But no intelligible account of its meaning is to be extracted from the concept of the continuous distribution of diverse (because extended) entities through space as an ultimate scientific fact. At some stage in our account of stress we are driven to the concept of any extended quantity of material as a single unity whose nature is partly explicable in terms of its surface stress.

1.4. In biology the concept of an organism cannot be expressed in terms of material distribution at an instant. The essence of an organism is that it is one thing which functions and is spread through space. Now functioning takes time. Thus a biological organism is a unity with a spatio-temporal extension which is the essence of its being. This biological conception is obviously incompatible with the traditional ideas. This argument does not in any way depend on the assumption that biological phenomena belong to a different category to other physical phenomena. The essential point of the criticism on traditional concepts which has occupied us so far is that the concept of unities, functioning and with spatio-temporal extensions, cannot be extruded from physical concepts. The only reason for the introduction of biology is that in these sciences the same necessity becomes more clear.

1.5. The fundamental assumption to be elaborated in the course of this inquiry is that the ultimate facts of nature, in terms of which all physical and biological explanation must be expressed, are events connected by their spatio-temporal relations, and that these relations are in the main reducible to the property of events that they can contain (or extend over) other events which are parts of them. In other words, in place of emphasizing space and time in their capacity of disconnecting, we shall build up an account of their complex essences as derivative from the ultimate ways. in which those things, ultimate in a science, are interconnected. In this way the data of science, those concepts in terms of which all scientific explanation must be expressed, will be clearly apprehended. But before proceeding to our constructive task, some further realization of the perplexities introduced by the traditional concepts is necessary.

2. PHILOSOPHIC RELATIVITY. 2.1. The philosophical principle of the relativity of space means that the properties of space are merely a way of expressing relations between things ordinarily said to be "in space." Namely, when two things are said to be "both in space" what is meant is that they are mutually related in a certain definite way which is termed "spatial." It is an immediate consequence of this theory that all spatial entities such as points, straight lines and planes are merely complexes of relations between things or of possible relations between things.

For example, consider the meaning of saying that a particle P is at a point Q. This statement conveys substantial information and must therefore convey something more than the barren assertion of self-identity "P is P." Thus what must be meant is that P has certain relations to other particles P′, P″, etc., and that the abstract possibility of this group of relations is what is meant by the point Q.

The extremely valuable work on the foundations of geometry produced during the nineteenth century has proceeded from the assumption of points as ultimate given entities. This assumption, for the logical purpose of mathematicians, is entirely justified. Namely the mathematicians ask, What is the logical description of relations between points from which all geometrical theorems respecting such relations can be deduced? The answer to this question is now practically complete; and if the old theory of absolute space be true, there is nothing more to be said. For points are ultimate simple existents, with mutual relations disclosed by our perceptions of nature.

But if we adopt the principle of relativity, these investigations do not solve the question of the foundations of geometry. An investigation into the foundations of geometry has to explain space as a complex of relations between things. It has to describe what a point is, and has to show how the geometric relations between points issue from the ultimate relations between ultimate things which are the immediate objects of knowledge. Thus the starting point of a discussion on the foundations of geometry is a discussion of the character of the immediate data of perception. It is not now open to mathematicians to assume *sub silentio* that points are among these data.

2.2. The traditional concepts were evidently formed round the concept of absolute space, namely the concept of the persistent ultimate material distributed among the persistent ultimate points in successive configurations at successive ultimate instants of time. Here "ultimate" means "not analysable into a complex of simpler entities." The introduction of the principle of relatively adds to the complexity—or rather, to the perplexity—of this conception of nature. The statement of general character of ultimate fact must now be amended into "persistent ultimate material with successive mutual ultimate relation at successive ultimate instants of time."

Space issues from these mutual relations of matter at an instant. The first criticism to be made on such an assertion is that it is shown to be a metaphysical fairy tale by any comparison with our actual perceptual knowledge of nature. Our knowledge of space is based upon observations which take time and have to be successive, but the relations which constitute space are instantaneous. The theory demands that there should be an instantaneous space corresponding to each instant, and provides for no correlations between these spaces; while nature has provided us with no apparatus for observing them.

2.3. It is an obvious suggestion that we should amend our statement of ultimate fact, as modified by the acceptance of relativity. The spatial relations must now stretch across time. Thus if P, P′, P″, etc. be material particles, there are definite spatial relations connecting P, P′, P″, etc. at time t_1 with P, P′, P″, etc. at t_2, as well as such relations between P and P′ and P″, etc. at time t_1 and such relations between P and P′ and P″, etc. at time t_2. This should mean P at time t_2 has a definite position in the spatial configuration constituted by the relations between P, P′, P″, etc. at t_1. For example, the sun at a certain instant on Jan. 1st, 1900 had a definite position in the instantaneous space constituted by the mutual relations between the sun and the other stars at a definite instant on Jan. 1st, 1800. Such a statement is only understandable (assuming the traditional concept) by recurring to absolute space and thus abandoning relativity; for otherwise it denies the completeness of the instantaneous fact which is the essence of the concept. Another way out of the difficulty is to deny that space is constituted by the relations of P, P′, P″, etc., at an instant, and to assert that it results from their relations throughout a duration of time, which as thus prolonged in time are observable.

As a matter of fact it is obvious that our knowledge of space does result from such observations. But we are asking the theory to provide us with actual relations to be observed. This last emendation is either only a muddled way of admitting that "nature at an instant" is not the ultimate scientific fact, or else it is a yet more muddled plea that, although there is no possibility of correlations between instantaneous spaces, yet within durations which are short enough such nonexistent correlations enter into experience.

2.4. The persistence of the material lacks any observational guarantee when the relativity of space is admitted into the traditional concept. For at one instant there is instantaneous material in its instantaneous space as constituted by its instantaneous relations, and at another instant there is instantaneous material in its instantaneous space. How do we know that the two cargoes of material which load the two instants are identical? The answer is that we do not perceive isolated instantaneous facts, but a continuity of existence, and that it is this observed continuity of existence which guarantees the persistence of material. Exactly so; but this gives way the whole traditional concept. For a "continuity of existence" must mean an unbroken duration of existence. Accordingly it is admitted that the ultimate fact for observational knowledge is perception through a duration; namely, that the content of a specious present, and not that of a durationless instant, is an ultimate datum for science.

2.5. It is evident that the conception of the instant of time as an ultimate entity is the source of all our difficulties of explanation. If there are such ultimate entities, instantaneous nature is an ultimate fact.

Our perception of time is as a duration, and these instants have only been introduced by reason of a supposed necessity of thought. In fact absolute time is just as much a metaphysical monstrosity as absolute space. The way out of the perplexities, as to the ultimate data of science in terms of which physical explanation is ultimately to be expressed, is to express the essential scientific concepts of time, space and material as issuing from fundamental relations between events and from recognitions of the characters of events. These relations of events are those immediate deliverances of observation which are referred to when we say that events are spread through time and space.

"Significance" is the relatedness of things. To say that significance is experience, is to affirm that perceptual knowledge is nothing else than an apprehension of the relatedness of things, namely of things in their relations and as related. Certainly if we commence with a knowledge of things, and then look around for their relations we shall not find them. "Causal connection" is merely one typical instance of the universal ruin of relatedness. But then we are quite mistaken in thinking that there is a possible knowledge of things as unrelated. It is thus out of the question to start with a knowledge of things antecedent to a knowledge of their relations. The so-called properties of things can always be expressed as their relatedness to other things unspecified, and natural knowledge is exclusively concerned with relatedness.

3.6. The relatedness which is the subject of a natural knowledge cannot be understood without reference to the general characteristics of perception. Our perception of natural events and natural objects is a perception from within nature, and is not an awareness contemplating all nature impartially from without. When Dr. Johnson "surveyed mankind from China to Peru," he did it from Pump Court in London at a certain date. Even Pump Court was too wide for his peculiar *locus standi;* he was really merely conscious of the relations of his bodily events to the simultaneous events throughout the rest of the universe. Thus perception involves a percipient object, a percipient event, the complete event which is all nature simultaneous with the percipient event, and the particular events which are perceived as parts of the complete event. . . . The point here to be emphasized is that natural knowledge is a knowledge from within nature, a knowledge "here within nature" and "now within nature," and is an awareness of the natural relations of one element in nature (namely, the percipient event) to the rest of nature. Also what is known is not barely the things but the relations of things, and not the relations in the abstract but specifically those things as related.

Thus Alciphron's vision of the planet is his perception of his relatedness (i.e., the relatedness of his percipient event) to some other elements of nature which as thus recalled he calls the planet. He admits . . . that certain other specified relations of those elements are possible for other percipient events. In this way he might be right or wrong. What he directly knows is his relation to some other elements of the universe—namely, I, Alciphron, am located in my percipient event "here and now" and the immediately perceived appearance of the planet is for me a characteristic of another event "there and now." In fact perceptual knowledge is always a knowledge of the relationship of the percipient event to something else in nature. This doctrine is in entire agreement with Dr. Johnson's stamp of the foot by which he realised the otherness of the paving-stone.

3.7. The conception of knowledge as passive contemplation is too inadequate to meet the facts. Nature is ever originating its own development, and the sense of action is the direct knowledge of the percipient event as having its very being in the formation of its natural relations. Knowledge issues from this reciprocal insistence between this event and the rest of nature, namely relations are perceived in the making and because of the making. For this reason perception is always at the utmost point of creation. We cannot put ourselves back to the Crusades and know their events while they were happening. We essentially perceive our relations with nature because they are in the making. The sense of action is that essential factor in natural knowledge which exhibits it as a self-knowledge enjoyed by an element of nature respecting its active relations with the whole of nature in its various aspects. Natural knowledge is merely the other side of action. The forward moving time exhibits this characteristic of experience, that it is essentially action. Thus passage of nature—or, in other words, its creative advance—is its fundamental characteristic; the traditional concept is an attempt to catch nature without its passage. (40)

In these quotations Whitehead critically analyzes the logical implications of certain fundamental presuppositional concepts used predominately in traditional Newtonian science. He shows that the spatio-temporal disconnective proclivity of mechanistic-materialism leads to very serious logical and pragmatic difficulties. Hence, to resolve some of these theoretical and methodological problems intrinsic to traditional materialism, Whitehead maintains that a more appropriate theoretical framework for science, one demonstrating considerably greater concordance with the facts ascertained in concrete experience, is that the perceived facts of nature must be considered as events connected by spatio-temporal relations and that these relations are directly derived from the factual properties of events. ". . . in the place of emphasizing space and time in their capacity of disconnecting, we shall build up an account of their complex essences as derivatives from the ultimate ways in which those things, ultimate in science, are interconnected."

These lengthy quotations have emphasized three very important considerations for us. First, they have provided a concise, but penetrating, account of fundamental conceptual shifts in contemplating certain primitive or axiomatic presuppositions of science in the twentieth century. Second, and this point is a consequent of the first, we have seen that the relativity conception of space-time is importantly more in accordance with the directly perceived facts in our individual concrete experience than in the materialistic view of the universe. Third, the quotations have served as a useful recapitulation of many of the concepts we have been developing, in addition to providing a brief and highly appropriate introduction to the relativity notion of space-time.

Now let us embark upon a more rigorous investigation of space-time and its relevant peripheral issues as they will have direct significance for a subjective psychology. We shall utilize Whitehead's own words for this explanation and in this way be assured of maximal conceptual and definitional clarity.

The following quotations suggest in a general way how what we have defined as event-components may be spatio-temporally related in each mental event. The definition of event as used here is conceptualized somewhat differently from that of Whitehead; our notion includes, in addition, those percepta standing over against the contributed percepta, as they are all directly perceived in determinate configurations. The contributed percepta, considered alone, are equivalent to what Whitehead will term the "prehensive unity" of perception, as distinct from what he defines as prehensive unity of a volume:

For simplicity of thought, I will first speak of space only, and will afterwards extend the same treatment to time.

The volume is the most concrete element of space. But the separative character of space analyzes a volume into sub-volumes, and so on indefinitely. Accordingly, taking the separative character in isolation, we should infer that a volume is a mere multiplicity of non-voluminous elements, of points in fact. But it is the unity of the volume which is the ultimate fact of experience, for example, the voluminous space of this hall. This hall as a mere multiplicity of points is a construction of the logical imagination.

Accordingly, the prime fact is the prehensive unity of volume, and this unity is mitigated or limited by the separated unities of the innumerable contained parts. We have a prehensive unity, which is yet held apart as an aggregate of contained parts. But the prehensive unity of the volume is not the unity of a mere logical aggregate of parts. The parts form an ordered aggregate, in the sense that each part is something from the standpoint of every other part, and also from the same standpoint every other part is something in relation to it. Thus if A and B and C are volumes of space, B has an aspect from the standpoint of A, and so has C, and so has the relationship of B and C. This aspect of B from A is of the essence of A. The volumes of space have no independent existence. They are only entities as within the totality; you cannot extract them from their environment without destruction of their very essence. Accordingly, I will say that the aspect of B from A is the mode in which B enters into the composition of A. This is the modal character of space, that the prehensive unity of A is the prehension into unity of the aspects of all other volumes from the standpoint of A. The shape of the volume is the formula from which the totality of its aspects can be derived. Thus the shape of a volume is more abstract than its aspects. It is evident that I can use Leibniz's language, and say that every volume mirrors in itself every other volume in space.

Exactly analogous considerations hold with respect to durations in time. An instant of time, without duration, is an imaginative logical construction. Also each duration of time mirrors in itself all temporal durations.

But in two ways I have introduced a false simplicity. In the first place, I should have conjoined space and time, and conducted my explanation in respect to four-dimensional regions of space-time. I have nothing to add in the way of explanation. In your minds, substitute such four-dimensional regions for the spatial volumes of the previous explanations.

Secondly, my explanation has involved itself in a vicious circle. For I have made the prehensive unity of the region A to consist of the prehensive unification of the modal presences in A of other regions. This difficulty arises because space-time cannot in reality be considered as a self-subsistent entity. It is an abstraction, and its explanation requires reference to that from which it has been extracted. Space-time is the specification of certain general characters of events and of their mutual ordering. (43)

It should be noted that in the second anticipated criticism Whitehead is saying that a distinction must be drawn between the prehensive unification located in the (percipient, for example) region A, consisting of a specific configuration of modal presences actualized in A at a given time, and those frames of reference, namely stimulus-objects or termini of sense awareness, from which the modal presences originate. Stated more simply, in order to avoid the solipsistic view of subjective idealism, Whitehead must prove that the natural world, apart from mind's perceptions, has spatio-temporal extensiveness. He must show that there is an external world whose entities can be comprehended in a relativity spatio-temporal framework. Although the following quotation does not embody a rigorous proof of the existence of the external world—a type which can be found in almost any of Whitehead's works— it is suitable for our present purpose in that it provides the reader with a more intuitively simple illustration of his spatio-temporal scheme.

An entity of which we become aware in sense perception is the terminus of our act of perception. I will call such an entity, a sense-object. For example, green of a definite shade is a sense-object; so is a sound of a definite generality and pitch; and so is a definite scent; and a definite quality of touch. The way in which such an entity is related to space during a definite lapse of time is complex. I will say that a sense-object has ingression into space-time. The cognitive perception of a sense object is the awareness of prehensive unification (into standpoint A) of various modes of various sense-objects, including the sense-object in question. The standpoint of A is, of course, a region of space-time; that is to say, it is a volume of space through a duration of time. But as one entity, this standpoint is a unit of realised experience. A mode of a sense-object at A (as abstracted from the sense-object whose relationship to A the mode is conditioning) is an aspect from A of some other region B. Thus the sense-object is present in A with the mode of location in B. Thus if green be the sense-object in question, green is not simply at A where it is being perceived, nor is it simply at B where it is perceived as located; but it is present at A with the mode of location in B. There is no particular mystery about this. You have only got to look in a mirror and to see the image in it of some green leaves behind your back. For you at A there will be green; but not green simply at A where you are. The green at A will be green with the mode of having location at the image of the leaf behind the mirror. Then turn round and look at the leaf. You are now perceiving the green in the same way as you did before, except that now the green has the mode of being located in the actual leaf. I am merely describing what we do perceive: we are aware of green as being one element in a prehensive unification of sense-objects; each sense-object, and among them green, having its particular mode, which is expressible as location elsewhere. There are various types of modal location. For example, sound is voluminous: it fills a hall, and so sometimes does diffused colour. But the modal location of a colour may be that of being the remote boundary of a volume, as for example is the locus of the modal ingression of sense-objects. This is the reason why space and time (if for simplicity we disjoin them) are given in their entireties. For each volume of space, or each lapse of time, includes in its essence aspects of all volumes of space, or of all lapses of time. The difficulties of philosophy in respect to space and time are founded on the error of considering them as primarily the loci of simple locations. Perception is simply the cognition of prehensive unification; or more shortly, perception is cognition of prehension. The actual world is a manifold of prehensions; and a "prehension" is a "prehensive occasion"; and a prehensive occasion is the most concrete finite entity, conceived as what it is in itself and for itself and not as from its aspect in the essence of another such occasion. Prehensive unification might be said to have simple location in its volume A. But this would be a mere tautology. For space and time are simply abstractions from the totality of prehensive unification as mutually patterned in each other. Thus a prehension has simple location at the volume A in the same way as that in which a man's face fits on to the smile that spreads over it. There is, so far as we have gone, more sense in saying that an act of perception has simple location; for it may be conceived as being simply the cognised prehension.

There are more entities involved in nature than the mere sense-objects, so far considered. But allowing for the necessity of revision consequent on a more complete point of view, we can frame our answer to Berkeley's question as to the character of reality to be assigned to nature. He states it to be the reality of ideas in the mind. A complete metaphysic which has attained to some notion of mind, and to some notion of ideas, may perhaps ultimately adopt that view. It is unnecessary for the purposes of these lectures to ask such a fundamental question. We can be content with a provisional realism in which nature is conceived as a complex of prehensive unifications. Space and time exhibit the general scheme of interlocked relations of these prehensions. You cannot tear any of them out of its context. Yet each one of them within its context has all the reality that attaches to the whole complex. Conversely, the totality has the reality as each prehension; for each prehension unifies the modalities to be ascribed, from its standpoint, to every part of the whole. Apprehension is a process of unifying. Accordingly, nature is a process of expansive development, necessarily transitional from prehension to prehension. What is achieved is thereby passed beyond, but it is also retained as having aspects of itself present to prehensions which lie beyond it.

Thus nature is a structure of evolving processes. The reality is the process. It is nonsense to ask if the colour red is real. The colour red is ingredient in the process of realisation. The realities of nature are the prehensions in nature, that is to say, the events in nature. (43)

Little need be said about the lucidity and profundity of this quotation except, perhaps, that the highly intimate relationship between what Whitehead has said in the above quotations and the various lines of argumentation we have explored throughout this discourse, although beginning from different points of departure and with somewhat different purposes in view, should be obvious to the reader.

Next, building upon the foundational concepts already introduced with regard to space-time and its relationship to human experience, let us briefly consider two additional abstract conceptualizations of this problem as they are formally developed by Whitehead. The purpose of this somewhat more advanced investigation is to suggest to those readers predisposed to formal scientific inquiry that the general theory of subjective psychological behavior here being developed is readily amenable to rigorous formulation.

First let us contemplate one way in which Whitehead geometrically schematizes the four-dimensional structure of events (see Figure 5). Here emphasis will be placed upon what we have termed mental event which closely approximates Whitehead's notion of thinking heterogeneously about nature: ". . . we are thinking heterogeneously about na-

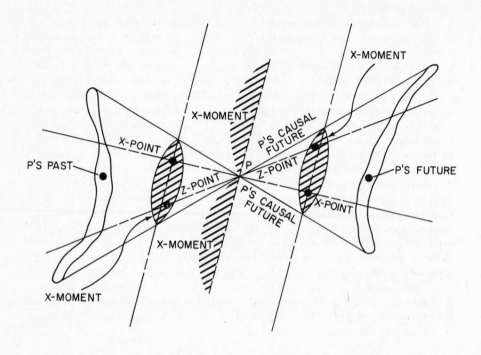

Figure 5. Whitehead's concept of formal four-dimensional
spatio-temporal restriction [42]

ture when we are thinking about it in conjunction with thinking either about thought or about sense-awareness or about both."(41)

(i) THE STRUCTURE OF THE CONTINUUM OF EVENTS. This structure is four-dimensional, so that any event is a four-dimensional hyper-volume in which time is the fourth dimension. But we should not conceive an event as space and time, but as a unit from which space and time are abstracts.

An event with all its dimensions ideally restricted is called an "event particle," and an event with only one dimension of finite extension is called a "route" or "path." I will not in this lecture discuss the meaning of this ideal restriction. I have investigated it elsewhere under the name of "extensive abstraction."

The structure is uniform because of the necessity for knowledge that there be a system of uniform relatedness, in terms of which the contingent relations of natural factors can be expressed. Otherwise we can know nothing until we know everything. If P be any event-particle, a moment through P is a system of event-particles representing all nature instantaneously contemporaneous with P. According to the classical view of time there can be only one such moment. According to the modern view there can be an indefinite number of alternative moments through P, each corresponding to a different meaning for time and space. A moment is an instantaneous three-dimensional section of nature and is the entity indicated when we speak of a moment of time.

The aggregate of event-particles lying on moments through P will be called the region co-present with P. The remainder of the four-dimensional continuum is divided by the co-present into two regions, one being P's past and the other being P's future. The three-dimensional boundary between P's past and P's co-present region is P's causal past, and the corresponding boundary between P's future and P's co-present region is P's causal future. The remaining portion of P's future is P's kinematic future.

A route lying entirely in one moment is called a spatial route, and a route which lies entirely in the past and future of each one of its event-particles is called a historical route.

. . . We gain great simplicity of explanation, without loss of any essential considerations by confining our consideration of events to routes. These routes are of course not true events, but merely ideal limits with only one dimensional extension remaining. (42)

Although this quotation provides an inadequate exposition of the highly systematic, formalized meaning implicit within the bare geometric construction presented above, a task that is largely executed in the third through fifth chapters of Whitehead's *Concept of Nature*, it at least presents sufficient elaboration, if contemplated in conjunction with the previous excerpts from his writings on space and time, to suggest the great possibilities for expressing relations delivered initially in concrete experience in mathematical, statistical, and geometrical form.

This last quotation concisely demonstrates how spatio-temporal abstract relations can be formally expressed as direct derivatives from concrete experience. Here Whitehead takes concrete external bodily perceptual apprehensions such as the apparent three-dimensionality of our momentary spatial perceptions and proceeds to demonstrate how the appearance of depth can be geometrically formalized. From this mental concepts of measurement such as simultaneity, parallelity, per- type of exposition geometric proofs may be proposed for certain funda- pendicularity, etc. The important point, however, is that these proofs may be shown to proceed from our concrete experiential perceptions of natural world phenomena (see Figure 6).

When we are conscious of nature, what is it that we really observe? The obvious answer is that we perceive various material bodies, such as chairs, bricks, trees. We can touch them, see them, hear them. As I write I can hear the birds singing in a Berkshire garden in early spring.

In conformity with this answer, it is now fashionable and indeed almost universal to say that our notions of space merely arise from our endeavours to express the relations of these bodies to each other. I am sorry to appear pigheaded; but, though I am nearly in a minority of one, I believe this answer to be entirely wrong. I will explain my reasons.

Are these material bodies really the ultimate data of perception, incapable of further analysis?

If they are, I at once surrender. But I submit that plainly they have not this ultimate character. My allusions to birds singing was made not because I felt poetical, but to warn you that we were being led into a difficulty. What I immediately heard was the song. The birds only enter perception as a correlation of more ultimate immediate data of perception, among which for my consciousness their song is dominant.

Material bodies only enter my consciousness as a representation of a certain coherence of the sense-objects such as colors, sounds and touches. But these sense-objects at once proclaim themselves to be adjectives . . . of events. It is not the mere red that we see, but a red patch in a definite place enduring through a definite time. The red is an adjective of the red time and place. Thus nature appears to us as the continuous passage of instantaneous three-dimensional spatial spreads, the temporal passage adding a fourth dimension. Thus nature is stratified by time. In fact passage in time is of the essence of nature, and a body is merely the coherence of adjectives qualifying the same route through the four-dimensional space-time of events.

But as a result of modern observations we have to admit that there are an indefinite number of such modes of time stratification.

However, this admission at once yields an explanation of the meaning of the instantaneous spatial extension of nature. For it explains this extension as merely the exhibition of the different ways in which simultaneous occurrences function in regard to other time-systems.

I mean that occurrences which are simultaneous for one time-system appear as spread out in three dimensions because they function diversely for other time-systems. The extended space of one time-system is merely the expression of properties of other time-systems.

According to this doctrine, a moment of time is nothing else than an instantaneous spread of nature. Thus let t_1, t_2, t_3 be three moments of time according to one time-system, and let T_1, T_2, T_3 be three moments of time according to another time-system. The intersections of pairs of moments in diverse time-systems are planes in each instantaneous three-dimensional space. In the diagram each continuous line accordingly symbolises a three-dimensional space; and the intersections of continuous lines, such as A or B or C, symbolises planes. Thus t_1 and T_1 are each a three-dimensional space, and A is a plane in either space.

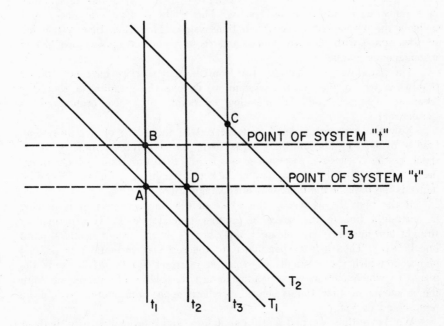

Figure 6. Whitehead's concept of interpenetrating spatio-temporal systems

Parallelism is the reflection into an instantaneous space of one time-system of the property of moments of some other system. Thus A and B are parallel planes in t_1, since T_1 and T_2 are moments of the same system which is not the system to which t_1 belongs.

But when we talk of space we are not usually thinking of the instantaneous fact of immediate perception. We are thinking of an enduring scheme of extension within which all these instantaneous facts are fitted. It follows that we ought to be able to find a meaning for the idea of a permanent space in connection with each time-system.

This conception must arise from our immediate observations of motion and rest. Both rest and motion have no meaning in connection with one mere instantaneous space. In such a space everything is where it is and there is an instantaneous end to it: to be succeeded by another instantaneous space. But motion and rest at once warn us that our perception involves something more.

The instantaneous moment is merely an ideal limit of perception. Have you ever endeavoured to capture the instantaneous present? It eludes you, because in truth there is no such entity among the crude facts of our experience. Our present experience is an enduring fact within which we discriminate a passage of nature. Now within this enduring fact we observe rest and motion. A body at rest in the space of our observation is tracing out a certain historical route intersecting the moments of our time-system in a sequence of instantaneous points. This route is what we mean by a point of the permanent space of our time-system. Thus each time-system has its own space with its own points, and these permanent points are loci of instantaneous points.

The paradoxes of relativity arise from the fact that we have not noticed that when we change our time-system we change the meaning of time, the meaning of space and the meaning of points of space (conceived as permanent).

Now the route of a small body at rest in the space of a time-system, that is to say, a point of that time-system, has a certain symmetry in respect to the successive instantaneous spaces of that system, which is expressed for us by the perception of lack of change of position. This symmetry is the basis of the definition of rectangularity.

If the body be at rest in the space of the time-system t, it is moving in a straight line in the space of another time-system T. This permanent straight line intersects any moment of T, say T_1, in an instantaneous straight line l_1 (say). Then l_1 is perpendicular to the series of instantaneous parallel planes in which the moments of system t intersect T_1. In other words the planes to which motion is perpendicular are the planes of intersection with the moments of that time-system for whose space and motion would be represented as rest.

We have thus defined both parallelism and perpendicularity without reference to congruence, but in terms of immediate data of perception. Furthermore, the parallelism of the moments of one time-system enables us to extend parallelism to time as also expressing the relation to each other of permanent points of the same time-system. It thus follows that we now possess a structure in terms of which congruence can be defined. This means that there will be a class of qualities L one and only one of which attaches to any stretch on a straight line or on a point, such that matching in respect to this quality is what we mean by congruence.(42)

This completes our sequence of quotations defining space-time, articulated in various works by Whitehead. Merely studying the relevant information on space-time presented in this discourse will not give the reader an exhaustive understanding of these quotations; that would require a meticulous and laborious examination of the original source materials. However, the reader can, through a reflective effort, gain from these quotations a substantial understanding of Whitehead's criticisms of traditional concepts of space and time, and the limitations and even distortions of concrete experiential facts that traditional materialistic-mechanistic theories impose upon our direct experience of the natural world and our inner bodily states. In fact, Whitehead's views provide an understanding of the importance and, moreover, the necessity of admitting the fourth dimension into our spatio-temporal characterization of mental events, regarded as theoretical units logically and empirically fundamental to a subjective psychology. This fact clearly reveals the primary reason for devoting prolonged attention to scrutinizing Whitehead's basic views on space and time. Also, in the most general sense, it can be said that Whitehead's discursive examinations of these concepts, regardless of the advanced nature of some of his speculative investigations, are essentially attempts to systematically show that all spatio-temporal conceptual formulations ultimately have their grounds in the perceptions of the individual's concrete experience.

The quotations examined with respect to space and time were primarily concerned with explaining the epistemological basis upon which the relations amongst natural entities may be validly established. But specifically for our purposes, we are also interested in exploring some fundamental considerations involved in ascertaining possible relations among directly accessible event-components that collectively constitute complete unified durations of subjective psychological experience. If we are to take Whitehead's general notion of an event, in the sense of thinking homogeneously about any given natural or bodily occurrence, which he defines as, "Wherever and whenever something is going on," then it must be conceded that such mental phenomena as ideas, for example, are events.(41) We have previously shown that ideas, now conceived in our bipolar conception of mind, have a substantial intrinsic nature defined as disciplined ideational feeling. Further, we have seen that all ideational states have a universal form characterized theoretically as the logical form of subjective psychological experience, and generally revealed as perceptual contributions from stimulus-objects concomitantly actualized with denotative and connotative symbolic meaning. Therefore, since individual thoughts, regardless of their intellectual content, occur as complete units of meaning, they can be conceived as particular events that embody a logical form. Since the actualization of subjective psychological events occurs throughout temporal durations, and because such events are comprised of event-components ascertained through exercising a reflective effort, it is possible to consciously locate and hence formally relate these components within a four-dimensional spatio-temporal scheme. In this way, mental events occurring within individuals can be spatio-temporally related to any other relevant components of reality whether located within or externally to the individual's bodily organism, and, in addition, analyzed according to their uniquely human developmental stages of origination. Let us now discuss some of the elementary considerations regarding this schematism.

In Figure 5, Whitehead suggests a model in which an event (now conceived as thinking homogeneously about nature) can be ideally restricted, for the purposes of formal and natural sciences, to a single mathematical point. The point abstractly conceived in this way can be contemplated in terms of its spatial and temporal routes, as these routes must be determined in conjunction with other relevant spatially and temporally separated entities. This idealized restriction does not, however, entail a distortion of the directly observable facts of nature as they have importance for the natural sciences because certain quantitative attributes of natural entities remain formally constant regardless of the extent to which restriction is effected. The arguments supporting this assertion are presented, as was mentioned, in the third through fifth chapters of Whitehead's *Concept of Nature*. But it must be kept in mind that his concern is primarily with demonstrating that the mathematical and statistical procedures for establishing certain relations among theoretical entities of the natural sciences are, in fact, capable of being derived from the perceptual deliverances of the natural world if we admit the relativity conception of space-time, a notion which is itself ultimately an abstract derivative from the intrinsic nature of concrete experience. However, our interest in four-dimensional space-time is primarily with the fact that it provides us with a theoretical framework in which the relevant relations manifested among all possible event-components constituting particular mental events can be ascertained as they evolve throughout temporal durations. Thus our center of interest is focused upon the intrinsic universal structure of mental events as atomic entities, in distinction to Whitehead's principal concern, which is in demonstrating the necessary relatedness among entities as a fact directly perceived in concrete experience. Therefore, instead of representing mental events as particular mathematical points as in Figure 5, we shall characterize them as a four-dimensional rectangular construction in which event-components can be related to one another in their modes of emergence throughout given temporal durations. The model can be simply illustrated as shown in Figure 7.

From the four-dimensional schematism, three-dimensional slices of theoretically conceived spatial routes can be abstracted in thought. It will be recalled that these spatial routes have instantaneous duration. Figure 8 portrays this concept.

Abstracted spatial routes may be used for specifying given reflectively ascertainable event-components constituting a moment in or-

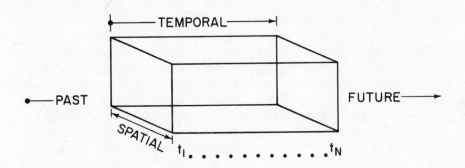

Figure 7. Four-dimensional subjective psychological events

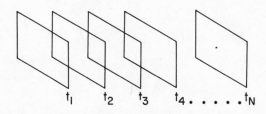

Figure 8. Theoretical restriction of subjective psychological events

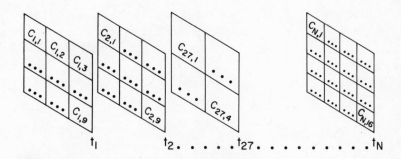

Figure 9. Theoretical specification of event-components

der to systematically study the relations among event-components within given events, and between mental events, as mental events occur in relation to stimulus-objects located in the natural world, or a percipient's bodily organism. Numerical equivalents of event-components occurring at given moments can be specified as shown in Figure 9.

It should be mentioned that, in principle, all possible event-components capable of spatio-temporal specification, apart from their unique mode of ingression, are elements depicted by the Categories. It is not difficult to see that from a simple four-dimensional spatio-temporal framework, considered in conjunction with such elaborate systems as Whitehead's geometrical and mathematical schemes, a great many variations from this basic model can be formulated in subjective psychological research.

We have now completed our systematic analysis of the concept of an event, and it has been shown that the four-dimensional schematism offers the greatest possibility for rigorously ascribing particularity to all conceivable concrete components of human experience.

Chapter eleven / Recapitulation of a developing concept of mind

The task to be undertaken in this chapter is initially to reconsider certain previously introduced constructs developed in order to systematically define mind, and then to submit them to moderate revision. In doing this we shall, in effect, be enhancing our understanding of originally formulated constructs through elucidating certain additionally important implications of the concrete experiential components that they represent. This constructive possibility arises from the fact that concrete experience is more extensively complex than the human intellect's ability to subject it to exhaustive exposition.

Heretofore we have been using a definition of mind simply defined as percepta concomitantly coming constructively to bear upon other percepta. From our previous discussion it is readily apparent that this deceptively elementary definition has an indeterminate number of ramifications. But apart from this, its great utility results from the fact that it demonstrates an important principle fundamental to our entire discussion on developing a concept of mind as it issues from the structure of directly perceived subjective psychological experience. Basically this principle necessitates that mind be regarded as more than a refined compounding of sense data that originate from the natural world and as organic bodily feeling. It accentuates the fact that emotion and, more specifically, highly disciplined symbolic emotion or ideational feeling is also a crucial factor in constructively generating human thought. Thus, beyond the sensory deliverance of percepta testifying to the sheer contemporaneity of the natural world and states of pure organic and emotional feeling, there is also a class of qualitatively more sophisticated percepta that symbolically represent previously acquired wisdom that is logically conceived to have correlative physio-chemical storage equivalents, in principle capable of empirical confirmation. This wisdom spatio-temporally endures, and comes constructively and synthetically to bear upon any relevant contemporary stimulus-occasion in a way that profoundly enhances the subjective psychological meaning of that event. This last class of percepta with their constructive characteristic will be our predominate concern in the remainder of the chapter. However, the problem to be initially confronted regarding this historically problematic issue is in describing accurately the universal manner in which the constructivity intrinsically characteristic of human thought is accomplished. However, we will not here undertake the task of presenting a plausible explanation of the subjective psychological mechanics of constructive cognitive synthesis, or of providing a possible explanation of how synthesis is accomplished during thought-in-process. The striking fact will emerge that our descriptive endeavor will also yield a final formulation of the logical form of subjective psychological experience, that essential structure universally embodied within all possible human experience. This will be our completed concept of mind.

The extraordinary nature of meaning-as-directly-felt-relatedness was emphasized earlier specifically by accentuating the logically distinguishable portion of our subjective psychological experience which fills out consciousness with the strange but undeniably efficacious classes of percepta constituting subjective psychological meaning. It was argued that the ontological emergence of this unique realm of meaning from intrinsically unconscious physio-chemical mechanisms is the result of organic concrescence involving the appearance of large numbers of relevant organic propensities that synthetically unite, hence yielding feeling, the novel emergent phenomena which permeate the human physiology. As concrescence increases, it was further argued, qualitatively more sophisticated levels of feeling also emerge, the highest grade being achieved in ideational feeling. This feeling, due to its intrinsic symbolic character, can, in turn, promote progressively higher-ordered organic concrescence even though mental processes themselves operate in accordance to a nonmaterialistic-mechanistic mode of causality logically distinct from that of physio-chemical phenomena. This is to say that ideas can cause higher-ordered physio-chemical synthesis, and vice versa. Conscious causality is rendered possible because of meaning-as-directly-felt-relatedness. To reiterate, consciousness adds a new dimension to reality over and above the unconscious physio-chemical domain. Meaning-as-directly-felt-relatedness arises from the possibility of human organisms experiencing qualitatively distinct emotional states and, further, of imposing a disciplined organization upon emotion by transforming it into an elaborate system of disciplined symbols. The essence of these symbols is the fact of their extensive relatedness with one another. At primordial levels of symbolic development, a triumphant realization is achieved by each human organism when it discovers that relevant groups of undisciplined but familiar emotion conjured by a given stimulus-object effect can be subsumed to a single symbolic utterance that represents the amorphous experiential unities. From this, the next equally important discovery occurs when the organism realizes that symbols can be organized into configurations that represent elements of experience, and eventually learns that symbols can be used to generate, hence in themselves become, novel experience. Obviously an immature mind comes to understand these extraordinary developmental advances on a level commensurate with its infantile capacities. The point in all this is that meaning-as-directly-felt-relatedness experienced as a major portion of symbolic meaning is primarily a vast, vaguely conscious network of relevant symbols synthetically actualized into an atomic unity qualifying a clearly conscious focal point of denotative symbolic meaning. In the dynamic process of thinking where denotative symbolic components have only ephemeral temporal duration, the enormous aggregation of connotative symbolic wisdom is conjured almost instantaneously to consciousness, hence filling out consciousness with a highly sophisticated yet vaguely conscious sense of far-reaching meaning. Thus the intrinsic nature of conscious experience with its unique mode of causality springs from the inextricably unified synthesis of myriad vague symbolic ideational propensities that reflexively accompany clear denotative symbolic components, the collective actualization of which is contingent upon the concomitantly appearing stimulus-object effect entering the consciousness of a human organism. Conscious understanding is in itself the indivisible, directly experienced net result of a bewilderingly complex configuration of ideational propensities synthetically emerging as its constitution. Since the total integrated unity is conscious experience, or more specifically, what we have defined as a mental event, all the logically possible constitutive ideational propensities or all the logically possible constitutive organic propensities, even if it were technically possible to formally express these conditions, could not capture the exact subjective meaning embodied in the original, ontologically particular occasion during which the event was actualized. This must be concluded for we have previously proven that only the individual within whose organism a given mental event occurs can, in principle, have direct immediate access to the event. Only individuals themselves can be the subjects of their own experience. Two dimensions of this issue become evident. First, it has been seen that from even a theoretically possible complete physio-chemical specification of the organic propensities underlying a given mental event, definitive statements of the correlative mental state could not be analytically deduced, hence rendering this mode of factual acquisition a matter of empirical inquiry. From this it follows that there are two logically distinct phenomenal domains. Since it was shown that all phenomenal ascertainment necessarily presupposes *a priori* a mind to perceive the phenomena, it must be concluded that mental events are causally efficacious in that minds cause knowledge, for example. Here we have, among other things, an argument demonstrating the impossibility of any behavioral science becoming capable, through intersubjectively verifiable means, or otherwise, of knowing the exact nature of any individual's mental event throughout any given time span. Although the argument for this view was presented in terms more appropriate to physiological sciences, it also is perfectly applicable to a behaviorism, in that the latter deals with more macroscopic behaviors, but neverthless, it methodologically accepts only those phenomena directly perceivable through the external bodily senses. Secondly, an argument predicating the partial privacy of mental events will be propounded with important implications for subjective psychological research procedures. Even if all the ideational propensities participating in a given mental event could be objectively ascertained through analyzing verbal reports made by a subject (an impossible feat because of the different spatio-temporal locations of individual percipients, because experience is more extensive than mind's capacity to symbolically represent its components, because of the transitory nature of mental events, and because there are emotional components of experience that are presymbolic), the exact nature of the mental event could not be exhaustively objectively characterized. Apart from the fundamental recognition that direct perceptual apprehension as experience-in-process is the ultimate indubitable basis for the definition of fact as that which is the case, there is the additional important consideration that the subject's verbal reports—the best indirect and practically the only means that we have for coming to know about his inner states—are perceived by external observers solely as spoken denotative symbolic components. This is to say that the heard verbalizations are the intersubjectively directly verifiable factual phenomena. However, behavioral scientists do not, and cannot in principle, have direct perceptual access to the *connotative* or *meaning-as-directly-felt-relatedness components of the spoken symbols*. In essence, they can directly perceive only a very small portion of a subject's subjective psychological experience for they have *direct access to only denotative* and not connotative aspects of symbols. Therefore it must be concluded that behavioral scientists can only come to know a subject's spoken symbols to the extent that the scientists as individuals ascribe their personal connotative meaning to the subject's contributed denotative symbolic utterances. Thus the accuracy of the observers' understanding is a function of the degree to which their individual connotative interpretation of subjects' contributed denotative symbolic component deviates from subjects' connotative ascriptions. The implications of this conclusion have enormous importance for any discipline studying the meaning and usage of language and other symbolic modes. Without belaboring the obvious ramifications of this issue, we have only to recall our past discussion on the meaning and method of symbolic discipline, and the diagrammatic representation of a hierarchy of symbolic endeavors, each manifesting an increased amount of symbolic discipline as one proceeded to higher hierarchical levels (Figure 1). From an organic point of view it was seen that increased symbolic discipline in a given system of inquiry is a matter of the participating human organisms developing commensurate concordance among the configurations of organic propensities that are constructively brought to bear to meaningfully enhance the bare contributed contemporaneous stimulus-object effects. From the perspective of conscious experience, considerable concordance is achieved by individuals with respect to their interpretive ideational propensities or, more specifically, the connotative meaning implicit within given denotative symbols. Practical instances of this disciplined state of affairs are evidenced in operational definitions, axioms, postulates, etc. All these devices are designed to effectively facilitate the extent to which individuals can develop similarity in their personal understanding of symbols and transformation rules.

The argument demonstrating the impossibility of exhaustively coming to know the intrinsic nature of subjective psychological meaning from an external observational perspective can be carried a step further. Over and above the information that could be derived from an ideally complete objective analysis of all the organic and ideational propensities capable of participating constitutively in any given mental event, there would be a class of information referring to the subjective psychological states of individuals as they are known through direct acquaintance by the individuals themselves. Therefore, it must be concluded that this additional information results from the experienced unique nexus of propensities as they are novelly actualized in ontologically particular events, and are thereby directly perceived in their full synthetic unity by individual percipient minds. "Unique nexus" refers to particular actualized configurations of propensities uniting during given occasions and is merely a term accentuating the fact that the emergent elements of conscious experience could not be completely understood in their full synthetic unity from even an exhaustive specification of all relevant organic and ideational propensities involved in a mental event. To scientifically study propensities abstracted from their total unified nexus is necessarily to delimit and hence distort in varying degrees the complete factuality of any given occasion. However, on the other hand, it is in this way that science progresses, for otherwise a discipline would be required to comprehend, theoretically, all relevant variables before it could proceed with its inquiries; a stipulation that is obviously unsatisfactory. Again, any given human organism has privileged, direct access to his mental states in the sense that since it requires time for complete thoughts to become formulated. Further, because even in simple mental events beyond the fact that there may be many denotative symbolic elements clearly evident in consciousness, there are also a multiplicity of substantive connotatively meaningful ideational propensities, any of which may suggest a new mode of thought. It should be evident to the reader that consciousness is an ontologically necessary condition for ascertaining any of the possible ideational variables that may causally influence the direction in which any given thought may develop, despite the fact that most of our thoughts are consciously habituative. Thus, to seriously think that a behavioral science, in the foreseeable future, could have direct access to the many possible variables that influence the course of developing behavior is ludicrous. However, since our behavioral patterns are most frequently habitual, whether in silent thought or in manifest behavior, a behavioral science can make important determinations about human behavior. The distinction is made to emphasize that even our theoretical concept of creative thinking is primitive, let alone our understanding of the cognitive processes involved in its actualization. It must be understood that in an individual's privileged position with respect to his subjective psychological experience, any denotative and connotative element of his vague-to-clearly conscious symbolic resources can operate constructively in clear consciousness by being reflectively considered in contrast to an extensive backlog of accumulated wisdom. This process results in either generating novel synthetic ideational products capable of serving as stimulus-objects for promoting further thinking or merely storing perceptual elements in memory and rendering them available for conjuration on a more propitious occasion. Therefore in addition to the denotative symbolic components periodically capable of direct intersubjective verification, there is at any given time an entire history of potential stimulus-objects serving as the largely private, predominating frame of reference from which individuals can make cognitive behavioral determinations. Today, most psychologists continue to contemplate

human behavior as habitual and reflexive; this seems to be a result, as
we have repeatedly seen in our previous discussion, of their unwarrantedly narrow conception of human behavior. It appears that with our
importantly broadened view of human behavior, as it is conceived by
subjective psychological theory, unpredictable though obviously constructive reflective modes of behavior ought to be systematically promoted through behavioral engineering, and not in fact denounced as
a weakness in the power of scientific explanation. We have only to
consider the large number of potentially provocative cognitive stimulus-
objects that are directly accessible to individuals on many given occasions, in contrast to the relatively few variables of this status controlled
by external observers, to appreciate the significance of this method for
promoting intelligent thinking. This is a fact that contemporary behavioral researchers must recognize and expeditiously capitalize upon, not
merely repress.

We have been briefly reconsidering the nature and significance of
meaning-as-directly-felt-relatedness as a distinct general class of percepta. Our predominant concern in analyzing this phenomenon has
been to designate its essential characteristic as the substance of subjective psychological experience. Beyond the fact that connotative symbolic meaning, arising from the synthetic actualization of innumerable
mutually relevant ideational propensities occurring in response to correlative stimulus-object effects, is the experiential essence of subjective
psychological meaning, there is the equally important fact that it executes a constructive and hence causal function. It has been repeatedly
argued that the wisdom of the past is brought constructively to bear
upon the present occasion, thus enhancing its psychologically experienced meaning. Previously established organic propensities or prior
learnings, having relevance for given contemporary stimulus-object effects, are reflexively and synthetically activated when stimulated. The
mechanistic basis for this possibility is in the physio-chemical structure
of the human organism and is subject to experimental investigation.
But an emergent manifestation of this remarkable physio-chemical synthesis also occurs as subjective psychological experience. However, in
many of our preceding inquiries a recurring conclusion has been that
emergent psychological phenomena are intrinsically different from their
physio-chemical correlates. If previously learned wisdom, occurring as
meaning-as-directly-felt-relatedness, consists of ontologically unique,
emergent, disciplined symbolic feeling, since it synthetically infuses contemporary perceptual deliverances with symbolic meaning that would
otherwise not be intrinsic to these contributions, the conclusion must be

drawn that connotative meaning causes contemporaneously contributed percepta to be meaningfully understood as intelligible actuality. This conclusion is in need of further explication if it is to be rendered systematically intelligible in the context of our evolving model. This elaboration will be made subsequently.

One of the most fundamental assumptions upon which our entire concept of mind rests is that in a reflective analysis of concrete subjective psychological experience the components of mind-in-process can be distinguished into logically and experientially distinct classes of percepta, ultimately reducible to the Categories which, if their intrinsic perceptual nature and relation to one another are carefully scrutinized, can yield an accurate definition and theory of mind. More specifically some implications of this statement are as follows:

1. In the analysis of conscious experience presented, it was discovered that to isolate the possible distinct classes of percepta that could participate in the constitution of any given mental event was in a fundamental sense to comprehend the logical form of subjective psychological experience. Any possible mental event must necessarily be a synthetic product of contributed perceptual components issuing from stimulus-objects located in the external natural or internal bodily environments, a connotative symbolic perceptual component including both vague symbolic and emotional percepta, and in most cases a denotative symbolic perceptual component.

2. Also an analysis of the percepta contributed directly as entities, properties, and relations comprising concrete experience, over and above revealing the concept of a logical form that is inherent to all possible human experience—a term implying permanence in that the form is universally constant throughout all time—can yield an understanding of the concrete synthetic process demonstrated in any given particular event. We have talked little of how mental events may be synthesized out of their basic possible components, for such investigations must presuppose a clear conception of the logical form of subjective psychological experience. This means that before a discussion of mind-in-process can successfully transpire, it is necessary to develop an accurate understanding of that which is in process. It is our purpose now to provide a final specification of the possible perceptual components of mind, and the logical form revealed in their distinctive modes of entry. Therefore it is only after this latter problem has been resolved that an inquiry into the concrete synthetic process of thinking can be successfully undertaken.

3. Hence a subjective psychology aspires to give its account of human behavior by initially indicating the logical form in which human experience concretely occurs, and the classes of perceptual contents with

their unique properties that embody the form; and at a second succes- sive ·stage to determine the conditions from which possible laws of ideational synthesis may be established to systematically characterize the process of thinking-behavior. This latter stage must rely upon both the powers of logical and philosophical analysis in developing theoreti- cal constructs and the experimental inquiry for validating hypothetical assertions.

It has been seen that all possible percepta synthetically constituting mind throughout any given time span can be classified as contributed percepta or stimulus-object effects, and connotative and typically de- notative symbolic meaning. In their experientially actualized state, the basic dipolar distinction characteristic of mind—percepta concomitantly coming constructively to bear upon other percepta—is in evidence. This essential dipolar character, as will be seen with increased specificity, is on one hand an apparently naïve view of cognition, yet on the other hand demonstrates an ultimately important principle that will underlie all our inquiries regardless of their technicality.

The remainder of this chapter will be largely devoted to ascribing new names to previously developed concepts, the principal modifica- tion being that the meaning of certain concepts will be extended, thereby rendering them more inclusive in their power to explicate cer- tain subtle dimensions of concrete human experience. An illustration of this was suggested in saying that we shall broaden the concept of mean- ing-as-directly-felt-relatedness by stressing not only its crucially impor- tant experiential quality of felt symbolic relatedness, but also the equally important property that this class of percepta actually causes our personal awareness of the reality to be subjective psychologically meaningful! Concisely stated, then, the term "presentationally immediate percepta" will be used interchangeable with the term "contributed percepta"; "causally efficacious percepta" will supersede the terms "vague symbolic connotative meaning" and "meaning-as-directly-felt- relatedness"; "emotional feeling" will be replaced by the term "causally efficacious emotional percepta" and will generally be regarded as im- plicitly contained within the notion of "causally efficacious percepta" un- less stated otherwise. Finally, the term "causally efficacious conceptual percepta" will be used in place of "denotative symbolic meaning." A further important consideration is that presentational immediacy (PI), causal efficacy (CE), causally efficacious emotion (CEE), and causally efficacious conceptual perception (CEC) are to be hereafter regarded as perceptual modes, whereas PI, CE, CEE, and CEC percepta will be considered as the classes of perceptual contents that enter via these modes. Therefore the notion of a perceptual mode merely indicates the way in which given classes of perception participate as event-components of particular mental events. Finally, although Whitehead in his later writings used the terms "presentational immediacy" and "causal efficacy" (and another term to be later introduced, "symbolic reference"), his definition of each perceptual mode, while having much in common with those to be now introduced, should not be considered as identical in meaning.

To reiterate, it should be remembered that since our concept of mind follows directly from a careful analysis of the percepta that constitute conscious experience, and because these percepta reveal themselves so that they can be subsumed to categorical classification, it must be clearly understood that in our analysis of distinct classes of percepta (PI, CE, CEE, CEC) we shall be discussing their intrinsic natures in abstraction from their concrete modes of occurrence. Single classes of percepta never occur in purely homogeneous independence; the general definition of mind as percepta concomitantly coming constructively to bear upon other percepta necessarily demands that perceptual actualization must occur in at least dipolar form. Thus we can never, in mature intellectual awareness, experience pure presentationally immediate percepta without the perceptual concomitants of causally efficacious emotion and causally efficacious perception, as they synthetically enter the contemporary emergent occasion. To be consciously aware at all logically and empirically demands that more than one perceptual mode be constructively activated; this is the principal implication of meaning-as-directly-felt-relatedness.

PRESENTATIONALLY IMMEDIATE PERCEPTA

An effective method for accurately understanding the distinct classes of percepta that synthetically constitute conscious experience is by pondering at length the properties of each class as if the percepta were to occur in complete homogeneity, unmixed with percepta from other classes. This may appear a rather questionable analytical procedure, but in fact it is merely a typical act of critical, constructive reflection. The method involved is no different from that operating when a geometer conceives of a perfectly straight line or a mathematician defines a point as that conceptual entity having no extension through which an infinite number of lines may be drawn. Similarly, we must

conceive of PI percepta as clearly and distinctly appearing in consciousness during the ever-emerging present experiential occasion. Further,
these PI percepta are to be regarded as referring to stimulus-objects
located in either the external natural world or internal bodily organism.
Also, since PI percepta are stimulus-object effects, and we have said
that these effects conjure relevant organic and hence ideational propensities to the present occasion to bring the wisdom of the past
constructively to bear upon the present occasion, the concomitant appearance of other classes of percepta over and above PI percepta is
necessarily contingent upon the occurrence of PI percepta. PI percepta
are logically prior to other classes of percepta in that given PI percepta, at least CEE and CE percepta, must also synthetically occur.
This matter of logical antecedence in distinction from temporal antecedence is a difficult one. Consequently we shall give careful consideration
to this distinction in future discussion for it is basic to many problematic philosophical and psychological issues. Finally, PI percepta must
be viewed as percepta contributed from externally or internally located
stimulus-objects. Therefore, there are five criteria that delineate PI percepta from other classes of percepta, namely:

> clarity in conscious awareness
> distinctness in conscious awareness
> contemporaneity of occurrence
> logical antecedence in occurrence
> contribution

The first criterion implies that entities and their concretely perceived properties and relations participate so vividly in consciousness
that their presence as elements of given events is unmistakable in their
participation as self-contained event-components. For example, to see a
green leaf as such in intuitive primordial experience, independent of
linguistic characterizations, light wave, and biochemical or botanical
theories, is an indubitable perceptual fact that will endure in self-
evident truth value beyond the changing theories that are developed to
explain its relatedness to other factors in nature. Even the words "green
leaf" are an abstract portrayal beyond the more primitive subjective
psychological experience of the stimulus-object effect in itself. However,
all PI percepta do not manifest the vividness of visual percepta. In fact,
it is possible to designate three general levels of vividness: those percepta delivered via the external bodily senses; those percepta delivered
as internal organic bodily feeling (e.g., pains, throbs, etc.); and
those percepta occurring as ideational stimulus-object effects, generally

occurring as denotative symbolic components or causally efficacious concepts formulated in previously actualized experience that enter contemporary events as PI percepta and subsequently acquire the status of
becoming stimulus-objects.

The second criterion of distinctness in conscious awareness is closely
related to clear awareness, but in the sense that perceptions of entities,
properties, and relations entering through the PI mode can be perceived as distinctly separate factors apart from the more complex context within which such factors necessarily occur. Thus, apart from the
vividness of PI perceptual occurrence, a phenomenon conceived in relation to the criterion of clarity, is the recognition that stimulus-object
effects appear as discernibly unto themselves. This is simply to say,
for example, that we do perceive chairs as distinct entities from the
immediately proximate table, floor, wall, and so on. We may hear a
sound as a distinct interruption in an enduring silence. Throbs are
distinctly variable in their felt intensity. A concept of green is clearly
recognized as distinct from the concept of automobile. Here we could
once again arrange these illustrations of distinctness into a hierarchical
order. For example, the concrete perceptual distinctness between a
table and a chair is more readily evident than the concepts of wisdom
and virtue as they apply to human behavioral states. Thus distinctness,
as it is in evidence in our perceptual experience and at much higher
levels in our cognitive discriminations among the distinct denotative
meanings of various ideational stimulus-objects, is intimately related to
the human organism's ability to discern contrast. The fact that we
perceive contrasting perceptions is, of course, largely contingent on the
structure of our bodies as well as the heterogeneity intrinsically characteristic of PI percepta. Thus, for example, if human organisms perceived only the colors black and white, many visually contrasting instances of perceptual differentiation would never have been made.

Since process is a fundamental fact testifying to the nature of
reality, the concept of an immediate perceptual presentation becomes
somewhat problematic, at least on logical grounds. We have seen that
the ultimate considerations upon which our entire concept of mind is
based are the perceptions revealed in direct concrete experience. More
specifically, we have theoretically analyzed experience into its constituent atomic components, namely events. Although events can be
analyzed into their constituent elements, it was stressed that this is
only achieved through critical and constructive reflection. We do not
experience event-components as distinct atomic unities; rather we experience complete events within determinate spatio-temporal durations.
The relevance of this for PI percepta is that concretely speaking such

perceptions enter into subjective psychological experience over time; we do not typically contemplate PI percepta as occurring in instantaneous temporal synthesis with concomitant CE, CEC percepta. Rather, this latter conception is a product of critical and constructive reflection, as is the notion of an atom, for example. During our experience, mind's gross, imprecise apprehension of percepta, occurring generally as change amid permanence, reveals nothing of the knife's edge of the absolutely instantaneously occurring present just as it has emerged from the past and is just about to proceed into the future as a newly emergent present. Rather, an experiential phenomenon that we, in retrospect, neatly characterize as a particular event is actually comprised of undercurrents of process, localized permanence, groups of elements readily amenable to symbolic characterization (which survive subsequently to constitute our recollections and characterizations of former experiential occasions), and finally numerous dimensions of only vaguely apprehended percepta which because of this quality frequently escape contemporary recognition. Thus it should be understood that the basis for the criterion of contemporaneity as well as the other four criteria are not to be found as immediately evident properties of events, for these criteria designate universally characteristic properties of classes of event-components, formulated only through careful analytical reflection. Therefore, these criteria essentially permit us to construct a hypothetical model accurately comprehending, from an ideally immutable frame of reference, the logical form of subjective psychological experience from the model itself, functioning as an instrument for facilitating the completeness coherence, and logical consistency of our reflective analyses. As a result of this theoretical possibility we are enabled, for example, to conceive of human behavioral circumstances with regard to thinking-behavior in which any given thought can be analyzed into its instantaneously concomitant components; that is, its logical form can be analyzed into PI, CE, CEC, and CEE perceptual deliverances and its experiential particularity can be empirically ascertained by consulting, either directly or by experiment, the subject in question. But since all perceptual components of an event occur concomitantly, how does the criterion of contemporaneity apply to PI perception? The problem may partially be resolved by saying that this criterion stresses the spatio-temporally unique character of the ever-emerging present occasion entering individual organisms as novel PI perception from external natural and/or internal bodily environments. More will be said about this criterion as additional qualifications are made in defining the nature of PI perception.

Beyond what has been said about the criterion of logical antecedence, we may simply mention that its chief utility is in accentuating the fact that we logically bring meaning to bear upon a stimulus-object only after the effects of the stimulus-object have entered the consciousness. This distinction is one of logical not temporal significance in that given stimulus-object effect A, relevant wisdom A' as a temporally concomitant accompaniment follows. A simple illustration of this is that we meaningfully recognize the green grass of the meadow where we are standing if we are, in fact, directly experiencing the natural perception. Thus given the perception of a grassy meadow, a subjectively meaningful awareness of the fact issues from the concomitant actualization of percepta entering a percipient's consciousness via the modes of PI, CEC, CE, and CEE. We do not, unless there is an incidence of hallucination, directly perceive meadows that are not, in fact, before our eyes. However, in the theory being developed, even such hallucinatory experiences can be reconciled with the criterion of logical antecedence. The reason for stressing the issue of logical antecedence is that we are bordering closely upon the philosophical problem of causality, certain aspects of which we are compelled to consider in the problem of mind as it is being conceptualized. However, it is inappropriate to discuss the causality issue at this time for our concept of mind has not yet been adequately developed. The logical antecedence issue will again arise in explicating the nature of CEC percepta.

Finally, it should be mentioned at this point that the criterion of contribution acknowledges the fact that percepta referring to natural and organic bodily stimulus-objects, revealing themselves as entities, properties, and relations, and considered theoretically as unsymbolized uninterpreted deliverances, are not caused or created by mind. They are obviously contributed effects or classes of percepta logically distinct from those termed denotative symbolic meaning or meaning-as-directly-felt-relatedness. Some additional qualification is required: causally efficacious conceptual percepta having in the past been already actualized, and hence ingressing into temporally successive events as stimulus-object effects, thereby participating in events as logically prior to other concomitant percepta, must also qualify as PI percepta for they fulfill the five relevant criteria. This matter shall be elaborated as we proceed.

In a more general consideration of presentationally immediate percepta, though still in light of the above criteria, it can be said that these perceptual data as directly presented in their barren uninterpreted state, logically prior to any symbolic characterization and antecedent to even emotional familiarity, would be mere transitory flux. Process would incessantly manifest itself amid permanence in the ever-emerging present. More explicitly, however, this is to say that PI perceptual configurations which mature intelligence entitled as trees, sounds, specific shapes, written words, pains, ideas, certain changes of state among entities and properties, and so on, conceived logically in their pure state, could never be meaningful objects of consideration apart from mind's symbolic power of representation. It will be recalled that our definition of symbol also includes emotion whether disciplined or undisciplined. In fact, it is logically contradictory to even raise the question of whether pure PI perceptual objects can be known apart from mind's ability to know them, for the concept of knowledge necessarily presupposes a system of symbolization to be organized as knowledge which in turn presupposes *a priori* minds that gain intelligent organization via symbols. The question of whether stimulus-objects exist independently of mind can be resolved, as we have generally seen, by understanding that stimulus-object effects are event-components, but components that are given or contributed from internally or externally located regions. Thus, since mind does not create in the sense of bringing into being these components, since minds do not create colors, sounds, pains, etc., in the same sense that minds create or cause subjective psychological meaningful definitions and concepts, it can be concluded that there are stimulus-objects that correspond to and underlie the effects that are contributed to our minds as perceptions. We are justified in considering PI percepta as logically distinct from other possible classes for this class is contributed and also, of course, because of the other criteria that distinguish them as a unique class of percepta. Further, the class may be conceived as logically distinct without necessarily being compelled to deny the independent existence of minds or an external world or to consider PI as the only possible perceptual mode.

Presentationally immediate percepta, then, are those contributions issuing from the ever-emerging present, completely devoid of any element testifying to stored learnings from the past. But considered logically in their independence as pure contributed percepta, they are by no means the entirely formless sensory "given" of which Kant speaks. For Kant, pure sensuous intuition delivered through the determinative modes of space and time demanded with *a priori* necessity that such intuition be subsumed to his Categories before the perceptual matter could acquire any intelligible form at all. But we differ from this view in that our concept of contribution by definition implies that external natural and internal bodily PI percepta come to us as event-components with their own independent *matter and form*, and thereby do not rely upon mind for their characteristic properties. An immediately and directly perceived PI perception of a table or a pain, apart from our subjective psychological symbolic characterization, is contributed to

mind with an intrinsic nature of its own from which it acquires particularity in the sense that it is ultimately the entity that it is and no other.
For example, the matter of a table considered as a visual presentation
would be the array of colors that distinguish it from other entities. However, the table is delivered as visually more than a mere haphazard
patch of colors; rather, the colors are presented in an organized, permanent form. Again in the case of a felt pain, the matter would be its
occurrence as a painful feeling as opposed to a pleasurable feeling. Thus
the perceptual consequences of placing our hand on a hot stove would
be such that the essential experience of the burning, painful perception
would be intrinsically undesirable whether we came to symbolically
characterize the brute PI sensation as a painful burning sensation or a
cooling breeze. The form of a painful perception would be its uniquely
characteristic quality, as a hot pain, a sharp or piercing pain, or a dull
persistent pain; and its temporal property, as sporadic, throbbing, or
momentary. The point to be made in the above illustrations is that the
direct PI experiential properties of the two perceptual states are intrinsic to the perceptions as directly contributed and are not, thereby,
dependent for their matter-form characters upon any constructive
power of mind even though, of course, it is contradictory and hence
meaningless to speak of percepta occurring without minds to concomitantly stand over against them. Further, this conceptualization of the
nature of contributed PI percepta also establishes a fundamental epistemological fact: that all our knowledge, existing psychologically as a
symbolic entity, with its properties and relations, ultimately acquires
its logical form from the entities, properties, and relations perceptually
entering our subjective psychological concrete experience as external natural perceptual deliverances, internal organic bodily feeling, and emotional feeling originally contributed via presentational immediacy.

Since throughout each of our personal conscious lives we constantly
entertain perceptions from our external and internal environments, it
must be concluded that PI percepta always participate as event-components in subjective psychological experience. Generally, most of these
percepta are so typical or matter-of-fact in our daily experience that
they are rarely symbolically represented due to their subtlety of occurrence and unimportant character. But, nevertheless, all such percepta
must be understood as legitimate event-components. Also as a further
technical distinction, it is only during the stages of early infancy that
anything approaching a pure experience of PI percepta is humanly
possible, for at this level of development stored wisdom is comparatively
minimal, with behavior manifesting itself as predominately reflexive
and wholly a function of externally natural and internally located organic

stimulus-objects. Beyond this early level of development, the progressive disciplining of emotion commensurately reduces the possibility of PI perceptual purity.

In our analysis of the first criterion that distinguishes PI percepta from other distinct classes, emphasizing the vividness of conscious percepta awareness, the point was made that although PI perception is experientially the most clearly manifested of the four possible classes of perception it is nevertheless possible to discriminate even more precisely among the levels of clarity manifested by the percepta specifically appearing through the mode of PI. A hierarchy of presentational vividness was posited in that percepta delivered via the external bodily senses were more forcefully evident and hence clearly distinguishable than those occurring as organic bodily feeling, and certainly ideational feeling experienced as stimulus-object effects. To these levels we may simply assign the definitional terms "natural PI percepta," "organic PI percepta," and "ideational PI percepta," thereby formalizing the within-mode distinctions not only to designate their particular degree of vividness, but also to increase the specificity of the term "PI percepta." Moreover, in analyzing the first criterion an area in need of further clarification was mentioned: namely, that clear denotative symbolic percepta, or what will be discussed in detail as causally efficacious concepts (CEC) can, after their inchoation, function as ideational stimulus-objects. These are concepts already having been synthetically actualized as such. CEC whose emergent particularity during the present occasion is less novel due to the fact that they were synthesized as genuinely unique ontological emergents in a spatio-temporally antecedent event. Although there has been little explanation of the nature of PI, CE, CEC, and CEE percepta, apart from the information pertaining to the previously developed concepts from which the present ones are refined derivatives, the explicative benefits to be derived from now analyzing the status of ideational PI percepta as stimulus-objects will outweigh the difficulties resulting from postponing the issue.

The question to be analyzed is the following: If ideational PI percepta are actualized CEC percepta functionally occurring as stimulus-objects spatio-temporally following their original inchoation as particular ideational entities, can they legitimately be regarded as PI percepta? It can be rightfully argued that they are not contributed in the same way that natural and organic PI percepta appear. Ideational PI percepta are, rather, synthetic *products* of mind, not independent contributions to mind. This question, although stated in a highly abstract way, is of fundamental importance in theoretically demonstrating how subjective psychological thought achieves coherence and continuity in its processes. These two considerations can be partially resolved through a reflective analysis of the logical form of human experience. A first step in answering this question, in order to clearly designate what we mean by ideational PI percepta, is to ask how it is possible, for example, to distinguish between the PI perceptual event-components entering into the two different mental events to which the following two statements refer:

"The house is brown."

"My concept of virtue caused me to . . ."

In the first case, we may assume that the stimulus-object effects of a house directly observed by an individual are entering his consciousness, and he chooses to linguistically characterize the effects by means of the first statement. Thus a perception of brown is participating as a constitutive component of the individual's mental event. But contrastingly, in the second case, there are no natural or organic PI percepta such as those linguistically represented as brown ingressing into the individual's conscious experience; rather there is a formerly learned concept of virtue ingressing as an ideational PI perceptual event-component that, in effect, participates in the present event in such a way as to determine the nature of the concomitant CE, CEC, and CEE percepta that will be synthetically united with the logically antecedent PI perception to produce a complete mental event. The ramifications of this conclusion are extremely complex and numerous and can only be adequately understood retrospectively pondering the preceding conclusion at length in light of the argumentation to be presented subsequently. For example, even though the ideational PI perception of virtue determines the nature of the additional necessarily concomitant CE, CEC, and CEE percepta that will be synthetically conjured as the relevant ideational propensities, hence organic propensities, required to produce a complete mental event, the PI percept itself is contingent upon meaning-as-directly-felt-relatedness (or more appropriately, what will be defined as CE percepta) for its principal attribute of being clearly and distinctly discernible in consciousness. This would be the case if the percept was occurring as a denotatively clear CEC perception. This merely means that ideational PI percepta must originate as projected, symbolically simplified, and consciously clear and distinct event-components in the same way that any denotatively clear symbolic components must arise from meaning-as-directly-felt-relatedness or CE percepta, for if objects of understanding could not be clearly and distinctly symbolically conceptualized, human thought would not be possible at all. Similarly, in the case of ideational PI percepta, if we could not conjure clearly to consciousness those concepts that have been formerly learned, human thinking could not occur.

The problem still before us is to formally prove that ideational PI percepta can validly qualify as PI percepta in the sense of being legitimately contributed, logically antecedent event-components. If we are to remain consistent with the definition of mind as percepta concomitantly coming constructively to bear upon other percepta, or as contributed percepta coming concomitantly to bear upon the symbolic resources of mind, then we must show that the definition when applied to pure cognition—that is, mental events theoretically containing no natural or organic PI perceptual component—still remains consistent with human behavior having no directly intersubjectively verifiable features indicative of its intrinsic nature as subjective psychological experience, if the behavior occurs as silent thinking. The primary importance of this issue is to demonstrate in a logically consistent way that the numerous ideational concepts which we develop, constituting a large portion of subjective psychological experience, are in fact causal determinants or stimulus-objects in intelligent thinking-behavior. The argument to be presented will essentially follow from the five criteria designating PI percepta as a logically and experientially distinct class of percepta.

1. Stimulus objects have been generally defined as those ontological factors that are inferred to yield stimulus-object effects. These are the event-components or perceptions that constititute our subjective psychological experience. Stimulus-objects can yield any of the effects encompassed within the domain defined as the Categories. Further, we have direct perceptual access to effects of stimulus-objects for they are known to us only through their possible modes of entering our mental events.

2. Figure 10 is a model that we shall frequently use hereafter to simplify and illustrate concomitant perceptual deliverance in any given mental events. Although the precise meaning of CE, CEC, and CEE percepta has not yet been discussed in detail, for the present discussion the reader can rely upon an understanding of the connotative and denotative symbolic meaning as an adequate basis for the following model. Figure 10 can diagrammatically represent any fully actualized mental event; thus,

2.1. PI are those percepta contributed by stimulus-objects located in the contemporary natural world, or bodily organism. They can appear as natural, organic, or ideational PI percepta and they must meet the demands of the five relevant criteria characterizing PI percepta.

2.2. CEC percepta have been defined as clear and distinct de-

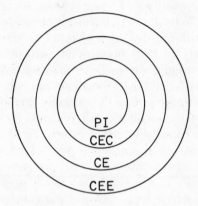

Figure 10. The logical form of subjective psychological events

notative symbolic components in that they are the bare symbols (usually linguistic) or groups of symbols conceptually embodying a single idea and conceived in their barren symbolic form as logically separated from meaning-as-directly-felt-relatedness or CE and CEE.

2.3. CE percepta are the vast configurations of vaguely apprehended symbolized percepta reflectively understood and implicitly felt as infusing CEC percepta with subjective psychological meaning. In fact, this infusion of relevant percepta causes the subjective psychological meaning of a mental event in that symbolic relatedness is the essence of clear conceptualization. Moreover, since symbols whether clear or vague are disciplined emotional feeling, to say that CE percepta cause subjective psychological meaning (thus rendering possible intelligent conscious awareness), means that the necessary conditions have been provided for symbolically understanding a given occasion as consciously intelligible. Thus CE percepta stand in concomitant relation to ideational PI and CEC percepta by causally producing their clear symbolic form as highly simplified symbolic focal points of clarity that enable mind to reduce the extraordinary complexity of a present moment to a simplified symbolic focal point of clearly conscious meaning. This sacrifices the causal importance of a great many event-components, though also retaining in great part myriad relevant symbolic components as they coexist with CEC percepta by vaguely, though powerfully, filling out those denotative percepta with meaning-as-directly-felt-relatedness.

This cognitive capacity enables thought to constructively proceed or advance as conceptual development, constituted, of course, of clear components accompanied by vague peripheries of symbolized-to-unsymbolized meaning that recedes in perceptual vagueness from each ideational PI and CEC perceptual focal point of clarity.

2.4. CEE percepta are those highly nebulous emotionally felt percepta too vague to be easily symbolized. However, when these percepta are symbolized by analytical, constructive reflection, they are thereby, by definition, relegated to the status of CE percepta. CEE percepta are powerfully efficacious in that they intuitively suggest novel modes of thought, but they are also conspicuously efficacious with reference to the highly nebulous though genuine perceptions constituting feelings of happiness, love, sorrow, qualitatively distinctive aesthetic feelings, and so on, in contrast to the highly intellectualized (hence clarified), precise linguistic definitions.

2.5. The above model, as it is graphically illustrated, generally indicates the relationships among distinct classes of percepta, regarding the degree of vividness or clarity and distinctness intrinsic to their characteristic nature as event-components. This is simply to say that the perception of a red house as visually perceived through PI is considerably more clear and distinct than a perception of one's feeling of hopelessness perceived via CEE. However, on the other hand, there are instances where an ideational PI perception of virtue may be less clear and distinct than its concomitantly emerging CEC symbolic definition, with its accompanying CE and CEE perceptual components that fill out the definition with substantive meaning, which may far exceed in definitional precision a former, more limited concept of virtue. Finally the area included within each concentric domain is not proportionate with the number of event-components functionally involved in each class of perception. For example, the statement, "The appreciation of beauty is the source of my greatest happiness in life," requires only thirteen words to be stated as a CEC. Yet undoubtedly the many hundreds of symbolized concepts concomitantly delivered as CE percepta constitute the connotative meaning that fills out the CEC percepta, hence causing the emotional-intellectual feeling of meaning intrinsically characteristic of subjective psychological experience. Consequently, if proportionate peripheral area were an important consideration, then the area included by CE percepta would be many units larger than that of CEC percepta.

3. We shall now demonstrate the basis for the conclusion that what we have defined as denotative symbolic or CEC components, initially synthesized as clear, distinct concepts on given determinable spatio-

temporal occasions, can, after their original actualization as particular ideational entities, reappear in three distinct ways:

3.1. As essentially the same CEC roughly discerned through reflection as reappearing in spatio-temporally different mental events, although logically speaking, sameness is impossible, if only because of the CEC. There is nothing problematic about this notion. We commonly rethink thoughts that have not changed fundamentally over the years. However, again in a strict sense, CEC that are roughly similar over time do undergo modification that is determinable via critical reflection. In this type of analysis it will invariably be discovered that our entire conceptual scheme of things constantly undergoes gradual, though not necessarily important, change. Technically stated, this slight but persistent change is a modification in the CE emotional and vague symbolic perceptual configurations that constitute the meaning-as-directly-felt-relatedness causing the substantive meaning of CEC. In fact such notions as positive and negative ideational habituations and organic and ideational propensities are grounded in the possibility of repetition, within general limits, of behavioral modes. This is to say that CEC can reappear as similar in the sense that the same PI perceptual stimulus conditions can conjure the same relevant CE percepta which in turn project the same simplified causally efficacious conceptions (CEC percepta), all of which enter spatio-temporally different occasions from the one of their original inchoation.

3.2. As perceptually transformed into a causally efficacious percept, in part filling out the substantive connotative meaning of some other CEC. Here the obvious fact is that any causally efficacious perception—vague by definition—has the potentiality of emerging as a clear, distinct CEC providing it has relevance for a PI percept. Thus a given PI percept, occurring logically prior to its concomitantly appearing classes of percepta and functioning as a stimulus-object, conjures relevant CE percepta as substantive meaning, and from these CE percepta a CEC emerges as a clear synthetic product. Conversely, if a once clear (by definition) CEC is not raised to a clear and distinct status upon a given successive occasion it is obviously conceivable that it may have some relevance for another CEC appearing concomitantly in a present occasion, and thereby achieve the less consciously distinct status of a CE percept.

3.3. As *ideational PI percepta*, in that after their original synthesis as CEC, CEC percepta may reappear as ideational PI perception occurring logically prior to other concomitant classes of percepta, hence functioning as a stimulus-object that determines which ideational propensities occurring as CE, CEE, and CEC percepta will be conjured as relevant to symbolically characterize the PI perception. Here the relativity in meaning of stimulus-object and stimulus-object effect are in evidence, namely, that logically speaking from the perspective of CE, CEE, and CEC percepta any PI percepta are stimulus-objects to the extent that they determine which other configurations of percepta will be conjured as relevant symbolic meaning. But from the perspective of concrete subjective psychological experience, PI percepta are experienced as stimulus-object effects arising from natural or bodily stimulus-objects that cannot in principle be directly known except through their effects.

4. Thus we are remaining consistent with the position that with the exception of mind stimulus-objects cannot be directly known in themselves but rather only as we directly experience their effects as perceptions, where the perceptions themselves are event-components. What meaning is to be understood by the concept of knowing things in themselves? It seems valid to say that knowing things by their effects means possessing an awareness of their mode of participation in individual consciousness, a view held by Whitehead, for example. Consciousness, then, is comprised of event-components each of which has a stimulus-object that determines their character as presentationally immediate or contributed perceptual components. Our thought does not cause the independently contributed unsymbolized PI perception of green, for example; rather, thought determines how green will be symbolically characterized and thereby interpreted. The case is similar for internal organic bodily phenomena such as pains, throbs, etc. Therefore, if our thought does not cause the nature of stimulus-object effects, and moreover, if the occurrence of these effects are contingent upon the presence of correlative stimulus-objects often located spatially apart from mind, hence existing independently of mind, then it may be concluded that the latter are the stimulus-objects that yield and hence determine the character of corresponding perceptual effects. Phenomena such as hallucinations are special cases, although still capable of consistent comprehension by our formulations. Therefore, knowing things in themselves, specifically in the limited sense of experience through direct acquaintance, would seem to mean somehow being the subjective psychological experience of stimulus-objects. But if this means perceiving internally and externally located stimulus-objects through their effects, as in the case of individual human beings, then we have made no progress in understanding this problematic issue. In any case, the notion of subjective psychological experience with organisms less developed than man seems purely a speculative issue, for man has no perceptions of such phenomena except indirectly, and inferentially, in those few instances in which we observe the behavior of dogs, apes, etc.

It may be noted that the case in which ideational PI percepta function as stimulus-objects was not considered so that special attention could be devoted to the problem, for it demands a moderate tempering of the contribution criterion.

4.1. Ideational PI percepta are stimulus-objects to the extent that they determine which relevant ideational propensities will be concomitantly conjured to meet the dipolar criterion required for actualizing a complete atomic mental event. For example, a formerly understood concept of virtue can ingress into the present occasion as ideational PI percepta and therefore acquire the status of a subjective psychologically meaningful concept by being synthetically united with meaning-as-directly-felt-relatedness or causally efficacious percepta.

4.2. But in this capacity as a unique class of stimulus-objects, ideational PI percepta do not possess the same degree of independence intrinsically characteristic of natural and organic PI perceptions, for the former are synthetically constructed by mind in a long process of symbolic discipline. Thus the subjective psychological meaning of virtue as a contributed event-component may have undergone an important definitional or evolutionary modification, while bare natural and organic PI percepta are not subject to this type of contingency on mind; they are as they are directly perceptually experienced. In this sense, then, in terms of the diminished independence of ideational PI perception compared to its other two counterparts as they relate to mind, the criterion of contribution is somewhat tempered.

4.3. Since the logically antecedent appearance of ideational PI percepta functioning as stimulus-objects determines the relevant CE, CEE, and CEC percepta that will be conjured to actualize a complete mental event, we may raise this question: Because ideational PI stimulus-objects are known intrinsically through direct perception, how is it that we do not directly understand their causal dynamics, entailing the actual process of conjuring relevant propensities? Generally, the entire conjurational process is directly experienced as reflexively actualized. More specifically, the problem may be resolved by saying that it is true that ideational PI percepta are known directly as stimulus-objects, thereby rendering our relation with these stimulus-objects as different from natural and organic bodily stimulus-objects in that we directly experience the effects of the latter. But in the case of ideational PI stimulus-objects we perceive the stimulus-objects in themselves. The question, then, is why do we not similarly perceive the dynamics of conjuration? Apart from physio-chemical considerations which are in principle inaccessible as direct perception, it can be said that conjuration is a temporally compressed associative process refined to such an extent that it is reflexively accomplished in thought, thus obscuring conjurational dynamics from conscious awareness. However, as a temporally extended counterpart we need only refer to typical reflective thinking which is not reflexively actualized. Since reflexive conjuration is too rapid for reflective ascertainment, although its associated elements must be regarded as elements of atomic thoughts, it may be concluded that we cannot in principle exclusively or directly perceive single ideational PI stimulus-objects for they are event-components, while mind is actualized only as complete events. In this sense, ideational PI stimulus-objects are rendered as singularly unknowable. The ideational PI percept is directly experienced within the entire context of a complete mental event, and can only be isolated as a distinct event-component through analytical reflection. Therefore it must be concluded that complete mental events occurring within the minds of individual human beings are the only cases in which stimulus-objects or things-in-themselves can be known through direct acquaintance, and therein be concretely experienced as causally generating other novel stimulus-objects —namely CEC percepta—which cannot singularly in themselves be understood as causal agents.

4.4. Another problem reveals itself at this point for it has been maintained that ideational PI percepta occur logically prior to concomitant CE, CEE, and CEC percepta because the latter acquire their unique conjurational determination as a group of synthesized propensities from ideational PI percepta occurring as a stimulus-object, thus designating which propensities out of the potentially vast available resource will be selected as relevant. To illustrate this function of PI percepta, using a natural PI stimulus-object, when the contributed color red, for example, enters our consciousness, the subjective psychological meaning reflexively ascribed to the stimulus-object effect is certainly not that designating dog, or the color blue, or the face of God; it is obviously the symbolic characterization, red. This simple illustration demonstrates the determinative effect of PI percepta in terms of which propensities will be reflexively deemed relevant. From this, the problem at hand can be clearly formulated. In past discussions on symbolic development it has been repeatedly affirmed that denotative meaning or what is now also termed CEC are simplified, emergent, clear symbolic elements that have been synthetically projected from meaning-as-directly-felt-relatedness or what we presently define as CE percepta. Therefore CEC percepta logically follow the appearance of CE percepta, for they are caused by CE percepta. We have also argued that ideational PI percepta are, in effect, CEC percepta occurring spatio-temporally after their original actualization. Thus the problem is the following one: we are compelled also to say that ideational PI percepta are caused by CE percepta, in the sense that as clear and distinct percepta they are simplified, projected products of CE percepta. Consequently, CE percepta must be regarded to occur logically prior to ideational PI percepta. This apparently leads us into a serious contradiction for it violates the fourth criterion designating PI percepta. To refer to our former illustration, how could it be that it was not the entry of red PI percepta that caused us to symbolically characterize the directly perceived phenomenon as, in fact, red? Similarly, using an example specifically involving ideational PI percepta, how could it not be true that in the train of thought "My name is John Stevens," for example, the subjective psychological meaning experienced by an individual in the initial stages of the event—"My name is"—did not enter into the later stage —"John Stevens"—in such a way as to determine the fact that "John Stevens" would be the name logically following "My name is"? It is a concrete fact of experience that coherence and continuity in thinking are evidenced in our thought processes, and that these rational properties result from the fact that individual minds are consciously and intelligently aware of their subjective psychological proceedings. An individual does not forget that his name is John Stevens when he has progressed to articulating the phrase, "My name is." More generally speaking, if we could not conjure relevant portions of past knowledge in their clear conceptual form as ideational PI percepta, thought could not advance at all. Is it not, for example, our previously established conception of virtue that, in effect, provides the preparational basis for a subsequently more clear or logically refined concept of virtue which springs into consciousness as a newly synthesized CEC perception? Thus the problem to be resolved— and it must be resolved, for logical antecedence of PI percepta is required to coincide with the concrete facts of experience—has been formulated. The resolution may be stated as follows:

It is true that ideational PI percepta presupposes the synthetic projective power of CE percepta, thereby rendering the latter class of percepta logically prior to the first.

But the crux of the matter lies in the fact that the CE percepta necessary for generating the ideational PI percepta in question were contributed by a temporally antecedent mental event which, in effect, overlaps the contemporary event, consequently entering into it, and thereby contributing the ideational PI perceptual component, functioning as a stimulus-object, and determining which propensities will be deemed relevant for completing the contemporary event. In this way the ideational PI perceptual component can still be regarded as logically prior to its concomitant CE, CEE, and CEC components for it arises from, so to speak, a more pervasive or spatio-temporally enduring substratum of causally efficacious perception that can temporally extend over many particular events. This enduring substratum of CE percepta will be analyzed and schematically represented subsequently.

It may be argued that this solution is an unsatisfactory one for it involves us in an infinite regress, logically speaking, for the solution has been inadequately developed; a condition, in turn, resulting from a heretofore insufficient exposition of the nature of CE percepta. It will be shown, however, that the durational characteristics of CE percepta and their modes of appearance are typically sporadic in their occurrence, primarily as a result of the unpredictable schedule in which external and internal stimulus-object effects enter human organisms thus commensurately disrupting, or, on the other hand, intruding novel factors into subjective psychological thought processes. Therefore from a purely logical point of view, at this point in the discussion, our proposed solution to the logical antecedence issue seems to lead to an infinite regress.

4.5. We are close now to a solution to the problem originally raised, to prove that ideational PI percepta, in the sense of being legitimate contributed, logically antecedent event-components, can qualify as genuine PI percepta similar to those presented immediately as natural and organic bodily PI percepta. The issue is an important one for although it is readily obvious to most of us that the entry into our conscious experience of a tree or throb stimulus-object effect, for example, is the causal basis for symbolically characterizing each as the tree or the throb, it is not so readily apparent that a formerly established concept (an ideational PI percept functioning as a stimulus-object) of virtue, for example, should be the causal basis for the emergence of an intellectually more suitable CEC of virtue originating in a successive mental event, into which the less adequate concept of virtue entered as an ideational PI perception. From the arguments presented above, we may now arrive at a conclusion by saying that:

We have tempered the contribution criterion by showing that ideational PI percepta fulfill the dipolar standard necessary for a mental event in basically the same way as natural and organic PI percepta do, except with the warranted qualification that ideational PI percepta do not possess the rigid ontological independence characteristic of natural and organic PI percepta, in the sense that their intrinsic nature as contributed percepta is contingent upon the synthetic power of mind.

Ideational PI percepta conceived as stimulus-objects cannot be directly perceived singularly as such for they are components of events and therefore must be understood (in their function of causally determining which CE, CEE, CEC propensities will be conjured to fill out the subjective psychological meaning of an event) as components, consciously ascertained only within the far broader perceptual context in which they occur: the entire mental event. Ideational PI percepta can only function as stimulus-objects within the consciously intelligible context of a complete mental event. The precise manner in which ideational PI percepta determine which propensities must be conjured as relevant cannot be explained at this time for we have not yet discussed the nature of CE percepta, their dynamics of synthesis, nor have we yet introduced the theory of layers. Hence, at this point, the ultimate appeal for determining the cogency of our theoretical formulations is concrete experience.

The logical antecedence issue was resolved by saying that ideational PI percepta arise from pervasively enduring CE and CEE percepta capable of persisting throughout many events as substrata constituted of vague yet powerfully efficacious percepta. Again the ultimate ground for verifying this contention is concrete experience, and the theoretical explanation for this view as it has relevance for mental events, conceived as concomitantly comprised of PI, CEC, CE, and CEE percepta, will be presented as the theory of layers. Specifically, for our present analysis, this means that it is possible for previously actualized event-components to enter contemporary events by overlapping them, thereby entering into the present occasion in a logically antecedent manner as an ideational PI element that can determine which additional propensities must be conjured, while yet remaining distinctly independent from the CE, CEE, and particularly CEC percepta that logically succeed the ideational PI percepta. Therefore our original problem has been resolved. The resolution although complex and often abstract is, however, in direct concordance with the testimony of concrete experience in that it is quite consciously evident to us that our previously developed, clearly conscious concepts are foremost in importance at the outset of our mental events, but then lose their position of prominence as this component is synthetically incorporated into its distinctly unique successor for which it has causally prepared the way, and which emerges in a later stage of the same mental event. A major reason for considering this phenomenon in such great detail is that we want its logically ascertainable basis clearly explicated so that the rigorous constructs to be developed for explaining this transformative process may rest upon a firm, logically consistent foundation.

4.6. In this last stage of our argument, a summary is in order, particularly with reference to how the resultant solution manifests itself in concrete subjective psychological experience. It should be realized from the preceding analyses that the term "CEC percepta," by definition and through experiential verification, presupposes that it is only as a result of ideational PI percepta, determinately conjuring relevant propensities that symbolically enhance and thereby make possible its clear, meaningful actualization as a subjective psychological event-component, that CEC can synthetically emerge as a logically successive event-component at all. In short, this is in a sense demonstrating the logical form for the constructive advancement or process of thought during future spatiotemporal occasions. Stated differently, if overlapping CE percepta did not frequently, though not always, synthetically project clearly and distinctly ascertainable ideational PI percepta into consciousness during the initial stages of mental events, then thought could not constructively proceed at all. For example, if the linguistic symbols "My name is" could not be clearly conceptualized, the subjective psycholgically meaningful phrase, "John Stevens," could never be meaningfully articulated. From this we can conclude that CEC acquire their emergent actualization by being synthetically projected (in coalescing organic propensities as transcendent concrescence) from that configuration of CE percepta designated as relevant to the ideational PI percepta which logically preceded its clear emergence as a stimulus-object. Of course an analysis of the hypothetically postulated mechanisms needed to explain this synthetic emergent process must be postponed until sufficient theoretical preparation has been made to systematically analyze such notions as projection, layers, and overlap.

Lest the reader think at this point that we are engaging in unwarrantedly abstract speculation, an undeniable fact of concrete experience is simply that thought constructively advances as a function of the consciously reflective determined efforts of individual human beings. Today's thoughts do not exactly repeat themselves in the future. Granted, human thinking does too often fall into seriously constrictive habituative modes when a problem is viewed macroscopically, but a meticulous scrutinization of the problem reveals that such is not the case. Any new learning is evidence of intelligent, consciously reflective ideational advancement. Theoretically conceived, our personal experience is necessarily unique with the passing of each moment if only because of the dynamic perceptual effects of the natural world and our bodily organisms as they are concomitantly actualized, as our experience, into coherent and continuous atomic events. Stated so generally, this fact can hold true for many high-ordered organisms. In a sense we obscure the uniquely distinctive nature of man by this partial characterization. For man experiences, more specifically, the effects of ideational PI percepta synthetically accompanied by the symbolic wisdom of past learning (as CE percepta) which in its extraordinary capacity for interrelation provides the powerfully profitable grounds for generating novel

CEC, clearly pointing the way for further cognitively constructive advancement. Thus not to recognize that our past symbolic learnings, occurring as CE and ideational PI percepta, enter into the present subjective psychological experiential occasion in such a way that there is the possibility of finding a novel solution to a given problem as a result of one's reflectively determined efforts during the contemporary occasion is to overlook one of the most obvious facts about human existence. However, to attempt to theoretically explain how this constructive endeavor specifically occurs is an undertaking of enormous difficulty and complexity—as our inquiries well indicate. The abstractness of this task is a necessary consequent of a tacit unwillingness to deny the fact that the conscious thoughts of individual human beings play a causally determinative role in influencing their behavior.

CAUSALLY EFFICACIOUS PERCEPTA

It is obvious by now that CE and CEE percepta are in evidence in our experience as event-components and are thereby accessible to direct reflective conscious analysis. Also, as we have recently seen, PI percepta are the meaningfully bare, symbolically uninterpreted, immediately presented contribution from the external natural world or the internal organism. Indirect reference was made to the fact that their clear, distinct, and contemporaneous mode of occurrence was also characteristic of CEC percepta. Thus it is in contrast with PI and CEC perceptions that CE percepta will be analyzed. Our method of explanation will systematically elaborate the concept of vague symbolic connotative meaning by introducing appropriate theoretical constructs emphasizing the causally constructive or synthetic character of this class of percepta as well as that of relatedness. It is this ideationally synthetic aspect of mental experience, whereby vast, previously learned relevant symbolic resources infusively enter consciousness as ideational propensities synthetically uniting with PI and CEC percepta as coherent and continuous mental events occurring in spatio-temporal succession, that contributes, beyond the felt CEE perceptual character, the intellectually innovative quality to human experience. Meaning-as-directly-felt-relatedness was a term specifically designed to accentuate and hence define the ontologically unique phenomenon of consciously intelligible emotional-symbolic awareness, invariably exceeding the limits of human understanding in terms of its subtle, ephemeral experiential breadth. We must now transcend this basically descriptive characterization and explore the constructive nature of meaning-as-directly-felt-relatedness; that is, the manner in which it causes subjective psychological meaning must be investigated. Because of this additionally important function, meaning-as-directly-felt-relatedness has been redefined as causally efficacious perception.

Minimal, dim conscious awareness is the first emergent appearance of what is definitionally regarded as CEE percepta. At this very low, presymbolic, amorphous emotional level, conscious awareness essentially means that in primordially felt subjective psychological experience given constituent components are directly perceived as being in some sense sufficiently important to gain an organism's attention. Thus it is in becoming aware that experiential components have variable conspicuousness and thereafter, in becoming capable of making gross discriminations among components, that the sense of importance arises. No doubt the primitive intrinsic desirability of pleasure and the undesirability of pain is a guiding factor in these emerging recognitions. Another way of conceiving minimal awareness is to conceptualize a given stimulus-object as being of sufficient intensity in its effect upon an organism that the stimulus-object effect is neurologically stored for future recollection. Of course it is impossible at this time to empirically verify this storing process; however, even from rough observation of organismic behavior it is easily determined that prior learnings do in fact effectively influence presently emerging behavior. The primitiveness of this learning process as it is inferred to represent infantile subjective psychological experience cannot be overstressed. We are engaging in the difficult and often erroneous endeavor of crudely portraying presymbolic subjective experience in which the only degree of consciousness that can be supposed to exist is a sporadic emotional class of percepta predominately determined, with regard to its differential qualitative states, by the nature of natural and organic PI percepta that are themselves, at best, only dimly evident. This domain lies far below the realm of symbolically disciplined emotion, and yet we are constrained to the instrument of language in attempting to accomplish this explanation. Thus much unavoidable linguistic sophistication permeates our analysis merely because we are using language as a means to conduct our speculations. Nevertheless, we have some understanding of infantile states through both careful observation and reflective analysis of our personal inner states. It is not being maintained that an immature human organism makes intentionally aware efforts to seek out meaningfully important elements to make certain that the important elements are rationally committed to memory for the specific purpose of utilizing them for future intelligent inquiry. These, obviously, are behavioral acts characteristic of mature symbolic intelligence. Rather, the primitive recognitions are undoubtedly far more consciously indeterminate and grounded in basic reflexive capacities spontaneously operative merely due to the human organism's intrinsic structure. It would seem at this low level of conscious awareness that the perceived effects of objects of importance are frequently unwittingly stored in an automatic, undeliberated, subtle, and cumulative manner. At the sign stage, the mere process of recording both unsymbolized and, later, symbolized data appears to be exclusively in evidence, while the more advanced concern for relating the collected, and hence stored, data must await the next major maturational advance.

The possibility for meaningfully relating neurologically stored perceptual information, as this phenomenon is contingent upon conscious experience, is solely a function of reflective consciousness. This next major intellectual advance in a human organism's symbolic understanding entails the capability of entertaining presently entering PI percepta while concomitantly recollecting an infusion of conscious perception pertaining to information learned in the past. Since PI percepta function as stimulus-objects—and this is clearly evident in concrete experience, whether in terms of natural, organic, or ideational, including emotional, PI percepta—all relevant stored ideational and/or emotional propentionalities are reflexively conjured to the ingressed effects thereby providing the grounds for reflexive conscious synthesis; resultantly, a more complex emotion or concept emerges, typically as CEC. At infantile presymbolic levels an infant would visually experience the mother stimulus-object effects while an infusion of concomitant CE percepta corresponding to the linguistic terms "happiness," "excitement," "security," "resolution of the painful feeling of hunger," etc., all learned in prior experiential encounters with the mother stimulus-object, would reflexively and synthetically come to bear upon the PI perception; hence enhancing its subjective psychological emotional meaning far beyond the meaning of the PI perception considered solely in itself, which, strictly speaking, would be inherently meaningless. At this stage of development, vaguely conscious familiarity of a given PI perception is the crude origin of reflective consciousness because the conditions for synthesis are in evidence. No longer is the PI mother perception an undifferentiated percept among innumerable others. Rather, due to the concomitant reflexive infusion of CE percepta, the mother perception is, additionally, caused to be experienced as "mother-is-happiness," "mother-is-pleasant excitement," "mother-is-security," "mother-is-pleasure," and so on. Thus when these many relevant associations, in conjunction with the bare PI mother perception, have been consciously understood as reciprocally related, reflective conscious synthesis has occurred. This same principle holds true for all subjective psychological experience regardless of its level of sophistication.

From this it can be seen that the emergent subjective psychological states in which infants experience the emotional urges of importance and later familiarity are possible in their functional capacity as emotional stimulus-objects because of a backlog of slowly accumulated recollected experience which, after a necessary amount of physiological maturation has occurred, is brought constructively upon PI percepta in such a way as to cause the phenomena of importance and familiarity in the sense of "bringing into being as an original, ontologically unique symbolic entity." Again, an illustration of this synthetic process is when an infant experiences the pleasurable feeling and taste of consuming food and, after repeated similar experiential feelings, the process becomes increasingly pleasurable as a result of having experienced feeling on many previous occasions. Each successive feeding experience is not an entirely new one for the infant because similar past instances, as CEE and CE percepta or wisdom, synthetically unite with PI percepta thereby increasing the importance and familiarity of the ever-emerging present. The crude, emotionally embodied information haphazardly recorded in past feeding experiences is constructively associated with present feeding-percepta ultimately as a result of the organismic physio-chemical structure which lends itself to the promotion of concrescence due to its interpenetrative relationship with inner and outer environments. In the higher-ordered case of familiarity, increased precision in conscious emergence is demonstrated when infants become excited in anticipation, for example, of the pleasure that will be experienced during feeding. Such anticipatory manifestations may be provoked by the natural PI percepta, the sight of mother, or the sight of the bottle, etc., entering the infant's consciousness. This example shows that CE percepta or past wisdom is playing an increasingly more powerful role in causally determining the subjective psychological meaning that is ascribed to bare PI percepta, for in both situations the PI percepta had not yet effected the concrete bodily felt impact that would cause pleasurable experiences as a direct result of actually touching mother and the bottle and tasting milk. The spatially distant perceptual appearance of mother or the bottle were very abstract in their meaningful implications in contrast to actually tasting food or touching mother.

Conscious awareness, then, at all levels of sophistication is essentially the behavioral act of taking account of, from a subjective psychological frame of reference, any given event-component of importance as it occurs in spatio-temporal passage. This important awareness is in some way transformed into a physio-chemical analogue that can be stored for future recollection, to be subsequently either conjured through a reflective effort or emerge reflexively as an event-component. Recorded awareness may be theoretically conceptualized as lying on a continuum of recognitional clarity and distinctness. As components of infant experience, these are indeed consciously vague; however, clarity increases with greater symbolic mastery. In reflective conscious awareness the situation is basically similar. When relevant previously learned CE percepta synthetically unite with contemporary PI and/or CEC percepta to causally determine the subjective psychological meaning attributed to the clear contemporary event-components, and further, when this concomitant perceptual emergence can be meaningfully understood as symbolically *interrelated*, the necessary conditions have been fulfilled for reflective conscious synthesis; a process beginning on an unconscious level and then, with increased concrescence, emerging into conscious experience as novel cognitive association. The degree to which relevant wisdom can be clearly consciously related in its concomitant appearance with contemporary event-components—the necessary condition for reflective conscious synthesis—is a phenomenon that can also be conceived to occur on a vague-to-clear continuum. In both categorical instances of conscious recording and reflective conscious synthesis the crucial factor to understand is that of consciousness, for this represents the emergent ontological frame of reference from which uniquely human symbolically meaningful determinations can be intelligently made, and hence transcends the lower-ordered realms of reflexive and physio-chemical causality such as mechanistic, presign, and sign behaviors.

As has been frequently said, emotional feeling, in its myriad degrees of discipline ranging from dim, sporadic emotion to emotion assuming the stable, determinate character of symbolic forms, is the substance or medium of mind-phenomena. We have also seen that the essence of intelligent mental behavior is in linguistic ideational forms or those entities that can be consciously organized into an indefinite number of relations. But in contrast to the entities, properties, and relations contributed to us as natural PI percepta, ideational entities, properties, and relations are very strange phenomena. Apart from the intuitively compelling materiality-spirituality issue, it is evident that ideational PI and CEC perceptual entities, logically conceived in themselves as spoken sounds, written words, or silently conceived thoughts, are clear and distinct symbolic components. Such words as tree, red, happiness, etc. are clearly and distinctly formulable as simplified symbolic elements when they are spoken, written, and silently thought. However, in this act of abstracting the denotative symbolic component from its connotative meaning, hoping thereby to accentuate the nature of the remaining clear and distinct element, a serious error is committed if our efforts are interpreted to mean that denotative symbolic elements can be meaningfully understood in disassociation from their necessarily concomitant connotative elements. An excellent example of this is when one is with individuals who are speaking an unknown foreign language. Here is an instance where the unknowledgeable listener is entertaining nearly pure denotatively clear symbolic percepta. Hence the spoken words are regarded by the listener as a mere unintelligible series of natural PI perceptual sounds, for no causally efficacious perceptual meaning can be synthetically brought to bear upon the natural PI perceptual sounds so that they may be rendered intelligible as subjective psychological meaning. This illustration basically reveals the dipolar nature of mental process. On one hand there are the unintelligible natural PI sounds, and in contrast there is an absence of what in normal intelligible linguistic communication would be defined as CEC, CE, and CEE percepta that fill out bare contributed PI percepta with substantive subjective psychological meaning. Again, the above example, as it isolates the PI perceptual domain from the unknown concomitant symbolic realm, forcefully demonstrates the fact that causally efficacious percepta truly do cause symbolic meaning. However, stated in this way, it is not yet evident that CEE and CE percepta are logically antecedent to the final clear, distinct, and simplified emergent or projected CEC perceptual product. It should be kept in mind, of course, that the whole logical chain of development as it occurs in its uniquely meaningful way is originally initiated by PI percepta functioning as a stimulus-object. In any case, the particular class of perception to which our analytical attention is devoted at this point has been clearly delineated. The reader is asked to contemplate those percepta designated as logically separate from all PI percepta and moreover those symbolic components defined as denotative or CEC percepta. We are left, of course, with symbolic components termed connotative meaning or meaning-as-directly-felt-relatedness; terms more recently defined as CE and CEE percepta.

Causally efficacious percepta manifest themselves as bewilderingly complex, integrated configurations of very vague to moderately conscious symbolic meaning, concrescently yielding concise emergent symbolic components functioning as denotative, clearly conscious focal points from which their multitudinous, constitutively vague symbolic and emotional components can be raised to a CEC status through conscious reflection. This means that highly succinct ideational PI or CEC percepta, in reponse to a given stimulus-object, can representatively organize vast complex symbolized histories of relevant learned human experience, portions of which can be recalled both reflexively and through a reflective effort, thus being symbolically re-enjoyed during the present. Every denotative symbolic element ephemerally appearing as an event-component has an accompaniment of immediately implicit though vaguely comprehended symbolic and emotional meaning, potentially capable of partial reflective explication as CEC in successive events, requiring years of learning for its development and efficacious implementation in intelligent problem-solving. The extensive storage, and hence synthetic, capacity of human cerebral mechanisms enables relevant accumulated wisdom of the past to constructively enhance the meaning of contemporaneously contributed perception. The essential meaningful nature of conscious and reflective conscious experience is not predominately in its PI and CEC perceptual aspects, although these dimensions are the most conspicuous facets of our experience, with the exception of natural PI perception (keeping in view, of course, that denotative symbolic components are absolutely essential for high-ordered intelligent behavior). It is rather the implicit CE perceptual concomitants emerging as experiential components from an enormous resource of relevant, disciplined past experience that reflexively infuse clearly conscious symbolic components with meaning-as-directly-felt-relatedness. Although this issue has been discussed earlier in some detail the distinction is so subtle that it warrants reconsideration for clarity.

The issue concerns specifically what has been analyzed as meaning-as-directly-felt-relatedness. The psychological phenomenon of consciously meaningful understanding as it is actualized by any individual human mind in any given conscious experience arises from gradually subsuming originally primitive, unwieldy, nebulously conscious emotional experience to extensive disciplining, hence transforming infantile primordial experience into highly sophisticated symbolic subjective psychological behavior. Further, at mature levels of intelligence, symbolic behavior gains its conscious clarity, precision, and extensive flexibility in its power of representation from denotative symbolic simplification. In saying this, it must also be understood, on the other hand, that the positive merits of denotative feeling are wholly contingent upon the concomitantly appearing, more vague symbolic components, CEE and CE percepta. Denotative understanding is possible because in its occurrence as CEC percepta, an accompaniment of CE and CEE percepta immediately reflexively infuse denotative percepta with the relevant, meaningfully enhancing wisdom of the past. The essence of this wisdom is in the consciously perceivable quality of vaguely perceivable relatedness that renders CEC or ideational PI perception experientially meaningful. This distinction, on a far more elementary level, is precisely the subjective psychological difference between Cassirer's sign and symbol stages. At the sign stage, it will be recalled, a child is capable of verbally responding to given stimulus-object effects. Thus when the mother articulates the word "mama," the child reiterates the sound. But at this stage of development there is no manifestation of anything that could be regarded as meaningful understanding. The child's behavior is essentially reflexive with no consciously accessible intervening symbolic components capable of functioning as ideational PI stimulus-objects for conjuring relevant wisdom in order that constructive, intelligent thought may temporally evolve. In short, there is no evidence of symbolic relatedness infusing the bare natural PI perceptual utterance of the child with subjective psychological meaning, which would have transformed the occasion into a meaningful mental event whereby the entry of PI perception was synthetically united with CEC perception, carrying with it a relevant history of CEE and CE perceptual wisdom to fill out the event with directly experienced subjective psychological meaning. In contrast, at the symbol stage or perhaps even the late sign stage, the child initially discovers that bare reflexive utterances do have significance beyond mere playful, pleasurable vocal activity. They are found to be concise representations of all the previously recorded relevant experiential meaning that the child has derived from interacting with given stimulus-objects. Thus, as has been stated previously, the term "mama" becomes a means for collectively subsuming under a single utterance such meaningful experiences as mama-pleasure, mama-food, and mama-warmth. Moreover, these experiences can be re-enjoyed and projected as a passionate, emotionally expressive urge toward the stimulus-object to which they refer. More important, at later stages of symbolic development, children, after having established a repertory of symbolic tags, can attain the highest form of linguistic achievement; they discover that the tags which they have been using as devices for re-enjoying past experience, categorically designating homogeneous experiences, and projecting emotionally meaningful expression, have meaningful relevance for one another in their unique existence as an independent symbolic realm; one that can be cognitively manipulated apart from a direct dependent association with immediately entering natural and organic PI perception. At this point the child may also have antecedently discovered a less abstract version of the phenomenon of relatedness in his more concrete experience involving the physical manipulation of natural objects. Beyond this triumphant discovery, the matter of further symbolic development becomes essentially one of learning additional symbols and developing an increased sophistication in their usage. Therefore, during the sign and symbol stages the groundwork for subjective psychological meaning as an experienced phenomenon and as an ontologically unique causal frame of reference is provided. In symbolically meaningful awareness we transcend reflexivity for words are no longer bare meaningless sounds. One now becomes consciously aware that reality in its appearance as entities, properties, and relations is being symbolically understood in a disciplined way; a way that can be subjectively comprehended and actively modified through a subjective effort. All this is possible from acquiring a number of symbolic tags and then discovering that the tags possess the potentiality for being interrelated. The symbols can be used to descriptively represent reality as it is PI perceptually contributed, and moreover, portions of internal and external environmental states can be modified in accordance to intelligently created intrinsically symbolic configurations. Thus, for example, the organic PI perception of thirst promotes the successive utterance "May I have a glass of water?"; here is a simple illustration of a human organism intelligently and actively endeavoring to modify his internal state of thirst. However, even more basic is the conscious subjective understanding that the denotatively clear symbol, water, for example, means something. Hence the subjectively understood meaning results from a reflexive infusion of CE percepta so that the individual implicitly understands that water has a presymbolic taste, tactile quality, distinctive appearance, etc., and the symbolic attributes of good, cool, wet, fluid, etc. These many properties are immediately, though vaguely, consciously present in the usage of the term "water" and constitute the wisdom that reflexively accompanies any symbolic term. Equally as important, however, is the fact that the many qualifications which define and set limits to the meaning of words, occurring as CE and CEE percepta, also experientally cause the subjective psychological meaning of symbols in their emergence as the symbolic entities-in-process constituting mind. It is this phenomenon which we shall consider next.

In analyzing the concept of causality specifically as it refers to CE and CEE percepta, a crude distinction is initially necessary in order to distinguish between what might be loosely regarded as natural and ideational causality. Natural causality will be considered, for argumentative purposes, in Hume's sense of perceived temporal succession of phenomenal occurrence. Ideational causality, however, will be defined in ontologically stronger terms; namely, in the sense of bringing into being or creating. Thus, in speaking of CE and CEE percepta as they come constructively to bear upon PI percepta, thereby generating projected causally efficacious concepts (CEC), it is our view that the former two classes of percepta together cause CEC to be subjectively psychologically meaningful. Of course it is evident that all mental percepta are emergents from underlying correlative physio-chemical processes and are in this sense comprehended in terms of natural causality. Therefore the concept of ideational causality applies exclusively to the conscious and reflectively conscious or the subjective psychological domain. The latter domain, then, has a mode of causality that can be delineated as occurring in three ways. First, there is the way indicated in our previous analysis on PI percepta whereby ideational PI perception can function as stimulus-objects, hence causally determining which CEE, CE, and CEC percepta will be deemed relevant for its symbolic elaboration. Second, there is the type of causality that is our present concern, where CE and CEE percepta reflexively infuse CEC percepta in such a way as to cause them to be subjective psychologically meaningful. Finally, there is the way in which CE and CEE percepta causally operate in projecting ideational PI and CEC percepta, a topic to be considered subsequently. Because of the structural nature of the human organism, concrescence involves, initially, synthetically uniting sensation with relevant pre-established organic propensities and then steadily proceeding to levels where physical processes yield emergent simplified perceptual stimulus-object effects that constitute and thereby efficaciously influence the evolvement of mental events through their unique mode of entry. It should also be said that in our analysis of the three types of ideational causality we are obviously conceptualizing an S-O-R model of human behavior as distinct from a behavioristic S-R view, for our concept of mind is, in effect, an elaborate exposition of the possible types of intervening variables that can possibly operate causally between S and R. Further, and this point is less evident, the effect of an ideational causality view is that a materialistic-mechanistic, natural concept of causality, such as that maintained in all exact empirical sciences and some behavioral sciences, is, in principle, inadequate to yield a full account of human behavior; Feigl's empirical identity thesis also implies this conclusion. However, it does not follow that a subjective psychology can, therefore, generate supernatural cause-effect explanations of human behavior. Rather, as is becoming apparent, our view is specifically designed to yield cause-effect explanations, but explanations involving different types of entities from those of the natural and biological sciences. Again, this point will be examined subsequently.

To demonstrate more clearly the nature of the second type of ideational causality, let us envision a circumstance where a man A upon having read in a newspaper about the death of a close friend, proceeds to write a letter of condolence to widow B. The causal sequence of the entire act may be expressed for maximal precision in the following abstract manner. The print embodying the death notification entered A as natural PI perception, hence conjuring relevant CEE, CE, and CEC reflexive infusive percepta actualized as a subjective psychological symbolic understanding of the death phenomenon. Then, the conscious understanding antecedently emerging most conspicuously as CEC percepta was successively transformed into ideational PI perceptual clarity functioning as a stimulus-object that conjured various relevant (CEE and CE perceptual) ideational propensities which, in turn, reflexively infused the PI perception with wisdom, thereby rendering the occasion intelligible and, moreover, raising such event-components as great surprise, sorrow from losing a friend, sympathy for the widow, etc. It was from considerations such as these that A was prompted to write to B. Initially we can say that the CEC clearly symbolically representing the natural PI percepta issuing from the print, and further, the CEC clearly symbolically representing the ideational PI percepta of surprise, sorrow, sympathy, etc., later when transformed to function as ideational PI perceptual stimulus-objects were functioning in accordance to the first type of ideational causality.

The third type of projective ideational causality was also efficacious in yielding the above ideational PI and CEC percepta. But there is yet infusive causality (the second type) which marks a decisive transcendence beyond materialistic-mechanistic or blindly reflexive causality such as that manifested by physio-chemical process, thermostats, electronic devices, and so on. Here, over and above the fact that stimulus-object effects (the PI perceptions of print, surprise, sorrow, sympathy, etc.) issuing from stimulus-objects located in the natural world and the organism's own internal body are efficaciously influencing the process of A writing to B, there still remains the fact that both the first and third causal modes are necessarily contingent upon the possibility of ideational infusive causality. The two key terms to be understood in explaining this phenomenon are wisdom and infuse. In considering the nature and function of ideational infusive causality we are discussing a matter that has been repeatedly contemplated in one way or another; perhaps the most relevant analyses were those pertaining to meaning-as-directly-felt-relatedness. It is now our purpose to complete our characterization of phenomenon of infusive causality. The illustration of man A acknowledging the death of a friend, thereby prompting him to communicate his sympathies to widow B, is in fact a very complex causal circumstance. Infusive causality represents the essence of all subjective psychological meaning as it ontologically occurs in sequential atomic units of human experience. We have seen that this experience is an ever-emerging synthetic product of perception analytically classifiable into the three psychologically universal Categories of directly accessible elements. It has also been demonstrated that these perceptual elements can enter the consciousness through diverse modes (PI, CEC, CE, and CEE), partially distinguishable in terms of the degree of perceptual clarity manifested by the percepta as they appear in consciousness. Thus in any given experiential occasion, percepta from diverse modes concomitantly emerge as an inextricable unity or event. A remarkable feature of mental events is the multitudinous number of percepta that synthetically constitute these conscious unifications. Beyond the criterion of degree of perceptual clarity, perceptual modes are also characterized by indicating the way in which their perceptual products function in generating mental events. PI percepta function as stimulus-objects in determining which propensities will be conjured as substantive event-components; CEC percepta function as the simplified emergent products projected from relevant CE and CEE percepta as a testimony of creatively advancing thought processes; and finally—and here we come to the issue of infusive causality—CE and CEE percepta function in mental events in such a way as to cause human experience to be subjective psychologically meaningful. These latter two perceptual modes define those directly accessible products whose essential attribute is their vaguely conscious relatedness to one another. In this sense, relatedness is wisdom and wisdom is all the relevant past learning that has been physio-chemically stored so that it functions reflexively, and through reflective conjuration wisdom functions to intelligently actualize all our myriad ideational behavioral endeavors. Metaphorically speaking, this creative, causally infusive process has been described as the relevant wisdom of the past concomitantly coming constructively to bear upon the present occasion. It can be more technically defined as the concomitant actualization of PI, CEC, CE, and CEE percepta during a particular event. Logically analyzed in terms of previous argumentation, let us say that physio-chemical or natural causality, in contrast to ideational causality, does not entail nor admit the inclusion of mental factors or variables in formulating various functional explanations for natural phenomenal occurrences.

Scientists need not introduce psyches as efficacious variables in explaining the behavior of single-cell organisms, thermostats, etc., and, more important, they do not have to introduce subjective psychological considerations in establishing these explanations. This latter point is, in effect, made by Whitehead in his definition of thinking homogeneously about nature. However, for reasons discussed earlier, such is not the case in explaining human behavior; mental phenomena do intervene as causal behavioral determinants. Human behavior cannot be exhaustively explained in the same methodological ways appropriate for natural phenomena. In fact, all explanations of physical phenomena and intelligent cognitive behavior in general must presuppose *a priori* subjective psychological behavior for their very possibility of occurrence. Basically, this is grounded in the fact that human intelligent behavior necessarily entails efficacious consciousness and reflective consciousness whose intellectually constructive powers result from their intrinsic symbolic nature. Therefore a discussion of symbolic behavior necessarily leads to the subject matter of a subjective psychology. The only facets of subjective psychological behavior that are legitimately accessible to an objective psychology are ideational presentationally immediate (PI) and causally efficacious conceptual (CEC) perceptual event-components, when they are verbally articulated, gesturally expressed, or manifestly written. Thus, an objective psychology cannot in principle have theoretical and methodological access to what we have defined as CE and CEE event-components, functioning in their causally infusive capacity, or to the other types of ideational causality, for that matter.

The extraordinary importance of this can be concretely understood with reference to our former example involving subjects A and B. It was absolutely necessary that subject A be capable of consciously understanding as subjective psychologically meaningful experience the printed death notification, and his experiences of surprise, sorrow, sympathy, etc., in order to communicate condolences to widow B. Thus the indeterminately large number of mental event-components (occurring as PI, CEC, CE, and CEE percepta in their inextricably related actualized states) that were necessary for A to write to B represent a completely unique class of ontological causal determinants that do not in principle intervene in natural causal relations. Therefore, the subjective psychological meaning, for example, of each word in the death notice and of surprise, sorrow, sympathy, etc., are infused through and through with a history of previously acquired relevant wisdom that causes the words, individually and in their collective form, to possess the meaning that they do. More specifically, the word "sorrow," for example, occurring as a bare transitorily entertained CEC perceptual event-component in a given train of thought, may implicitly contain in its moment of subjectively meaningful actualization in the mind of subject A the CE percepts of great sadness, personal loss, waning enthusiasm about living, the recollection of losing a loved one, many enjoyable experiences that will no longer be shared, etc. All these vaguely conscious, implicit CE perceptions, and undoubtedly many more similar cognitive factors, would concomitantly accompany the mere thought of sorrow. Further, subject A in pondering his inner state of sorrow would be simultaneously seized by highly vague but powerfully efficacious substrata of experientially potent CEE percepta that may yield sporadically fearful, despairing, or compassionate attitudes about his own existence. This illustration merely hints at the profound complexity and existential uniqueness of human experiential phenomena, whether intense or matter of fact, that arise from causally infusing CEC and/or ideational PI percepta with relevant CE and CEE perception. Thus it is in this way that what each human being understands through direct acquaintance as subjective psychological experience is constructively synthesized, thereby yielding an ontologically unique realm of phenomena possessing their own characteristic entities, properties, and modes of relation whose dynamic cognitive configurations are structurally symbolically concordant with those of natural, organic, and emotional presentational immediate perceptual deliverances. Anyone who ponders these distinctions will understand that the notion of natural or materialistic-mechanistic causality can have only limited applicability in systematically investigating human behavior unless the presuppositional basis upon which this theory is predicated is modified to consistently incorporate those entities ontologically demanded by ideational causality, efficaciously operative within a subjective psychological framework.

It should be clear at this point that even what we may regard as the simplest of linguistic concepts are thoroughly infused with vaguely conscious CE and CEE percepta, over and above their merely denotatively evident symbolic form. Thus, CE and CEE percepta in their infusive function are so numerous and synthetically potent that an individual's originally amorphous emotional experience is subsumed to extraordinary discipline to an extent that meaningfully intelligent subjective psychological experience gradually emerges. Moreover, CE and CEE percepta can be said to cause subjective psychologically meaningful experience; i.e., due to the relatedness among symbols—the intrinsic property that enables linguistic symbols to be subjectively meaningful—these percepta infuse denotatively clear symbolic components in such a way as to render the clear elements personally meaningful by uniting them with other relevant though vaguely conscious linguistic symbols. Thus, denotative clarity is synthetically coexistent with connotatively vague symbolic and emotional meaning. In saying this we are actually maintaining that denotative symbolic components acquire their substantive subjective meaning from, or are caused to be personally meaningful as a result of, a concomitant infusion of previously learned wisdom. In conjunction with this infusive process, it was previously implied that infusion occurs in two distinct ways: through reflexive and reflective conjuration. The most conspicuously apparent distinction to be made in distinguishing the two types of functions from one another is their temporal difference; that is, the former synthetic process occurs almost instantaneously, while the latter requires more time for conscious reflective analysis. As an example, let us psychologically examine the question "What is man's true nature?" in light of reflexive and reflective infusive causality. First, it is evident that the subjective psychological meaning of each particular word is understood almost instantaneously merely upon consciously attending to the linguistic terms. Mature readers typically do not have to exert as great an intellectual effort to understand the term "man," for example, as that required of them when initially learning the word during childhood. Therefore, CE, CEE, and CEC percepta are nearly instantaneously actualized when bare (PI perceptual) printed words enter the consciousness. The case is similar when comprehending the words collectively as a complete question, although this requires more time. Again, the CEC man is immediately infused by the CE percepta, a term designating human beings; men, women, and children conceived collectively; all men at all time; an intelligent species of animal; a class of creatures generally possessing two legs, a head, two hands, etc., not to mention many possible CEC percepta. There is little discernible consciously deliberate effort required for understanding the words individually or collectively. However, in contrast to this easily executed process which essentially involves conjuring past wisdom to come to bear upon the present occasion, there is the far more complicated but in principle similar process entailing temporally prolonged analytical reflection. This is a situation in which solutions, understandings, etc., are not reflexively yielded; rather, careful, gradual, constructive deliberation is required for problem-solving. The two experientially distinct ways in which CEE and CE percepta may be conjured as causally infusive can also be understood by saying that reflexively infusive causality characterizes those percepta whose entry into the mind as event-components is so spontaneous and massively pervasive that they provide an enduring, uninterrupted, qualitatively suggestive flow of perception which we directly perceive as meaningful, familiar, typical subjective psychological experience. Of course, stated in this way, we cannot discriminate precisely amongst PI, CEC, CE, and CEE perceptual event-components. Hence, we must make a determined effort to focus our analytical attention particularly upon the causally infusive dimension of experience.

We must develop a deep and accurate sensitivity to the truly profound complexity of our personal conscious events, and understand how experientially barren and, in fact, logically and psychologically unintelligible, our awareness would be, devoid of past wisdom. Again, in contrast to reflexive infusive causality which causes our many matter-of-fact event-components to be spontaneously intelligible because of automatically conjured wisdom that enhances conscious awareness with an enduring substratum of experiential intimacy with our inner and outer environments, reflective infusive causality yields an overriding stratum of CEE and CE percepta lacking the properties of spontaneous and enduring symbolically meaningful enhancement characteristic of CEC and PI perceptual event-components. Rather, reflective infusive causality is far more sporadic, meaningfully unpredictable, qualitatively variable in its perceptual enhancement and, moreover, difficult to constructively conjure. Reflective infusive percepta are, in fact, the transcendent crest of organic concrescence as directly perceived in subjective psychological experience. But this frontier of ideational synthetic emergence necessarily presupposes the faithfully enduring substratum of reflexive infusive causality, for it is only from this subordinate preconditional conscious frame of reference that reflective synthesis can be fruitfully actualized at all. Metaphorically speaking, it is only in light of past wisdom that we may intelligently understand the present and hence imaginatively proceed into the future. In more technical terms, this means that higher-ordered conjuration of reflectively infusive CEE and CE percepta can emerge only if reflexive infusive causality has antecedently meaningfully elucidated CEC perception so that it can be transformed into ideational PI perceptual stimulus-objects, thereby designating which CE, CEC, and CEE percepta will be conjured as relevant ideational propensities—and further, which CE and CEE percepts will emerge in a transcendent reflectively infusive capacity. We are now discussing some of the causal dynamics of mental events, the only stimulus-objects that can be known in themselves, in their ontologically unique function as stimulus-objects. It has been proven by the empirical identity thesis that mental events are not logically identical to their correlative underlying physio-chemical processes. One extremely important implication of this conclusion is that mental events can function as a logically distinct class of stimulus-objects over and above those characteristic of materialistic mechanism.

We have shown earlier that this distinct type of ideational causality arose from the phenomenon of meaning-as-directly-felt-relatedness, operating synthetically in conjunction with denotative meaning in the actualized symbolic, largely linguistic state. We have also demonstrated that connotative symbolic meaning has reflexively and reflectively infusive causal characters. It is primarily through these latter two functional modes that mental events acquire their ontologically unique ideational causal status, hence transcending physio-chemical or natural causality. Briefly stated, this means that the less consistently productive, though synthetically potent, mechanism of reflective infusive causality must necessarily function contingently upon preconditional reflexively infusive causality which, through CEE and CE perceptual enhancement, provides a basic subjective psychological frame of reference that initially consciously isolates an object of importance for human organisms. The significance of this seemingly trivial point is that if an object of concern could not be clearly and meaningfully conceptualized at the outset of its perceptual apprehension, then more profoundly analytical successive thinking would not be possible. Since human beings can, however, easily conceptualize many objects of importance as a result of gradually developed reflexively infusive causality, and because clear initial conceptualization of PI perceptual phenomena is a necessary precondition for higher-ordered reflection, it follows that conscious understanding is a logically prerequisite factor over and above natural causal considerations in producing humanly intelligent behavioral responses to given stimulus-conditions. In the latter section of Part Two it was argued that although conscious events were necessarily contingent upon underlying physio-chemical correlates for their possible emergence, on the other hand, further increased organic concrescence or intellectual development was also contingent upon the synthetic power of conscious events in themselves through their capacity to function as stimulus-objects. This means that mental events can additionally cause physio-chemical synthesis in the transcendent process of concrescence. Therefore, in initially clearly and meaningfully conceptualizing a given object of importance—an elementary action whose very possibility rests in great part upon the fact that the PI perception can be thoroughly reflexively infused with CEE, CE, and CEC perception—we are, in effect, conjuring a multitude of relevant organic propensities that consciously emerge as our meaningful apprehension of an object of concern. In the more sophisticated process of reflecting analytically upon the object, we are, roughly speaking, conjuring all those relevant organic propensities that will yield us a spontaneous understanding of the object. Moreover, there are distinct additional propensities that consciously emerge as reflectively infusive CEE and CE percepta corresponding to any possible consciously determinable relations that the object of concern may have with any previously established relevant wisdom. Reflective infusive causality, in its sporadically fecund and temporally prolonged mode of affective-cognitive actualization, is clearly in evidence when, in its appearance as determinately transcending a stratum of subordinate reflexive infusively meaningful awareness, it occurs in consciously evident distinction from the former as CEE and CE percepta representating novel or atypical, infusively conjured relations with objects formerly not recognized as possessing relevant mutual relations. High-ordered reflectively infusive causality has its originative basis ultimately in unconscious physio-chemical processes. This means, more specifically, that when a reflective effort is devoted to some object of concern, a large number of reflexively infusive ideational propensities are conjured to consciousness. But frequently as the reflective effort persists, an increasing number of atypical propensities begin to consciously emerge, indicative of novel modes for relating objects. This is the essential manifestation of reflectively infusive causality. Our theory of cognitive synthesis implies that when objects of importance are reflectively contemplated, the objects, perceived as PI stimulus-object effects, activate, concomitant with conscious understanding, correlative physio-chemical processes which when perceptually entertained in conscious experience, as a result of reflexive infusion and because of those correlative states corresponding to "persistent reflective effort," begin to progressively engage in physio-chemical concrescent synthesis. Starting initially at an unconscious level of purely organic cerebral functioning, and as this mode of integration becomes steadily more complex and interrelated with other previously established relevant processes, the newly synthesized products emerge into conscious experience as reflectively infusive CE and CEE percepta. The typical concretely conscious manifestation of this complex underlying process occurs when, for example, after we have reflected upon a matter of concern for given periods of time, much to our surprise the answer unexpectedly springs into consciousness. If we carefully analyze this matter-of-fact phenomenon it will be seen that we do not intentionally cause a specific novel ideational synthesis; rather, through the ability to consciously focus attention upon a specific object of concern as a result of reflexive infusion, and because of the ability to consciously reflect upon the problem as a result of reflective infusion, the necessary preconditions for emergent ideational synthesis, originating in unconscious physio-chemical regions, have been established. This is the process of setting the stage for creative ideational emergence as rendered possible by the preconditional factors of consciousness and reflective consciousness as well as operative physio-chemical mechanisms. Thus we do not personally cause ideational synthesis, in the sense of knowing precisely which elements will be synthesized by mind, and thereby proceed to deliberately unite them as though it were a carefully controlled chemical experiment where components are known and hence the synthetic results can be accurately predicted. The causal role of mind is to set the stage for cognitive synthesis, having readily available as reflexive and reflective infusive CE and CEE percepta all the relevant wisdom that can be conjured at that time for constructively resolving problematic circumstances. We cannot rid ourselves, in conceiving our model for mind, of the classical Greek notions of functional harmony and virtuous behavior as important factors in the global execution of intelligent behavior and the resultant enjoyment of genuinely humane personal experience.

The phrase "persistent reflective effort" was used above as the general enduring event-component empirically identical with a large group of physio-chemical processes that, in conjunction with those corresponding to reflexive infusive percepta, were alleged theoretically to unite in concrescence so that ultimately novel, reflectively infusive perception would emerge into consciousness, thereby promoting cognitive advance. We must at this point devote our attention to clarifying the notion of exercising a persistent reflective effort, for this is a central aspect of the consciously deliberate behavior termed intelligent problem-solving. It was said that the reflexive infusion of percepta is a process readily capable of being perceived as providing a basic, temporally enduring substratum of perceptually meaningful familiarity in response to our direct experience of reality. This was said to be the case because reflexively infusive percepta caused the possibility of symbols, primarily linguistic symbols which enable primitive emotional feeling to be subsumed to discipline and render intelligent behavior possible, by enabling PI perception to be concomitantly united with denotative symbolic components and reflexively infused by numerous connotative components. Therefore it can be said that reflexively infusive perception synthetically united with clear and distinct symbolic perceptual components constitutes a major portion of the event-components comprising complete mental events at any given time. In fact, the only possible components that remain available to fill out complete events are natural and organic PI percepta and those defined as reflectively infusive perception that must actually be regarded as atypical or novel CEE and CE percepta that emerge in contrast to those deemed as reflexive infusively relevant by PI perception functioning in their capacity as stimulus-objects. From this, it was previously maintained that reflective infusive perception, because of its contrasting, unpredictably novel, sporadically occurring character, concomitantly transcended its consistently enduring reflexively infusive perceptual substratum, with respect to its conspicuously novel ideational character. We saw that this transcendent synthetic mode of entry was, so to speak, the crest of novel concrescent emergence as it manifests itself in conscious percep-

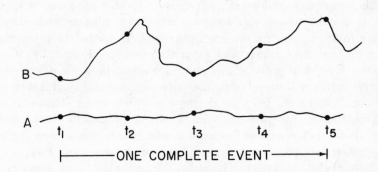

Figure 11. Reflexive and reflective infusive perceptual modes

tion. The two concomitantly occurring contrasting modes of reflexive
and reflective infusive CEE and CE perception are diagrammatically expressed in Figure 11 which represents the topology of a complete event
(t_1-t_5) involving the entry of reflexive (line A) and reflective (line B)
infusive perception as they function in consciously ascertainable contrast with one another during reflective conscious behavior. Line A
represents the spontaneously understood meaning that is brought to bear
upon PI perception as the meaning symbolically participates in consciousness as reflectively infusive perception. Line B represents the
sporadically occurring, potently suggestive CEE and CE perception,
symbolically indicative of novel ways for relating objects of concern
to other relevant known objects in order to promote a more intelligent
comprehension of the former's nature, as they originate in consciously
ascertainable contrast to the reflexively infusive perceptual substratum
necessarily persisting during conscious reflection. In answer, then, to
the original problem of technically defining the mental act of exercising
a persistent reflective effort, as this behavior could be regarded as a
particular configuration of event-components having, in principle, determinate physio-chemical correlates, let us say that it essentially consists
in the concomitant, consciously ascertainable contrasting entry of reflexive and reflective infusive perception into our mental events. More
specifically, what we directly experience in reflective consciousness,

over and above PI and CEC event-components, is a consciously distinguishable variable amplification of meaningful understanding embodied within reflective infusive CEE and CE perception consisting of
the novel relations perceived among given objects of concern as this
information emerges into consciousness from unconscious synthesis, and
as this temporally prolonged awareness is vividly accentuated in contrast to a substrate of spontaneous, reflexively infusive understanding
issuing from the constitutive linguisitic symbols needed to conceptually
effect the reflective effort throughout its existence. Essentially, we are
emphasizing the cognitively experienced contrast between reflective and
reflexive infusive perception as they are concomitantly actualized with
relevant PI and CEC percepta during a complete event. Thus it is from
this contrasting, the preconditions of which necessarily presuppose *a
priori* that consciousness and conscious reflection be considered as *causal
determinants* in producing human behavioral responses, that perceptual testimonies of novel relatedness among objects of concern are
permitted to emerge into conscious experience. Within this phenomenon
lies the synthetic power of human intelligence. All this was metaphorically implicit in the phrase, the wisdom of the past is concomitantly
brought constructively to bear upon the present occasion so as to enhance
its meaning.

In our distinction between natural and ideational causality, it was
said that we know the former type in the sense of perceived temporal
succession. At this point, the latter type of causality, specifically as it
is embodied within subjective psychological phenomena as reflexive
and reflective infusive CEE and CE perception, can be directly
perceived as creatively causal in the sense of causing PI and CEC perceptual deliverances to be subjective psychologically meaningful. We
directly experience causality as it pertains to the modes of synthesis by
which event-components are actualized as complete events, distinct
from directly experiencing temporal succession. In the former case we
directly experience causal synthesis in the sense of having direct intelligible awareness of reflexive and reflective infusive CEE and CE
percepta uniting in unique nexus with PI and CEC percepta.

We may conclude our analysis of causally efficacious perception at
this point by saying that from an early concept of regarding the subjective psychologically substantive portion of linguistic symbols as constituted by connotative meaning, then meaning-as-directly-felt-relatedness,
and finally, causally efficacious and causally efficacious emotional perception, it must be understood that the very possibility of humanly
conscious, intelligible experience as an ontologically unique class of
phenomena is contingent upon the possibility of reflexive and reflective

infusive causality being operative factors in human behavior. This assertion still concords with a fundamental assumption underlying our entire analytical enterprise, namely that the intrinsic nature of mind as a unique entity, and thereby thought, can be exhaustively explicated, in principle, by reflectively analyzing its perceptual constitution and then the various ways in which percepta enter consciousness; an analytical process principally revealing the logical form of subjective psychological experience that, in effect, universally characterizes the structure of all possible mental events. This initial stage of analysis provides the basis for a logically successive stage of inquiry involving a systematic investigation of the actual concrete experiential modes of relation among event-components during particular spatio-temporal occasions occurring within given individuals and groups of individuals. This latter stage of inquiry entails two distinct types of methodological investigation:

1. A philosophical psychological mode of analysis, similar to the first stage of inquiry, that will systematically reflectively explicate the consciously ascertainable modes of relation among the components of complete events in response to given stimulus-conditions.

2. A subjective psychological, genuinely experimental approach to investigating modes of relations among the components of complete events in response to given stimulus-conditions. Subjective psychological inquiry will have frequent occasion to draw upon the theoretical constructions devised through philosophical psychological analysis for formulating testable hypotheses, as well as upon its own unique resources in pursuing, in conjunction with an objective psychology, the ultimate ideal goals of presenting a complete explanation of human behavior, and moreover, developing effective means for promoting behavioral functional virtue.

Reflexive and reflective infusive CEE and CE perception can only be understood as causally functional or operative within the context of complete unified mental events, and it is only in this mode of perceptual synthetic actualization that mental events can be regarded as a class of stimulus-objects that are directly knowable in themselves. Complete mental events are stimulus-objects in the sense that:

1. Because of reflexive infusive causality, subjective psychologically meaningful concepts can be consciously entertained spontaneously as CEC with accompanying substantive CEE and CE perceptual wisdom when they come synthetically to bear upon PI percepta. This establishes the first precondition of consciously attending to a matter of concern, in itself an ontologically unique phenomenon capable of occurring only within the context of mental events.

2. The second precondition is met when executing a persistent

reflective effort based upon the emergent occurrence of reflective infusive percepta whose suggestive implications are sporadically meaningful and mode of occurrence is time-consuming, because these percepta embody novel suggestions for relating relevant objects that are not manifestly obvious, and hence demand that all relevant perceptions be pondered at length in their concomitant conceptual proximity with one another. Due to this fact of inostensible relation, reflective infusive percepta are not habitually or spontaneously implicit within CEC as in the case of reflexive infusive percepta. However, if reflective infusive percepta are repeatedly entertained and hence critically pondered, they are frequently transformed into reflexive infusive percepta. This is a necessary condition for intellectual development, where formerly difficult concepts are later understood with intuitive ease as a function of intervening growth promoted through reflection.

3. Fulfilling the two preconditions sets the stage for the emergent occurrence of additional novel reflective infusive CEE and CE percepta, over and above preceding reflective infusive percepta, suggesting constructively unique ways for relating relevant objects with one another.

4. In fulfilling condition 3 above, a single developing event demonstrates the following concomitant properties:

4.1. PI percepta are functioning in their ideationally causal role as stimulus-objects, hence conjuring conditions 4.2 through 4.5 below.

4.2. CEC percepta, functioning as simplified clear and distinct consciously symbolic focal points, are projected from logically antecedent CEE and CE percepta, and in their denotative clarity generally symbolically represent conditions 4.3 through 4.5 below.

4.3 CEE and CE percepta arise as reflexive infusive event-components.

4.4. CEE and CE percepta arise as reflective infusive event-components.

4.5. Novel reflective infusive percepta arise whose synthetic origin begins in unconscious physio-chemical processes and hence emerge as ideationally unique event-components.

5. When conditions 4.1 through 4.5 have been concomitantly actualized in the development of a single event, the requirements have been met for novel ideational synthesis or transcendent concrescence; and mind proceeds to a new level of understanding. Thus,

5.1. due to the fact that factors 4.1 through 4.5 developed to a state of concomitant conscious proximity with one another,

5.2. and because the occurrence of these concomitant conditions was in great part due to both a long-term preparational as well as a contemporary enactment of conscious awareness and reflective conscious analysis,

5.3. or generally, as a result of the view that underlying physio-chemical conditions or correlates provide the basis for all consciously emerging event-components, and that mental events also cause transcendent organic concrescence which is to say that as developing conscious awareness, promoted by conscious reflection, achieves the state posited in 4.1 through 4.5 the underlying physio-chemical correlates are also being spatio-temporally resynthesized until state 4.1 through 4.5 is achieved.

5.4. Thus it may be concluded that when state 4.1 through 4.5 has been actualized in a given developing event, the entire configuration of components—each with its unique perceptual properties and functional mode of entering events—acquires a consciously unique nexus of relations so that a new associative understanding (often termed as an insight) is consciously realized. Further, this newly synthesized idea, clearly understood as a CEC, is henceforth capable of functioning as an ideational PI perceptual stimulus-object.

5.5. But the synthetic process, understood from a physio-chemical concrescent perspective, more fundamentally indicates that conscious and reflective conscious processes were necessarily instrumental in spatio-temporally ordering correlative physio-chemical processes to the extent that state 4.1 through 4.5 was attained, thereby providing the requisite spatio-temporal proximity among organic processes propitious for transcendent physio-chemical synthesis which, from a perspective of conscious experience, yielded the insightful understanding.

5.6. To understand the way in which consciousness can order empirically identical correlative physio-chemical processes so that their spatio-temporal proximity is propitious for concrescent synthesis, one must at once possess an acute, integrated conceptualization of all of the various arguments presented heretofore; these are merely contrived to explain the intrinsic nature of the subjective psychological meaning available to almost any human being during any conscious moment of his life.

CAUSALLY EFFICACIOUS EMOTIONAL PERCEPTA

Our characterization of CEE percepta will be brief for the nature of this class of perception was adequately covered in previous discussions on emotional feeling, storing mechanisms, and our previous analysis of CE perception, at least with respect to reflexive and reflective infusive causality. To avoid redundancy, let us merely enumerate the most important features of CEE percepta. However, as we proceed to analyze and devise constructs that to some extent reveal the synthetic mechanics of conscious reflection and extend our analytical interests to the process of thinking as distinct from our present concern with defining the perceptual entities that are in process, it will be seen that CEE percepta play a crucially important role in establishing enduring coherence and continuity among our thoughts, as well as provide an indeterminately rich resource for novel reflective infusive perception that often suggests new ways to promote ideational relatedness.

From the perspective of mature intelligence, unquestionably the most indigenous directly experiential property of CEE perception is its extraordinarily pervasive, yet powerfully efficacious, vaguely felt presence. These percepta unite with other more high-ordered percepta to concomitantly form inextricable units of experience, or mental events. Subjective psychological theory demands that CEE percepta be prelinguistic. On purely logical grounds, if the profoundly subtle experiential quality of these percepta are adequately linguistically represented, it must be concluded that they are CE percepta, hence potentially capable of achieving the status of ideational PI and CEC percepta. This, of course, is a possibility that in fact portrays the intrinsic process of symbolic development. The transformational process of CEE acquiring symbolic discipline is particularly evident in infantile linguistic acquisition where children proceed through the sign and symbol stages. But the question may be raised, How is it possible to linguistically designate the nature of CEE if it is by definition prelinguistic? This question prompts a reconsideration of the illustration in which it was shown that the direct experience of consuming a fine steak dinner could not be linguistically communicated to another sufficiently adequately to enable the listener to vicariously grasp the full implication of what is intrinsically an experiential understanding derived through direct perceptual acquaintance. This is ultimately the grounds upon which the view is propounded that all mental events are private in that percepta of any type can only be known through direct acquaintance. Further, the tenet that mental events are the only possible stimulus-objects that can be known in themselves by the individual within whose organism the phenomena occur, follows from the fact of privacy. These conclusions arise from the obvious fact that only individuals themselves can be the subject of their own experience. Each of us has privileged access to our perceptions and, more important, is the undeniable fact that minds stand over against percepta, or percepta concomitantly come constructively to bear upon other percepta, or finally, as our formulation exists in its present form, PI percepta enter human organisms, concomitantly conjuring CEE, CE, and CEC percepta, and collectively providing the necessary and sufficient conditions for a complete mental event. The steak dinner example reveals that having direct experience and listening to another describe his own direct experience are two categorically distinct phenomena. The subject of the experience has percepta directly available to his consciousness that are not in principle available to the listener. Thus, assuming subject A, who is eating a steak, is informing percipient B, who has never eaten a steak, about the experience, let us proceed to show in what way having direct experience differs from listening to another describe his own direct experience. This difference can be designated through a rough enumeration of the possible classes of percepta that are directly experienced by percipients A and B.

1. It may be said that A has direct access to the following classes of percepta:

1.1. natural PI percepta that are defined as taste of steak, and also the organic PI percepta characterized as the internal feeling of consuming food.

1.2. CEE percepta defined as deep satisfaction, enjoyment and/or pleasure, derived from the eating process. These percepta are prelinguistic and, moreover, intuitively felt or experienced in a way which was so subtly extensive and experientially forceful that the domain of linguistic comprehension is exceeded. We have previously discussed this issue in analyzing the nature of mental events, saying that experience is broader than the capacity of individuals to fully symbolically characterize it. In our present illustration, A's experience roughly involves both eating a steak and verbally describing the experience of eating the steak. Hence it would be a mistake to say, as linguistic philosophers have maintained, that experiential facts as they are expressed within verbal statements can be understood exhaustively by analyzing the way that we use words in given contexts, for words, which are intersubjectively used symbolic instruments, are the only means by which we can come to organize and thereby understand experience. While it is true that words are the basic means we have for organizing, communicating, and explicating our experience, it is not correct to maintain that our statements about reality can be exhaustively understood by analyzing the way in which words are used to make factual assertions. There is, of course, value in attempting to encourage clear and precise statements of fact that are subject to acceptable procedures for verification. But to devote exclusive interest to the usage of words as they occur in statements of fact and hence in their commonly accepted modes of usage, is to de-emphasize the basic fact that words are used to organize, clarify, and report on our experience. Words are linguistic instruments designed to representatively characterize the entities, properties, and relations of inner and outer expereince. CEE, CE, and CEC percepta are to be most precisely regarded as linguistic symbols that concomitantly come to bear upon PI percepta which contribute data about the nature of entities, properties, and relations; data, in the cases of natural and organic PI percepta, that exist wholly independent from symbols with respect to their intrinsic contributed character. Therefore, to increase the precision of word usage and statements of fact, we ordinarily begin by very carefully scrutinizing the presentationally immediate perceptual portion of our experience to make certain that our words accurately characterize what we directly perceive as PI percepta. This cannot be adequately ascertained through mere analysis of verbal statements regardless of the way in which they are used.

1.3. CEC percepta equivalent to A's clear and distinct denotative concepts of the complete steak-eating experience: what is being consumed, the taste of the food, the feeling of consuming the food, the properties of what is being consumed, how the experience may be best communicated to B, and so on.

1.4. CE reflexive and reflective infusive percepta equivalent to all the relevant past wisdom symbolically referring to 1.1 through 1.3 above: eating steaks, usage of language as a descriptive and communicative instrument, previously relevant occasions, etc.

2. On the other hand, listener B has only the articulated sounds of A, embodying his verbal report to B, and A's manifest behavioral movements or gestural expressions as these phenomena ingress into B as natural PI percepta from which to make vicarious determinations about the direct experience of consuming a steak, using A's communications as a basis for inference, and what are natural PI percepta for B would be CEC percepta in the mind of A. These percepta would generally consist of:

2.1. The natural PI percepta embodying the verbal articulations and other manifest behaviors of A.

2.2. CE percepta corresponding to the connotative meaning of A's verbalizations that would be attributed to A's words by B from B's past experience and learning, not A's.

2.3. CEE percepta embodying B's past pleasurable experiences of eating food other than steak, and other relevant types of felt meaning.

3. Thus in terms of even the very crude preceding perceptual analysis of both A's and B's direct perceptual experience as the two domains

of experience related to the steak-eating phenomenon, it can be easily understood that if B had never eaten a steak it would be impossible for B to have a very clear concept of A's steak-eating experience. In fact, it is in principle impossible for B to fully understand A's experience because this demands knowing through direct acquaintance, hence necessitating the contradictory condition of B being A. It may be concluded, then, that B's understanding of A's dierct experience is necessarily constrained to B's natural PI perceptions of A's manifest behaviors as these natural PI perceptions are caused through B's reflexive and reflective infusive CEE and CE percepta to be subjective psychologically meaningful through their concomitant synthesis with B's previously learned wisdom.

4. There is also the fact, over and above the one that B can understand a very small portion of the subjective psychological meaning inherent in A's words through their manifest effects as natural PI perception, that A himself can clearly and distinctly linguistically characterize only a comparatively small portion of his directly accessible experience of eating a steak. Experience is broader than our capacity to exhaustively characterize it in linguistic terms.

5. Now we are in a position to deal with a question formerly raised regarding the methodological analysis to which the class of CEE perception is being subjected, viz., How is it possible to linguistically designate the nature of CEE if by definition it is prelinguistic? The answer to this problem is suggested in steps 1 through 4 above.

5.1. As the problem specifically refers to this discourse, the reader presently has only the bare printed words on white pages as a means of understanding the writer's concept of CEE percepta, for example.

5.2. The printed words are, in effect, natural PI percepta embodied in a permanent medium and are thereby directly accessible to both readers and the writer who, if the natural PI percepta were not immediately available, would have to entertain the words more haphazardly in thought as ideational PI perception.

5.3. But the vastly important difference in subjective psychologically comprehending the intersubjectively ascertainable natural PI perception as printed words, however great or minimal it may be among any given percipients, and assuming they all knew the language embodied in the natural PI perception, arises wholly from the fact that all individuals' CEE and CE perceptual domains are ontologically unique as they are concomitantly actualized with PI perception as subjective psychological experience.

5.4. The writer's reflexive and reflective infusive percepta infuse natural PI perception with a distinctive type of wisdom that embodies a disciplined way or theoretical predisposition for understanding mental phenomena; one gradually developed from many hours of reflecting upon personal experience and the writings of numerous thinkers who address themselves to similar problems.

5.5. The readers in contrast, although many may have read extensively and pondered at length the nature of mind or ideational phenomena, will infuse the same natural PI percepta with importantly different reflexive and reflective infusive percepta, primarily because they are unique individuals with highly personalized mentalities, developed as a function of greatly dissimilar experiential backgrounds, physiological differences, and unique modes of perceptual synthesis during subjective psychological experience. With all these sources of variability as operative factors in influencing personal understanding of identical natural PI perception, one must expect significant difference in conceptualizing or interpreting phenomena that given individuals directly experience in common.

5.6. Steps 5.1 through 5.4 are mere prefatory remarks that must be kept clearly in view before we proceed to consider the problem of how we are to methodologically linguistically conceptualize that perceptual domain which is in principle prelinguistic. Let us now proceed to this task.

5.7. In coming to understand the nature and efficacity of CEE perceptual states, the writer reflectively analyzes his subjective psychological experience. After having classificationally subdivided and definitionally explicated the most conspicuous perceptual classes constituting mind as PI, CEC, and CE percepta, the writer is yet aware that there remains a very subtle and powerfully efficacious aspect of subjective psychological experience that is not comprehended by the preceding perceptual classifications. This remaining perceptual class includes a very intimate portion of the writer's experience (or any human being's experience if he exercises a sufficiently precise reflective effort within the theoretical framework proposed) which is immediately, reflexively or intuitively, emotionally felt, possessing such experiential authenticity and efficacy as a synthetic agent in consciousness that to deny its efficacious perceptual presence would be to regard subjective psychological experience as unreal or a mere delusion. Directly apprehending mental events entails perceiving them as inextricable experiential unities and it is herein that CEE plays its decisive role as a class of synthetic perceptual agents that infusively cause the inextricable quality. Thus, direct concrete experience seems to appropriately characterize the inextricable unity of our conscious apprehensions of reality. But this holds true only if an individual possesses a deep sensitivity to the definitionally impre-

cise CEE perception providing the intimate experiential basis for effecting this profoundly felt unity. This mode of designation may appear
logically doubtful in contrast to sound operational definition, yet we
must necessarily appeal to such indirect linguistic methods, placing
great emphasis upon intuitively evident illustrations similar to the
previously cited steak-eating example. Directly perceived moments of
intense experience resulting from conditions yielding unmitigated happiness, deep hatred, successful psychotherapy, powerfully humane communication with another human being, etc., all include the extraordinary
CEE perceptual, emotive dimension of human experience. In fact, one
does not come to initially achieve an understanding of these percepta
merely by argumentatively isolating them as components of experience.
Rather one has many opportunities to intensely perceive these components long before they are reflectively isolated within a theoretical
framework as CEE perception, for example. We have only to ponder
the many implications of the theory of symbolic development proposed
in Part Two to understand the present issue. It will be recalled that
two major tenets were that subjective psychological experience during
infantile levels of development is pure causally efficacious emotion, and
further, it is only through the human organism's capacity for conscious
reflective behavior, the intellectual efficacy of which must obviously be
regarded as commensurate with the organism's level of development,
that amorphous, unwieldy, primordial CEE can be subsumed to
symbolic discipline. Thus all acts of creative intelligence can be conceived as rendering more clear and distinct, precisely in the sense of
generating causally efficacious concepts, certain aspects of our perceptual
experience. Therefore if CEE is contemplated as an indeterminately
complex and hence profound domain of suggestibility, containing innumerable possibilities for establishing unique modes of cognitive relation, then its functional relevance and enormous importance for intellectual growth becomes manifestly apparent when pondered in
conjunction with the mechanism of reflective consciousness. The concepts that are presently being analyzed are very closely related to
John Dewey's thesis of intelligent thinking: the human organism after
having reflectively formulated a sound hypothetical program of activity
for solving a given problem, based upon the best available factual information, proceeds to the overtly active phase of intelligent inquiry
where the hypothetical program is experientially and/or operationally
implemented to test its pragmatic efficacy. In this second crucial
phase the organism has an opportunity to experience the reciprocal impact of his conceptual efforts as their efficacy is determined through
concrete implementation. Once again, the relevance of this latter phase

for our view can be easily understood because we maintain that experience, specifically with respect to CEE perception, must be contemplated as broader than man's capacity to subject it to exhaustive symbolic characterization. This fact, considered in conjunction with the possibility for indeterminately great ideational relatedness, provides the basis of mind's commensurate capacity for development.

Although some of the examples used to illustrate the nature and efficacity of CEE perception were atypical of daily matter-of-fact experience, CEE perception does not occur exclusively on occasions of intense emotional activation. Rather, this class of perception is the fundamental source of consciously felt inextricable unity in mental events. This gross perceptual discrimination is indicative of an experiential substratum whose efficacious presence is the most experientially vague and subtly pervasive dimension of meaning-as-directly-felt-relatedness, a theoretical concept characterizing a level of understanding including both CEE and CE percepta. CEE perception, then, introduces an undeniable felt unity to concrete experience, hence rendering consciousness incapable of, division without destroying its intrinsic nature as a stimulus-object capable of being known in itself through its concomitantly unified perceptual constitution.

5.8. Thus the writer, in attempting to communicate his systematic understanding of mental experience specifically with respect to CEE perception, can ultimately rely only upon linguistic symbols as instruments to effect this communication, endeavoring to organize them in a way that will accurately suggest, over and above the clear and distinct natural PI perceptual specification of symbols in written form, the writer's directly accessible CE and CEE perception which in essence constitutes the substantive meaning of the manifest printed words. The printed words must be organized so that, functioning initially as natural PI stimulus-object effects and then as ideational PI perceptual stimulus-objects in the mental events of readers, they will conjure relevant reflexive and reflective infusive wisdom in readers reasonably concordant with that of the writer. This, of course, is a subjective psychological principle that holds true for all possible intersubjective communication. Thus the prelinguistic perceptual domain is designated, though unquestionably inadequately, by attempting to present the reader with a highly systematic theoretical framework that comprehends human experience in terms of universally applicable categories, collectively defined as the logical form of subjective psychological experience, that refer to directly accessible perceptual components constituting mental events. Then each perceptual category is explicatively characterized in a way amenable to precise analysis until the last category of perception is reached, one whose nature and efficacy can only be subtly felt as primordial subjective psychological experience because of its extremely vague mode of occurrence. Therefore, by rigorously defining those perceptual classes that can be rendered linguistically determinate, we are able to analyze mental events in such a way that sufficient uniformity can be achieved among the reflexive and reflective infusive perceptual domains of individuals who have learned subjective psychological terminology. From this, they can partially reflectively isolate the presence of CEE perception as distinct from their understanding of PI, CEC, and CE percepta, and then use their own personal conscious experience as an ultimate basis for feeling the unique nature and efficacy of CEE.

CAUSALLY EFFICACIOUS CONCEPTUAL PERCEPTA

As has been said, the notion of CEC percepta can be regarded as a refined derivative from the concept of denotative symbolic meaning. Ensuing discussion about CEC perception should be considered in light of this consideration.

The most distinctive experiential property of CEC percepta is their clearly and distinctly perceivable occurrence as discrete concepts or ideas. Of course, as is the case with all other classes of percepta, this characterization is the product of reflective analysis, which indicates that we cannot in principle directly perceive CEC as pure clear and distinct perception apart from concomitantly occurring CEE, CE, and PI perceptual event-components. The natural PI perceptual spoken sound of the word, or the ideational PI perceptual thought of, red, conceived in itself as a bare entity has absolutely no reference to the natural PI perception of red unless considered in conjunction with reflexive and reflective infusive CEE and CE percepta which render the spoken word of silent thought subjectively psychologically meaningful. The extraordinary importance of linguistic relatedness was emphasized earlier. We are now concerned with accentuating the ontological strangeness of symbolically representative phenomena where spoken, written, silently thought, or otherwise manifested, highly abbreviated, intrinsically discrete CEC entities serve as clearly and distinctly simplified conscious focal points from which vast amounts of concomitant, connotatively implicit wisdom can be consciously represented and hence constructively manipulated with extraordinary facility, rendering thought and communication possible. It is unnecessary to elaborate the numerous implications involved in characterizing this subjective psychologically meaningful mental phenomenon for, in effect, the entire foregoing discourse has been devoted to this end. Let us merely emphasize the tenet that CEC are the most highly refined, disciplined emergent ideational entities produced by the process of transcendent concrescence. As was mentioned in discussing the onset of the symbol stage, an enormous intellectual advance is made when an organism discovers that symbols can tag or represent large quantities of generally relevant past and present direct experience. Subsequently, of course, further developments in the symbol stage enable human organisms to establish relations among linguistic symbols. To better appreciate these two necessary conditions for intelligent behavior, we have only to imagine circumstances where the deceptively simple capacity to meaningfully tag a bare natural PI perception with an abbreviated symbol is absent, as in the case of animals. Speculation of this type accentuates the incredible linguistic interrelatedness that implicitly accompanies even the mere utterance of a single meaningful verbalization. In this simple fact lies the essence of subjective psychological experience and thereby the possibility of all genuinely intelligent inquiry. If the human brain lacked its neurological complexity and interrelated character, consciousness would be forever limited to vague CEE perceptual awareness of external natural and internal organismic states. Concrescence would never achieve the level where reflective awareness transcends the sign stage; the level which only a few species of animals below man achieve.

In the analysis of the distinctive nature of PI perception, a moderate, indirect understanding of CEC percepta was derived and it was shown that ideational PI perception was logically distinct from CEC percepta. PI perception was said to embody the properties designated by the following five criteria: clarity in conscious awareness; distinctness in conscious awareness; contemporaneousness in occurrence; logical antecedence in occurrence; and contribution. Although, as was seen, there are important differences between PI and CEC percepta, it will be instructive to briefly consider CEC perception in terms of these five criteria in order to promote a clearer understanding of CEC.

With respect to the first two criteria of clarity and distinctness of conscious awareness, CEC percepta would manifest these properties to at least the same extent as ideational PI percepta, but not to the same extent as natural or organic PI perception. This maintains the distinction made by Hume when he stressed the obvious fact that directly perceived sensory impressions are more vividly clear and distinct than our ideas of direct impressions. Thus the two criteria as they apply to CEC are perhaps more in accordance to the Cartesian definition of clarity and distinctness: that CEC can be clearly entertained in consciousness and conceived as distinct from other CEC.

Again, with the third criterion, CEC percepta share much in common with ideational PI perception. But the commonality refers to the limited discriminative power of the contemporaneousness criterion. The question was raised earlier that since all perceptual components of mental events occur concomitantly in a logical form, how does the criterion of contemporaneousness apply to PI perception? The answer was that the criterion emphasized the spatio-temporally unique, independent character of the ever-emerging present occasion entering organisms as novel PI perception from the external natural and internal bodily environments. However, at that point it had not yet been demonstrated that PI perception also included ideational PI perception; a distinction requiring a moderate relaxation of the contribution criterion. Moreover, the concepts of CE and CEE perception were not considered. The point to be made is that with respect to natural and organic PI perception, the criterion of contemporaneousness does strictly hold true in that these perceptual deliverances do in fact testify to the spatio-temporally unique, independent character of ever-emerging, contemporary natural world and internal bodily felt states. These two subclasses of PI percepta portray relevant entering reality as it contemporaneously exists, but do not in any way refer to past occasions. However, beyond this point, as the criterion applies to ideational PI perception and, more recently, to CEC percepta, we discover that these latter two modes of perception do not in most instances testify to novel circumstances. Logically speaking, from our theoretical point of view, we must concede that all percepta—PI, CEC, CE, and CEE percepta—are ontologically unique during every emerging occasion simply due to the fact that they are spatio-temporally separated. But there is also the consideration that CE and CEE perception, by definition, are percepta testifying to the learned wisdom of past experience. While it is true that percipient A feels a throb and sees green grass that are organic and natural PI percepts indigenous to contemporary reality and, further, that the reflexive infusive CE and CEE percepta enabling the two recognitions to be intelligently understood also occurred concomitantly with the PI percepta, the fact remains that the subjective psychological meaning embodied within the reflexive infusive perception was not learned during the present occasion, but rather, in past occasions. From this the conclusion follows that the criterion of contemporaneousness disqualifies, at least in this narrow sense, CE and CEE perception from being regarded as PI perception for they are contributed data not uniquely intrinsic to the present occasion. But we may quickly indicate that all ideational PI percepta are temporally previously formulated CEC, successively rethought in the sense of entering into present occasions as ideational PI stimulus-objects. This, of course, means that the ideational PI entities are never unique perceptual contributions from contemporary reality though, nevertheless, we must necessarily persist in regarding them as legitimate PI perception for they do function as ideational stimulus-objects determining which CEC, CE, and CEE percepta will be concomitantly conjured to render contemporary events subjective psychologically meaningful. The point, then, is that the criterion of contemporaneousness has limited applicability for designating causally efficacious concepts, because CEC percepta also often occur as repetitions of past thoughts. There is, however, the not infrequent situation when engaging in reflective analysis that novel reflective infusive percepta may prompt the projected synthesis of a novel CEC; hence in this case the criterion would also strictly apply to CEC perception for the novel synthesis would be a creation occurring during the contemporary, inner environmental occasion.

The foregoing remarks should suffice to indicate to what extent these two criteria are relevant to CEC percepta. It will be recalled, however, that CEC were said to be synthetically projected from causally efficacious percepta originally conjured by PI perception functioning as stimulus-objects. Since the notion of projection refers to the dynamic or process dimension of mental activity, as distinct from our present concern which is with explicating the nature of the entities that are in process, an analysis of this theoretical construct must be postponed. Yet in terms of the CEC mode of perceptual entry it is well to mention that the process of projection is a reflexive one in typical conscious awareness of reality. That is, when we perceive familiar stimulus-object effects such as a chair, the taste of sugar, the odor of smoke, the feeling of nausea, etc., CEC percepta are spontaneously representatively ascribed to them without a reflective effort. This discussion of the nature of CEC percepta may be concluded by saying that in the vast majority of instances CEC are those components of symbolic meaning that literally embody our thoughts as manifestly spoken and silently thought bare linguistic forms, logically conceived as completely devoid of all PI, CE, and CEE perception.

SYMBOLIC REFERENCE

It has been emphasized many times that PI, CEC, CE, and CEE percepta occur concomitantly throughout every possible instantaneous spatio-temporal moment during which conscious experience is actualized in any given human mind. However, as will be demonstrated, a CEC component is not always necessarily present and, moreover, during infancy it seems that only natural and organic PI and CEE perceptual components are present. Therefore the term "symbolic reference" will be used to define the phenomenon of concomitant actualization amongst given classes of percepta during any possible theoretically instantaneous moments of space-time. Symbolic reference places greater emphasis upon the implication of concomitant actualization of percepta that constitute mind at any given instant than the previously defined concepts of experience or mental event. As a directly perceivable phenomenon within a mental event, symbolic reference would be subjective psychological experience in its evolving inextricable durational unity. It is emergent concrescent experience, or the subjective psychological perspective of unique nexus among relevant organic propensities, the latter occurring as the physio-chemical empirical correlates to mental events. Stated still differently, symbolic reference is perceptually unified direct apprehension or experience of symbolically disciplined understanding (CEC, CE, and CEE percepta) coming constructively to bear upon the present occasion, ideationally enhancing the present with the relevant wisdom of the past.

Speaking now with a more mechanistic emphasis, we have seen that when stimulus-object effects enter as PI perceptual event-components, they concomitantly conjure relevant CEE, CE, and CEC as reflexive infusive and reflexive projected perception that, in effect, renders the stimulus-object effect initially intelligible. Further, as the spatio-temporal occasion evolves into the future the PI stimulus-object effect, occurring within the inextricably integrated context of the complete consciously intelligible mental event-in-process (and hence meeting the necessary conditions of knowing a stimulus-object, namely, that it can be known directly in itself) is transformed into a PI stimulus-object concomitantly determining which CEE, CE, and CEC perception will be deemed relevant to enhance its meaning. It must be understood that throughout this complex reflective experience—a behavioral act that human organisms can generally execute with ease—we may theoretically conceive of an unchanging basic structure persisting throughout each possible successive instant during an event. This consideration should be kept clearly in view because it is of fundamental importance to our final formulation of the logical form of subjective psychological experience and for an elaborated exposition of the distinction drawn between natural and ideational causality. In reference to the issue of causality, it can be said that our concept of mind will render erroneous the unquestioningly accepted notion, applied to uniquely human behavior, that a stimulus can be conceived as spatio-temporally preceding a response in the Skinnerian sense, for example. It will be seen that our concept of concomitant actualization provides the basis for a severe criticism of traditionally conceived stimulus-response theories of human behavior.

It should be re-emphasized that although the preponderance of analytical attention was devoted to our directly perceivable experience, it was implicitly maintained that, at least logically prior to the emergence of conscious perception, there exists the vast organic functional domain of unconscious physio-chemical processes. A fundamental precondition for conscious emergence is that quantitatively sufficient activated organic mechanisms in qualitatively adequate integration are concomitantly activated to yield conscious perception, however minimally sophisticated the events may be. This is what is meant by the term "emergent concrescence." In the massively complex domain of, necessarily, unconscious processes, we may nevertheless conceive, as in the case in physiological scientific inquiry, of concrescence beginning as sensation, for example from light impinging upon the retinal region of an individual's eyes (the beginning of a stimulus-object effect), and hence ultimately emerging as the consciously intelligible perception of a particular color and form. However, consciously perceiving, for example, a red apple as an intelligible object of concern, with the original physio-chemical change occurring as a modification in retinal states, initiated an extraordinarily complex synthetic concrescent process whereby the resultant consciously intelligible product occurring as a complete event presupposes all the physio-chemical correlates underlying PI, CEC, CE, and CEE perception. Presupposing our entire foregoing subtly evolving argument, a concise theoretical formulation of the logical form of subjective psychological experience or mind can now be presented. A final brief argument, accentuating a consideration that was perhaps only implicit in the preceding analyses, shall now be propounded in order to arrive at a formulation of the logical form of mind. The argument again utilizes the concepts of form and matter, contemplated as universal principles of organization in their application to the entities, properties, and relations constituting our perceptual experience of reality, comprised of percepta issuing from stimulus-objects located in both inner and outer environments. It may be stated as follows:

1. Any possible mental event must necessarily demonstrate at least a dipolar structure with regard to its constitutive classes of perceptual event-components. It may be assumed that early infant mentality consists merely of natural and organic PI perception, concomitantly occurring with CEE percepta. In their mature, functional state, mental events generally embody the concomitant structure of PI, CEC, CE, and CEE perception.

2. It has been said that natural and organic PI perception are unique, spatio-temporally contemporary contributions to mind in that their bare intrinsic perceptual nature is not contingent upon CEC, CE, and CEE for their distinctive character as entered perception.

3. The intrinsic perceptual nature of natural and organic PI perception may be further analyzed in terms of matter and form. For example, when we perceive a red apple, the natural PI perception of red cannot be directly perceived apart from its apple shape. More generally, the entire visually perceived natural world is, throughout space-time, a kaleidoscopic process of determinate colors included within determinate forms. This type of analysis may be applied similarly to the remaining external bodily senses, and further, to the internal modes of perceptual experience yielding all types of organic and ideational PI perception.

4. It was further stated, however, that ideational PI percepta do not possess the same degree of independence from CEC, CE, and CEE percepta as natural and organic PI perception. Moreover, ideational PI percepta necessarily originally emerge as unique ontological existents from CE and CEE percepta functioning in their infusive roles, as novel projected CEC during spatio-temporally prior occasions. But we have demonstrated that even though the contribution criterion had to be somewhat relaxed in the case of ideational PI perception, ideational PI percepta do function in mental events as ideational stimulus-objects, effectively determining which CEE, CE, and CEC percepta will be conjured as relevant for actualizing a complete event.

5. Therefore, the same matter-form distinction deemed appropriate for natural and organic PI perception is suitable for ideational PI percepta occurring as stimulus-objects. That is, for example, the subjective psychologically entertained idea of red has as its form the denotatively clear and distinct spoken sound, written word, bare silent thought, or behaviorally manifest gesture representing the linguistic symbol, red, hence designating the symbol as uniquely distinct from any other linguistic symbol. Further, the subjective psychological idea of red has as its matter the myriad connotatively meaningful, or, more specifically, the CE and CEE percepta that constitute its substantive meaning.

6. Thus far we have only considered one half of the dipolar character of mind, PI perception, and have not devoted attention to the second portion, CEC, CE, and CEE, collectively conceived as unitary symbols concomitantly brought to bear upon PI perceptual contribution. Stated differently, when we see a red apple the stimulus-object effects participate in our consciousness as directly perceived natural PI perception to which we concomitantly, as reflexive infusive percepta, ascribe the

THE STRUCTURE OF MIND OR SUBJECTIVE PSYCHOLOGICAL EXPERIENCE
"PERCEPTA STANDING OVER AGAINST PERCEPTA"

The categories of all possible event-components	Stimulus-object effect		Symbolic reference	Language (symbols)	
	Matter Independent contribution (Matter)	→ Form (Form)	→ Symbolic reference	Form Emotional-ideational feeling (Form)	Directly experienced meaning-as-directly-felt-relatedness, i.e., CEE and CE perception (Matter)
Sight	Particular color as a directly experienced event-component	Form that defines the boundary of the color Relation Process	Symbolic reference	The particular form of the symbol as clear and distinct CEC perception	Directly experienced meaning-as-directly-felt-relatedness, i.e., CEE and CE perception
Sound	Particular sound as a directly experienced event-component	Duration of sound; beginning and end points Form of durational process, e.g., structure of music	"	"	"
Taste	Particular taste as a directly experienced event-component	Duration of taste; beginning and end points Form of durational process	"	"	"
Touch	Texture: i.e., smooth, coarse, etc. Temperature: i.e., hot, cold, warm, etc. as a directly experienced event-component	Relation: solid, flexible; liquid, gas; straight, curved, etc.	"	"	"

Smell	Particular smell as a directly experienced event-component	Duration of smell Form of durational process	"
Organic or Bodily Feeling	Particular internal feeling as a directly experienced event-component	Duration of feeling; beginning and end points Form of durational process	"
Ideational Feeling	Ideational PI percepta as a directly experienced sublimated disciplined emotion CE percepta CEE percepta	The particular form of the symbol as clear and distinct ideational PI percepta Duration	"

Figure 12. Double form-matter structure of mind

linguistic terms "red apple" (terms ontologically constituted by CEC, CE, and CEE percepta). In effect, from what has been said above, the CEC perceptual component of unified symbols could be regarded as the symbol's form, and the CE and CEE perceptual components could be contemplated as the symbol's matter.

7. The conclusion, then, is that our concept of mind implies a twofold form-matter distinction, with regard to PI perceptual event-components as they concomitantly come to bear upon PI perceptual stimulus-object effects functioning also as PI stimulus-objects designating which CEC, CE, or CEE percepta will be relevant for actualization into a twofold form-matter relation.

8. Both form-matter units are concomitantly actualized as symbolic reference in experience throughout space-time, as a universal logical form for all possible mental events. All our previous argumentation reduces to this concept of mind, a view that shall be defined as the double form-matter theory.

9. Again it should be noted that our concept of mind, in principle, entirely follows from an analysis of the direct perceptual deliverances, actualized as subjective psychological experience.

DOUBLE FORM-MATTER STRUCTURE OF MIND

We have arrived at a stage in our argumentation where a highly formalized specification of mind, surpassing in precision those heretofore defined, can be concisely presented. The final theoretical deduction will be an important instrument for facilitating a complete understanding of the concept of mind propounded throughout this discourse. The schematization outlined in Figure 12 essentially embodies the basic formula developed early in our inquiry, namely, percepta concomitantly coming constructively to bear upon other percepta. Once again, it should be mentioned that the double form-matter scheme cannot be understood as a means for avoiding a careful reflective scrutiny of preceding arguments. Rather, it is hoped that the double form-matter formulation will be regarded as an obvious consequent and simple expression of the developing train of previous thought, aimed at proceeding to progressively higher levels of clear understanding. Hence, with this latter attitude, the ensuing greatly simplified formalization of the logical form of subjective psychological experience (see Figure 12) is merely a precondition and instrument for future, more elaborate, and more precise investigations of the intrinsic structure and process of mind.

Chapter Twelve / Recapitulation

Let us reflect briefly upon the major points made in the previous line of argumentation. It was seen that the principal claim to be refuted was that human behavior could be exhaustively explained, in principle, in terms of its intersubjectively directly accessible perceptual manifestations occurring within natural environmental contexts. Thus if it were true that all causal factors underlying human behavior are directly accessible to scientific observers, then psychologists would not need to introduce mentalistic intervening variables into their behavioral models for they would be extraneous and, moreover, confusing to behavioral inquiry due to the fact that they are not directly perceivable by scientists. In holding this position, proponents are necessarily compelled to an epiphenomenalistic conception of mind-body—that mind can be exhaustively explained in terms of physical and/or reflexive processes. It has been held that this is a seriously erroneous view for it demands, as was shown in an earlier illustration, that the thoughts or mental states occurring in our heads particularly during silent meditation, when we are personally demonstrating merely neutral overt behavior, are, in a behavioristic account, for example, not to be regarded as causal factors in the production of human behavior. Thinking is to be equated with solely intersubjectively manifest behavior and, more specifically, with verbalizations that can be heard aloud. Hence there is no more to human behavior; it is literally what it appears to be, insofar as the needs of a behavioristic psychology are concerned. The only data suitable for psychological inquiry are those directly ascertained through the external bodily senses of psychologists. Such a view is seriously discordant with the facts of concrete experience, for its implications carried to their extreme demand that the notion of human subjective perspective or subjective understanding be purged from psychological vocabulary, since the behaviors of observational psychologists as well, for example, cannot be conceived as involving anything more than their mere appearances. Surely this is an error for the obvious fact is that individuals' experiences in one definite sense must be minimally understood as a spatio-temporally extended sequence of conscious awarenesses, each sequence collectively comprising single-life histories. This latter concept of human experience is a fundamental fact from which Whitehead's and similarly the position here being propounded followed.

We have developed a view diametrically opposed to that of behaviorism. It was maintained that all humanly perceivable events must necessarily be regarded as mental events to the extent that an individual mind must be logically presupposed to entertain any possible phenomenal occurrence. Thus it is illogical to speak of a human organism having an intelligible awareness of an external natural or internal bodily occurrence unless we presuppose *a priori* a consciousness and reflective consciousness that directly perceives the phenomenon. From this, the metaphorical expression of mind standing over against percepta followed. In this dichotomized portrayal, it was not maintained that a dualism was implicit; rather the converse was emphasized. That is, the mind factor was conceived to include the two general classes of percepta—denotative and connotative perceptual meaning—that constituted the personal perceptual contribution necessarily ascribed for example to heard verbal utterances by both the subject articulating the utterances as well as those hearing them as natural world sounds. Thus the mind factor and the percepta factor were regarded as inextricably related components in producing manifest verbal behavior. Then the traditional subject-object relationship was reformulated to the degree that stimulus-objects were said to yield stimulus-object effects. The effects were then conceived to be the perceptual elements entertained by an individual consciousness. Therefore mind was metaphorically posed as standing over against stimulus-object effects. Stimulus-object effects were to be regarded as occurring from two different spatial regions: from stimulus-objects located in the external natural world, and from stimulus-objects located in an individual's personal bodily organism. From this, the conclusion followed that intersubjective verification of phenomenal occurrence is based on the fact that individual percipients have direct perceptual access to the effects of stimulus-objects located in the external natural world. Conversely, those effects occurring within an individual's own organism were in principle directly inaccessible to externally located percipients. The two categorically distinct spatial regions of stimulus-objects led to the division of two methodologically distinct approaches to psychological inquiry: one termed an objective psychology or a nonepiphenomenalistic behaviorism dealing with human behavior as it appears directly through the external bodily senses of observers; the other a subjective psychology utilizing a system of hypothetical constructs designed to represent the form and dynamics of the subject's internal bodily and essentially ideational experience. It was noted that since internal behavioral dynamics are directly inaccessible to externally located observers, the constructs must ultimately be subject to verification through phenomenal occurrences directly intersubjectively confirmable.

The principal objection that could be raised against this view would be in questioning the nature of the entity—namely, a mind or consciousness and reflective consciousness—that is alleged metaphorically to stand over against percepta or what has also been defined as stimulus-object effects. However, all types of individuals' linguistic and symbolic behavior have two aspects if such behavior has an intersubjectively manifest dimension (although in the case of silent thinking, there is often no intersubjectively accessible manifestation of linguistic behavior. Thus obviously this class of behavior cannot serve as data for scientific psychology for it is directly accessible only to those individuals within whose organisms the states occur). One aspect is the dimension that is directly ascertainable by externally located observers, as in the case of any natural world phenomenon. But also there is a very complex dimension to symbolic, and particularly linguistic, behavior directly accessible only to individual subjects themselves. This dimension is essentially equivalent to the highly complicated relevant personal history of learned information implicitly associated with each articulated linguistic sound heard by listeners located spatially separate from subjects. These implicitly contained meaningful components of linguistic symbols, which are reflexively and synthetically associated with subjects' vocal utterances, are directly accessible only to subjects themselves for they arise as internal bodily ideational perceptions. Due to the fact that there is relatively high concordance in the definitional meaning ascribed to elements of given languages shared in common by groups of individuals, intersubjective communication is rendered possible. These two aspects of linguistic behavior are rightfully the subjectmatter of an objective and subjective psychology, together capable, in principle, of providing a complete account of human behavior. To better understand the necessity for admitting the two-perspective approach for investigating linguistic behavior, a phenomenon roughly equated with mind, let us briefly reconsider the line of argumentation developed.

In Part One it was argued that since Skinner does not hold that mental states have a causally efficacious status in determining human behavioral modes, these states must be regarded as epiphenomena. But it can be shown that this view must necessarily logically presuppose as part of its axiomatic basis that mental states do possess causal efficacity, for otherwise the system as logically proposed becomes seriously contradictory. The essence of these criticisms can be expressed in the following way. First, given only those behavioral phenomena delivered through the external bodily perceptual modes of behavioristic observers, it cannot be demonstrated that a full account of human behavior can, in principle, be experimentally established. This was made evident in the example of subjects engaged in the typical act of silent thinking, while exhibiting the appearance of merely neutral behavior to onlookers. Observers would have, in this case, no way of knowing what events were occurring in the heads of the subjects unless the subjects themselves verbally described the personally experienced phenomena. Moreover, the limitations of behavioristic methodology can be more importantly seen in investigating linguistic behavior. In hearing the verbal utterances of subjects, for example, all that is strictly heard by observers are the natural world sounds of words, in themselves having no intrinsic meaning apart from a consciously aware human being to understand the words. Over and above being bare natural world sounds, spoken words stimulate meaningful understanding in percipients who both articulate and hear the words. Therefore in order for subjective understanding to be accomplished by or actualized in any individuals, it is necessary that each person make a personal interpretive linguistic contribution concomitant with the natural world sounds as they are either subjectively emitted or directly heard by externally located percipients. However, it is essential to note that the exact meaning, whether true or false, vaguely expressed or eloquent, of the personal contribution to the natural world sound shared in common is directly accessible only to the subject emitting the verbal utterances. Hence there may result great concordance or discordance among the personal interpretive contributions ascribed to the heard verbalizations by listeners, in contrast with the subject's personal contribution. This condition also indicates that there are, in addition to natural world variables, intersubjectively nonmanifest variables operating in the personal production of linguistic behavior as well as in understanding heard utterances. Hence it must be concluded that behaviorism cannot, in principle, directly ascertain all the variables causally operative in human behavior solely through the external bodily senses of scientific observers. Furthermore, since the behavioristic enterprise itself, like all intelligent human endeavors, is dependent upon the usage of linguistic symbols, it must also be concluded that the internal bodily states which it presumes to methodologically exclude from its procedures are necessarily logically presupposed *a priori*, and, in fact, operationally implemented for its possibility as a systematic mode of inquiry.

The views of Ernst Cassirer and Alfred North Whitehead were

introduced in order to elaborate theoretically upon the view that linguistic symbols when overtly expressed have both an intersubjectively accessible dimension and an aspect directly accessible only to each individual entertaining the sound, whether he personally generates the utterance or merely hears it—that is, the relevant personal history of meaning reflexively and reflectively brought constructively to bear upon the natural world linguistic components, hence, actualizing a complete meaningful verbal utterance. Explicitly contained in each thinker's position is the view that emotion, as it is directly accessible to individual human beings, is a crucial factor in acquiring and effectively using language. Cassirer and Whitehead generally hold that emotion subjectively experienced during the acquisition of speech in early life undergoes a radical disciplined transformation whereby linguistic behavior is gradually learned, consequently enabling human organisms to characterize and meaningfully develop their experience. Here experience is regarded as an inextricable synthesis of external and internal bodily perception.

It can also be shown that from scientific statements about behavior generated by a Skinnerian behaviorism and by those relevant sciences which provide human behavioral accounts in physio-chemical terms statements referring to mental phenomena cannot be deduced analytically, since both approaches can be regarded generally as delivering data via the external bodily senses of scientific observers. Therefore the correlations that can in principle be established between mental events and physio-chemical states said to underlie the mental events must be established by empirical, not purely logically deductive, correlative procedures. An alternate argument arriving at the same conclusions was also proposed by Herbert Feigl.(13)

The above criticisms have great methodological importance for the behavioral sciences in that they clear the way for two logically distinct procedures for systematically investigating human behavior. First, there is the approach designated essentially by traditional behavioristic methods: investigating those behavioral phenomena that can be ascertained directly via the external bodily senses of behavioristic psychologists. There is also a second approach, defined as a subjective psychology, investigating those phenomena perceived directly only by individual human beings themselves and hence perceived indirectly by subjective psychologists. These inner states are classifiable into three distinct types of perception: bodily feelings, emotional feelings, and ideational feelings.

Thus a subjective psychology, although not having the methodological advantage of a behaviorism in that the phenomena with which it deals are not intersubjectively directly ascertainable by subjective psychologists, can deal with inner behavioral elements essentially through an analysis of verbal reports of subjects referring to their inner states. The primary difference in this approach from a behaviorism is that a different theoretical interpretation is ascribed to these verbal reports. This is the general theory developed in Parts Two and Three. Thus the methodological procedure of collecting data having reference to subjects' inner perceptual states that are not directly experienced by subjective psychologists, in light of an appropriate explanatory theory and carefully controlled experimental conditions, is not a serious methodological handicap. The highly precise science of physics, as it was proven in the introduction, for example, cannot directly observe the nature of its theoretically postulated entities such as atoms, electrons, and molecules, and yet, through the utilization of well-formulated theoretical constructs amenable to mathematical expression, penetrating investigations are conducted into the nature of hypothetical entities that are in principle unobservable.

In Part Two a model for conceptualizing human behavior was presented which is consistent with the aim of both an objective and a subjective psychological approach to investigating human behavior, that is, a system for explaining the dynamics of human behavior in terms of experimentally ascertained dependent relations among behavioral components. Essentially the model demonstrated that individual human organisms are to be conceived as unified functional mechanisms actively behaving interpenetratively in a physical and social environment. Next, it was shown in detail that there are two categorically distinct ways that an individual can be stimulated: through the external bodily senses as external bodily sensation and perception; and through internal bodily modes yielding organic bodily feeling, emotional feeling, and ideational feeling.

It should be repeated that we are here, in a sense, developing an S-O-R model, for it has been logically demonstrated that by omitting the O factor, a behavioral science can provide only a partial, very limited account of human behavior because the second category of factual perceptual phenomena must be methodologically excluded from a behaviorism. This second category of percepta, then, becomes the prime concern of a subjective psychology. Both objective and subjective psychological approaches can, in principle, provide a full account of human behavior if their knowledge claims are considered jointly. Thus all possible percepta capable of functioning as causally efficacious variables in determining human behavioral responses must be delivered through the two categories of perceptual modes. A human organism can, in effect, be stimulated from internal bodily regions and from the external natural world. A small set of theoretical concepts was thus developed, possessing cybernatic generality, in order to comprehend the vast number of physio-chemical systems involved in behavioral processes, hence demonstrating, at least in principle, how organic bodily mechanisms can operate in conjunction with conscious processes. If it has been proven that, given a set of scientifically appropriate statements referring to states said to underlie a particular mental state (a logical possibility for a very highly developed neurophysiology), it is not logically possible to deduce analytically the nature of the correlative mental state from the scientific statements, and vice versa, then it follows that two logically distinct perceptual domains exist. From this, it must be concluded that an emergentism is in evidence: from physio-chemical bodily processes, a logically and experientially distinct class of internal bodily phenomena emerge, namely, feeling of qualitatively different grades. However, this is regarded to be a scientifically predictable emergentism.(27)

From the previous discussion, this concept of mind follows: in investigating human behavior there are three possible ways in which individual human behavioral phenomena may be systematically studied:

1. From the point of view of the biological, and more generally, the natural sciences.

2. From the point of view of the behavioristic sciences, dealing with human behavior as it directly appears to investigators through their external bodily senses, hence methodologically purging statements referring to inner subjective psychological states from their explanations as scientifically irrelevant because of verificational reasons.

3. A subjective psychology similar to the Gestalt and phenomenological schools of psychology, yet importantly different, but using theoretical and methodological procedures more in accordance with those of the natural sciences than particularly the latter schools.

Thus from a subjective psychological point of view, a concept of mind is advocated arguing that mental phenomena do in fact emerge from underlying physio-chemical conditions. But since statements referring to the two classes of percepta representing each domain are not logically equivalent, the correlations to be established between the two domains by a logically possible feat of a highly sophisticated neurophysiology must necessarily be empirical correlations. This situation leads to the conclusion that with the emergence of a mental perceptual domain logically distinct from a correlative physio-chemical domain, there results also a mutually exclusive realm of causality over and above the lower-ordered mechanistic causality of physio-chemical processes. Thus individual persons, apart from the indeterminately large number of physical environmental contingencies that may influence their behavior, do consciously determine many of their own modes of behavior. One ramification of this conclusion is that the theoretical concept of conditioned reflex has only limited, although important, relevance for systematically studying human behavior, for consciousness, working conjointly with its reflective capacity, also acts as an ontologically unique frame of reference for generating a causally efficacious class of mental variables that act in conjunction with conditioned reflexive factors in determining human behavioral modes.

In Part Three it was seen that because the domain of inner bodily perception had been demonstrated to be a causal realm distinct from the physio-chemical realm, yet obviously working in conjunction with it in producing individual behavior, it was possible to devise a system of constructs suitable for experimentally investigating the dynamics of personally accessible conscious and reflective conscious processes. A theory was subsequently presented showing that given the human organism with its capacity for ideational synthesis, and given merely those percepta delivered through the two categorically distinct modes of perception, it is possible to demonstrate the logical form intrinsic to all possible subjective psychological experiences (defined as those inextricably unified perceptual configurations issuing from both internal bodily and external natural regions, directly experienced by individual human beings throughout given spatio-temporal durations). The logical form of subjective psychological experience is that theoretical framework within which all subjective psychological behavior can be understood, in terms of the various possible ways that any configuration of mental event-components may be actualized within a particular mental event. In essence, human conscious experience embodies a small number of determinate classes of event-components out of which any given subjective psychological state may be synthetically actualized. Further, there are a limited number of ways in which these components may be organized into subjective psychological experience: as determined by the form of the natural world, perceptually expressed as entities, properties, and relations; the physio-chemical structure of the human organism; the operational function of memory and conscious reflection with their perceptual content; and so on. Therefore, if we understand the possible components of human experience and the various ways in which these components may be related as partially revealed by the logical form of subjective psychological experience, important advances in dealing with the general problem of behavior modification can be made, primarily as a result of gaining a clearer and more comprehensive understanding of the many possible variables that can causally influence human behavior. Finally, from understanding the logical form of subjective psychological experience, many additional theoretical constructs can be developed and hence subjected to experimental verification. As was seen in the preceding discussion, a subjective psychology would deal —by means of appropriately formulated theoretical constructs—with human experience as it is factually and concretely actualized in individual human beings, in distinction to an objective psychology which seeks to experimentally ascertain the lawlike regularities in behavior as it directly appears to externally located observers. The difference in viewpoints is essentially one of perspective. The former approach attempts to view and hence systematically explain individual experience as it is directly entertained by subjects themselves. The latter view endeavors to explain this process in terms of its intersubjectively directly available appearance.

References

(1) Nagel, Ernest and Newman, James R. *Gödel's Proof*. New York: New York University Press, 1960.

(2) Feigl, Herbert; Scriven, Michael; and Maxwell, Grover, ed. *Minnesota Studies in the Philosophy of Science*, Vol. II: *Concepts, Theories, and the Mind-Body Problem*. Minneapolis: University of Minnesota Press, 1963.

(3) Burtt, Edwin Arthur. *The Metaphysical Foundations of Modern Physical Science*. 2d ed. rev. Garden City, N.Y.: Doubleday & Company, 1955.

(4) Skinner, B. F. *Science and Human Behavior*. New York: The Free Press, 1965.

(5) Titchner, E. B. *A Textbook of Psychology*. New York: Macmillan, 1910.

(6) Köhler, Wolfgang. *Gestalt Psychology*. New York: Liveright, 1929.

(7) Tymieniecka, Anna-Teresa. *Phenomenology and Science in Contemporary European Thought*. New York: Noonday, 1962.

(8) Sellars, Wilfrid. "Intentionality and the Mental," ed. Feigl, Scriven, and Maxwell, II.

(9) Whitehead, Alfred North. *Adventures of Ideas*. New York: Macmillan, 1933.

(10) Skinner, B. F. *Cumulative Record*. New York: Appleton-Century-Crofts, 1959.

(11) Dewey, John. *Democracy and Education*. New York: Macmillan, 1916.

(12) Dewey, John. *Experience and Nature*. 2d ed. rev. LaSalle, Ill.: Open Court, 1929.

(13) Feigl, Herbert. "The 'Mental' and the 'Physical'," ed. Feigl, Scriven, and Maxwell, II.

(14) Nagel, Ernest. *The Structure of Science*. New York: Harcourt, Brace & World, 1961.

(15) Whitehead, Alfred North. *Process and Reality*. New York: Macmillan, 1929.

(16) Buber, Martin. *I and Thou*. 2d ed. rev. New York: Charles Scribner's Sons, 1958.

(17) Ashby, W. Ross. *An Introduction to Cybernetics*. New York: John Wiley & Sons, 1963.

(18) Ryle, Gilbert. *The Concept of Mind*. New York: Barnes & Noble, 1964.

(19) Cassirer, Ernst. *An Essay on Man*. New Haven: Yale University Press, 1965.

(20) ———. *The Philosophy of Symbolic Forms*, Vols. 1–3. New Haven: Yale University Press, 1965.

(21) ———. *Substance and Function*. New York: Dover, 1953.

(22) Bergson, Henri. *Creative Evolution*. New York: Henry Holt, 1911.

(23) Maritain, Jacques. *Education at the Crossroads*. New Haven: Yale University Press, 1943.

(24) McKeon, Richard. *The Basic Works of Aristotle*. New York: Random House, 1941.

(25) Haldane, Elizabeth S. and Ross, G. R. T. *The Philosophical Works of Descartes*. New York: Dover, 1931.

(26) Ashby, W. Ross. *Design for a Brain*. New York: John Wiley & Sons, 1963.

(27) Oppenheim, Paul and Putnam, Hillary. "The Unity of Science Working Hypothesis," ed. Feigl, Scriven, and Maxwell, II.

(28) Kant, Immanual. *Prolegomena To Any Future Metaphysics*. New York: Bobbs-Merrill, 1950.

(29) Bandura, Albert. "Psychotherapy as a Learning Process," *Psychological Bulletin*, 58 (1961).

(30) Wolpe, John. *Psychotherapy by Reciprocal Inhibition*. Stanford: Stanford University Press, 1958.

(31) Murray, Edward. "Learning Theory and Psychotherapy: Biotropic vs. Sociotropic Approaches," *Journal of Counseling Psychology*, 10 (Fall, 1963).

(32) Truax, Charles B. "Effective Ingredients in Psychotherapy: An Approach to Unraveling the Patient-Therapist Interaction," *Journal of Counseling Psychology*, 10 (Fall, 1663).

(33) Hobbs, Nicholas. "Sources of Gain in Psychotherapy," *American Psychologists*, 17 (1962).

(34) Bergin, Alan E. "The Effects of Psychotherapy: Negative Results Revisited," *Journal of Counseling Psychology*, 10 (Fall, 1663).

(35) Chappell, V. C., ed. *The Philosophy of Mind*. Englewood Cliffs, N.J.: Prentice-Hall, 1962.

(36) Zener, Karl. "The Significance of Experience of the Individual for the Science of Psychology," ed. Feigl, Scriven, and Maxwell, II.

(37) Butler, J. A. V. *The Life of the Cell*. New York: Basic Books, 1964.

(38) Butler J. A. V. *Science and Human Life*. New York: Basic Books, 1957.

(39) Robson, J. W. "Whitehead's Answer to Hume." *Alfred North Whitehead: Essays On His Philosophy*, ed. George L. Kline., Englewood Cliffs, N.J.: Prentice-Hall, 1963.

(40) Whitehead, Alfred North. *An Enquiry Concerning the Principles of Natural Knowledge*. Cambridge: University Press, 1919.

(41) Whitehead, Alfred North. *Concept of Nature*. Cambridge: University Press, 1920.

(42) Whitehead, Alfred North. *The Principles of Relativity*. Cambridge: University Press, 1922.

(43) Whitehead, Alfred North. *Science and the Modern World*. New York: Macmillan, 1925.

Index

Analytical philosophy, criticism of, 257-263

Anticipation, 235
  infantile, 58

Apriori, argument of, 20, 23-27, 30-34, 40, 72, 80, 115, 116, 122, 123, 153, 180, 181, 274

Aristotle, 63, 77, 84, 85, 90
  concept of virtue, 90

Ashby, W. Ross, 38, 39, 67

Awareness, 36, 37, 39, 233, 235, 236
  infantile, 57, 58

Bandura, Albert, 94-96, 98, 99

Behavior, definition of, iii, iv
  human, 110
  generic concepts of, 5
  instrumental, Dewey's concept of, 15
  origins of intelligent growth, 144
  reflexive, 218, 226, 227
  subjective psychological definition of, 103, 274
  Skinnerian concept of, 7
  therapy, 94-98

Behavioral sciences, iii

Behaviorism, xiv, xvi-xx, 2, 3, 121, 122, 241
  criticism of, 46, 50, 51, 53, 65, 180, 181, 206-209, 257-263, 267, 268, 273-281
  See also, Skinnerian Behaviorism

Biological Theories, xiv-xx
  See also, mechanistic biology

Bergson, Henri, 48

Buber, Martin, 36, 81

Butler, J. A. V., 116-120

Cassirer, Ernst, 40, 41, 46-56, 65, 84, 86, 122, 128, 167, 169, 276, 277

Causal efficacity, of mental events, 70, 72
  of mental event-components, 75, 106-111
  of mind, 124

Causality, 216
  direct subjective psychological experience of, 252
  ideational, 106-110, 204-207, 211, 219-232, 235-255
  defined, 240, 241
  three types, 241-255
  mental, 182
  natural, 240, 241, 243-255
  projective ideational, 242-255
  reflexive infusive ideational, 241-255

Change, 180

Clarity, in perception, 213, 214

Client-centered Psychotherapy, xvii, xviii

Cognitive
  functioning, the four levels of, 78-89
  repetition, 224
  synthesis, 204-209, 222, 223, 236-255

Coherence, 215, 256-263

Communication, 207

Completeness, 215

Concrescence, 88-90, 94, 100, 102, 103, 153, 268
  definition of, 79
  organic, 79, 82, 204
  transcendent, 106-111
  transcendent ideational, 241-255
  transcendent organic, 254, 255

Concrescent synthesis, 16

Conditioned reflex, 31

Conscious processes, human, xiv-xx

Conjuration, 220, 224-231

287

Repetition, 231
Ryle, Gilbert, 39, 63

Science, descriptive nature of, 7, 8
Scientific reductionism, iv
    unwarranted, xvi
    See also, reductionism
    Scientific verification, xii-xx
Sellars, Wilfred, 3, 4
Sensation, 71, 102, 103, 106, 109, 162
Sign behavior, 50, 51, 56, 58-60
Sign stage, 130, 131, 234, 238, 239
Simplification, 101, 147, 149, 154, 158,
    167, 222
Skinner, B. F., 63, 72
Skinner, operant conditioning, theory
    of, 94, 95, 97

Skinnerian, Behaviorism, xvi-xx, 10, 15-
    19, 24
    refutation of, 17-28, 31-35, 273-
        281
    See also, behaviorism
    functional analysis, x
    Psychology, 6-8, 10
    psychology, 6-8, 10
    criticism, 267, 268
Socrates, 47
Space, Whitehead's criticism of the
        Traditional concept, 175-179,
        184-189
Space–time, four dimensional, 179-202
    modal character of, 176, 191, 192,
        193
    prehensive character of, 176, 190-193
    separative character of, 176, 190,
        192, 193
    Whitehead's concept of, 184-199
Stage, presymbolic, 233

Stimulus–response, 6-8, 267, 268
    –object, 25, 29, 70-72, 80, 106, 162,
        221
    effects, 31, 70-72, 88, 102, 103,
        106, 147, 160, 161, 162, 213,
        220, 221, 225-227
        defined, 25
        natural, 161, 162

ontological status of, 217-219
–objects, ideational, 80, 89, 208, 225-
    227, 243-247
    location of, 25, 31, 36, 37, 155
    natural, 216
    occuring as ideational PI per-
        cepta, 219-232
    ontological status of, 217, 218
    organic bodily, 80, 216
    in themselves, 37, 225-227
        conditions for, 253-255
    occasion, 37
Storing, 82, 86, 129, 140, 141, 233, 234
    mechanisims, 62
Subject-object relationships, 274
Subjective experience, xv-xx
Subjective psychological, data, xv-xvi
    events, a schematization, 29
    experience, 63, 103, 158, 159, 168
        catagories of components, 142,
            143
        dipolar structure of, 172, 237,
            269-272
        logical form of, 124, 125, 145,
            160, 169-175, 210-212, 215,
            218, 267-272, 280, 281
            a diagramatic representation,
                222
    meaning, 19, 20, 37-39, 65, 204-206,
        224
    mechanistic model, 72, 111, 153, 207-
        209, 248-255
    schematic representation, 112
    thought, 41
Subjective psychology, 3, 15, 24, 31,
        33, 35, 145, 146, 206-208, 210,
        211, 241, 244, 253, 274, 275,
        277-281
    a method of perceptual analysis, 212,
        213
Sublimation, 82, 84, 85, 139-142
Substratum theory of matter, 157, 158
Symbol stage, 130-132, 238, 239
Symbolic, behavior, 50-56, 60-65
    discipline, 204, 205, 207
    reference, 212, 266-272
    relatedness, 130, 131, 133-143, 236
Synapse, 7
Synthesis, transcendent concrescent, 88,
    89, 94-111